THE SEVENTH
OLD HOUSE CATALOGUE

Cover photograph: *Entryway of Aquia Church, c. 1750, Stafford, Virginia, by Ford Peatross. The pediment and beautifully carved surround is of locally quarried sandstone.*

THE SEVENTH
OLD HOUSE CATALOGUE

Lawrence Grow

A Sterling/Main Street Book
Sterling Publishing Co., Inc.   New York

Library of Congress Cataloging-in-Publication Data

Grow, Lawrence.
 The seventh old house catalogue / compiled by Lawrence Grow.
   p.   cm.
 "A Sterling/Main Street book."
 Includes index.
 ISBN 0-8069-7436-2
  1. Historic buildings—United States—Conservation and
restoration—Catalogs.   2. Buildings—United States—Conservation
and restoration—Catalogs.   I. Title.   II. Title: 7th old house
catalogue.   III. Title: Old house catalogue.
 TH3411.G7633   1991
 728.3′7′0288029473—dc20   90–28644
                                                          CIP

Designed by John Murphy
Typeset by Upper Case Limited, Cork, Ireland

10   9   8   7   6   5   4   3   2

A Sterling / Main Street Book

© 1991 by Lawrence Grow
Published by Sterling Publishing Company, Inc.
387 Park Avenue South, New York, N.Y. 10016
Distributed in Canada by Sterling Publishing
% Canadian Manda Group, P.O. Box 920, Station U
Toronto, Ontario, Canada M8Z 5P9
Distributed in Great Britain and Europe by Cassell PLC
Villiers House, 41/47 Strand, London WC2N 5JE, England
Distributed in Australia by Capricorn Ltd.
P.O. Box 665, Lane Cove, NSW 2066
Manufactured in the United States of America
All rights reserved

Sterling ISBN 0-8069-7436-2

Contents

Introduction

For this, *The Seventh Old House Catalogue*, an entirely new format has been adopted for the first time since the launching of the series in 1976. Presented in encyclopedic form are thousands of useful products and services for restoring, renovating, and re-creating period buildings, and advice on how to make use of these myriad sources. The improved alphabetical arrangement makes it much easier to locate any particular kind of item needed by the old-house resident. Through the use of cross-references, the reader is also led to other related subject entries which may provide useful supplementary information.

No one-volume work can cover every single architectural and decorative detail that goes into the creation of a period structure, particularly those of its interior spaces. *The Seventh Old House Catalogue*, nevertheless, attempts to cover all major elements of domestic architecture and many minor aspects. Windows, doors, flooring, glass, lighting, paints, floor coverings, fabrics, wallpapers, paneling, porches, fencing and gates, moldings, stairs, fireplaces and mantels, siding, ceilings, furniture, cabinetry, columns, and hardware are discussed and illustrated in detail with a wide variety of currently available products described for each. The work of restoration consultants and contractors is also given primary coverage. At the same time, much less important but no less interesting subjects as andirons, balusters, chimney pots, firebacks, old-fashioned garden plants and seeds, greenhouses, hitching posts, medallions, pumps, radiators, shutters, stained glass, stoves, and tiles, to name but a handful, are given due and respectful attention. Small details such as these serve to define a property's period character.

The Seventh Old House Catalogue, presenting products and services from the United States, Canada, and Great Britain, is the only *selective* sourcebook available. Approximately 500 sources – companies and individuals – are surveyed in the book, having been selected from over 2,000. There is no advertising in these pages. Suppliers are here because they deserve to be. In gathering as accurate and up-to-date information as possible, we found most suppliers in the ever-growing old-house market cooperative and generous in their responses, but we have also encountered rudeness or an aloofness that ill-becomes people whose business, after all, is serving the public. When this has occurred, we have simply dropped the supplier from consideration, however big and important the firm. If this happens to us, it is likely to happen to you.

As in the past, we again urge readers to send in suggestions regarding suppliers and subjects that should be covered in future editions, as well as any complaints about service or products from firms mentioned in this book. The old-house market has grown very large since the mid-1970s when we first began surveying it, and while compromise is often the name of the game, eternal vigilance as to reasonable authenticity is a necessary requisite of the informed consumer.

With the high-flying '80s and all its attendant up-market hype behind us, we hope that a new spirit of conservation will emerge. We have come a long way from the days when real estate agents referred to old houses as "used," but there is still a strong tendency to destroy evidence of past craftsmanship, to waste material and artistic resources. Economically bad times can have benefits for those who can creatively turn their attention to making the best of a bad situation by adapting what is in hand at a reasonable cost. Fewer new speculation houses will be built in the 1990s, and there will be an increase in home renovation and restoration. It is already clear that funds for building new roads and improving public utilities will be severely limited. This will mean less destruction of the built environment. European visitors to North America frequently comment on the extraordinary variety and vitality of New World period architecture. This is a reflection of our enterprising past and can be the foundation of a much brighter future.

In compiling this entirely revised *Old House Catalogue*, we have turned to a completely new corps of helpers. We are extremely grateful to John Woodside of Sterling Publishing Co. for his considerable assistance in contacting numerous suppliers for us; John Murphy and Eamonn MacGabhann for their design services; Finbarr Langford of Lee Press for supplying camera-ready photographs; and the hard-pressed but always good-humored staff of Upper Case Ltd. for their diligent typesetting.

THE SEVENTH
OLD HOUSE CATALOGUE

Entrance arch, Oaklands, Murfreesboro, Tennessee. Photograph by Jack E. Boucher, Historic American Buildings Survey.

Anaglypta. *See* **Wallcoverings.**

Anchors. *See* **Tie Rods and Plates.**

Andirons. Simply used to hold logs in a fireplace, andirons can be decorative as well as practical accessories. In many period houses, especially those of Colonial inspiration, the fireplace

is the central feature of a room. The size of the opening will determine the proper dimensions for andirons. These may range from a little more than a foot high to as much as a yard. As the name andiron implies, at least some part of this fixture should be made of iron forged or cast to with-

stand intense heat. Sets of andirons can be found in fireplace and antique shops and are also staples of the decorative housewares trade. Additionally, there are specialty dealers of note.

HISTORIC HARDWARE LTD.
This maker of period hardware, lighting, and decorative accessories offers three models of andirons, including the "Knifeblade" set shown here. The design dates from the 18th century and is both practical and attractive. Solid brass finals top solid cast-iron bases. Height 21", depth 15".

Catalog available, $3

HISTORIC HARDWARE LTD.
PO Box 1327
North Hampton, NH 03862
(603) 964-2280

LEMEE'S FIREPLACE EQUIPMENT
A major supplier of accessories for the fireplace, Lemee's is a convenient source for the products of many manufacturers. Ten andiron designs are featured from the very simple (all cast iron) to the elegant (solid brass with cast-iron backs.) The set illustrated here is termed the "Colonial

Key" design and is super sturdy. Height 14", depth 14". Lemee also offers a pair of "log dogs" which are protective iron covers for the back rests of decorative andirons.

Catalog available, $2

LEMEE'S FIREPLACE EQUIPMENT
815 Bedford St.
Bridgewater, MA 02324
(508) 697-2672

Other recommended andiron suppliers: HAMMERWORKS, KAYNE & SON CUSTOM FORGED HARDWARE, LAWLER MACHINE & FOUNDRY CO.

Arbors. Designed to support climbing plants, an arbor usually consists of a framework and latticing. Often a simple arched form, the arbor provides a picturesque focus to an old-fashioned garden. Structures of this sort appeared in both Colonial and Victorian gardens and in recent years have found a new popularity, especially as an arched entryway. The framework may be of metal or wood. Simple arched metal frames are offered by such garden catalog houses as SMITH & HAWKEN. *See also* **Trellising.**

KENNETH LYNCH AND SONS
Among the many garden features supplied by this famous firm is a 10' wide frame for a grape arbor. It can be made in any length. The spheres on top are optional. The frame, of course, is suitable for almost any type of climber plant.

Book of Garden Ornament, $9.50

KENNETH LYNCH AND SONS
78 Danbury Rd., Box 488
Wilton, CT 06897
(203) 762-8363
Fax (203) 762-2999

STICKNEY'S GARDEN HOUSES
     AND FOLLIES
The function of an arbor is combined with that of a neoclassical garden house in Stickney's model #10. The structure may serve as a pass-through archway or – with a back latticed panel in place – as a garden house. The manufacturer also cleverly suggests its use as a door surround with some adjustment and the addition of plinth base blocks. The basic unit measures $6\frac{1}{2}$" wide x 5' deep x $9\frac{1}{2}$' at keystone.

Brochure available

STICKNEY'S GARDEN HOUSES
     AND FOLLIES

1 Thompson Sq., PO Box 34
Boston, MA 02129
(617) 242-1711
Fax (617) 242-1982

Other recommended arbor suppliers:
BOW HOUSE, INC., OUTDOOR DESIGNS & SERVICE.

Arches. One of the basic forms in almost every type of architecture, the arch can take a number of configurations. It is most often seen in houses as a gentle elliptical span which may or may not make use of a keystone. Other types used for openings such as windows and doors as well as for dividing a space are pointed or Gothic arches and elongated Victorian arches similar to spandrels. The classic arch of the past was of plasterwork, but today it is more than likely made of wood or even a polymer material. The typical arch is a

series of moldings joined together. Nearly every supplier of traditional moldings can produce arches suitable for window and door casings as well as more ornamental uses. *See also* **Moldings.**

SILVERTON VICTORIAN MILLWORKS
This firm's moldings are made to order – as they must be for a proper fit – but there are still three standard shapes: chord, half circle, and quarter circle. Silverton will also make up other shapes such as the elliptical.

VINTAGE WOOD WORKS
The wood arches manufactured by Vintage are suitable for late-Victorian interiors. Similar in form to a spandrel, the arch extends down only 26" or 30" and not to floor level. The "Sun Ray" model shown is 62" wide and 26" high; it is composed of two brackets and a drop. Both narrower and wider versions of this design are also available., Premium pine is used.

Catalog available, $2

VINTAGE WOOD WORKS
513 S. Adams
Fredericksburg, TX 78624
(512) 997-9513

Other recommended suppliers of arches:
FOCAL POINT, HICKSVILLE WOODWORKS CO.

Architectural Antiques. *See also* **Bathtubs, Beams, Chandeliers, Clapboards, Columns, Doorknobs. and Plates, Doors, Etched Glass, Fencing and Gates, Garden Ornaments, Lamps, Mantels, Moldings, Paneling, Posts, Registers, Sconces, Sinks, Stained Glass, Stairways and Parts, Stone, Tiles, Toilets, Windows.** As indicated by the list of entries, the term *architectural antiques* embraces a wide variety of structural and decorative objects. Not too long ago such used materials were known as "salvage." Earlier, the term was "junk."

Illustrated is a doorway composed of two quarter-circle arches. The use of keystone and corner blocks makes the installation much easier. The widths range from 1" to 5" and materials used are pine, premium pine, oak, or premium oak. There are at least four different molding profiles to choose from in each of the five widths.

Catalog, $4

SILVERTON VICTORIAN MILLWORKS
PO Box 2987 - OC7
Durango, CO 81302
(303) 259-5915

SUNSHINE ARCHITECTURAL
    WOODWORKS
Sunshine's basic arch design for doors and windows is similar to that of Silverton but differs in the possible use of a decorative carved keystone as shown here. Sunshine will produce arched wood casing moldings for openings as small as 2' in diameter and as large as 8'. The firm can also supply eliptical arches.

Catalog available, $4

SUNSHINE ARCHITECTURAL
    WOODWORKS
2169 Sunshine Dr,
Fayetteville, AR 72703
(501) 521-4329

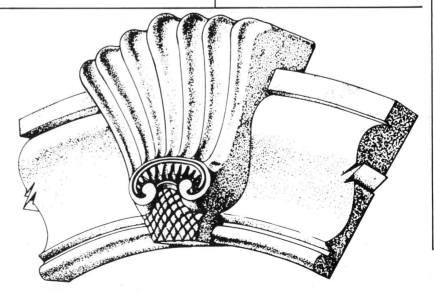

The Brass Knob

In the 1990's architectural "antiques" are also used by modern architects and interior designers to add ornamental touches to otherwise boring interiors. Restorers of old houses have a genuine antiquarian interest in recycled materials. Prices, once very reasonable for "junk," have soared with demand. Anyone seeking authentic materials should shop with caution. Especially in the field of lighting fixtures, new parts may be married to old, and the difference glossed over.

Shopping for antique objects requires patience and persistence. Most dealers have lists available of their current holdings, and if a particular item is not in stock, it will be added to the dealer's "wants" list. The network of architectural antiques dealers is quite closely knit throughout North America, and if a part or component isn't available in one place, the customer is often directed to another seller.

Restorers of old houses on the East Coast may also find it to their advantage to contact British dealers, many of whom ship across the Atlantic on a regular basis. While it may not be practical to import heavy items such as columns or cast-iron stoves, it can be advantageous to bring in wood moldings, small ornamental objects, and windows.

Many dealers both here and abroad are specialists in various fields such as wood flooring, paneling, doors, windows, garden furniture, and stained glass. The names of these firms and a description of their general stock is found under the subject entries. Among the general dealers who are often likely to have a wide assortment of almost every type of object are the following: ARCHITECTURAL ANTIQUE CO., ARCHITECTURAL ANTIQUES EXCHANGE, ARTEFACT ARCHITECTURAL ANTIQUES, THE BANK, BRASS KNOB, IRREPLACEABLE ARTIFACTS, QUEEN CITY ARCHITEC-

TURAL SALVAGE, SALVAGE ONE, UNITED HOUSE WRECKING, VICTORIAN REVIVAL/ARCHITECTURAL ANTIQUE WAREHOUSE, and THE WRECKING BAR OF ATLANTA.

EAGLE EYE TRADING CO.
Offering a useful search service along with restoration consultation and reproductions is Eagle Eye. The firm will locate and deliver items for you using its computerized Resource Library which lists thousands of dealers, traders, and resources throughout North America and Europe. This service is also useful for customers who want to sell. Eagle Eye calls its service "Rapid Search Inquiry" and sets up possible contacts through its computer bank between buyer and seller almost immediately upon receipt of an inquiry and payment of a low handling charge for each item the buyer or seller lists with them. There is no limit to the number of objects that can be listed. Negotiations as to price, terms of sale, etc., are then handled solely between the two parties.

Brochure available

EAGLE EYE TRADING CO.
PO Box 17900
Milwaukee, WI 53217
(414) 374-1984

OLD-HOUSE JOURNAL
A popular venue for advertising architectural antiques as well as placing "wanted" inquiries is *Old-House Journal*. It is published six times a year and classified ads in "The Emporium' section are free to current subscribers. Deadline is the first of the month, two months prior to publication. Ads must be submitted in writing along with a current mailing label.

OLD-HOUSE JOURNAL
Advertising Office
123 Main St.
Gloucester, MA 01930
(800) 356-9313

Ashlar. *See* **Stone.**

Awnings. Canvas awnings are a traditional and practical way of providing shade for windows and doors of Victorian and early 20th-century houses. Until the mid-1800s, it was customary to employ interior or exterior shutters to provide the same amenity, and they continue to be used today on Colonial period dwellings. Awnings fell from favor after World War II as air-conditioning units came on the scene. This expensive, and often wasteful, modern "improvement" has increasingly been called into question. It is very difficult to centrally air-condition most old houses, and the usual alternative, window units, can be unsightly and unwieldy. Awning suppliers are now to be found in every major region and service both commercial and residential customers. If, however, enlightenment regarding this traditional means of keeping a house cool has not reached your area, contact THE ASTRUP CO., a firm that has been in business for over 114 years. Astrup can provide the material and the necessary hardware.

Free literature

THE ASTRUP CO.
2937 W. 25th St.
Cleveland, OH 44113
(216) 696-2820

Axminster Carpets. *See* **Carpeting.**

Gothic Revival arch, John F. Singer House, Pittsburgh, Pennsylvania. Historic American Buildings Survey.

Fourposter bed, Arnold-Temple House, near West Chester, Pennsylvania. Photograph by Ned Goode, Historic American Buildings Survey.

Balconies. These romantic and attractive architectural features are found on rural and urban dwellings of the 18th and 19th centuries. Of wood or ornamental iron, they are composed of railings and balusters or panels, and may be supported either internally (tied in to the main structure) or by the use of brackets. Balconies are common features on many Southern townhouses and plantation dwellings, the climate encouraging the use of such open-air platforms. The fanciful wrought-iron work seen in Charleston and New Orleans is done on only a very limited basis today, cast versions of the same designs being preferred because of cost and durability. One can, however, still special order hand-forged work of artistic merit. Balconies of wood construction may be as elaborate in execution, and any number of firms can supply the elements needed (*see* **Balusters, Balustrades, Railings**) if they cannot be fabricated locally. Ornamental iron (steel) will hold up better over the long run.

NEW ENGLAND TOOL CO
Members of the Artist-Blacksmith Association of North America have given a new lease on life to traditional forged metalcraft. New England Tool is a prominent member of this guild and prides itself on custom work in metal which combines old-fashioned hand-forging methods with modern joinery. The balcony design shown might be as appropriate for a Charleston town-house dating from the early 1800's as for a modern dwelling.

Resource file of architectural metalwork design, $2

NEW ENGLAND TOOL CO.
PO Box 30
Chester, NY 10918
(914) 782-5332
(914) 651-7550
(914) 783-2554
Fax (914) 783-2554

STEWART IRON WORKS CO.
In business since 1886. Stewart has enjoyed an opportunity to replace cast-iron fencing made by the company more than 100 years ago. Its castings are solid and traditional in design. Stewart's basic balcony model (M-280) uses simple iron railings and

corner posts with ball tops. A more elaborate design, however, could easily be substituted.

Catalog, $2

STEWART IRON WORKS CO.
PO Box 2612, 20 W. 18th St.
Covington, KY 41012
(606) 431-1985

Other recommended metal balcony suppliers: ARCHITECTURAL IRON CO., LAWLER MACHINE and FOUNDRY CO., INC.

Balls. Ornaments used primarily for outdoor posts are supplied by all the ornamental ironwork manufacturers (*see* **Fencing and Gates**) as well as

major garden accessory firms. These may be of iron or stone and handsomely cap a pair of gateposts. Other forms such as pineapples, urns, and eagles are used in the same manner. Whatever the choice, the object should be proportioned to the base on which it stands and not be, as is often unfortunately the case, top heavy. *See also* **Finials.**

KENNETH LYNCH & SONS
Lynch supplies a large variety of ornaments in cast stone, including balls ranging in dimension from 1" to 72".

Book of Garden Ornaments, $9.50

KENNETH LYNCH AND SONS
78 Danbury Rd., Box 488
Wilton, CT 06897-0488
(203) 762-8363
Fax: (203) 762-2999

Balusters. Balusters or spindles are one of the essential elements of an enclosure, whether porch, balcony, fencing, a stairway balustrade, or other space dividers inside or outside the house. Balusters used in stairways are often called banisters.

Balusters may be of nearly any material and of a flat or turned profile. They are supported by a horizontal rail at the top and sometimes a bottom rail as well. The most common form of baluster is made of wood by a turner working on a lathe. Carved work was once also common and is still executed on a custom basis by exceptionally skilled craftsmen.

Wood and metalwork suppliers of balusters are found throughout North America as there is a great demand for these elements for stairways and porches *(see also* **Stairways).** Since these elements are structural as well as decorative, it is important that they be of the most solid construction and be fitted into place with care.

BLUE OX MILLWORKS
Situated in Northern California, Blue Ox has a ready supply of that most durable material – redwood – for an endless variety of products. Illustrated are but two baluster designs of many offered as standard; custom turnings or flat design models are also available as are other similar components such as posts and columns.

Literature available

BLUE OX MILLWORKS
Foot of X St.
Eureka, CA 95501
(800) 248-4259
(707) 444-3437
Fax (707) 444-0918

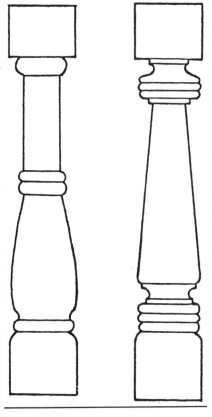

GOTHOM, INC.
This Canadian firm specializes in "gingerbread," millwork for exterior use; it also provides interior ornaments. The balusters illustrated are sawn, have a flat profile, and are Victorian in style. From left to right, the designs are: Regal, Circles and Spears, Flying Swans, and Diving Swans. Gothom also supplies a variety of turned balusters appropriate for interior use.

Catalog, $5

GOTHOM, INC.
Box 421, 110 Main St.
Erin, Ontario N0B IT0
Canada
(519) 833-2574

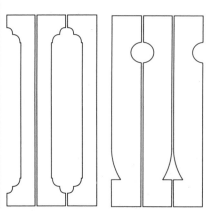

PAGLIACCO TURNING AND MILLING
As the name states, wood turnings are an essential part of this firm's output. California redwood is used primarily and is superb for exterior balusters, For interior use, mahogany, oak, or other fine woods may be substituted on a custom-order basis. The standard baluster models are available in 30" and 36" lengths and widths vary from $2\frac{1}{4}$" to 6". Pagliacco, like many other millwork companies, offers matching newel posts. Balusters are shipped sanded.

Catalog, $6

PAGLIACCO TURNING AND MILLING
PO Box 225
Woodacre, CA 94973
(415) 488-4333

SILVERTON VICTORIAN MILLWORKS
A very useful supplier of standard millwork, Silverton ships all over North America. Although or perhaps because selection is somewhat limited, prices are lower than those of other suppliers. Shown are two of the pine-sawn exterior baluster designs; at left, #37-1; right, #37-2. Each is 33" long, $5\frac{1}{2}$" wide, and $\frac{3}{4}$" deep. There

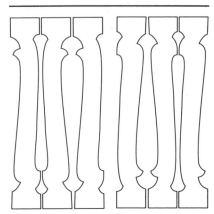

are also two turned baluster models for exterior use. In addition, Silverton supplies custom-molded (rather than turned) interior balusters in oak, pine, or poplar.

Catalog, $4

SILVERTON VICTORIAN MILLWORKS
PO Box 2987-0C7
Durango, CO 81302
(303) 259-5915
Fax (303) 259-5919

STEPTOE & WIFE ANTIQUES LTD.
Best known for its imaginative iron staircases *(see* **Stairways***)*, Steptoe supplies the parts needed for these stairs. Its balusters are also appropriate for balconies and landings. The standard baluster is named the Colonial and is a simple

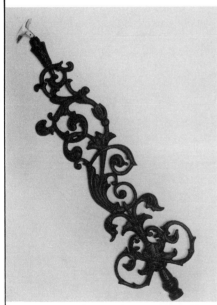

Windsor

turned iron column. The Windsor model is much more decorative and is supplied with an aluminum or brass fitting or saddle.

Catalog available in U.S. and Canada, $3

STEPTOE & WIFE ANTIQUES LTD.
322 Geary Ave.
Toronto, Ontario M6H 2C7
Canada
(414) 530-4200
Fax (414) 530-4666

VINTAGE WOOD WORKS
Both sawn-pine balusters for outdoor use and hemlock turned balusters suitable for interiors or exteriors are standard offerings of Vintage. Illustrated are two "Traditional" designs and two turned "Heritage" designs. The Traditional range from 7½" to 36" in length and are 2" or 3" in diameter; the Heritage are either 32" or 36" long and 2" or 3" in diameter.

Catalog, $2

VINTAGE WOOD WORKS
513 S. Adams
Fredericksburg, TX 78624
(512) 997-9513

Other recommended suppliers of balusters are: ARCHITECTURAL LATHE & MILL, CUMBERLAND WOODCRAFT CO., HICKSVILLE WOODWORKS CO., MARK A. KNUDSEN, NEW ENGLAND WOODTURNERS, W.F. NORMAN CORP., SACO MANUFACTURING & WOODWORKING, SHEPPARD MILLWORK, INC., and THE WOODSTONE CO.

Balustrades. A series of balusters held in place by a handrail, a balustrade may be an exterior or interior feature of a period house. Federal-style houses sometimes have a balustrade edging the roof line; a balustrade may also serve to enclose a widow's walk at the top of the house. While usually of wood, metal, or stone, balustrading can be produced effectively in fiberglass *(see* **Balusters***)*.

THE WORTHINGTON GROUP LTD.
Worthington supplies balusters, corner posts, and rails for a

balustrade that might very well suit a terrace, roof, porch, or balcony. The standard design illustrated is of fiberglass with an end post height of 36", baluster height of 26", and a handrail height, after installation, of 33¼". The hand and base rails come in 13' sections. Worthington will also supply concrete balusters on a special order basis and build them to the customer's design.

Luxury Architectural Details Catalog, $3

WORTHINGTON GROUP, LTD.
PO Box 53101
Atlanta, GA 30355
(404) 872-1608 (Atlanta)
(800) 872-1608
Fax (404) 872-8501

Banisters. *See* **Balusters.**

Bargeboards/Vergeboards.
Decorative millwork used to cover the joint between the gable end of a house and its roof is known variously as bargeboards, vergeboards, or, simply, gable-end ornaments. The boards, usually cut out in some fashion, take the place of cornice moldings on the exterior of many early to mid-Victorian houses. The Gothic Revival cottage designs popularized by A.J. Downing and Calvert Vaux in the mid-1800's frequently featured such decorations as did seaside vacation houses. With the use of a jigsaw, a Victorian carpenter could create quite intricate openwork designs. This type of ornamental feature should be used only sparingly for modest Victorian-style cottages or farmhouses with pronounced gables.

GOTHOM, INC.
This firm has made a specialty of bargeboards and offers twelve designs ranging from repeating scroll patterns to paneled Gothic forms. Illustrated are two of the latter designs: The Duncan Gothic (BA 008) and The Gothic Panel (BA 009). Both are representative of a traditional 19th century gable-end treatment. All of the Gothom bargeboards are custom-made, as they must be, since a roof or pitch slope differs from building to building.

Catalog, $5

GOTHAM INC.
Box 421, 110 Main St
Erin, Ontario N0B IT0
Canada
(519) 833-2574

Other recommended suppliers of bargeboards/vergeboards are: BLUE OX MILLWORKS, HICKSVILLE WOODWORKS CO., SILVERTON VICTORIAN MILLWORKS, *and* VINTAGE WOOD WORKS.

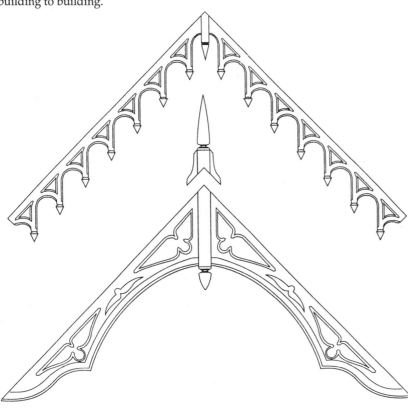

Barns. Buildings meant for housing animals or storing grain and produce weren't intended for human occupation, but such is the charm of many old outbuildings that they have been put to domestic use. Converting a barn into a dwelling gained popularity in the 1960's and '70s at the same time that industrial lofts and churches were rediscovered by city dwellers. Many barns were not built to last for generations. Notably subject to fire because of the combustible nature of the materials stored therein, the barn, nevertheless, has survived against the odds. Those particularly well built in mortise-and-tenon fashion before the advent of

balloon framing are the prizes of rural areas. These are increasingly difficult to find. If a barn is the structural form you are seeking, one option is to build one anew; there are firms that will assist.

THE BARN PEOPLE, INC.
This company has made its reputation by locating, dismantling, and reassembling antique timber-frame outbuildings such as the Bridport Hay Barn illustrated. A three-bay, 30' x 40' barn with hand-hewn beams and round tree rafters, it is one of fourteen structures currently inventoried. This inventory, of course, almost constantly changes

and the firm can locate other models which might better suit a customer's needs.

The post and beam method of construction proved its worth over many years and may be as appropriate for new structures. The Barn People will consequently provide new hand-hewn frames from native Vermont pine. The beams of these are also hand-hewn. Shipping of components from the Vermont shop is not as expensive or difficult as it might seem. Most frames will fit on one truck and costs run approximately $1.75 a mile. If the customer does not wish to handle assembly, this can also be arranged by Barn People.

Barn Frame Planning Portfolio, $10

THE BARN PEOPLE, INC.
PO Box 217
Windsor, VT 05089
(802) 674-5778

THE HOUSE CARPENTERS
Timber barn frames using traditional joinery with mortise and tenon, dovetailing, and fastening throughout with oak pegs are also built by this firm, Massachusetts red oak and white pine are among the variety of native woods employed. Frames can be shipped ready for assembly or erected on site by a company team.

Brochures, $6

THE HOUSE CARPENTERS
PO Box 281
Leverett, MA 01054
(413) 367-2189

Other recommended suppliers of antique barn frames are: SYLVAN BRANDT *and* THE NEW JERSEY BARN CO.

Barn Siding. Material from abandoned or derlict barns has been used in old and new homes for years, unfortunately not always with sufficient attention given to its preparation. Barn siding is most likely to have a round, weathered texture appropriate for a *barn* but unsuitable for a house interior. If it is a barn that needs residing, any one of the timber framing outfits may be able to help you (*see* **Barns**). For interior use in a house, there are two alternatives: use of carefully selected – select Grade A – siding with little or no nail marks or remilled beam stock.

DIAMOND K. CO.
Among the longtime suppliers of quality barnwood is Diamond K. It is also a source for virgin Canadian pine in widths from 12" to 20" for flooring. The barnwood is available in a choice of color and grain with random widths of up to 1' and random lengths to 16'

Brochure available

THE DIAMOND K. CO., INC.
130 Buckland Rd.
South Windsor, CT 06074
(203) 644-8486

RAMASE
This company is typical of firms dealing in a wide variety of architectural salvage (*see* **Architectural Antiques**) which can often supply barn siding and wallboards. Again, the quality of the siding is paramount if it is to be used in an interior. Harold Cole of Ramase has a large inventory of old building materials and is worth contacting.

RAMASE
Rte. 47
Woodbury, CT 06798
(203) 263-3332

Remilled lumber is a speciality of several firms in the South. Their stock in trade is longleaf or yellow heart pine removed from old farm buildings and mills. Each of the following firms supplies a variety of recycled products; it is not real barn siding, having been derived from beams, but that makes it better for many purposes: E.T. MOORE, JR. CO., MOUNTAIN LUMBER CO., and OLD SOUTH CO. Old South can also supply real barn siding, as can ROBERT W. BELCHER and VINTAGE LUMBER.

Bars. Dealers in architectural antiques report a steady demand for bars, the kind that people drink at. Why any tavern or restaurant would wish to part with its antique bar is unfathomable, but enough of these lengths of polished wood turn up each year to satisfy the demand. Most, of course, are used in pubs or are the centerpiece of a trendy restaurant-lounge. A few may even be used in homes – in a basement or family room. Any number of architectural antique emporiums offer old bars as well as reproductions.

ARCHITECTURAL ANTIQUES EXCHANGE Front and back bars – antique and reproduction – are a speciality of this outlet. Some models are modest in size, like that illustrated, and others could serve easily for a Dodge City tavern. Inventory is always changing. Customers who would prefer a new old-style bar unit can choose from several models or other custom designs. These feature fine hardwoods and raised panels.

Literature, $3

ARCHITECTURAL ANTIQUES EXCHANGE
709-15 N. Second St.
Philadelphia, PA 19123
(215) 922-3669

SPIESS ANTIQUE BUILDING MATERIALS Greg Spiess has now turned his attention to antique back and front bars and interior architectural woodwork. Located in an old industrial and trading town which has suffered its share of urban "renewal," the firm loses no opportunity to save and recycle what it can.

Brochure available

SPIESS ANTIQUE BUILDING MATERIALS
228-230 E. Washington St.
Joliet, IL 60433
(815) 722-5639

Other specialist suppliers of bars are: FLORIDA VICTORIAN ARCHITECTURAL ANTIQUES *and* SALVAGE ONE.

Base blocks. *See* **Door Casings.**

Baseboards. Sadly lacking in many modern interiors, baseboards are an essential feature of a period room. The English call baseboards "skirting," and this term aptly describes the decorative effect of hiding the joint between floor and wall. A tiny little shoe molding – today's usual substitute – just does not provide the same decorative effect or protection from the scrapes of chair and table legs against a wall. Baseboards vary in size from 2" to over a foot in height and are sometimes capped. A shoe molding can be used along the base to add more of a profile.

Any good woodworking shop or supplier of lumber should be able to provide a basic selection of baseboards. Most common is a plain board 6" or so high with beading as a cap and a shoe molding at the base. For something more elaborate, it may be necessary to turn to one of a number of specialty suppliers.

AMERICAN CUSTOM MILLWORK, INC. American offers an almost unlimited variety of baseboard assemblies. Illustrated are but three of these which make use of plain and

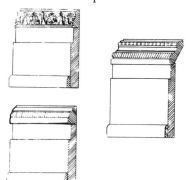

embossed moldings. These are available in Appalachian poplar, walnut, oak, cherry, and mahogany. They are shipped in 4' to 16' lengths.

Literature available

AMERICAN CUSTOM MILLWORK, INC.
3904 Newton Rd., PO Box 3608
Albany, GA 31706
(912) 888-3303 or 6848
Fax (912) 888-9245

AMHERST WOOD WORKING & SUPPLY, INC.
Amherst provides simple baseboards. Thickness can vary between $1/2$" to $13/16$". Height is what you choose to make it, although 6" is probably a minimum for these graceful profiles. The woods stocked are white ash, birch, aromatic red cedar, mahogany, red oak, Eastern poplar, butternut, cherry, Western red cedar, hard maple, white oak, and white pine. Amherst is also willing to reproduce custom patterns if the need is to patch or replace preexisting base.

Moldings catalog available

AMHERST WOODWORKING & SUPPLY, INC.
Box 718, Hubbard Ave.
Northampton, MA 01061
(413) 584-3003
Fax (413) 585-0288

ORNAMENTAL MOULDINGS LIMITED
Two baseboard designs – one of them #765, illustrated here – are offered. Because these are stock items with the company, prices are reasonable and supply immediate.

Number 765 is 5" wide and $11/16$" thick; the companion design, #763, is another inch wider. Both have embossed repeating patterns and are made of white hardwood oak.

Ornamental Mouldings Designer Kit with 4" samples of all architectural patterns, $12; wood moldings brochure, no charge

American inquiries:
ORNAMENTAL MOULDINGS LTD.
PO Box 7123
High Point, NC 27264

Canadian inquiries:
ORNAMENTAL MOULDINGS LTD.
PO Box 336
Waterloo, ONT N2J 4A4
(519) 884-4080
Fax (519) 884-9692

SILVERTON VICTORIAN MILLWORKS
True to its name, Silverton offers baseboards with a particular late 19th- century touch. Model 22-5 is shown with outside and inside base corner beads *(see also* **Corner Beads***)*.

This is an 8"-wide board, $11/16$" in thickness. There are three other stock baseboards. Silverton will also supply custom-made baseboards and baseboard assemblies of moldings to the width desired. The stock bases are available in premium or commercial Northern red oak or Southern yellow pine. Just about any commonly available wood can be specified for the custom work.

Complete catalog package, $4

SILVERTON VICTORIAN MILLWORKS
PO Box 2987 - OC7
Durango, CO 81302
(303) 259-5915
Fax (303) 259-5919

Other recommended suppliers of baseboards are: BENDIX MOULDINGS, INC, BLUE OX MILLWORKS, CLASSIC ARCHITECTURAL SPECIALTIES, OLD WORLD MOULDING & FINISHING CO., SAN FRANCISCO VICTORIANA, INC., *and* SUNSHINE ARCHITECTURAL WOODWORKS.

Baskets. Of minor importance in any period interior, natural fiber baskets can nonetheless add an extra note of substance in various areas of the house. Before plastic bags and containers became ubiquitous, straw, reed, and wicker baskets had multiple uses – for laundry, eggs and produce, flowers, bread, and shopping.

JONATHAN KLINE
The black ash baskets produced by Kline in upper New York State are small pieces of art. Nearly 200 baskets

are woven each year and come in every size and form. These are harvest, laundry, bread, fruit , storage, mail, flower, carrier, and berry baskets – a selection almost as extensive as that offered by a 19th-century basketmaker. Handles and rims are formed from hickory. Illustrated is a nest of three harvest baskets in diameters of 12", 15" and 18".

Brochure, $2

JONATHAN KLINE
5066 Mott Evans Rd.
Trumansburg, NY 14886
(607) 387-5718

SHAKER WORKSHOPS
Baskets of the type woven in 19th-century Shaker communities comprise the selection offered by this firm. Three of them – a 7" berry basket, a 14" cheese basket, and an 8" melon basket – are also available in kit form along with complete instructions for assembly. These are made of reed splint. Other finished baskets are intended for herbs, apples, pies, and laundry and are made of white oak with carved handles.

Catalog $1

SHAKER WORKSHOPS
PO Box 1028
Concord, MA 01742
(617) 646-8985

Another recommended supplier is
MARTHA WETHERBEE BASKET SHOP. Ms.
Wetherbee is also the co-author of
Shaker Baskets, an authoritative
history.

**Bathroom Accessories and
Hardware.** It is hard to forget the
advice of one of our early
contributors to *The Old House
Catalogue:* "Don't tart up the john."
We've never believed in trying to
achieve period bathrooms. There is
no reason, however, that fixtures and
accessories can not have a handsome,
even antique, appearance as long as
they do function in a modern fashion.
Increasingly, manufacturers of
fittings and fixtures are taking into
account a desire for a bit of charm in
the bathroom in keeping with the rest
of the house. Not included among
these suppliers are purveyors of
Pennsylvania-Dutch sayings, corncob
toilet paper holders, wicker thrones,
or other "period" kitsch.

A. BALL PLUMBING SUPPLY
This firm has grown year by year into
one of the largest and most
discerning mail-order suppliers of
fine bathroom fixtures and fittings.
Among the items offered are faucets
of porcelain and brass for sinks and
tubs that are guaranteed to last for
several years, porcelain and brass
toilet trip levers, mirrors, hooks, a
footed tub soap/sponge basket, a
solid-brass toilet tissue holder, a
pedestal soap dish, and a pedestal
toothbrush and cup holder. All are
useful and well-designed items.
Many others are also available.

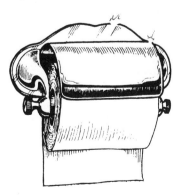

Catalog available

A. BALL PLUMBING SUPPLY
1703 W. Burnside St.
Portland, OR 97209
(503) 228-0026
Fax (503) 228-0030

HISTORIC HARDWARE LTD.
Hand-forged iron bars from this
enterprising small firm serve as
attractive towel and toilet paper
holders., Mounting hardware is
included with each item.

Catalog, $3

HISTORIC HARDWARE LTD.
PO Box 1327
North Hampton, NH 03862
(603) 964-2280

KOHLER CO.
One of those enlightened major
manufacturers of bath fixtures and
accessories, Kohler has recognized
the need for something more than the
purely functional. The Antique Artist

Editions lavatory faucet set may be
somewhat grandiose in name, but it
is attractive to the eye. Made of
beaded brass with ceramic bases and
matching handle insets, the set would
be fitting for a high-style bathroom in
a late 19th- or early 20th-century
home. Kohler products are available
through bath and plumbing
suppliers. If you can't find this
fixture, write directly to Kohler.

KOHLER CO.
Kohler, WI 53044
(414) 457-4441
Fax (414) 459-1656

WATERCOLORS
Watercolors imports some of the best
bathroom hardware made in the UK
and Italy. Among the very best faucet
sets are those included in the
Edwardian Range from England.
They are individually hand cast, one

set at a time, from solid brass. And perhaps most important, these sets will fit standard American or Canadian plumbing; installation should be easy for any plumber. The brass is finished in polished chrome, nickel, 18K gold plate, or available as simple polished brass. Illustrated are a bath filler and a basin set.

Catalog, $1

WATERCOLORS
Garrison on Hudson, NY 10524
(914) 424-3327
Fax (914) 424-3169

Other recommended sources for bathroom accessories or hardware are: ACORN MANUFACTURING CO., ANTIQUE BATHS AND KITCHENS, FANEUIL FURNITURE HARDWARE, HEADS UP SONOMA WOODWORKS, INC., KAYNE & SON, OMNIA INDUSTRIES, RESTORATION WORKS, INC., ROY ELECTRIC ANTIQUE LIGHTING CO., SUNRISE SALVAGE CO., TREMONT NAIL CO., and WEST HARTFORD LOCK.

Bathrooms. In the long history of the house, a bathroom is a fairly recent development. Prior to the introduction of central heating and plumbing in the late 1800s, bathing was more likely to be performed in a bedroom or even a parlor. Other functions were consigned to a water closet, chamber pot, or outhouse. The dilemma facing most old-house owners is that of deciding on what period the bathroom should be. Fixtures that are of real utility, however, will not be terribly old-fashioned unless one is willing to put up with the discomfort of a wooden or galvanized tub and a basin and pitcher. Some of the first fixtures used in the modern bathroom – the claw-foot tub and the pedestal sink – are just as appropriate today. There are suppliers of reproduction fixtures as well as purveyors of the antique *(see* **Bathtubs and Sinks***).* A cold, impersonal modern bathroom is immediately transformed by the introduction of antique fixtures.

The overall design of a bathroom can also add to its comfort and attractiveness. This may involve wainscoting the walls or ceiling, paneling around the tub, or the

introduction of brass accessories *(see* **Bathroom Accessories and Hardware***).* If one is at a complete loss as to what might be done, there are designers of bathrooms (and, often, kitchens as well) who can come to the rescue. Two of the most imaginative are located in England; both are essentially cabinetmakers. Each is prepared to serve customers on both sides of the Atlantic. For American suppliers of similar services, *(see* **Contractors, Restoration***).*

PIPE DREAMS
The use of a simple diamond pattern ceramic tile and a claw-foot tub with brass fittings sets this bath off from the ordinary. The tub is supplied by the British fixture manufacturer, Sanitan. Other rooms designed by

Pipe Dreams involve hand painting, special cabinetwork, and joinery.

Literature available

PIPE DREAMS
72 Gloucester Rd.
London SW7 4QT
England
(071) 225-3978

ROBINSON AND CORNISH
This firm makes use of its considerable skill in cabinetry to create warm, inviting baths. The typical model contains a mellow antique pine lavatory and tub enclosure. Victorian-style ceramic tiles are used to form a splashguard around the basin and the tub. The use of a wood such as pine in a bathroom was once considered unthinkable because of its moisture-absorbent nature. Today's sealers and preservatives make woodwork as easy to care for as vitreous china.

Literature available

ROBINSON & CORNISH
The Old Tannery
Hannaford Lane
Swimbridge, Devon EX32 0Pl
England
(0271) 830732

Bathtubs. Old tubs – mainly claw-foot Victorian models – are among the most popular architectural "antiques." Many firms regularly stock a supply of reconditioned tubs that are as useful and comfortable as they were a century ago. Hardware specialists can supply fittings for showers and other accessories. Because of the widespread demand for these fixtures, today's manufacturers have introduced new tubs in old-fashioned form. These are not strictly authentic, but in the bathroom, practicality should be given precedence before authenticity.

A. BALL PLUMBING SUPPLY
Just about everything needed for an old-fashioned bathroom can be purchased from A. Ball, including a cast-iron claw-foot tub. The tub is available in two sizes – 60" long x 30" wide and 68" long x 30" wide – and features brass-plated or chrome-plated feet. Various fittings, such as shower rings, faucets, waste and overflow plates, and shower heads, are made of brass, chrome, or porcelain.

Catalog, free

A. BALL PLUMBING SUPPLY
1703 W. Burnside St.
Portland, OR 97209
(503) 228-0026
Fax (503) 228-0030

KOHLER CO.
The Vintage Suite of bathroom fixtures from this leading manufacturer includes a cast-iron tub which is Victorian in form. It sits, however, on a wood base rather than claw feet. The wood towel rails are optional. The tub is spacious – 72" long x 42" wide x 22" deep – and is shown with Kohler's Antique faucet set.

Kohler fixtures are distributed through-out North America; contact Kohler for the nearest supplier.

KOHLER CO.
Kohler, WI 53044
(414) 457-4441
Fax (414) 459-1656

ROY ELECTRIC ANTIQUE LIGHTING CO.
Despite its name, Roy features
antique bathroom fixtures in addition to its regular line of lighting devices.
The claw-foot tub shown is restored
and is fitted with a two-valve antique shower unit and 24" shower ring.

Plumbing fixtures catalog, $6

ROY ELECTRIC ANTIQUE LIGHTING CO.
1054 Coney Island Ave.
Brooklyn, NY 11230
(718) 434-7002
Fax (718) 421-4678

Other suppliers of antique tubs are:
THE BRASS KNOB, FLORIDA VICTORIAN
ARCHITECTURAL ANTIQUES, SALVAGE
ONE, and VINTAGE PLUMBING &
SANITARY SPECIALISTS. Vintage also
restores claw-foot fixtures and can
supply missing parts.

Two additional suppliers of new
"Victorian" tubs are: ANTIQUE BATHS
AND KITCHENS and CUMBERLAND
GENERAL STORE.

Beams. Good solid members strong
enough to support floors can often be
retrieved from derelict buildings.
Dealers in recycled lumber depend
on such a supply, barns and old mills
providing most of their antique
harvest. Many of the beams end up
being remilled for flooring. There are,
as well, suppliers of newly milled
beams, craftsmen who know the
difference between a mass-produced
ornamental beam and a substantial
one hand-hewn with an axe. Nothing
appears quite as ridiculous in an old
house as a fake beamed ceiling made
up of strips of wood often no thicker
than lathe. Beams should declare
their structural function and be
exposed only when a higher ceiling is
needed. It was never a builder's
intention to leave wood beams
exposed during the Colonial period
and early 19th century. If the beams
were not boxed in or a plastered
ceiling not put up, this was a result of
a lack of money or the skill of a
plasterer and not a conscious
aesthetic choice.

CONKLIN'S AUTHENTIC ANTIQUE
    BARNWOOD AND HAND HEWN
    BEAMS
The name of this supplier says it all.
Leo Conklin, of rural northwest
Pennsylvania, will supply beams in
oak, hemlock, and pine. He has 8,000
to 10,000 running feet in stock at most
times, The sizes will vary, and the
customer must be precise in his
needs. The beams are all from old
barns.

Flyer available

CONKLIN'S AUTHENTIC ANTIQUE
    BARNWOOD AND HAND HEWN
    BEAMS
RD 1, Box 70
Susquehanna, PA 18847
(717) 465-3832

TIRESIAS, INC.
Tiresias is one of a number of
Southern suppliers of yellow heart
pine for flooring, paneling and
beams. These can be obtained rough
sawn or hand hewn, random sawn to
the customer's specifications. Again,
this is recycled material saved from
old barns, mills, and other industrial
structures.

Brochure available

TIRESIAS, INC.
PO Box 1864
Orangeburg, SC 229116
(803) 534-8478 or 3445
(800) 553-8003
Fax (803) 533-0051

Other suppliers of recycled beams are:
ROBERT W. BELCHER, DIAMOND K. CO.,
INC., E.T. MOORE JR., CO., MOUNTAIN
LUMBER CO., and PAGLIACCO TURNING
AND MILLING. *Additional suppliers of
new beams made in the old manner
are:*THE BARN PEOPLE, INC., and
BROAD-AXE BEAM CO.

Bed Hangings. The use of bed
hangings for privacy and protection
from insects and drafts is an ancient
practice which continued in various
forms until the late 19th century.
Beds in the 17th and 18th centuries
were often encased in fabric – from
the dust ruffles or flounces below to a
canopy or valances above. Curtains
might also hang from all sides. In
order to support hangings, a superstructure was necessary, a four-
poster with a tester was the common
form. Not all beds, of course, were as
elaborately draped. Those occupied
by children or servants were likely to
be much simpler, low, and
uncurtained.

The type of fabrics used for hangings
in the 17th century was somewhat
limited because of availability. Calico
or serge was the most common
material. In the 1700s cheney, a
worsted fabric, became almost as
popular as calico. By the early 1800s
printed (copperplate) textiles had
come into use. Net or candlewick
material for canopies dates from
some time in the 19th century.

The making of bed hangings is today
a speciality of needleworkers with a
knowledge of historical fashions.
Museum curators responsible for
authentically furnishing period
rooms are often a good source of
information on craftspeople who will
fabricate bed hangings. Two firms
that supply various types of hangings
are described below.

CARTER CANOPIES
Fishnet canopies and valances for
four-poster beds with testers are
offered by this firm. The style is one
that was popular in the mid- to late
19th century. There are six patterns to
chose from in the 100% cotton fabric.
Illustrated is a bed with valances in
the large scallop design. Carter will
also custom-make dust ruffles and
hand-tied fringe.

Color brochure, $1

CARTER CANOPIES
PO Box 808, Rte 2, Box 270G
Troutman, NC 28166
(704) 528-4071
Fax (704) 528-6437

COHASSET COLONIALS
Cohasset offers an arched fishnet
canopy in antique white or pure
white cotton. It is available in two
sizes for a full-size or queen-size bed.
Dust ruffles can be ordered as well,
along with hardware needed to hang
the fabric from rods.

Catalog, $5

COHASSET COLONIALS
Cohasset, MA 02025
(800) 288-2389

THE COUNTRY BED SHOP
One of the rare suppliers of
traditional Colonial bed hangings is
this old New England company. The
firm will even provide handwoven
fabrics similar to these of the past, but
these are understandably quite
expensive. Printed fabrics may do
just as well for non-museum settings.
Included in the list of hangings
available are valances and tester
covers, head cloths, curtains, and
skirts or dust ruffles. Curtains are
made to be hung from the tester
frame by tape loops or brass rings.
For an illustration of one of the shop's
draped beds, *see* **Beds.**

Catalog, $4

THE COUNTRY BED SHOP
RR1, Box 65, Richardson Rd.
Ashby, MA 01431
(508) 386-7550

SERAPH WEST AND SERAPH EAST
Reproduction homespun fabrics are
used by Seraph West and Seraph East

for bed curtains and swags. There are 25 patterns to choose from.

Catalog available, $3

SERAPH EAST
PO Box 50, Rte. 20
Sturbridge, MA 01566
(617) 347-2241

SERAPH WEST
5606 St. Rte. 37
Delaware, OH 43015
(800) 233-1817

BED HARDWARE AND PARTS

Converting or repairing antique beds for modern use can be a frustrating task if the right parts are not in hand. The number of people who wish to make do with rope supports are few in number and it may take a bit of adjustment to fit an antique wood bedstead with proper box spring and mattress. Similarly, a brass bed can require special parts or even new rails. There are speciality dealers who can help.

BEDLAM BRASS

Bedlam is one of the largest suppliers of solid-brass tubing, ornaments, bends, caps, balls, and scrolls. It can also supply such essential, and sometimes difficult to find, elements as threaded rods, tee fittings, and pop-in threaded fasteners.

Bed part replacement catalog, $1

BEDLAM BRASS
137 Rte. 4 Westbound
Paramus, NJ 07652
(201) 368-3500
Fax (201) 368-1850

PAXTON HARDWARE

Speciality bed hardware such as bed bolt covers in brass, brass balls for iron and brass beds, forged steel bed bolts, cast-iron as well as wrought steel bed rail fasteners, and steel spring supports for a conventional spring and mattress are available from Paxton. The supports are neccessary for converting an antique wood bedstead which has never had modern appointments.

Catalog 10, $4

PAXTON HARDWARE LTD.
7818 Bradshaw Rd.
Upper Falls, MD 21156
(301) 592-8505
Fax (301) 592-2224

Another recommended supplier of bed hardware is A CAROLINA CRAFTSMAN.

Beds. Since the average person spends almost a third of his life in bed, it is especially important that a bed be not only sturdy but comfortable. This does not mean, however, that one has to settle for a futon or a frameless modern box spring and mattress. Almost any antique bed can be adapted for modern use. And there are makers of traditional-style beds that are not only authentic in appearance but are handsome pieces of furniture in their own right.

G. R. CLIDENCE, 18TH CENTURY WOODWORKS

Beds produced by this furniture maker are built to fit all standard mattress sizes. The beds can be given various support systems – traditional roping, a recessed mattress support, a

raised mattress support, or a drop support for a mattress and box spring. Clidence offers six different beds, although he is willing to use features from one in another on a custom basis. The basic designs are a New England pencil post bed, a Sheraton field bed, a cannonball bed with turned blanket roll, a low post bed, a half-canopy bed, and a folding bed. Twin, double, and queen sizes are available in most styles. The pencil post, Sheraton, and cannonball beds are also available in king size. Cherry and maple primarily are used for a variety of headboard, rail, and post designs, but tiger maple, walnut, and mahogany can be substituted . Illustrated is one stock design , a cannonball bed, and two custom adaptations, a Sheraton field bed with a trundle and a folding half-canopy bed.

Brochure and photographs, $3

G.R. CLIDENCE , 18TH CENTURY
    WOODWORKS
Box 386, James Trail
West Kingston, RI 02892
(401) 539-2558

THE COUNTRY BED SHOP
The founder of the shop, Charles
Thibeau, and his successor, Alan
Pease, are as knowledgeable about
the development of the bed over the
centuries as anyone could be. Their
careful study has allowed them to
faithfully re-create bedsteads from

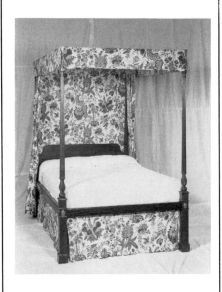

the late 17th century to the mid 19th.
Most of their models are based on
18th-century examples and, typically,
are made up of several woods, maple
and pine being among them. All the
frames are of bolted mortise-and-
tenon construction. Any carving is
done by hand, and turnings are made
in one piece, freehand on the lathe.
Beds are sized for standard
mattresses. Shown is what is called
the Goddard Chippendale bed after
the 18th-century Newport craftsman,
John Goddard. The design dates from
c. 1760. Other styles include pencil
post beds with flat testers, low post
beds, a paneled bed and turned
Pilgrim bedstead from the late 1600s,
Sheraton and Hepplewhite field beds,
trundle beds, and a Queen Anne
tester bed. The Bed Shop's catalog is a
model of clarity, providing both
historical and technical information
of value.

Catalog, $4

THE COUNTRY BED SHOP
RR1, Box 65, Richardson Rd.
Ashby, MA 01431
(508) 386-7550

SPRING HOUSE CLASSICS
Included among the furniture
carefully handcrafted by
Pennsylvanian Dan Backenstose is a
pencil post bed with or without a
tester for a canopy. Poplar is the
usual wood used, although walnut or
cherry can be specified. Sizes are
based on standard mattress sizes for
double, queen, or king-size beds.
There are four headboard styles to
choose from, and three post styles.

*Catalog, $3 (refundable on first
    purchase)*

SPRING HOUSE CLASSICS
PO Box 541
Schaefferstown, PA 17088
(717) 949-3902

*Other recommended suppliers of period
beds are:* BEDLAM BRASS, COHASSET
COLONIALS, JEFFREY P. GREENE,
FURNITUREMAKER, MURPHY DOOR BED
CO., SERAPH EAST AND SERAPH WEST,
SHAKER WORKSHOPS, and SWAN BRASS
BEDS.

Bell Pulls. In the days when servants
were plentiful and could be
summoned whenever needed, a bell
pull was a useful accessory. Its utility
is rather limited today, but in a
stately home a fabric pull might have
a place, even if the bell system has
disappeared or fallen out of use.

DECORATIVE TEXTILES OF CHELTENHAM
Four different designs are produced –
paisley, brocade, needlework, and
tapestry. Each fabric pull is
handmade and, as shown in the
illustration, includes the handle. If
one of these designs doesn't seem
right, the workshop will create
something entirely unique by special
order.

Brochure available

DECORATIVE TEXTILES OF CHELTENHAM
7, Suffolk Parade
Cheltenham, GL 50 2AB
England
(0242) 574546
Fax (0242) 222646

Benches, Outdoor and Indoor. A
garden or patio bench must be of
very sturdy construction because of
its exposure to the elements.
Depending on the climate, however,
it may be wise to store furniture in a
less exposed place such as a shed or
garage during the winter. That being
the case, lightness will also be a
virtue. Strength and ease of handling
can be combined. Stone benches are
not, of course, meant to be moved
and will survive even the effects of
acid rain. Benches for indoor use –
usually with a dining table – can be
of almost any material and weight.
They range from small pieces hardly
larger than a footstool to lengths
appropriate for a trestle table. *See also*
Settles.

GREEN ENTERPRISES
Popular desire for attractive, well-
built outdoor furniture led to the
founding of Green in the 1970s. It was
a time when a customer could choose
only between aluminum models with
all the durability and style of
flypaper. Since then, molded
synthetic furniture has also come on

the market and it, too, has the grace of a high school shop class production and will endure for only a season or two. Green's handsome benches, on the contrary, are made of either red oak or maple; those given a white enamel finish are of maple, and the oak models are finished with a clear polyurethane treatment. The width of Green's "Victorian" bench is either 68" or 20".

Brochure available

GREEN ENTERPRISES
43 S. Rogers St.
Hamilton , VA 22068
(703) 338-3606

KENNETH LYNCH AND SONS
As a source for benches of all types, Lynch is unsurpassed. There are over 500 designs to choose from, and of special interest and value are those of stone. Illustrated is No. 108 which can be curved or straight. It has what is termed an Irish safety leg at each end so that it cannot possibly topple. Lengths of 4' and 5' are offered. Once this bench or any of the other stone models are in place, you won't want to move it, but, then, there would be no necessity of doing so.

Book of Benches, $6.50

KENNETH LYNCH AND SONS, INC.
78 Danbury Rd., Box 488
Wilton, CT 06897
(203) 762-8363
Fax (203) 762-2999

Other recommended suppliers of garden benches are: ARCHITECTURAL ANTIQUES EXCHANGE, ARCHITECTURAL IRON CO., BRANDYWINE GARDEN FURNITURE, *and* LAWLER MACHINE & FOUNDRY CO. (Steptoe and Wife Antiques, Ltd., in Canada). *A number of architectural antiques firms carry an inventory of antique cast-iron benches. A source for*

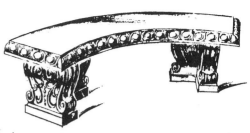

indoor wooden benches is SHAKER WORKSHOPS.

Beveled Glass. Glass that has been cut with one of a series of sloped or canted surfaces, beveled glass is made today in great variety. It is also regularly stocked by many architectural antiques outlets already installed in doors and windows. Glass panels of this type were popular in the late 1800s and early 20th century for transoms, sidelights, doors, and windows. In an entryway, a degree of privacy is wanted, and the cutting of the glass diffuses light penetration. Elaborately beveled glass is expensive and the work of artists; glass panels edged with a bevel only – still often used for mirrors – is available from many

GLOSTER LEISURE FURNITURE
Gloster is typical of English manufacturers of teak outdoor furniture who have kept the tradition of fine woodworking alive in an age of ersatz. All of the firm's furniture is made of solid teak from Java. Illustrated is one of the most popular models, the 5' Sandringham bench. There are several other types available, including a new bench design, the Sunray, with sunburst motifs on twin back panels. It is made in 5' and 6' lengths.

Canadian customers, contact:
STEPTOE AND WIFE ANTIQUES, LTD.
322 Geary Ave.
Toronto, ONT M6H 2C7
(414) 530-4200
Fax (414) 530-4666

American customers, contact:
UNIVERSAL GLOSTER INC.
1555-57 Carmen Dr.
Elk Grove Village, IL 60007
(708) 362-9400
Fax (708) 362-9430

window glass dealers.

ARTEFACT ARCHITECTURAL ANTIQUES
Artefact is one of the salvage dealers who offer an assortment of beveled glass panels at almost any given time. Shown is a design of the type popular in the early 1900s for entrances and stair landings. Artefact will provide a profile sheet on the firm and photos of inventory at no cost.

ARTEFACT ARCHITECTURAL ANTIQUES
130 S. Main St.
Doylestown, PA 18901
(215) 340-1213

CAIN ARCHITECTURAL ART GLASS
The company uses its 1915 machinery to produce custom orders for beveled glass panels. This is a particularly good source to turn to if there is a need to duplicate a period piece. On the other hand, if you have no idea of what to choose, Cain can provide its own design services.

Photographs available on request

CAIN ARCHITECTURAL ART GLASS
Cain, Inc.
Bremo Bluff, VA 23022
(804) 842-3984

ELEGANT ENTRIES
Hardwood doors, sidelights, and transoms are the primary product of this firm , and beveled glass is the stock material used for inserts. The panels are highly ornamental, as the Town and Country entryway shows.

Transoms are available in rectangular, true radius, and compound radius forms.

Catalog available

ELEGANT ENTRIES
240 Washington St.
Auburn, MA 01501
(800) 343-3432

Other recommended suppliers of new beveled glass panels are: BACKSTROM STAINED GLASS & ANTIQUES, CHERRY CREEK ENTERPRISES, MORGAN-BOCKIUS STUDIOS, INC., POMPEII & CO., J. RING GLASS STUDIO, INC., SUNFLOWER GLASS STUDIO, and WILLIAMS ART GLASS STUDIO, INC.

Additional sources for antique beveled glass are: THE BRASS KNOB, FLORIDA VICTORIAN ARCHITECTURAL ANTIQUES, and SALVAGE ONE.

Birdbaths, Houses, and Feeders. No old house garden is complete without a provision for songbirds. Beautiful accommodations for birds were designed in the past and many of them are handsomely reproduced today.

LAZY HILL FARM
This company is the creation of bird lover Betty Baker. Houses and feeders of cypress with cedar shingle roofs are made in her North Carolina workshop. Shown is the Lazy Hill House styled after an English dovecote. It is 16" in diameter, 28" high, and has eight compartments. it is available painted white or stained

gray. All houses except for The Bluebird House come with a mounting bracket. A 7' post can be provided for the Lazy Hill House.

Brochure, $1

LAZY HILL FARM DESIGNS
Lazy Hill Rd.
Colerain, NC 27924
(919) 356-2628

KENNETH LYNCH AND SONS
Lynch has a superb assortment of traditional birdbaths in stone, cast stone, and lead. There are sculpted shells, fonts, and other kinds of basins. Many of the designs are based on antique English models.

Book of Garden Ornaments, $9.50

KENNETH LYNCH AND SONS
78 Danbury Rd., Box 488
Wilton, CT 06897
(203) 762-8363
Fax (203) 762-2999

Blinds. *See* **Venetian Blinds.**

Bluestone. *See* **Stone.**

Bolection Moldings. *See* **Moldings.**

Bolts. Often called a slide bolt, this type of hardware is used in the place of, or in addition to, a lock to secure a door. It may be placed on an entry door, inner door, cabinet, or cupboard door. Inexpensive brass bolts can be purchased in almost any hardware store; heavier and stronger iron bolts of various types are available from a growing number of blacksmiths and ironmongers.

FORGERIES
This company is proud to be copying antique hardware. Each piece produced is hand-wrought, as the slight irregularity evidences. This is hardware with texture and color (gray) with only a turpentine preservative wax. Most items are in stock, including a selection of door bolts with fishtail pulls. The slide has a back-spring to facilitate ease of handling. Each bolt is supplied with a standard or a mortise-plate keeper.

Brochure available

FORGERIES
Old Butchery, High St.
Twyford, Hants SO21 1RF
England
(0962) 712196 (Telephone and Fax)

HISTORIC HARDWARE LTD.
In addition to slide bolts, Historic Hardware fabricates canebolts, as illustrated, which are suitable for

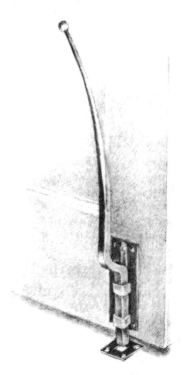

securing French doors, barn doors, and garden gates. The device is made in three sizes – 10", 14", and 18" with a 6" x 1 3/4" plate. Each is supplied with a flush keeper for floor or ceiling mount; a surface mount keeper can be substituted.

Catalog, $3

HISTORIC HARDWARE LTD.
PO Box 1327
North Hampton, NH 03862
(603) 964-2280

KAYNE & SON, CUSTOM FORGED
    HARDWARE
Steve Kayne prides himself on custom-produced hardware. Seventeen of the type of bolts illustrated were recently made for use on stable doors. He also produces

forged bolts for use on Dutch doors and windows, French doors, and standard doors. Kayne additionally carries a line of cast bolts.

Forged hardware catalog, $2; cast $3; both, $3.50

KAYNE & SON, CUSTOM FORGED
    HARDWARE
76 Daniel Ridge Rd.
Candler, NC 28715
(704) 667-8868 or 665-1988

Two other recommended suppliers of forged sliding bolts are: THE ARDEN FORGE CO., *and* THE WOODBURY BLACKSMITH & FORGE CO.

Bookcases. Display shelves for books need not be DIY quickies. While attractive units can now be found at such outlets as IKEA, The Workbench, and The Door Store, custom-designed shelving is to be preferred for any permanent home. If books are an important possession, they should be displayed attractively. In a period room this means that there should be an attempt to integrate the shelving with the architectural character of the space, perhaps making use of moldings and a finish that imitates the woodwork. Carpenters or cabinetmakers sensitive to period detail can sometimes be entrusted with this type of work. There are also specialists in shelving at some of the woodworking and restoration contracting firms.

SUNSHINE ARCHITECTURAL
    WOODWORKS
Imaginatively designed bookcase units are included as stock items by this enterprising millwork firm. Illustrated is the 510CS series of units. The stock height is 95" and the widths are 2', 2 1/2', and 3'. The units are a foot deep. Raised panels are used in the arches and cabinets; they can also be incorporated in an exposed end. Sunshine produces a second design with a similar dentil cornice, but without the arches. It is made in the same sizes.

Catalog, $4

SUNSHINE ARCHITECTURAL
    WOODWORKS
2169 Sunshine Dr., Dept. C.
Fayetteville, AR 72703
(501) 521-4329
(800) 628-8004
Fax (501) 521-8863

MARION H. CAMBELL, CABINETMAKER
This Pennsylvania craftsman has made his reputation from fine cabinetwork – shelves, built-in cabinets, mantels – as well as from the design, construction, and finishing of paneling, cornices, valances, doors, and shutters. Large pieces of furniture such as desks and tall clock cases comprise yet another form of his craftsmanship in woods such as walnut, cherry, and Honduras mahogany. Shelving or cabinets for books are designed with a room's overall character clearly in mind. Since bookshelves are often also used for storing audio equipment and displaying objects, provision may be made for these uses.

Brochure available, 50¢

MARION H. CAMBELL, CABINETMAKER
Barber & Plymouth Sts.
Bath, PA 18014
(215) 837-7775 (shop)
(215) 865-3292 (home)

Borders. *See* **Wallpapers.**

Brackets. Brackets are used for innumerable decorative and functional purposes, and are fabricated of wood, plaster, composition, metal, and synthetics. Presented here are sources for brackets which are used primarily in an ornamental fashion; *See also entries for* **Stairways** *and* **Fencing and Gates.** Outdoors, brackets can be used effectively in porches, cornices, and as part of gable-end decorations. Indoors, brackets are used to support or hide the joint between a beam and a wall, as embellishments for doorways, and as supports for shelving and hanging objects.

Particularly heavy brackets are often termed corbels.

THE DECORATORS SUPPLY CORP.
Decorators is the granddaddy manufacturer of composition, wood fiber, and plaster ornaments used by the interior design trade. Until the resurgence of restoration work in the 1960s, this firm was one of the few that could supply a wide assortment of decorative architectural

appointments. Brackets are made in fibrous plaster or two varieties of composition for interior or exterior use. Use of these materials allows items to be produced at much less expense than if they were carved in wood or stone. Composition or fibrous plaster brackets are, of course, not intended for structural purposes. The designs range from neoclassical Greek and Roman to Rococo.

Illustrated catalog of Composition Capitals and Brackets, $3

THE DECORATORS SUPPLY CORP.
3610-12 S. Morgan St.
Chicago, IL 60609
(312) 847-6300
Fax (312) 847-6357

NEW ENGLAND TOOL CO. LTD.
Forged steel brackets for load-bearing objects such as shelves, window boxes, and heavier elements are supplied by New England. Different gauges of steel are used for light, medium, and heavyweight loads. They are shipped pre-drilled for installation and have a black satin finish.

Sale sheet available

NEW ENGLAND TOOL CO. LTD.
PO Box 30
Chester, NY 10918
(914) 782-5332
(914) 651-7550
Fax (914) 783-2554

W. F. NORMAN CORP.
A firm best known for its metal ceilings, Norman also supplies a full line of ornamental brackets in sheet zinc. Its 1892 catalog, reissued recently, includes over 50 designs, including brackets termed "modillions" which **are** used below as fascia.

Sheet Metal Ornaments catalog, $5

Canadian customers, contact:
STEPTOE AND WIFE ANTIQUES LTD.
322 Geary Ave.
Toronto, ONT M6H 2C7
Canada
(414) 530-4200
Fax (414) 530-4666

U.S. customers, contact:
W.F. NORMAN CORP.

214 N. Cedar
Nevada, MO 64772-4038
(800) 641-4038
(417) 667-5552 (MO)

SAN FRANCISCO VICTORIANA
The principals of Victoriana pioneered in the restoration business in the San Francisco area. Today it continues as a major supplier of authentic reproduction materials, but has expanded to serve a national market. Its architectural castings are produced as shells with fiber reinforcement. Castings intended for interior use are of cast gypsum plaster; castings to be used outside are hydrocal. There are over 30 bracket designs to choose from, the vast majority of them being appropriate for mid- to late-Victorian buildings. Illustrated are three recently introduced designs.

Book of Architectural Building Materials, $5

SAN FRANCISCO VICTORIANA, INC.
2070 Newcomb Ave.
San Francisco, CA 94124
(415) 648-0313
Fax (415) 648-2812

SILVERTON VICTORIAN MILLWORK
The company's popular corner brackets are intended primarily for exterior use – on porches, as gable-end decoration, and as support for window boxes – but are useful above or in the corners of doorways and as shelf brackets. They are also produced in oak or pine. All are available in 1 1/8" or 3/4" thickness and range in height from 9" to 16". This is true gingerbread for a Victorian house.

Catalog, $4

SILVERTON VICTORIAN MILLWORKS
PO Box 2987-OC7
Durango, CO 81302
(303) 259-5915
Fax (303) 259-5919

TENNESSEE FABRICATING CO.
Corner brackets are an integral part of all the decorative cast-iron and aluminum parts intended for porches produced by Tennessee and other metalwork firms (*see* **Porches**). There are also other bracket types such as those made for affixing handrails, window boxes, shelves, and mailboxes.

Catalog, $5

TENNESSEE FABRICATING CO.
1822 Latham St.
Memphis, TN 38106
(901) 948-3354
Fax (901) 948-3356

WORTHINGTON GROUP LTD.
Cast plaster brackets for use indoors under a support beam or outside under a soffit are handsome appointments. The supplier also suggests their use as side table bases. From left to right, the designs are: 79118, 16 3/4" high, 12" deep, 12" wide; 74299, 12" high, 11 3/4" deep, 7 3/4" wide; and 79115, 18" high, 11" deep, 7 1/2" wide.

Other suppliers of brackets are: wood – BLUE OX MILLWORKS, GOTHOM INC., HICKSVILLE WOODWORKS CO., THE OLD WAGON FACTORY, and VINTAGE WOOD WORKS; *cast plaster* – THE BALMER STUDIOS; *metal* – LAWLER MACHINE & FOUNDRY CO., INC. and TREMONT NAIL CO.

Brick. The warmth and irregularity of brick contributes greatly to the character of many old house facades. This is an appearance which is hard to duplicate with new material, as most new brick is singularly dull in finish and uniform in shape. This applies as much to the brick used as pavers as it does for those used for walls. Home restorers in need of a limited number of bricks for rebuilding or repairs often turn to suppliers of antique material, of which there are many. Much of this material can be recycled after being removed from a demolition site.

Luxury Architectural Details catalog, $3

WORTHINGTON GROUP LTD.
PO Box 53101
Atlanta, GA 30355
(404) 872-1608
(800) 872-1608
Fax (404) 872-8501

Local suppliers of building materials will often have leads to such antique supplies. For major projects, however, it probably will be necessary to contact one of the manufacturers of new brick in traditional forms and colors.

CUSHWA BRICK, INC.
The foremost producer of traditional brick materials in North America, Cushwa has been in business since 1872. Both hand- and machine-molded bricks are in their product line. The top of line are the Calvert hand-molded facing bricks of Maryland shale. They are formed in sand-coated wooden molds in a wide range of colors from a whitish-brown to a dark red. All are made in what is termed "oversize"– 4" x 2 3/4" x 8 1/2". The National Park Service has used this brick in its restoration work. Only slightly less superior are Cushwa's Antique Collection bricks which are machine-made. These are

available in an even wider range of colors than the hand-molded bricks and come in three sizes – standard, 3 5/8" x 2 1/4" x 8"; modular, 3 3/8" x 2 1/4" x 7 5/6"; and oversize, 3 5/8" x 2 3/4" x 8". These two types of brick can be used for paving purposes as well. Cushwa also makes an easier to handle and install paver that is only 1 5/8" in thickness rather than the standard 2 1/4" and is available in the same colors as the face brick. In addition, the company can supply special shaped bricks needed for fireplace surrounds, arches, sills and copings, stair treads, watertables, and for angled or curved surfaces. The photograph shows all of Cushwa's product lines; the handmade oversize and the Antique Collection machine-made bricks are shown in the lower left, above and below, respectively.

For a list of distributors, contact:

Cushwa Bricks, Inc.
PO Box 160
Williamsport, MD 21795-0160
(301) 223-7700

Other recommended manufacturers of traditional brick are: Glen-Gery Corp., Kane-Gonic Brick Corp. *and* Old Carolina Brick Co. *Among the architectural salvage firms carrying a regular supply of old bricks are:* The Brickyard, Florida Victorian Architectural Antiques, E. T. Moore, Jr. Co., *and* Ramase.

Brownstone. *See* **Stone.**

Building Inspection Services. When buying an old house nothing is more important than a thorough knowledge of its workings – or non-workings. Anyone with construction experience probably does not need to avail himself of the services of a building inspector, but for the rest of mankind, other people's expertise is most helpful. An investment of $1,000 or even a bit more for a thorough inspection report can very well save

the future home owner many thousands. Inspectors of houses are found throughout North America, but caveat emptor – not all know what to look for in an old house. Old wood window sash, for example, should be retained if at all possible, but some inspectors will recommend that they be replaced with vinyl or even aluminum. These misguided inspectors completely ignore the value of those elements which give a house its character and which can be restored to their former glory.

Among the recommended inspection firms in the United States is HouseMaster of America with franchises across the country; in Canada, Carson, Dunlop & Associates is particularly recommended. Local contractors are also sometimes of value for inspection purposes, but remember that since their primary business is remodeling or restoration rather than inspection, their report may be unduly gloomy.

Bull's–Eye Panes. Glass of this type is often used for transoms and sidelights in Colonial entryways. Of a heavy substance rich in lead, a bull's-eye pane takes its name from the pontil mark at the center. There are several sources for these handmade panes.

Historic Hardware Ltd.
This firm's panes are made in the same way they were 200 years ago – by hand-blowing, spinning, and cutting. The Colonists considered the discs from which the panes were cut leftovers or waste fit only for transoms and rear windows. Today the panes may add the character needed for a Colonial farmhouse entryway. Historic Hardware stocks five sizes: 6 x 6, 8 x 8, 10 x 10, 10 x 12, and 12 x 12, and will cut custom sizes as well.

Catalog available, $3

Historic Hardware Ltd.
PO Box 1327
North Hampton, NH 03862
(603) 964-2280

Kraatz Russell Glass
This firm has made its name as a supplier of bull's-eye panes made in the traditional manner since 1976. Some sample sizes are 6 x 6, 6 x 8, 8 x 10, 10 x 10, 10 x 12. The workshop, however, cuts the glass to the customer's specifications on a custom basis.

Literature available, SASE with 45¢ postage

Kraatz Russell Glass
Grist Mill Hill
FRD 1, Box 320C
Canaan, NH 03741
(603) 523-4289

Details, gable-end decoration with bargeboard, Design XXV, "Cornice, etc., of the Gables," An Ornamental Cottage, from The Model Architect *(1852) by Samuel Sloan.*

Fig. 1

Fig. 2

Fig. 3.

Fig. 4.

Fig. 5.

Fig. 6.

Fig. 7.

Fig. 8.

Fig. 9.

Scale ½ inch to the foot.

Clapboards, Joiner Farmhouse, near Suffolk, Virginia. Historic American Buildings Survey.

Candles, Electric. The use of real beeswax is certainly to be preferred in sticks and sconces; dripless candles can also be used in chandeliers and other hanging fixtures. The expense and the risk of fire, however, may recommend that electric "candles" be substituted. Tiny flame-tipped bulbs as low as 10 watts and as high as 25 provide a soft glow not unlike that of candlelight. These are available from many lighting shops or through the mail from PAXTON HARDWARE LTD. These may be used with candle or socket covers which give the appearance and texture of a real candle. Entire electric candle units are also available from a longtime supplier – ELCANCO.

ELCANCO, LTD.
This firm has supplied ingenious electric fixtures and fittings to museums and homeowners for many

years. There are two models – the Starlite and the Morelite – to choose from. The former is entirely handmade, making use of either an ivory European beeswax or a true, unbleached beeswax cover. The Starlite must be used with Elcanco's Candlewick bulb and with a six-volt transformer. The Morelite is also handcrafted but will accept any candelabra-base bulb and does not require a transformer. Illustrated is the Starlite model. Elcanco is also a good source for beeswax candlecovers to be used with other types of fixtures.

Brochure available, $1

ELCANCO, LTD.
PO Box 682
Westford, MA 01886
(508) 392-0830

Candlestands and Accessories. The revival of blacksmithing and tinsmithing in recent years has brought with it the production of numerous traditional objects such as candlestands, candle boxes, match holders, and candle molds. Antique examples are hard to find and, when located, may be unaffordable.

THE VILLAGE FORGE
Michael D. Sutton produces a handsome line of Colonial-period lighting fixtures, including three iron candlestand models. They are very reasonably priced and completely hand wrought. All the fixtures are wired, the stands being supplied with candelabra sockets. If, however, an unwired stand is desired, this is available on request. The two-arm model shown is 60" in height; there is a second two-arm fixture that is also 60" in height as well as a one-arm

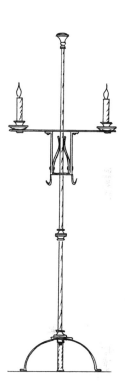

model measuring 48".

Brochure available, $1.50

THE VILLAGE FORGE
Country Club Rd.
Rte. 4, Box 124
Smithfield, NC 27577
(919) 934-2581
Fax (919) 934-3298

THE TINNER
A superb source for tinwear, The Tinner is Jim Barnett, a knowledgeable craftsman. His restored 19th-century tin shop is a pleasure to visit. Among the decorative and useful objects he produces are a candle box (illustrated), single and six-candle molds, a snuffer, and several types of

candlestands ranging in height from 1' to 3'.

Catalog, $1.50

THE TINNER
PO Box 353
Spencer, NC 28159
(704) 637-5149

SHAKER WORKSHOPS
Tables for holding a candlestick may also be known as candlestands. Shaker Workshops is a convenient supplier of simple 25 1/2" high candlestands in either finished or kit form. The company can also supply a Shaker shoemaker's candlestand in wood which will hold two interdependent sticks. It is made of rock maple and has a threaded center post so that the height of the two-arm platform can be adjusted. It is available in finished or kit form.

Catalog, $1

SHAKER WORKSHOPS
PO Box 1028
Concord, MA 01742
(617) 646-8985

Canebolts. *See* **Bolts.**

Caning Materials. Cane or other natural fiber materials for chair seats and backs are supplied by a number of mail-order firms. It is always a pity to discard an old caned chair because of its worn condition. Unfortunately, the number of individuals reweaving chair seats is limited, and it may take months to find a craftsman to take on the work and to complete it. One solution is to learn caning – a fairly easy hobby for the handy. If this is a hopeless alternative, replacement seats can always be purchased (*see* **Chair Seats**).

PAXTON HARDWARE, LTD.
A variety of weaving materials – cane, reed spline, flat reed, and twisted fiber rush – as well as caning pegs are featured in Paxton's catalog. The firm also offers copies of Ruth B. Comstock's three instruction primers: *Cane Seats for Chairs, Spline Seats for Chairs,* and *Rush Seats for Chairs.*

Catalog available, $4

PAXTON HARDWARE, LTD.
7818 Bradshaw Rd., PO Box 256
Upper Falls, MD 21156
(301) 592-8505
(301) 592-2224

Other suppliers of caning materials include: THE CANING SHOP, NEWELL WORKSHOP, PEERLESS RATTAN, WOODCRAFT SUPPLY CORP., and THE WOODWORKERS' STORE.

Canopies, Bed. *See* **Bed Hangings.**

Canopies, Fireplace. A canopy over or within a fireplace is an extremely useful and decorative accoutrement which has been used only rarely in North America. Such a device is sometimes found in a Craftsman-period house or one built in the English Tudor or French Gothic manner. The canopy serves to direct heat out into the room and smoke up the flue. Its use will result in a better-burning fire overall.

THE CANOPY CO.
A leading British manufacturer of these units, this firm creates several different models by hand in steel, brass, or copper. They are banded in steel or brass and riveted in the same materials. Each is supplied with a spigot for connecting to a chimney flue liner. The canopies are heat-resistant and are left plain or given a hammered finish. In addition to the standard canopy, there is a "sweep" canopy for central, freestanding fireplaces and a smoke hood similar to that used above a cook top.

Literature available

THE CANOPY CO.
Platts Rd., Amblecote
Tourbridge, Worcestershire DY8 4YR
England
(0384) 370997
Fax (0384) 442128

For other suppliers of canopies, see
Fireplace Accessories

Capitals. *See* **Columns and Capitals.**

Caps. *See* **Fencing and Gates, Newel Posts, Porches.**

Carpeting. *See* **Rugs and Carpets.**

Carpet Rods and Hardware. There is little sense in putting down carpeting on stairs unless the material is given an extra incentive to stay in place. Use of the rods will also ensure that since the carpeting will not shift, it will last much longer. The brass rods used to keep a run of carpet in place are also handsome additions to any staircase. They can be found now in many quality hardware stores or purchased from speciality sources.

BEDLAM BRASS
The "Carpet Hardware Systems" from Bedlam are deservedly well known. Solid-brass tubing can be used with a number of different bracket designs from the very simple to the ornate. Both 5/8" round and 5/8" quarter-round steel reinforced brass tubing are offered. The brackets are hinged so that the tubing can be removed when the carpet needs cleaning.

Carpet Hardware Systems brochure, $1

BEDLAM BRASS
137 Rte. 4 Westbound
Paramus, NJ 07652
(201) 368-3500
Fax (201) 368-1850

Other recommended direct-mail suppliers of carpet rods and hardware are:
H. PFANSTIEL HARDWARE CO. and RENAISSANCE DECORATIVE HARDWARE CO.

Cartouches. Ornaments of this type are more likely to be used in a hotel or restaurant lobby or dining room than in a domestic interior. A cartouche is basically a framed oval tablet somewhat like a shield. Use of the form in plaster or composition could be appropriate for high-style late-Victorian interiors as well as in homes built in the English Tudor style during the early 1900s.

THE BALMER STUDIOS
A limited selection of cartouches made of gypsum plaster are offered by Balmer. These are shields with ornate frames, the center oval space left blank in most designs. Sizes

range from as small as 14" to 3' in height and from 10" to 3' in width.

Catalog, $20

THE BALMER STUDIOS
9 Codeco Court
Don Mills, ONT M3A IB6
Canada
(416) 449-2155
Fax (416) 449-3018

W. F. NORMAN CORP.
Metal ornaments in sheet zinc are a specialty of Norman. In its 1892 catalog reprint, these, appropriately, are referred to as "shields." They range in size from 7" square designs to highly embellished models, 2' high and 3' wide.

Sheet Metal Ornaments catalog, $5

Canadian customers:
STEPTOE & WIFE ANTIQUES LTD.
322 Geary Ave.
Toronto, ONT M6H 2C7
Canada
(416) 530-4200
Fax (416) 530-4666

American customers:
W. F. NORMAN CORP.
214 N. Cedar, PO Box 323
Nevada, MO 64772-0323
(800) 641-4038
(417) 667-5552 (MO)

Another recommended supplier of ornamental cartouches in fibrous plaster is THE DECORATORS SUPPLY CORP.

Carvings. This term is used to describe true hand-carved ornaments and objects as well as machine-made embossed carvings of wood or wood fiber. Similar in form to many of these "carvings" are plaster, sheet metal, and composition ornaments (*see* **Ornaments**). Both hand-carving in relief and applied carvings are used to decorate window heads, fireplace mantels, window and door surrounds, porticos, and porches. Even such common architectural elements as moldings, baulsters, and railings can be hand-carved in wood if expense will allow for this.

THE DECORATORS SUPPLY CORP.
Both wood fiber and composition carvings in a broad range of period styles can be found at Decorators. These are appropriate for mantels, cabinetwork, and trim. The most

common designs are rosettes, urns, festoons, garlands, and shells.

Wood Fiber Carvings catalog, $5

THE DECORATORS SUPPLY CORP.
3610-12 S. Morgan St.
Chicago, IL 60609-1586
(312) 847-6300
Fax (312) 847-6357

SILVERTON VICTORIAN MILLWORKS
Embossed carvings of commercial oak and white hardwood are particularly useful for mantels and door and window heads or caps. Many Queen Anne and Colonial Revival interiors display such decorative ornamentation as rosettes and swags. Silverton provides a selection of a dozen designs.

Complete catalog package, $4

SILVERTON VICTORIAN MILLWORKS
PO Box 2987-OC7
Durango, CO 81302
(303) 259-5915
Fax (303) 259-5919

FREDERICK WILBUR, WOODCARVER
Wilbur executes all designs by hand whether they are simple signs or complicated floral rosettes and garlands. Among the woods used are mahogany, basswood, walnut, and white pine. His list of clients includes the University of Virginia, Library of Congress, Caswell-Massey, and numerous architectural and design firms. These are demanding customers requiring the services of an artist.

Brochure available

FREDERICK WILBUR, WOODCARVER
PO Box 425
Lovingston, VA 22949
Tel. and Fax (804) 263-4827

Other recommended suppliers of embossed wood carvings are: WOODCRAFT SUPPLY CORP. *and* THE WOODWORKERS' STORE. DIXON BROTHERS WOODWORKING *and* DIMITRIOS KLITSAS *are sources for hand-carved decorations.*

Casement Windows. *See* **Windows.**

Casings. *See* **Door Casings and Window Casings.**

Cast Iron. *See* **Ironwork.**

Ceiling Fixtures. Devices mounted flush with or suspended from the ceiling can be attractive and are especially useful in such areas as a foyer or entry hall. Not included in this category of fixtures are chandeliers or lanterns, either of which can be used as a hall light as well as a fixture for the dining room, parlor, and even a bedroom. *See also entries for* **Chandeliers, Hanging Fixtures** *and* **Lanterns.**

CLASSIC ILLUMINATION, INC.
For a small area with a low ceiling a flush-mounted fixture may be the only option. Classic's Colonial Revival-style fixture was a popular design from the early 1900s until

World War II. The fitter or frame is available in polished brass, polished brass with lacquer, antique brass lacquer, verdigris, or classic bronze. There are two fitter sizes – 10" and 12". There are two corresponding sizes in the shades – 12" and 14". These drop from the ceiling a maximum of $6^{1}/_{2}$". Classic can also supply a slightly larger shade in the Art Deco style which fits into a 14" base. These models by no means exhaust the possibilities. Other Classic options are Art Deco and Art Nouveau dish fixtures suspended from three stems and frosted glass one-stem fixtures.

Catalog, $5

CLASSIC ILLUMINATION, INC.
2743 9th St.
Berkeley, CA 94710
(415) 849-1842
Fax (415) 849-2328

HAMMERWORKS
Depending on the size of the space and its general decor, Hammerworks offers several options appropriate for Colonial and early 19th-century interiors. The simplest of these are made of copper, brass, or antique tin and consist of glass panels with thin strips dividing them (models CL113, 114, and 115). These fit flush against the ceiling and are made in three shapes – square, rectangular, and hexagonal. More elaborate are the hanging fixtures – an open three-light lamp suspended from a chain (model TL-1) and a ceiling onion lamp (OCL 106). The open-frame lamp is offered in 11" and 14"-high models in antique tin; the onion lamp is available in copper or brass in heights of 12", 14", and 17".

Catalog, $3

HAMMERWORKS
6 Fremont St.
Worcester, MA 01603
(800) 777-3689
(508) 755-3434
or
798 Boston Post Rd., Rte. 20
Metro-West Plaza
Marlboro, MA 01752
(508) 485-6721

HISTORIC HARDWARE LTD.
The Wetherfield Foyer Light is especially suitable for a hall or other small space which should be well lit. Its style is suitable for any Colonial period house. As illustrated, the

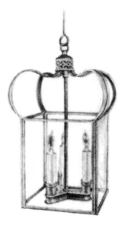

design is a simple one featuring a graceful crown. Shown is the medium-size model, 15" high, 7" wide, and 7" deep. Historic Hardware also makes a smaller version, 11" high, 4 1/2" wide, and 4 1/2"

deep, as well as a larger model. 24 1/2" high, 12" wide, and 12" deep. Both the small and medium lights are offered in tin or antique brass finish. The fixtures can be either electrified or fitted for candles. A canopy and enough chain for an 8-foot ceiling is supplied with each of these hanging fixtures.

Catalog, $3

HISTORIC HARDWARE LTD.
PO Box 1327
North Hampton, NH 03862
(603) 964-2280

REJUVENATION LAMP & FIXTURE CO.
Lighting for late-Victorian and early 20th century homes is a speciality of Rejuvenation. Included in The Craftsman Collection is an art glass lantern ideal for halls or porches. Of solid brass, it can be finished in a number of ways, including verde antique shown here, which gives an

appearance of age and weathering. The shade is available either frosted or in four colors. A canopy and solid-brass chain come with the fixture. The fixture measures 17" in diameter. Rejuvenation also manufactures late-Victorian and other 20th-century ceiling-mounted fixtures as well as hanging bowl lights.

Catalog, $3

REJUVENATION LAMP & FIXTURE CO.
901 N. Skidmore
Portland, OR 97217
(503) 249-0774
Fax (503) 281-7948

Other recommended sources for ceiling or hall lights are: COHASSET COLONIALS, CONANT CUSTOM BRASS, INC., A. J. P. COPPERSMITH & CO., RENOVATOR'S SUPPLY, *and* VICTORIAN LIGHTCRAFTERS LTD.

Ceilings. Most ceilings are simply expanses of plaster applied in sections to joists. The use of ceilings, even in early Colonial houses, is much more common than often thought, the exposure of beams or joists considered until recently a primitive practice. The extent of ceiling decoration is limited to a large extent by the overall style of the house. A centerpiece for a lighting fixture may be the only element used, but one can also add corner and side ornaments. A coffered ceiling and what is termed an "Old English ceiling" of ornate plaster relief is usually found in only late-Victorian and early 20th-century mansions as well as public buildings. Tin or pressed-metal ceilings were introduced in the late 1800s as a less expensive substitute for an ornate plaster ceiling. Their use, however, is also limited domestically, despite their popularity today. If adopted, a tin ceiling may be best used in a kitchen or bathroom. Wood ceilings are another period alternative for plaster. Ceilings made up of beaded oak or pine boards are known as wainscoted ceilings and were used in the kitchen of many vernacular houses. *See also* **Beams, Ornaments, Wainscoting.**

THE DECORATORS SUPPLY CORP.
As a source of ceiling ornaments and complete designs, Decorators is hard to surpass. Eight overall designs are included in the firm's plaster ornaments catalog, including Empire, Louis XIV, Louis XV, Italian coffered, Old English, and a Colonial Revival or a Beaux Arts pattern worthy of an Edith Wharton sitting room. Just about any design can be created from the firm's vast assortment of ornaments.

Catalog of Plaster Ornaments, $3

THE DECORATORS SUPPLY CORP.
3610-12 S. Morgan St.
Chicago, IL 60609
(312) 847-6300
Fax (312) 847-6357

FRANK J. MANGIONE
Mangione, seen at work on a plaster barrel ceiling, is an expert at

plastering and restoring walls and ceilings. He and his crew have a number of distinguished credits to their name, including the Lockwood-Mathews Mansion Museum in Norwalk, Connecticut; Montgomery Place in Barrytown, New York; and continued work at the National Trust property, Lyndhurst, in Tarrytown, New York. Mangione also lectures at Eastfield Village, East Nassau, New York. *(see* **Workshops***)*.

FRANK J. MANGIONE
21 John St.
Saugerties, NY 12477
(914) 246-9863

Canadian customers:
STEPTOE & WIFE ANTIQUES LTD.
322 Geary Ave.
Toronto, ONT M6H 2C7
(414) 530-4200
Fax (414) 530-4666

J. P. WEAVER CO.
Composition ornaments for ceilings have been made by this California-based firm since early in this century. Weaver possesses a molding collection of close to 8,000 ornaments from which just about any design can be created or re-created. Although of composition, the components are especially strong and may have been pressed or cast as many as three times. Illustrated is one ceiling design made up of a centerpiece, corner and side pieces, and bands. It is suggested that the inner band be made up of one of Weaver's new products, a special polyester molding.

W. F. NORMAN CORP.
Hi-Art Designs, the trade name for Norman's tin ceilings, are almost as popular today as they were when introduced in 1909. All of the elements are created through use of original dies. The largest components are main panels – usually 2'x4' – and around these borders, fillers, moldings, medallions and cornice pieces of tin may be used. Altogether there are 140 components to choose from which are used to create 60 different patterns. In style these range from what was called "Colonial," in 1909 (in truth much closer to Colonial Revival) back through time to Victorian Gothic, Empire, "Oriental," Rococo, and several more. The components are made of 30-gauge matte-finished tin plate which can be left natural with a coat of polyurethane or painted in any color. There are also optional plated finishes such as bright brass, antique brass, bright copper, and antique copper.

Hi-Art Steel Ceilings catalog, $5

American customers:
W. F. NORMAN CORP.
214 N. Cedar, PO Box 323
Nevada, MO 64772-0323
(800) 641-4038
(417) 667-5552 (MO)

Brochure available

J. P. Weaver Co.
23011 W. Victory Blvd.
Burbank, CA 91506
(818) 841-5700
Fax (818) 841-8462

Other suppliers of ceilings and ornaments are : metal – AA Abbingdon Affiliates, Inc., Chelsea Decorative Metal Co., *and* Renovator's Supply; *plaster –* Balmer Studios; *and wood –* The Barn People, Inc., Craftsman Lumber Co., *and* Cumberland Woodcraft Co.

Ceramic Tiles. *See* **Tiles.**

Chair Rails. Part of the family of moldings, chair rails are used to define a lower section of the wall and to protect the wall from scraping furniture. When used in conjunction with paneling or wainscoting, the rail serves as an ornamental cap. Casing and panel moldings may be used in place of what are usually considered chair rails, although the design of the latter is usually too simple. Many lumberyards stock three or four types of chair rail in simple profiles. For more imaginative types, as well as moldings in plaster and polymer, one can choose from a number of millwork suppliers and manufacturers.

American Custom Millwork, Inc. A firm that specializes in embossed moldings, American Custom offers a wide selection of stock designs, but can custom make anything desired. These are available in common woods as well as a variety of fine woods. Illustrated are three stock

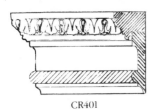

CR401

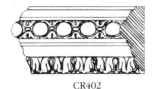

CR402

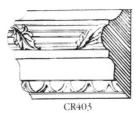

CR403

embossed chair rails. Plain moldings are also available; in this case, panel moldings may serve the purpose as well as those designated "chair rails."

Catalog, $5

American Custom Millwork, Inc.
3904 Newton Rd., PO Box 3608
Albany, GA 31706
(912) 888-3303 or 6848
Fax (912) 888-9245

Ornamental Mouldings Limited Embossed moldings are also the specialty of this firm. All are produced in quality kiln-dried poplar. They range from the plain (pattern #710), which would well fit many early 19th century interiors to the very ornate, appropriate for a high-Victorian villa (pattern #693). The first pattern illustrated measures $2\frac{1}{8}$" by $\frac{27}{32}$"; the second is 3" by $\frac{27}{32}$".

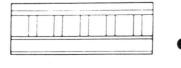

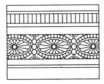

Designer Kits (4" sample pieces of all patterns), $12

American customers:
Ornamental Mouldings Limited
PO Box 7123
High Point, NC 27264

Canadian customers;
Ornamental Moldings Limited
PO Box 336
Waterloo, ONT N2J 4A4
(519) 884-4080
Fax (519) 884-9692

San Francisco Victoriana, Inc. Chair railings called as such comprise only a small part of Victoriana's millwork offerings. This fine firm also terms them wainscot caps an appropriate name since the railings are often used in the Far West to top off a beaded panel wall section. The numerous panel moldings and base cap designs shown in the catalog are almost all suitable for use as chair rails. In addition to the primary assortment of plain molding designs, there is also a small selection of embossed moldings suitable for use as chair rails.

Book of Architectural Building Materials, $5

San Francisco Victoriana, Inc.
2070 Newcomb Ave.
San Francisco, CA 94124
(415) 648-0313
Fax (415) 648-2812

Sheppard Millwork, Inc. This general millwork company prides itself on custom work, and makes up its own molding knives used to create the necessary profile requested. The four chair rail moldings shown, however, are

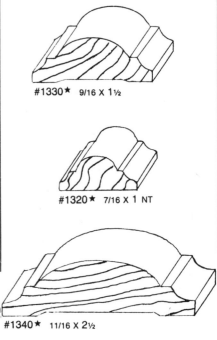

#1330 ★   9/16 X 1½

#1320 ★   7/16 X 1 NT

#1340 ★   11/16 X 2½

#380 ★   11/16 X 2 13/16

carried in stock and need not be custom-ordered.

Free brochure

SHEPPARD MILLWORK, INC.
21020 70th Ave. W.
Edmonds, WA 98020
(206) 771-4645
(206) 283-7549
Fax (206) 642-1622

SUNSHINE ARCHITECTURAL
WOODWORKS
The overall appearance of an interior space is of utmost importance to those who produce Sunshine's millwork. Moldings – including chair rails – are presented in the firm's catalog together with door and window casings and wainscoting so that the customer can see just how the elements come together in a pleasing manner. Chair rails, as Sunshine suggests, can be made up of two or three moldings, what millworkers term an assembly. The cost, of course, is much greater for these complex combinations. Poplar is the stock wood for all moldings, but oak, cherry, walnut, or Honduras mahogany can be substituted.

Catalog, $5

SUNSHINE ARCHITECTURAL
WOODWORKS
2169 Sunshine Dr.
Fayetteville, AR 72703
(800) 628-8004
(501) 521-4329
Fax (501) 521-8863

Among other recommended suppliers of chair rails are: Wood – BLUE OX MILLWORKS and SILVERTON VICTORIAN MILLWORKS; plaster – THE BALMER STUDIOS and WORTHINGTON GROUP LTD; polymer – FOCAL POINT and FYPON, INC.

Chair Seats. An alternative to cane materials which have to be woven are ready-made pressed fiber seats. These are particularly fitting for chairs made in the early 1900s. Yet another option are tapes of the type used by Shakers and these are appropriate for any plain ladderback or rocking chair of 18th-century inspiration.

A CAROLINA CRAFTSMAN
Three designs in chair seats are offered. Of fiber material, they can be cut with scissors or a knife and

attached with upholstery nails. It is suggested that they be stained and given a protective finish. The size of two of these seats is $14^1/_2$" square; the third is $12^1/_2$" square.

Catalog, $3 (refundable with first order)

A CAROLINA CRAFTSMAN
975 S. Avocado St.
Anaheim, CA 92805
(714) 776-7877
Fax (714) 533-0894

SHAKER WORKSHOPS
Chair tape weaving is a great deal easier than working cane or rush. Shaker Workshops supplies the material, a foam rubber cushion to be inserted in the seat, upholstery tacks, and complete step-by-step instructions. The tapes are available in ten solid colors, two stripes, and a natural white. Traditionally, Shaker seating furniture was often taped in two contrasting colors. The tape itself is 100% cotton canvas webbing.

Catalog, $1

SHAKER WORKSHOPS
PO Box 1028
Concord, MA 01742
(617) 646-8985

Other suppliers of pressed fiber chair seats are: THE CANING SHOP and RENOVATOR'S SUPPLY. Another source for chair tapes is NORTH WOODS CHAIR SHOP.

Chairs. A strong, well-built chair of graceful lines is a possession to be prized. Too many times antique chairs – even of early 20th-century vintage – fail to hold up under daily wear. This is as true for spacious wing chairs as it is for more delicate ladderbacks and Windsors. Fortunately, it is not necessary to depend only on restored seating furniture for dining room tables, desks, and other uses. Chairmaking is an art that has never died in North America and nearly every style is recreated by able craftsmen in reproductions that are works of art themselves.

STEPHEN P. BEDARD
Authentic in every detail as Windsor chairs produced in the 18th century, Bedard's could only be handmade. Seats are hand planed and carved from a single piece of pine; spindles and legs are hand turned; bows are individually steam bent. The joinery is mortise and tenon. Illustrated from left, rear, are a bow-back side chair, fan-back writing arm chair, and a bow-back armchair; front row, a fan-back youth armchair and a bow-back youth armchair. Seat heights are approximately $17^1/_2$" on the full-size chairs, and proportionately lower on the children's models.

Catalog, $3

STEPHEN P. BEDARD
Durell Mountain Farm
PO Box 2

Gilmanstown Iron Works, NH 03837
(603) 528-1896

CANDLERTOWN CHAIRWORKS
Traditional chairmaking is an art still seriously pursued in western North Carolina. Maple, hickory, red oak - the principal woods used - are in plentiful supply; so, too, is the splint that is woven for seats. Illustrated are but three of more than a dozen chair models produced by hand. From left to right are a Shaker Mt. Lebanon ladderback side chair or maple (39$^1/_2$" high), a Pilgrim ladderback side chair (43" high), and a High Country ladderback side chair of maple, hickory, or red oak (40" high). There are armchairs which match each of these designs. Candlertown also produces children's chairs, highchairs, and stools, and has added most recently a plank seat chair termed a "thumb back" with bamboo-turned spindles and legs. All of the chairs are available in a natural oil finish or may be given a milk paint worn finish.

Catalog, $2

CANDLERTOWN CHAIRWORKS
PO Box 1630
Candler, NC 28715
(704) 667-4844

SHAKER WORKSHOPS
The No. 5 shawl-back dining chair shown was first produced at the Shaker South Family factory in Mt. Lebanon, New York, in the 1860s.

There was and is also an armchair of the same style. Both are made in superior grade hard maple. In addition, the workshops offer nine other chair designs. All are available in finished or kit form. The shawl-back side chair and armchair are 40$^3/_4$" in height. The seats are of fabric tape.

Catalog, $1

SHAKER WORKSHOPS
PO Box 1028
Concord, MA 01742
(617) 646-8985

Other suggested makers of chairs in various 18th- and 19th- century styles are: COHASSET COLONIALS, THE COUNTRY BED SHOP, GERALD CURRY, CABINETMAKER, JEFFREY P. GREENE, FURNITUREMAKER, DIMITRIOS KLITSAS, NORTH WOODS CHAIR SHOP, *and* SERAPH WEST AND SERAPH EAST.

E. RUMSEY
"I build Windsor chairs because I love their lightness and their fluid grace of line," explains Ed Rumsey. He does not add, as he should, that he also builds Windsors because he possesses a sure sense of proportion and detail and an ability to translate this by hand. His chair designs are based on fine historical examples and if they were not branded on the seat bottom might be confused for the antique. Shown is a comb-back armchair, New Englsand style, with a carved crest.

Brochure, $3

E. RUMSEY
721 E. Shore Dr.
Ithaca, NY 14850
(607) 272-3020

Chandeliers. No lighting fixture is more popularity used in a period interior. The very presence of a hanging light seem to signal that something "old" is in the air. Chandeliers can be modern in design but there is little allowance for them in contemporary architecture and design. Sometimes it does appear that a bit too much attention is devoted to chandeliers in period rooms. A fixture can overwhelm an interior and its light can destroy any suggestion of intimacy or scale. Care, therefore, must be taken in the selection of a fixture, that it be sized properly, that its style be compatible with the period of the interior, and that it be wired in a way that it can be both subdued as well as brilliantly lit. There are as many types of chandeliers as there are styles in chairs and tables. Different terms have been used over the years such as gasoliers (for gas-fueled fixtures), hanging lamps, pendants, and showers. Suppliers are many and these producers are often extremely knowledgeable about what is appropriate for a particular period room. The same cannot be said about the run-of-the-mill retail lighting emporiums found in every metropolitan area. What they have to offer is often high-priced junk. Better to be in contact with one of the specialized suppliers. Or, if a real antique is desired, contact one of a number of dealers in antique lighting.

AUTHENTIC DESIGNS
As the name suggests, this firm is commited to copying lighting fixtures from the past in a faithful fashion. The models they have chosen to imitate are handsome to begin with , and, although adapted for electricity, retain the best qualities of the original design. All are handmade of solid brass. Electrification is standard, but the same fixtures can be fitted for candles. All brass parts are burnished and then given a lacquer coating or left plain. There is also an option of having the metal plated pewter or gunmetal. Illustrated are, in order of appearance, a five-arm chandelier, CH-400, 16" high and 20" in diameter; a three-arm chandelier, CH-155, 17$\frac{1}{2}$" high and 12$\frac{1}{2}$" in diameter; and a three-arm chandelier CH-289, 16$\frac{1}{2}$" high and 10$\frac{1}{2}$" in diameter. All are shown in brass.

Catalog, $3

AUTHENTIC DESIGNS
The Mill Rd.
West Rupert, VT 05776

(802) 394-7713
Fax (802) 394-2422

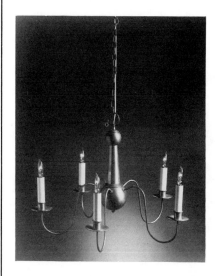

THE BRASS KNOB
A number of architectural antiques suppliers regularly stock an assortment of old lighting fixtures. Shown is just one of the type usually

available from well-stocked The Brass Knob. This is a six-arm fixture that was originally a gas-burning device; it has since been electrified. ₁

Brochure, free

THE BRASS KNOB
2311 18th St., NW
Washington, DC 20009
(202) 332-3370

CLASSIC ILLUMINATION , INC.
In addition to a large selection of late-Victorian gas, electric, and combination gas-electric chandeliers, Classic offers an inverted fixture with three arms that epitomizes 1930s lighting design. It is as a close to a modern chandelier as any offered by a reproduction manufacturer. Model 1938-3, it features a center etched-glass bowl and three arms with hand-blown French glass shades. The same basic design is available with two to five arms. The standard size is 26" square. The height from the ceiling, of course, can vary depending on the length of the stem.

Catalog, $5

CLASSIC ILLUMINATION, INC.
2743 9th St.
Berkeley, CA 94710
(415) 849-1842
Fax (415) 849-2328

GATES MOORE
Chandeliers appropriate for Colonial and early 19th-century interiors are a specialty of this concern. One of the oldest reproduction lighting fixtures in business, Gates Moore has an enviable reputation for authenticity and craftsmanship. Shown is their model 12 A, a double-decker metal chandelier with four arms over eight arms. It can be pewter-coated, painted, or left plain in what the maker calls a "distressed tin" finish. The fixture is 15" high to the hook and 24" in diameter. It is supplied with a canopy and hollow hanging hook.

Catalog, $2

GATES MOORE
SIlver Rd., Silvermine
Norwalk, CT 06850
(203) 847-3231

HAMMERWORKS
Wooden chandeliers are featured in Hammerworks' line of Colonial period fixtures. These feature either antique tin or antique brass arms. Model CH 123 is a seven-arm wooden fixture 17" high and 27" wide. The center hub is hand-turned, painted, and given an antique glaze. There is a choice of a dozen paint colors.

Catalog, $2

HAMMERWORKS
6 Fremont St.
Worcester, MA 01603
(800) 777-3689
(508) 755-3434
or
798 Boston Post Rd., Rte. 20
Metro West Plaza
Marlboro, MA 01752
(508) 485-6721

HURLEY PARENTEE MANOR
It is hard to outdo Hurley when it comes to primitive early American fixtures of character and charm. Stephen and Carolyn Waligursky know the early history of lighting better than almost anyone in the country. As is evident from the photograph of the Bird Hook chandelier (CH115), the iron is hand-

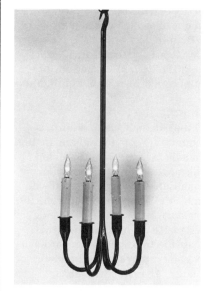

forged. This fixture could be used as effectively with real candles. The height is 24"; the width, 10".

Catalog, $3

HURLEY PATENTEE MANOR
RD 7, Box 98A
Kingston, NY 12401
(914) 331-5414

KING'S CHANDELIER CO.
For high-style Victorian glass chandeliers, go no further than King's. Its selection is unparalleled; the reproduction fixtures make use of

fine Venetian crystal. Be sure, however, that the surroundings in which the chandelier selected is centered are as brilliant as the fixture itself. The prisms and festoons on the model shown, for example, will dazzle any eye. This is Whitaker-4, a gaslight reproduction that has been wired. The frosted gas shades carry a rose design, and in the hub are four cast-bronze American eagles. The brass fixture is 28" wide by 35" long.

Catalog, $3

KING'S CHANDELIER CO.
PO Box 667, Dept. OHC-VII
Eden, NC 27288
(919) 623-6188
Fax (919) 623-1723

NEW ENGLAND TOOL CO.
There are only a few stock lighting designs in this company's portfolio, but each is choice. The hanging light or chandelier illustrated is unique in the offerings of reproduction

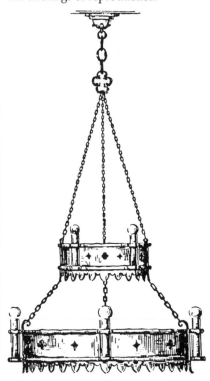

craftsmen. It could take its place in a Tudor-style mansion of the early 1900s. Like the rest of the company's work, this piece is hand-wrought metalwork at its finest.

NEW ENGLAND TOOL CO.
PO Box 30
Chester, NY 10918
(914) 782-5332
(917) 651-7550
Fax (914) 783-2554

NOWELL'S INC.
The company's credentials in reproduction lighting are hard to beat. Among the projects for which it has supplied fixtures are the U.S. Treasury Building and the Old Executive Office Building in Washington, D.C., and the Hotel Del Coronado in San Diego, Caliifornia.

The brass Tivoli (#306) is typical of the restrained, delicate Victorian chandeliers offered. It is used with etched glass shades carrying a rose deign and cut-glass prisms.

Catalog, $3.50

NOWELL'S INC.
PO Box 295
Sausalito, CA 94966
(415) 332-4933

REJUVENATION LAMP & FIXTURE CO.
In the early 1900s electric fixtures called "showers" made their appearance. They are, in effect, chandeliers and as such were used in dining parlors and dining rooms well into the 1930s. The model shown is The Laddington Court and features five arms; a model with three, four, or six arms is also available. The center bowl and shades are of satin

etched glass. The diameter is 27" and the standard length, with chain, is 36"; add 5" for the canopy.

Catalog, free

REJUVENATION LAMP & FIXTURE CO.
901 N. Skidmore
Portland, OR 97217
(503) 249-0774
Fax (503) 281-7948

ROY ELECTRIC CO. INC.
An extraordinary selection of well-made and historically accurate Victorian fixtures is always on offer at Roy. Particularly well represented are single-stem pendants and combination gas and electric multi-arm chandeliers. Illustrated is a combination fixture (GES R 6-6) with very fine brass rope tubing and filigree work. Fixtures of this type date from the 1890s.

Lighting catalog, $5

ROY ELECTRIC CO. INC.
1054 Coney Island Ave.
Brooklyn, NY 11230
(718) 434-7002
Fax (718) 421-4678

VICTORIAN LIGHTCRAFTERS, LTD.
The proprietors of Victorian
Lightcrafters traveled the road from
collecting antique lighting to
reproduction of rare examples. The
gas chandelier shown is typical of

their craftsmanship, employing very
fine metalwork of solid brass; cast
parts only are used. The model
shown is C-900-3 and is wired for
electricity.

Catalog, $3

VICTORIAN LIGHTCRAFTERS. LTD.
PO Box 350
Slate Hill, NY 10973
(914) 353-1300

WATERTOWER PINES
Antique fixtures make up the
inventory at this country shop. Since
the owners excel at repairing and
rewiring period fixtures, they are also
frequently called upon to resuscitate
pieces brought to them. Some
reproduction lighting dealers can do
the same, but Watertower Pines is set
up solely to make the truly old useful
again.

Brochure available

WATERTOWER PINES
Rte. 1 South, PO BOx 1067
Kennebunk, ME 04043
(207) 958-6868

*Among other recommended suppliers of
reproduction chandeliers are:* A
CAROLINA CRAFTSMAN, A. J. P.
COPPERSMITH, HISTORIC HARDWARE
LTD., RENOVATOR'S SUPPLY, SERAPH
EAST AND SERAPH WEST, SHAKER
WORKSHOPS, THE TINNER and THE
VILLAGE FORGE. *Other companies
offering antique chandeliers are:*
ARCHITECTURAL ANTIQUES EXCHANGE,
CENTURY HOUSE ANTIQUE LAMP
EMPORIUM AND REPAIR, CITY LIGHTS,
SALVAGE ONE, and WESTLAKE
ARCHITECTURAL ANTIQUES.

Chests. Next to chairs, chests are
among the most useful pieces of
furniture. There are various types –
small chests of drawers which can be
used as night stands and end tables,
blanket chests for storage, dressers,
chests of drawers such as highboys,
huntboards and silver chests for the
dining room. It's nice, of course, to be
able to afford to have antique chests
rather than reproductions. Cost and
availability, however, may weigh
against such a choice. And, besides,
there are some cabinetmakers today
whose work is every bit as good as
their forefathers.

COHASSET COLONIALS
For chests which are practical and
reasonably priced, Cohasset is a good
choice. The firm offers three types – a
pine chest on stand, a pine four-
drawer dresser, and a pine blanket
chest. Each is offered in finished or
kit form. The chest on stand is based
on a 17th-century Virginia piece
which was used as both a seat and a
storage chest. It measures 24 3/4" high,
30" long, and 14 1/2" deep. It would be
useful in a bathroom for towels or
linens or as a children's toy box. The
dresser is in the Chippendale style,
the original design dating from 1740.
Polished-brass drawer pulls are
provided. The chest's dimensions are
34 3/4" high, 38" wide, and 18" deep.
The blanket chest is best used in the
bedroom, although it can also be
given a cushion top and used as a
hall seat. It measures 22" high, 46"
wide, and 16" deep.

Catalog, $5

COHASSET COLONIALS
Cohasset, MA 02025
(800) 288-2389

JEFFREY P. GREENE, FURNITUREMAKER
Greene is one of those craftsmen
whose work is as good as that of the
Colonial cabinetmakers he emulates.
His speciality is 18th-century pieces
of museum quality. This is a good
description of his Queen Anne
highboy with sunburst carvings
shown here. It is a Connecticut

design dating from c. 1730 and is
executed in tiger maple. Cherry and
mahogany are other woods Greene
frequently uses. Measurements of the
piece are 78" high, 38" wide, and
19 1/2" deep. For those seeking
reproduction chests of less imposing
stature, Greene offers five different
18th-century designs, ranging in
simplicity from a four-drawer New
Hampshire chest to an elaborate six-
drawer bombé chest with sunburst
carving from the Salem, Massachusetts, area.

Catalog available

JEFFREY P. GREENE, FURNITUREMAKER
97 James Trail
West Kingston, RI 02892
(401) 783-6614

Chimney Breasts/Overmantels.
A chimney breast is the projecting
section of a wall that contains the
fireplace and flue. This feature is to
be found only in homes where the
chimney is internal and forms part of
the wall rather than being attached to
the outside of the building. In

Colonial and early 19th-century interiors, the upper part of the chimney breast is often paneled or is ornamented with panel moldings. Later in the 1800s, mantels were sometimes extended high up the wall, well beyond the fireplace opening. The upper part, or over-mantel, was often fitted out as a set of tiered shelves or with a framed mirror. Both the Colonial and Victorian treatments emphasize the central importance of the fireplace in a period room's layout and decoration.

Architectural antiques firms are often a good source for Victorian one-piece mantels and overmantels (*see* **Mantels**). An ornamental chimney breast is usually offered only as part of a room-end wall assembly by those antique dealers specializing in Colonial paneling (*see* **Room Ends**). Either type of treatment, of course, can be reproduced by an able craftsman.

ARCHITECTURAL ANTIQUES EXCHANGE
This is one of a number of salvage firms that have a fairly constant supply of Victorian overmantels in stock. The basic model is a very elaborate mirror framed on three sides, the fourth resting on the mantel top. The Exchange, of course, is also a good source for Victorian mantels.

Literature, $3

Architectural Antiques Exchange
709-15 N. Second St.
Philadelphia, PA 19123
(215) 922-3669

ARCHITECTURAL COMPONENTS, INC.
A firm well versed in traditional joinery and paneling, Architectural Components can handle the design and fabrication of Colonial and early 19th-century fireplace walls. A raised panel design over a fireplace without a mantel might be appropriate for a 17th-century or early 18th-century interior. Mantels gradually came into use during this period. Architectural Components usually makes use of $1^5/_6$" clear kiln-dried eastern white pine, but also will employ poplar, cherry, or oak.

Flyer, free; brochure, $3

ARCHITECTURAL COMPONENTS, INC.
26 N. Leverett Rd., Dept. OHC
Montague, MA 01351
(413) 367-9441
Fax (413) 367-9461

SUNSHINE ARCHITECTURAL
    WOODWORKS
Both lower and upper sections of a Colonial chimney breast may be of one unit, this being composed of elements such as those illustrated here – raised panels, pilasters, and a cornice-type shelf. This is one of several designs available from Sunshine, and can be modified in all directions. The stock hardwood is kiln-dried poplar; walnut, cherry, mahogany, or oak can be substituted. The fireplace opening would require some sort of tile or stone surround. The dimensions of the design illustrated (113FW) are 95" high, 78" wide at base, opening height, $39^1/_4$", and opening width, 50".

Catalog, $4

SUNSHINE ARCHITECTURAL
    WOODWORKS
2619 Sunshine Dr., Dept. C.
Fayetteville, AR 72703
(501) 521-4329
(800) 628-8004

Other possible suppliers of Victorian overmantels include such architectural antique firms as THE BRASS KNOB, IRREPLACEABLE ARTIFACTS, NOSTALGIA, INC., SALVAGE ONE, *and* UNITED HOUSE WRECKING, INC. *Room ends, including paneled chimney breasts, are also included in the inventory of* RAMASE *and* WALCOT RECLAMATION LTD. *Among fabricators of room ends, including chimney breast ornamentation, is* MAURER & SHEPHERD JOYNERS.

Chimney Pots. These extensions of a chimney flue above the roof can be not only functional objects but highly decorative ones as well. They crown the chimneys of many British and Irish buildings, but have had limited use in North America. This is to be regretted as these earthenware or metal pots serve to improve the draft and to disperse smoke.

SUPERIOR CLAY CORP.
The leading manufacturer of chimney pots in North America, Superior offers twenty different styles, most of them cylindrical. All are made of selected ceramic materials fired to a temperature of 2,000°F. In size they range from the 12" Essex to the 45" Magnum. Corresponding weights range between 25 and 420 lbs.

Brochure, $2

SUPERIOR CLAY CORP.
PO Box 352
Uhrichsville, OH 44683
(800) 848-6166

WALCOT RECLAMATION LTD.
At any given time this British architectural antiques firm is likely to have over 100 pots in stock. Sets can be made up if some advance notification is given. The most common are the red or buff Victorian clay cylinders; there are also square, louvered, and octagonal shapes. All are functional and decorative.

WALCOT RECLAMATION LTD.
108 Walcot St.
Bath BA1 5BG
England
(0255) 444404
Fax (0255) 448163

Christmas Decorations/Lights.
Christmas has been so commercialized and plasticized that any return to decorations of the past is welcome. Handmade tree ornaments of wood and metal are regularly offered by a number of catalog suppliers. Sets of old-fashioned electric lights are also a refreshing reminder of a more graceful past.

BRADFORD CONSULTANTS
This is the source for blown-glass figural light bulbs and nostalgic bubble lights. Each set of figural bulbs has fifteen lights, each bulb lighting independently. Up to three sets can be connected together. A spare bulb is included with each set. Bubble sets include seven lights. Bradford will also supply replacement light strings if an heirloom set has become weak or defective.

Free brochure

BRADFORD CONSULTANTS
PO Box 4020
Alameda,. CA 94501
(415) 523-1968

THE COPPERSMITH
Metal angels and stars for treetops and animal cutouts in tin make attractive decorations. The Coppersmith specializes in small country items, including such Christmas-oriented objects as metal door wreath holders and rings fitted with a tiny candle socket to hang in windows.

Catalog, $3

THE COPPERSMITH
Rte. 20, PO Box 755
Sturbridge, MA 01566
(508) 347-7038 or 9509

RED FERN GLASS
This firm produces brilliant glass ornaments as well as reproductions of early Midwestern objects such as glasses, bottles, bowls, and pitchers. The decorations are handblown in two forms – icicle and ball – and in the warm and authentic shades of aquamarine, amethyst, cobalt blue, and teal green.

Brochure with SASE

RED FERN GLASS
HCR 68, Box 19-A
Salem, AR 72576
(501) 895-2036

Another supplier of old-fashioned Christmas ornaments (in wood) is THE CANDLE CELLAR AND EMPORIUM.

Cire-Perdue. *See* **Door Hardware.**

Clapboards. The use of aluminum siding in imitation of clapboarding is enough to drive a grown man to tears. The practice creates an excrescence for which there is no excuse. No artificial siding yet offered has the profile or feel of real wood and little or none of the true protective qualities of a natural material. Despite the introduction of vent holes, artificial siding does not "breathe" well – that is, allow for air and moisture to be released; the old siding beneath merely rots. And then, there is the appearance of the metal material which seems to attract dents and rust spots like flies to honey. Wood clapboards cut to fit almost any type of building are available from mills in various areas of the country, and more and more outlets are opening up for their products. Old clapboards are also available, but these are best used for patch jobs as supply is limited. *See also* **Siding.**

DONNELL'S CLAPBOARD MILL
Clapboards of eastern white pine are likely to last 200 years or more. In the 18th century they were hand sawn, but now they are produced by machine or radially-sawn. The effect is much the same – boards that will not warp or twist and will have a flat, tight fit. Donnell's standard board size is $5^1/_2$" but $3^1/_2$", $4^1/_2$" and 6" clapboards can be produced by special order. There are two grades – #1 premium clear, recommended for restorations and new buildings; and #2 New England Cape, which is ideal for repair work and for small outbuildings or modest cottages.

Brochure available

DONNELL'S CLAPBOARD MILL
County Rd., RR Box 1560
Sedgwick, ME 04676
(207) 359-2036

GRANVILLE MANUFACTURING CO., INC.
A $4^1/_2$" to 5" clapboard is the standard at Granville. These are quartersawn to eliminate warping and cupping problems. Both spruce and pine are used. Boards in $5^1/_2$" and 6" widths are also available.

GRANVILLE MANUFACTURING CO., INC.
Rte. 100
Granville, VT 05747
(802) 767-4747

Other suppliers of new clapboard siding include: BLUE OX MILLWORKS, CRAFTSMAN LUMBER CO., CUSTOM MILLWORK, INC., REMODELERS & RENOVATORS, *and* WARD CLAPBOARD MILL. *One source for antique clapboards is* DIAMOND K. CO., INC.

Clocks. No old house "sounds" right without the ticking of an old clock or two. The digital timepieces produced today are typical of the age – of limited life and so quiet as to suggest that the passage of time is something to be ignored. America was the world's prime producer of clocks in the 19th century, and there are thousands to be had in shops. Getting them to keep accurate time is another matter. If that is vitally important, a new traditional clock might be in order.

MARION H. CAMPBELL, CABINETMAKER
Among the exceptional pieces produced by Campbell is a tall case or grandfather's clock. Antique models of this type are not plentiful,

and a reproduction case fitted with either old or new works may be the best alternative. Most of the new grandfather clocks offered by retail outlets today are rather ungainly specimens, often being bottom heavy. And, unfortunately, they are usually fitted with tiny electronic works. Campell's reproduction is authentic through and through.

Among the firms offering smaller clocks (shelf, mantel, wall) in finished or kit form are COHASSET COLONIALS *and* SHAKER WORKSHOPS *(see photograph of the wall clock from the New Lebanon, New York, Shaker community).*

Clothing, Period. Why anyone needs to dress up in period garb in an old house or museum setting is anyone's guess. Role-playing, however, is a modern obsession and if it is to be done, it might as well be done well. Wearing of a Colonial mobcap or Victorian bonnet will not suffice, especially when these are combined with a bouffant hairdo or rhinestone glasses.

AMAZON VINEGAR & PICKLING WORKS
       DRYGOODS
Janet Burgess has put together a most astonishing collection of authentic clothing and accessory patterns from the past and offers a good number of ready-made or custom-order items.

The variety in women's hats – at least thirty three styles – is matched as well in other areas, such as ladies' dresses, blouses, hoop skirts, men's vests and coats, collars and shirts, and hats. There is also a fine selection of ladies, men's and boy's shoes and stockings.

Pattern catalog, $7; general catalog, $3

AMAZON VINEGAR & PICKLING WORKS
       DRYGOODS
2218 E. 11th St.
Davenport, IA 53803
(319) 322-6800
(309) 786-3504
Fax (319) 322-4003

Columns and Capitals. With the revival of neoclassical ornamentation in postmodern architecture, manufacturers and suppliers of columns and capitals have increased measurably. This is a most welcome enrichment. During most years of the 20th century, columns have been used externally only as porch posts or as supports for a Gone-with-the-Wind type of portico; their interior use has been almost nonexistent since the turn of the century and the Beaux Arts or Colonial Revival Period. The Roman orders – Tuscan and Composite – and the Greek – Doric, Ionic, and Corinthian – form the early history of column use and its revival at various times. Each of these

columns, except for the Doric, is comprised of a base, shaft, and capital, the Doric being without a base. A column would appear to be the simplest of architectural forms, yet even the least ornamental have to be given proper shape and dimension. Entasis, the slight bulging out which occurs in a column to compensate for straight lines, must be carefully calculated for each style of column and allowed for in the production. The classical orders, however, do not constitute the sole members of the column family, there having been as many column designs as architectural styles in the past. The type of column which often appears on an American Greek Revival building of the 1840's or '50s, for example, is square with only a slight capital. This is true of what was originally a law office in Flemington, New Jersey, designed by Mahlon Fisher. Others of his buildings in this county seat, however, have elaborate fluted columns and ornate capitals.

External columns are usually made of wood, although stone or cement have been and are still used. These columns are load-bearing structural members and must be unusually strong. Capitals, inside or outside, however, are usually of a molded composition material. Carved capitals in wood or stone are not unknown, but, because of the complexity of the designs, it is easier and less expensive to mold them of a pliable but sturdy material. Inside the house, columns and capitals of just about any type of material can be used. *See also* **Pilasters.**

CHADSWORTH INC.
PO Box 53268
Atlanta, GA 30355
(404) 876-5410

NOSTALGIA, INC.
A major supplier of architectural antiques in the Southeast, Nostalgia is also the U.S. distributor of plaster ornamentation from Sorte & Chasle, Nantes, France. Colums are for interior use and are plain or fluted. There is no attempt to reproduce exact classical types; rather, the columns are stock architectural forms.

Catalog available

NOSTALGIA, INC.
307 Stiles Ave.
Savannah, GA 31401
(912) 232-2324
(800) 874-0015
Fax (912) 234-5746

PAGLIACCO TURNING AND MILLING

California redwood is used for the columns produced by Pagliacco in four parts – plinth, base, shaft, and

CHADSWORTH INC.
This manufacturer of columns and capitals emphasizes that its work closely adheres to the classical proportions and details outlined by Giacomo Barozzi de Vignola in the 16th century. Similarly, some of America's earliest architects and carpenter-builders sought to follow Vignola's dictates in the revival of classical decoration of the 18th and early 19th centuries. Worthington's standard columns are produced of Ponderosa pine, although clear heart redwood or other species can be specified. All styles are available plain or fluted. The truest designs are Greek Doric, Roman Doric, or Tuscan; Chadsworth also produces what it terms an Art Deco and a contemporary column for which the firm, and not Vignola, has set the rules. Any column with a diameter greater than 1' and a height greater than 12' is supplied with a cast-marble base molding and cast-aluminum (exterior) or wood (interior) plinth. Each column comes with a capital of a plaster-fiberglass composition or of wood.

Catalog, $2

capital – except for the Greek Doric which is without plinth or base. The other styles are Tuscan, Greek Doric, Roman Doric, Doric cap and Attic base, and what is termed the Pagliacco cap and Attic base. All columns are available fluted or plain. In addition to wood capitals, more complex composition capitals can be ordered. They are supplied with load-bearing plugs to transfer the load and to securely tie the column into the structure. These assemblies can be used both inside and outside.

Catalog, $6

PAGLIACCO TURNING AND MILLING
PO Box 225
Woodacre, CA 94973
(415) 488-4333

SACO MANUFACTURING &
    WOODWORKING
Eastern white pine, plentiful in northern New England, is used for standard columns from Saco. These are made in the usual tapered stave design and with tongue-and-groove joinery. Custom work is a speciality of Saco, in business for over 117 years, and just about any style column can be produced.

Free brochure

SACO MANUFACTURING &
    WOODWORKING
39 Lincoln St.
Saco, ME 04072
(207) 284-6613

SOMERSET DOOR & COLUMN CO.
Somerset is a major supplier of structural and decorative columns made of Northern white pine, clear heart redwood, Pennsylvania sound knotty white pine, or poplar. Stock styles are a plain architectural column, Doric cap and Attic base, Tuscan, Roman Doric, and Greek Doric. These are made up plain or fluted. Each is available with a plain cap or an ornamental capital. Ventilated plinths are made of fiberglasss, aluminum, or wood; bases are wood or fiberglass; plain caps are wood or fiberglass; and ornamental capitals are of composition. Somerset is also a good source for square columns.

Free brochure

SOMERSET DOOR & COLUMN CO.
Box 328
Somerset, PA 15501
(814) 445-9608

WORTHINGTON GROUP LTD.
Two basic column types – Doric and Tuscan – are manufactured by Worthington. It is one of the few companies that has made a special effort to include a typical 18th-century American column design, "Colonial," which incorporates a simple two-piece capital. The Doric Colonial columns are made in diameters of 6" to 14". The Tuscan columns, with a Doric Tuscan capital, measure 16" to 30" in diameter. All columns have a two-piece Tuscan base; Attic bases can be substituted. Ponderosa pine is used for these elements. As the photograph shows,

ornamental capitals can be used instead of the plain two-piece caps. Shown are columns with Greek Erechtheum capitals, one of the seven designs made up in a composition blend of plaster and fiberglass with strengthening fibers.

Catalog, $3

WORTHINGTON GROUP LTD.
PO Box 53101
Atlanta, GA 30355
(404) 872-1608
(800) 872-1608
(404) 872-8501

Ornamental capitals are a speciality item offered by all column manufacturers but capitals are also supplied separately by firms whose only business is ornaments.

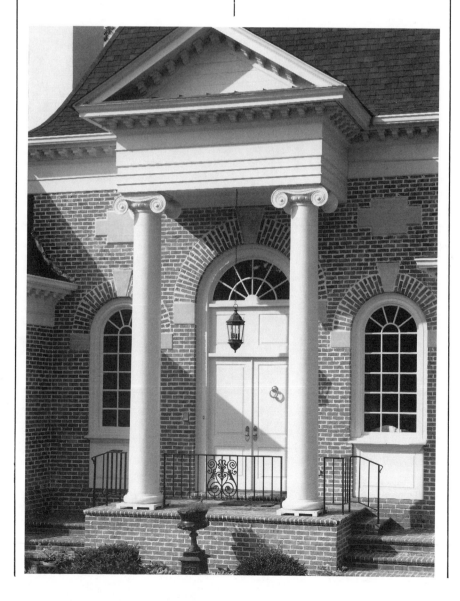

THE DECORATORS SUPPLY CORP.
At least two dozen capital designs for columns, including Gothic, French Renaissance, and Italian Renaissance, are included in Decorators' collection. They are cast in plaster for interior use and in stucco plaster for exterior. Many of these same designs are also available for pilasters (see **Pilasters**).

Catalog of Capitals and Brackets, $3

THE DECORATORS SUPPLY CORP.
3610-12 S. Morgan St.
Chicago, IL 60609
(312) 847-6300
Fax (312) 847-6357

W. F. NORMAN CORP.
Capitals in stamped sheet zinc are useful only for ornamental purposes with pilasters or other relatively flat relief decoration. Norman offers many designs for round or square pilasters or engaged columns.

Architectural Sheet-Metal Ornaments catalog, $5

American customers, contact:
W. F. NORMAN CORP.
214 N. Cedar, PO Box 323
Nevada, MO 64772-0323
(800) 641-4038
(417) 667-5552 (MO)

Canadian customers, contact:

STEPTOE & WIFE ANTIQUES LTD.
322 Geary Ave.
Toronto, ONT M6H 2C7
(414) 530-4200
Fax (414) 530-4666

SAN FRANCISCO VICTORIANA
Among the architectural plaster castings produced by Victoriana are three capital designs, two Ionic and one Corinthian, for use with columns and pilasters. Castings for exterior use are hydrocal; for interior, cast gypsum plaster. Victoriana also provides a custom casting service that can duplicate just about any design devised.

Catalog, $5

SAN FRANCISCO VICTORIANA
2070 Newcomb Ave.
San Francisco, CA 94124
(415) 648-0313
Fax (415) 648-2812

Other suppliers of columns in wood are:

AMERICAN WOOD COLUMN CORP., BAILEY'S ARCHITECTURAL MILLWORK, INC., BLUE OX MILLWORKS, DIXON BROTHERS WOODWORKING, HARTMANN-SANDERS CO., KENTUCKY MILLWORK, NEW ENGLAND WOODTURNERS, A. F. SCHWERD MANUFACTURING CO., and TURNCRAFT. *Suppliers of plaster colums are:* THE BALMER STUDIOS, GIANNETTI STUDIOS, and FRANK J. MANGIONE. *Sources for antique columns include:* IRREPLACEABLE ARTIFACTS and SALVAGE ONE.

Concrete, Restoration. Although concrete would appear to be a fairly modern building material, it has been used in various forms for 150 years or more. Since the introduction of Portland cement in the 1800s, concrete – a mixture of cement, aggregates, and water – has been used for floors and steps, walls, and walks. Although extremely durable, over time it requires maintenance and even restoration as do other building materials.

ABATRON, INC.
An epoxy patching and resurfacing cement/grout – Abocrete – is strongly recommended for restoration and resurfacing. It is many times stronger than the usual building cement and hardens to a very smooth surface. A five-gallon kit of Abocrete contains one can of liquid epoxy resin, one can of liquid hardener, and sufficient sand to blend about four-and-a-half gallons of mix. None of the elements are toxic or volatile. The resin and hardener blend can also be used without sand to form a thin coating; this is useful where patches have been made and a uniform surface is desired.

Free Literature

ABATRON, INC.
33 Center Dr.
Gilberts, IL 60136
(708) 426-2200
Fax (708) 426-5966

Conductor Heads/Fittings. These devices direct or conduct rainwater from gutters to downspouts. They are usually found on public buildings and mansions of the late 1800s and early 20th century and are made of metal.

W. F. NORMAN CORP.
Conductor heads are still produced by this firm. Norman has the molds necessary to fabricate over twenty designs and the fittings necessary for attaching them. Illustrated is one

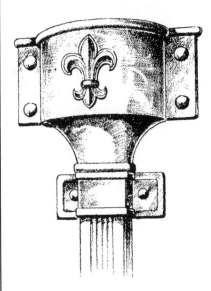

design, No. 922. The heads are made in lead-coated or plain copper.

Architectural Sheet Metal Ornaments catalog, $5

American customers, contact:
W. F. NORMAN CORP.
214 N. Cedar, PO Box 323
Nevada, MO 64772-0323
(800) 641-4038
(417) 667-5552 (MO)

Canadian customers, contact:
STEPTOE & WIFE ANTIQUES, LTD.
322 Geary Ave.
Toronto, ONT M6H 2C7
(414) 530-4200
Fax (414) 530-4666

Conservation, Fine and Decorative Arts. The expertise developed by conservators can be of value to old-house owners. This applies to such areas as fabrics, ceramics, painted finishes, wood products, and lighting fixtures. *See also* **Consultants, Restoration.**

BERNHEIMER'S CONSERVATION & RESTORATION
Training in naval architecture and the sciences has led Mark Bernheimer from England to the United States and from theory to practice of restoration techniques in a number of areas. This involves objects of such

materials as wood, glass, clay, marble, and metal. Architectural restoration work is also undertaken. Among the firm's clients are Dade Heritage Trust, Miami, Florida; the Marriott Corp.; and the Radisson Hotel, Miami.

BERNHEIMER'S CONSERVATION & RESTORATION
6439 Miller Dr.
Miami, FL 33155
(305) 770-6641

TEXTILE CONSERVATION CENTER
The Museum of American Textile History in Massachusetts' historic textile mill region is suitably committed to preserving antique fabrics. To this end, the Textile Conservation Center was founded in 1977. The center cleans, fumigates, and dries such fabrics and performs chemical analyses, photographic documentation, and light microscopy on historic textiles. Services include on-site inspections and work on textiles so large or so delicate as to prohibit transport. Appraisals, dating, and authenticating services are not available, but "first aid" and emergency assistance, as well as specific lectures and workshops, are offered.

Free brochure

TEXTILE CONSERVATION CENTER
800 Massachusetts Ave.
North Andover, MA 01845
(508) 686-0191

HELENE VON ROSENSTIEL, INC.
Experienced as a museum conservator, Helene Von Rosenstiel has developed an enviable reputation as one of America's leading private textile consultants. She and her skilled assistants care for all types of old textiles – costumes and accessories, coverlets and quilts, tapestries, samplers, embroideries, and other forms of needlework. They are knowledgeable in the history and development of the decorative arts.

Free Literature

HELENE VON ROSENSTIEL, INC.
382 11th St.
Brooklyn, NY 11215
(718) 788-7909

Conservatories. *See* **Greenhouses.**

Consultants, Restoration. Anyone contemplating more than minor restoration is advised to seek the assistance of a consultant. The approach to restoring a building is not unlike that of building a new one in which a detailed plan by an architect or builder is worked out in advance. The task of restoring a house, indeed, may be more complex than that of building anew since a knowledge of today's techniques must be wedded to a thorough knowledge of past practice. Some restoration consultants are also contractors; others are architects with a special expertise in historic architecture. And yet others may be architectural historians well-versed in the building technology of yesterday and today. There are also consultants in particular areas such as paint research, wood and metal restoration, and textile conservation. Private and public preservation groups can sometimes be helpful in providing educational materials, hands-on workshops, and lectures concerned with restoration skills; a few will also consult for private homeowners. *See also* **Building Inspection Services; Conservation, Fine and Decorative Arts;** and **Workshops and Courses.**

THE COLOR PEOPLE
An historically appropriate and pleasing exterior color scheme has transformed many period houses. The Color People is one of the leading national consulting firms specializing in Victorian and early 20th-century structures. While on-location consulting is available, most clients work through the mail, supplying "before" photographs of the building along with bits of pertinent information.

Brochure available

THE COLOR PEOPLE
1546 Williams St.
Denver, CO 80218
(800) 541-7174

OEHRLEIN & ASSOCIATES ARCHITECTS
This Washington, D.C., based firm is representative of a large group of professional architects who regularly consult on old house projects. Having seen some of the buildings for which it has supplied restoration expertise,

we can unreservedly recommend Oehrlein. This firm provides technical consulting and architectural design, including condition surveys, materials conservation analysis, maintenance programming, preparation of construction drawings and specifications, and continuing construction supervision services. As with many other consultants, Oehrlein can also help in the preparation of historic structure reports and state and federal tax certification applications.

Literature available

OEHRLEIN & ASSOCIATES ARCHITECTS
1702 Connecticut Ave., NW
Washington, DC 20009
(202) 387-8040
Fax (202) 265-0883

TRADITIONAL LINE LTD.,
    ARCHITECTURAL RESTORATION
In addition to its expert contracting services, Traditional Line is also ready to provide consultation. This means anything and everything from structural analysis to planning the work of electricians and plumbers so that modern improvements do not disturb the true period character of a building. Traditional Line will also undertake historic research.

TRADITIONAL LINE LTD.,
    ARCHITECTURAL RESTORATION
143 W. 21st St.
New York, NY 10011
(212) 627-3555
Fax (212) 645-8158

HENRY PAGE, HOUSE RESTORATION
    CONSULTANT
A thoroughly experienced restoration craftsman, Henry Page has the requisite know-how and expertise to plan and supervise the work of others. He draws on the work of various specialists and his own broad knowledge in consulting and managing house restoration projects. "I can become involved in so many more projects," he explains "rather than spending much time in doing the work itself." A special interest of his is structural work, finding ways of piecing a building back together so that it will stand at least another 200 years.

Video of completed projects, $15

HENRY PAGE, HOUSE RESTORATION
    CONSULTANT
PO Box T419
Gilmanton, NH 03237
(603) 542-0963

SOCIETY FOR THE PRESERVATION OF
    NEW-ENGLAND ANTIQUITIES
The SPNEA, as it is better known, has
served the New England preservation community for generations,
having been founded by architectural
historian William Sumner Appleton
in 1910. Through its Conservation
Center, homeowners throughout
North America can avail themselves
of SPNEA's technical expertise. There
are also special conservators in such
areas as furniture, textiles, woodwork
and decorative finishes, and
metalwork available for consultation.

Literature available

SOCIETY FOR THE PRESERVATION OF
    NEW-ENGLAND ANTIQUITIES
185 Lyman St.
Waltham, MA 02154
(617) 891-1985

Other consultants include: ALLEN
CHARLES HILL, AIA; ALVIN HOLM
AIA. ARCHITECTS; THE PRESERVATION
PARTNERSHIP; RESTORATIONS
UNLIMITED, INC.; and WIGGINS
BROTHERS INTERIORS. *For consultation
and paint research, contact:* MATTHEW
MOSCA.

Contractors, Restoration. During
times when the economy is in a
slump, contractors handling
restoration work, renovation, and
rehabilitation are busier than ever.
The instinct to want to "improve" a
building is strong and not easily laid
to rest. To improve used to mean to
tear down or "remodel" completely.
There are still too many general
contractors around who have no
interest in or respect for a building
that has survived many years and
may be in need of renewal only. The
expense of restoring or rehabilitating
a building can be very high,
depending on the condition of the
structure. A majority of buildings,
however, usually require only
selective work, perhaps those
elements such as windows, doors,
porches, roofs, and chimneys which

are more subject to the elements than
interior appointments. A general
contractor experienced in restoration
work who can oversee all of the work
to be done is to be preferred. He may
not perform each task, but assumes
the responsibility for lining up
craftsmen and overseeing their work.
This can save the homeowner many
headaches and hours of time passed
in arranging for work to be
performed. Most general contracting
firms have a crew of specialists who
can be called into action when the
need arises. Only if the restoration
work is limited to such areas as
plumbing or painting is it wise to
contract directly with the workmen
involved. There are, of course,
contractors who specialize in
particular aspects of restoration work
who can oversee even a limited
amount of work. *See also*
**Conservation, Fine and Decorative
Arts; Consultants, Restoration;** and
Painting, Decorative.

ANDERSON BUILDING RESTORATION
Masonry structures are prime
candidates for the state-of-the-art
cleaning and restoration techniques
employed by Anderson. Whether of
brick or stone, masonry buildings are
subject to the damage of weathering
and pollution, including acid rain.
Sandblasting was once considered
the only way to clean masonry, but
this method often pits the stone or
brick on which it is applied. There are
now more sensitive and effective
washing techniques which employ
nontoxic chemicals. These can be

applied overall or used in limited
areas such as decorative elements,
stairs, and lintels. Cleaning, however,
is likely to be only part of the task.
Walls may have to be repointed,
decorative details patched, or even
missing segments fabricated. A firm
such as Anderson is set up to handle
each step of a complete restoration
job.

ANDERSON BUILDING RESTORATION
923 Marion Ave.
Cincinnati, OH 45229
(513) 281-5258

ARCHITECTURAL RECLAMATION
Among the best of the restoration
contracting firms are those that are
run as a family business, the
members personally supervising and
physically working on each project.
This is as good a description of
Architectural Reclamation – headed
by brothers Andy and Bruce Stewart
– as can be given. The Stewarts
undertake complete projects,
including plastering, carpentry,
masonry, custom woodwork, roofing,
heating, and plumbing. In their own
words, "We have strengthened floor
joists, repaired box gutters, repointed
chimneys, reproduced old doors,
matched moldings, stair spindles,
and even Greek column capitals."
The majority of their projects have
been commercial, but they especially
enjoy working on private homes.
Again, the Stewarts explain: "We use
modern materials off the shelf, but
we also fabricate new materials to
match the old and we reuse old
materials salvaged from demolished
buildings. When necessary to achieve
the desired effect, we have learned
traditional crafts and used tools
common to an earlier time in
history." Architectural Reclamation
will be glad to supply what it calls its
"Experience Statement," a
description of the major projects it
has completed.

ARCHITECTURAL RECLAMATION
312 S. River St.
Franklin, OH 45005
(513) 746-8964

EARLY NEW ENGLAND ROOMS &
    EXTERIORS/SUTHERLAND
    PERIOD HOMES
Custom millwork – windows, kitchen
cabinetry, entrances, raised panel

walls, doors, and moldings – is the specialty of Early New England. These elements are, for the most part, based on traditional 18th-century designs. Sutherland Period Homes is that arm of the business which does the basic work of dismantling old buildings and reconstructing them from top to bottom, and of building reproduction period houses along the lines of documented originals. Both the reconstructed and the new houses make use, where necessary, of Early New England's reproduction millwork. The firm also has its own blacksmith shop for producing authentic hand-forged hardware. Bringing together so many skills and facilities allows the company to manage almost any kind of project effectively and imaginatively.

Brochure available

EARLY NEW ENGLAND ROOMS &
    EXTERIORS/SUTHERLAND
    PERIOD HOMES
37 McGuire Rd.
South Windsor, CT 06074
(203) 282-0236

THE HOUSE CARPENTERS
This versatile firm produces custom millwork for restorations and builds new homes with traditional timber frames and fittings. Moldings, window sash, doors, and casings are the primary items fabricated. Clear eastern white pine is used for most millwork, but other woods can be specified. Illustrated is one of the

traditional houses designed and built by the firm.

Brochures, $6

THE HOUSE CARPENTERS
Box 281
Leverett, MA 01054
(413) 367-2189

METROPOLIS
Rigorous training in decorative painting, carpentry, masonry, plasterwork, and electrical work has equipped the owner of Metropolis, Guenter de Vincent, to undertake the most complex of restoration projects with confidence. He is European-trained, as are his two assistants. Metropolis has acted as the painter and remodeler for a large San Francisco property investment firm which manages over twenty buildings.

METROPOLIS
1210 46th Ave.
San Francisco, CA 94122
(413) 564-5776

CONRAD SCHMITT STUDIOS INC.
For over 100 years this firm has provided invaluable assistance in the restoration of public buildings such as theaters, hotels, courthouses, and churches. Its special expertise is in the areas of architectural and stained glass and decorative finishes. The research and documentation undertaken by Schmitt Studios before it begins any work is thorough and may include miscroscopic examination of paints and other finishes. The company is also well-suited to handle the restoration of murals, lighting, furnishings, screens, sculptures, and mosaic work.

Brochures available

CONRAD SCHMITT STUDIOS INC.
2405 S. 162nd St.
New Berlin, WI 53151
(414) 786-3030

STRASSER & ASSOCIATES, INC.
A background as a master restorer at the Metropolitan Museum of Art and as a principal in a restoration company serves Peter Strasser well. In 1990 he formed his own company devoted to restoration and conservation. Working with him is a dedicated and well-trained staff of associates who will take a project from the planning and design stage through to fabrication, installation, and finishing. Special interests are consultation and fine furniture restoration in wood, metal and stone.

STRASSER & ASSOCIATES, INC.
35 Hillside Ave.
Monsey, NY 10952
(914) 425-0650
Fax (914) 425-1842

TRADITIONAL LINE LTD.
    ARCHITECTURAL RESTORATION
The firm's highly-trained restoration team is comprised of cabinetmakers, carpenters, stonecutters, welders, carvers, draftspeople, and artists who can execute fine decorative finishes. Antique tools are used on some work, and traditional techniques are employed to produce effects which are in keeping with a period interior. Among the important projects this firm has completed are over a dozen apartments in the landmark Dakota apartment building on New York City's Central Park West. Work here has ranged from simply reproducing missing hardware to the re-creation of an elaborate interior. This last project included all details from sub-floor to the creation of matching ceiling medallions in ten different sizes. Illustrated is the fine

woodwork executed by Traditional Line for a Regency period library in a Westchester County, New York, residence.

Brochure available

TRADITIONAL LINE LTD.
ARCHITECTURAL RESTORATION
143 W. 21st St.
New York, NY 10011
(212) 627-3555

Vintage, Inc.
336 N. 10th St.
Easton, PA 18042
(215) 258-0602

WINANS CONSTRUCTION INC. Quality craftsmanship knows no period restraints, and Winans is as good a contracting firm for a contemporary building as it is for a period structure. Winans reflects a refreshing recognition of the responsibilities of a good contractor. In Paul Winans' words, he began his own company to provide quality service in an industry "where all too frequently contractors provide their clients with unanticipated delays, rude workmen, surprise expenses, gross inconveniences, and continual excuses." The company's many satisfied and demanding customers in the San Francisco area will testify to Winans' ability to hold to a schedule and a budget. A kitchen created for a 1926 house in what Winans calls "retro-dec" is seen in "before" and "after" shots. It combines up-to-date appliances with cabinetry and detailing of the '20s. The "before" photo is seen below; the "after" photo, on the opposite page.

Presentation folders, $5 (refundable with placement of order)

WINANS CONSTRUCTION INC.
5515 Doyle St., No. 9
Emeryville, CA 94608
(415) 653-7288
Fax (415) 653-0823

Other recommended restoration contractors include: JOSEPH CHILLINO; DODGE, ADAMS & ROY LTD; JON EKLUND RESTORATIONS; M. J. MAY BUILDING RESTORATION; MONTCLAIR RESTORATION, INC; RAMBUSCH; RESTORATIONS UNLIMITED; RIVER CITY RESTORATIONS, INC.; BARRY ROSE, ART IN ACTION; SKYLINE ENGINEERS OF MARYLAND, INC.; DONALD STRYKER RESTORATIONS; and W.J.B. & ASSOCIATES.

VINTAGE, INC.
Gerald Mazzetta has carefully carved out a career for himself as an all-round restoration craftsman in Pennsylvania and New Jersey. Like many others who have chosen the calling of restoration work, he has refined his skills on his own home, a late 19th-century residence in Easton, Pennsylvania's historic district. Mazzetta and his associates specialize in kitchen and bathroom design, but will also undertake painting, papering, plumbing, heating, and electrical work.

Corbels. *See* **Brackets.**

Corner Beads. Until recently the use of simple moldings or beading to protect the corners of a wall had fallen into disuse. Corner beads are a feature of the interior woodwork of many Victorian houses where it was important to protect expensive wallpaper or a special painted surface. Corner beads, however, can be used just as effectively to prevent gouges or scrapes wherever there is a critical projecting corner. Many suppliers of millwork now carry these moldings.

SILVERTON VICTORIAN MILLWORK
The corner beads offered by Silverton

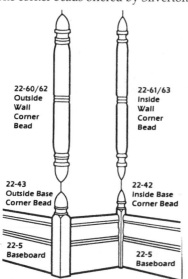

22-60/62
Outside
Wall
Corner
Bead

22-61/63
Inside
Wall
Corner
Bead

22-43
Outside Base
Corner Bead

22-42
Inside Base
Corner Bead

22-5
Baseboard

22-5
Baseboard

come in two types – those used with wainscot and smaller moldings (as illustrated) which can be attached to either an inner or outside corner. The beads are available in 36" and 48" lengths and are designed to match Silverton's base corner beads. The wainscot corner beads are designed for Silverton's $1/4$" wainscot and can be used with up to $4^1/_2$' of wainscoting. All beads are available in pine, premium pine, oak, or premium oak.

Complete catalog package, $4

SILVERTON VICTORIAN MILLWORKS
PO Box 2987-OC7
Durango, CO 81302
(303) 259-5915
Fax (303) 259-5919

Among other firms which feature corner beads are: BLUE OX MILLWORKS *and* SAN FRANCISCO VICTORIANA.

Corner Blocks/Rosettes. *See* **Door and Window Casings.**

Cornices. *See* **Moldings.**

Counter Tops. Anyone who has to make do with kitchen counter tops of a plastic or other synthetic material has learned that these surfaces are difficult to keep clean and can be

easily marred. Butcher block may be substituted in some sections, especially in areas where food is prepared. But this is not the only option. Counter tops of soapstone, slate, and other stone that has been treated for staining are handsome additions to any kitchen, and may prove much easier to maintain than an artifical surface. A polished stone suitable for this purpose – slate or a low-grade marble – may be found at most quarries; suppliers of stone for flooring and outdoor paving often can custom cut large pieces of stone in a requisite thickness.

THE STRUCTURAL SLATE CO. Architectural slate in gray, the color ranging from a blue-gray to a gray-black, is Structural's stock in trade. This is available directly from the firm or through stone and tile distributors throughout North America. The slates are custom-cut from one of two grades – ribbon stock or clear stock, the latter being preferable for counter tops. There are also various finishes, the honed probably being the best for kitchen or bathroom use. Honed slabs are similar to those used for sills. Any length up to 7' is available; widths are as required. In thickness, the slabs can be $3/_4$", 1", $1^1/_4$" $1^1/_2$" or 2".

Brochure available

THE STRUCTURAL SLATE CO.
PO Box 187, 222 E. Main St.
Pen Argyl, PA 18072-01
(215) 863-4141
(800) 67-SLATE
Fax (215) 863-7016

For other slate colors – red, gray-green, purple – contact: EVERGREEN SLATE CO., INC. *or* VERMONT STRUCTURAL SLATE CO.

VERMONT SOAPSTONE CO. Soapstone is an extraordinary material mined in only a few areas of North America. It is a variety of talc and takes its name from its slightly slippery and soft feeling. Soapstone has been used for years to make washtubs, sinks, drainboards, and counter tops. It is very durable and a nonporous heat-resistant material. Vermont Soapstore, miners and manufacturers since 1850, custom cut and make counter tops in a thickness of 1¹/₄" and a maximum size of 30" by 48". The natural color is a light gray; this will darken with age. Vermont Soapstone can advise on changing this color if desired. No sealing or treatment is needed, whatever the shade.

Literature available

VERMONT SOAPSTONE CO.
PO Box 168, Stoughton Pond Rd.
Perkinsville, VT 05151-0168
(802) 263-5404
Fax (802) 263-9451

Other suppliers of stone for counter tops, by type, are: slate – RISING & NELSON SLATE CO.; *marble* – GEORGIA MARBLE CO.; *slate and marble* – BERGEN BLUESTONE CO., INC., DELAWARE QUARRIES, INC., NEW YORK MARBLE WORKS, INC., *and* PASVALCO.

Cove Moldings. *See* **Moldings.**

Coverlets. Antique coverlets are so highly sought-after that it is only natural for craftspeople to take to weaving them again. Some are woven on old-fashioned Jacquard looms; plain coverlets are turned out on simple looms. Quilts are now distinguished from coverlets as not being woven, but, technically, they are bed coverings or coverlets. Suppliers of antique or reproduction quilts, however, are not included in the following listings as both types are still commonly available in shops throughout the world. It is unlikely that the weaving of coverlets, a much more intricate process than quilting, will ever become a popular pastime.

FAMILY HEIR-LOOM WEAVERS
Jacquard and plain woven coverlets are among the prizes produced by David and Carole Kline and their assistants in rural Pennsylvania. They work on old mill equipment to produce two pictorial Jacquard designs, as illustrated, left, "House Border," and right, "Bird and Bush." The same type of cotton warp or vertical thread, wool weft or horizontal thread, and process of assembly are used that were introduced more than 150 years ago. A personalized signature block can be included with each, a feature of many antique examples. "Plain" coverlets include an all-white or a geometric block twill named after

weaver Heinrich Leisy. There is a selection of one, two, or three wool color combinations for each of the Jacquard and plain designs. Sizes differ from coverlet to coverlet, but include a child's size, double, and queen or full size for most.

Brochure, $2.50

FAMILY HEIR-LOOM WEAVERS
RD 3, Box 59E
Red Lion, PA 17356
(717) 246-2431 (shop)
(717) 244-5921 (residence)

RASTETTER WOOLEN MILL
Plain wool and cotton coverlets in what Rastetter terms Colonial patterns are made in designs that date from the early 19th century; these are "Morning Star," "Whig Rose," and "Lovers Knot." "Whig Rose" is offered in two sizes – 90" or 78" by 108" – and the other two designs in a 90" by 108" size only. Colors to choose from include navy blue, delft blue, red, and rose. All are worked on a white background. Rastetter also supplies 90" material in the "Whig Rose" and "Lover's Knot" designs for use as throws, draperies, and upholstery.

Brochure available

RASTETTER WOOLEN MILL
State Rte. 39 and 62
Millersburg, OH 44654
(216) 674-2103

Other suppliers of plain coverlets include CARTER CANOPIES *and* VIRGINIA GOODWIN

Cradles. A special bed for a baby can be the kind of heirloom which families pass down from generation to generation. Few of these treasures, however, have survived use over time, and those that have are more likely to be found in museums than in homes. The classic cradle has rockers, the motion of which is intended to calm or delight the most belligerent baby. Fortunately, skilled woodworkers are still turning out cradles, and the result of their labors is well-enough designed and built to serve well into the 21st century.

STEPHEN P. BEDARD
Bedard is a craftsman who could not resist creating a cradle in a classic

Windsor style. It has a base of pine, curved ash bows, and maple spindles. All the work is done by hand, including the turnings. The standard model is 18¹/₂" high, 39" long, and 24" wide, including the carved rockers.

Catalog, $3

STEPHEN P. BEDARD
Durrell Mountain Farm, PO Box 2
Gilmanton Iron Works, NH 03837
(603) 528-1896

THE COUNTRY BED SHOP
It is appropriate that this longtime supplier of period beds should also take into consideration the needs of infants. An exact copy of a late 18th-century hooded cradle in clear pine is the standard model offered. Country Bed Shop is also prepared to custom make other cradle styles from Pilgrim Century paneled oak to Windsor and swinging types.

Catalog, $4

THE COUNTRY BED SHOP
RR 1, Box 65, Richardson Rd.
Ashby, MA 01431
(508) 386-7550

Cranes. Fireplace cranes were useful objects when cooking was performed over an open fire, as was the practice in many homes well into the 19th century. Of wrought- or hand-forged iron, these bars swung out from one side of the fireplace and provided a place to hang cooking utensils. Today cranes have little more than decorative use, but they are appropriate for a kitchen fireplace or in any fireplace that may have been used at one time for cooking.

KAYNE & SON CUSTOM FORGED
    HARDWARE
A crane is a simple form for a blacksmith to forge – if you can find such a craftsman these days. Steve Kayne is one of them and a member of the Artist-Blacksmiths' Association of North America. His basic design can measure up to 30" wide, and he supplies the pintels that hold the vertical bar on which the horizontal crane swings. The usual crane is one-half the width of the fireplace.

Hand Forged Hardware catalog, $2

KAYNE & SON CUSTOM FORGED
    HARDWARE
76 Daniel Ridge Rd.
Candler, NC 28715
(704) 665-1988
(704) 667-8868

LEMEE'S FIREPLACE EQUIPMENT
A general supplier of fireplace equipment, Lemee's features a simple crane design in four widths from 22" to 41". It is, of course, made of wrought iron, and Lemee also supplies the face-mounting supports for securing the vertical member. Instructions for installing the crane are included with each order.

Catalog, $2

LEMEE'S FIREPLACE EQUIPMENT
815 Bedford St.
Bridgewater, MA 02324
(508) 697-2672

Other suppliers of fireplace cranes include HAMMERWORKS.

Cresting. Ironwork which decorates the roof lines of 19th-century buildings is known as cresting. This usually takes the form of a series of repeating perforated panels which, in effect, fence off the top of a building or a portion of it such as a tower. The designs are often highly elaborate. A similar treatment in wood, seen on some Federal and early Victorian houses, is also termed cresting. This can be worked in solid panels similiar to fencing or as ornate carved decoration.

ARCHITECTURAL IRON CO.
This firm is America's premier producer of cast-iron cresting. As Architectural Iron correctly points out in its catalog, most of the decorative ironwork used on buildings in the 1800s was cast or a combination of cast and wrought members. It was the availabilty of relatively inexpensive cast work rather than the hand-wrought which contributed to its widespread use. Among Architectural Iron's stock items are four cresting designs. Any number of other designs can be made on a custom basis, and the firm stands ready to fabricate replacement parts where needed.

Brochure, $4

ARCHITECTURAL IRON CO.
Box 126, Schocopee Rd.
Milford, PA 18337
(717) 296-7722
(212) 243-2664
Fax (717) 296-IRON

Kayne and Son Custom Forged Hardware

W. F. NORMAN CORP.
Sheet-metal crestings from the late 1800s are an essential part of Norman's production today. These are stamped designs, a few of which are pierced. Most of the crestings feature a series of classic forms such as shell and leaf and fleur-de-lis. Sizes range as low as 4" to as high as 22". There are over fifty stock designs in Norman's catalog, and each may be made up in sheet zinc or can be stamped of copper, aluminum, bronze, lead-coated copper, hard lead, and other alloys.

Catalog, $5

American customers, contact:
W. F. NORMAN CORP.
214 N. Cedar, PO Box 323
Nevada, MO 64772-0323
(800) 641-4038
(417) 667-5552 (MO)

Canadian customers, contact:
STEPTOE AND WIFE ANTIQUES, LTD.
322 Geary Ave.
Toronto, ONT M6H 2C7
(416) 530-4200

Other suppliers of cast-iron cresting include: ROBINSON IRON CORP., THE STEWART IRON WORKS CO., and TENNESSEE FABRICATING CO.

Crewelwork. *See* **Fabrics.**

Crown Moldings. *See* **Moldings.**

Cupboards and Cabinets. Built-in and freestanding cabinets and cupboards should reflect, whenever possible, the general architectural style of a house. There are no hard and fast rules, of course, but style in cabinetry is usually dictated by the type of millwork which is used to define such structural elements as doors, windows, and ceilings. In any early Colonial dwelling, for example, cupboards might be fashioned with simple beaded boards and the use of wrought-iron hardware. In a later Georgian Colonial house, a raised panel design and brass fittings would be more appropriate. most restoration consultants and contractors understand how very important it is to achieve an overall consistency of interior design, and are well equipped to provide the means to achieve this aim.

RICHARD A. BRUNKUS, CABINETMAKER
Fine painted and grained American furniture and fine art of the 18th and 19th centuries are passions of this talented cabinetmaker. He has studied the actual pieces so carefully that his reproductions are hard to detect from the antique. All of his work is custom and commissioned and includes cupboards of various types. Illustrated is a small grained

and painted hanging cupboard of pine and poplar. It is painted blue. Brunkus used early glass for this piece as he does for other cupboards, including a very handsome freestanding corner cupboard. The size of the hanging cupboard is 34" high, 21³/₄" wide, and 7" deep. This master cabinetmaker also restores antique pieces to perfection.

Literature available

RICHARD A. BRUNKUS, CABINETMAKER
PO Box 451
Frenchtown, NJ 08825
(201) 996-7125

EARLY NEW ENGLAND ROOMS & EXTERIORS, INC.
Both stock and custom-designed cupboards and cabinets are available from this restoration woodworking firm. All pieces are hand-built and reflect or duplicate exactly styles of 18th-century cabinetry. Included in the stock designs are a hutch or china cupboard, a drygoods cupboard, and corner cupboards.

Catalog, $10

EARLY NEW ENGLAND ROOMS & EXTERIORS, INC.
37 Maguire Rd.
South Windsor, CT 06074
(203) 282-0236

FIRESIDE REPRODUCTIONS
John Glenn of Fireside has been slowly expanding his line of reproduction furniture and now offers an early New England pine pewter cupboard. No reproduction could be more "real." The wood used is anywhere from 150 to 200 years old. The shelves are hand-beaded, and hand-cut spoon notches are included. The cupboard, measuring 6'6" high, 26" wide, and 14" deep, is available in either an aged natural finish or in a worn buttermilk paint.

FIRESIDE REPRODUCTIONS
4747 Winterset Dr.
Columbus, OH 43220
(614) 451-7695

TRADITIONAL LINE LTD.
   ARCHITECTURAL RESTORATION
The importance of cabinetry which blends in with the architectural appointments of an interior is recognized in all of Traditional Line's work. All projects are custom-designed and built. Illustrated is cabinetry installed in a New York City apartment dating from the 1880s. Traditional Line also restores period pieces and built-in cabinetry.

Brochure available

TRADITIONAL LINE LTD.
ARCHITECTURAL RESTORATION

143 W. 21st St.
New York, NY 10011
(212) 627-3555
Fax (212) 645-8158

Other makers of cupboards and cabinets include: ARCHITECTURAL COMPONENTS, INC., BAILEY'S ARCHITECTURAL MILLWOEK, INC., BLUE OX MILLWORKS, MARION H. CAMPBELL, CABINETMAKER, THE COUNTRY BED SHOP, GERALD CURRY, CABINETMAKER, MAURER & SHEPHERD JOYNERS, RESTORATIONS UNLIMITED, SPRING HOUSE CLASSICS, *and* DONALD STRYKER RESTORATIONS.

Cupolas. This most attractive of roof-top structures has become something of a visual cliche. It is now perched atop just about any building – garage, shed, ranch-style house – to give it a folksy "Colonial" appearance. Banks and nursing homes seem particularly prone to cupolamania. In addition to such inappropriateness, cupolas are often strikingly under- or over-sized in relation to the buildings on which they sit. That being said, there still remain buildings for which a properly-proportioned cupola would be a handsome addition, and these include true Colonial residences, real carriage houses, and barns. The best argument for a cupola, however, is its original *raison d'etre,* to serve as conduit for ventilation. Large and powerful exhaust fans in the roof can often cool an old house more successfully than air-conditioning, and a cupola can be used not only to vent the attic but also to serve as a superstructure for the equipment. A cupola remains, nonetheless, only appropriate for a barn or a Colonial building.

DENNINGER CUPOLAS AND WEATHER VANES

Wood – not aluminum – cupolas are the standard at Denninger. Solid redwood or cedar are used for their durability and appearance. Roofs are made of heavy gauge, 16oz. copper with handmade standing seams. The only synthetic material employed is fiberglass for screens inside the louvers to keep out insects. Illustrated is the handsome hexagonal Mt. Vernon model. It and

three square models are available in two approximate sizes; each of the cupolas comes with a base sized to fit the pitch of a roof – from low to steep. Louvers and roofs are also sized accordingly to maintain proper proportions between the elements. As an extra bonus, a copper arrow weather vane is included free with each order.

Literature, $1

DENNINGER CUPOLAS AND WEATHER VANES
RD 1, Box 447
Middletown, NY 10940
(914) 343-2229

GOOD DIRECTIONS, INC.
Cupolas in finished or kit form can be purchased from this firm. The Windsor is a traditional square box in base sizes ranging from 16" to 36"; Canterbury differs in having a pagoda-style roof. The other two models – Newmarket and Buckingham – are six-sided, the first with a bell-shaped roof and the second, a pagoda form. All roofs are of copper. Good Directions provides this rule of thumb for determining the proper size for a cupola: "the base of the cupola should measure NO LESS THAN one inch for every foot length of uninterrupted ridge of the building it is to be installed upon. This is the MINIMUM size acceptable. The next size larger will usually be more pleasing." As the firm comments, "If too small, it will look like a birdhouse on your roof! A cupola, like anything else, always looks smaller when installed on the roof."

Catalog, $1

GOOD DIRECTIONS, INC.
24 Ardmore Rd.
Stamford, CT 06902
(203) 348-1836 (CT)
(800) 346-7678
Fax (203) 357-0092

Other producers of cupolas are: BAILEY'S ARCHITECTURAL MILLWORK, INC., CAPE COD CUPOLA CO., INC., THE COPPERSMITH, *and* FYPON, INC.

Curtains. *See* **Draperies.**

Cushions. It hardly seems essential to include this category of furnishings in *The Old House Catalogue.* Decorating magazines are full of plump varieties which, curiously, in interior photos, move from room to room. But the cushions made by one company are so distinctive and attractive that they should be mentioned. The firm is DECORATIVE TEXTILES OF CHELTENHAM, and, as the photograph illustrates, there are a number of types available: toile de Joy, floral chintz, 17th- and 19th-century tapestry weaves, Victorian beadwork, and 19th-century needlepoint, brocade,

Aubusson, and crewelwork. Antique textiles are used and, necessarily, each cushion is handmade.

Brochure available

Decorative Textiles of Cheltenham
7 Suffolk Parade
Cheltenham GL50 2AB

Stair hall chandelier, Wickham-Valentine House, Richmond, Virginia. Historic American Buildings Survey.

Door casings, Reading-Large House, Flemington, New Jersey. Photograph by Jack E. Boucher, Historic American Buildings Survey.

Dentils. *See* **Moldings.**

Desks/Secretaries. Old-fashioned desks, ranging from pediment-top secretaries to massive rolltops, have an undeniable charm for many people, including those who have no interest in other aspects of the antique world. Wanting to possess and display a handsome, substantial desk at home is one of those true, unexplainable passsions. Competition for antique desks is therefore severe. A desk-bookcase or secretary is more difficult to find than a low desk or bureau. Machine-crafted reproductions of all desk types are available commercially, but few are really worth the price. The work of individual craftsmen, however, guaranteed to be enjoyed for many years, may actually cost little more than that supplied by a new furniture dealer or department store.

GERALD CURRY, CABINETMAKER
The secretaries and desks made by Curry will take their place some day alongside the antiques on which they

are modeled. So that there will be no confusion, Curry's signature, the buyer's name, and the date of purchase appears on each of his pieces. A Chippendale block front secretary in mahogany is the most elegant and expensive of Curry's hand-carved furniture. It is made in two sections, the bottom desk also being available as a separate piece. The fan carved domes, blocked main drawers, candleslides, flame finials, and sculpted pilasters are superbly worked. A walnut Chippendale slant-front dest is only slightly less elegant.

Brochure, $2

GERALD CURRY, CABINETMAKER
Round Hill Rd.
Union, ME 04862
(207) 785-4633

JEFFREY GREENE, FURNITUREMAKER
Eight 18th-century reproductions are included in the repertoire of desks

made by Greene. The largest – 90" high by 42" wide by 23" deep – is the Chippendale six-shell block-front secretary illustrated. Smaller units are various slant-top desks which range in height from 42" to 44" and vary proportionately in width. These include a reproduction of a c. 1760 bombé desk made in Boston and a Queen Anne desk-on-frame based on a Massachusetts piece dated 1750-60. All pieces carry historically accurate brass hardware and fittings. Mahogany, cherry, and maple, including tiger maple, are used for various pieces.

Catalog available

JEFFREY GREENE, FURNITUREMAKER
97 James Trail
West Kingston, RI 02892
(401) 783-6614

Other master fruniture craftsmen inlcude MARION H. CAMPBELL, CABINET MAKER, *and* DIMITRIOS KLITSAS.

Domes. The term "dome" suggests a rather grand and monumental use of space befitting a church or other public building. Domes on a smaller scale, however, have been used in homes of the past, especially in entry halls and dining rooms. These features add interest to any interior and, in a confined area, create an illusion of space. Domes can be custom made of stained glass, an attractive option when the circular or oval form is placed in a position to receive light. Most domes, however, are of solid plaster or fiberglass construction.

THE BALMER ARCHITECTURAL ART
STUDIOS
Six different types of domes are featured by Balmer in its illustrated catalog. Of gypsum plaster, these are

only a few of many sizes and shapes available from the firm. Each dome has a trim ring and can also be made with a center hole so that a chandelier can be hung, the dome being used, as it often is, as a centerpiece.

Full catalog, $20

THE BALMER ARCHITECTURAL ART
    STUDIOS
9 Codeco Ct.
Don Mills, ONT M3A 1B6
Canada
(416) 449-2155
Fax (416) 449-3018

FOCAL POINT, INC.
Domes in two types of materials are included in Focal Point' s collection of molded ornamentation. Two sizes – outside diameters of 37$1/_2$" and 61$1/_2$" – are offered in the stock Endure-All material, a polyurethane formula. Rims are separate items and are available in three styles. Domes are also made with integral rims in Fabucast, a fiberglass-reinforced polyester. Three size are offered in this form, with outside diameters of 35$7/_8$", 59$3/_4$", and 89$1/_4$". Focal Point domes will need only light sanding after installation; they take paint easily.

Catalog, $3

FOCAL POINT, INC.
PO Box 93327
Atlanta, GA 30377-0327
(800) 662-5550
(404) 351-0820
Fax (404) 352-9049

WORTHINGTON GROUP LTD.
A dome and trim ring in one piece is available in various sizes from Worthington. These are constructed of fiberglass.

Catalog, $3

WORTHINGTON GROUP LTD.
PO Box 53101
Atlanta, GA 30355
(404) 872-1608
(800) 872-1608
Fax (404) 872-8501

Expert plastering contractors such as FRANK J. MANGIONE can also provide dome units and undertake their installation.

Doorbells. Doorbells are not high on the list of priorities in many old-house households. It is useful, nevertheless, to have a contrivance which does not require electrical wiring and which, in itself, is an attractive period accessory. A mechanical doorbell is guaranteed to function and the ring to be heard.

A. BALL PLUMBING SUPPLY
Ball supplies a decorative Victorian mechanical doorbell with a twist key mechanism. A rectangular plate with the twist is placed on the outside of a door and the bell assembly on the inside. Two screws hold the pieces together in place. The plate is 6" high and 3$1/_4$" wide.

Free catalog

A. BALL PLUMBING SUPPLY
1703 W. Burnside St.
Portland, OR 97209
(503) 228-0026
Fax (503) 228-0030

DOMUS DOORBELLS LTD.
Only in England would the manufacture of such a contrivance as a mechanical doorbell *system* continue today. The standard model consists of a solid-brass pull rod and handle, cast-iron brackets for the rod, a pulley bracket, cable, a bell assembly mounted on an oak or mahogany plaque, and all other necessary fittings. The pull rod and handle can

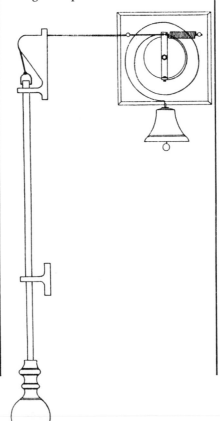

also be supplied in wrought iron. The cast, turned, and polished bell is 3$3/_8$" in diameter and is produced in bell metal by one of England's oldest foundries. What Domus refers to as a "shop" door bell is also available. This is the same bell and coil spring apparatus mounted on a plaque, but it is activated by a door trigger.

DOMUS DOORBELLS LTD.
PO Box 190
Haywards Heath, Sussex RH17 5YG
England
(0444) 417571
Fax (0737) 773650

TREMONT NAIL COMPANY
Simple round mechanical doorbells in brass or nickel plate are supplied by Tremont. These work on a twist mechanism on the outside of the door. The turn piece is offered in iron on an iron or brass base. Two screws hold the assembly together.

Free brochure

TREMONT NAIL CO.
8 Elm St., PO Box 111
Wareham, MA 02571
(508) 295-0038

Door Casings and Window Casings.
To case-in a door or window is to enclose it with a molding or a series of moldings. These are termed casings and are included in the repertoire of almost all millwork suppliers. Casings range from very simple beaded boards to a highly complex series of profiles. In general, the style of casings accords with the overall architectural period or style of the house, and will blend in with the millwork used elsewhere in the home. For plain casings, a local lumberyard may suffice; high-style assembllies of moldings may have to be custom-produced and/or ordered from a specialty supplier. In addition to moldings, a door or window casing might also include such elements as corner blocks or rosettes, a keystone, and base blocks. *See also* **Arches, Door Heads and Window Heads, Pilasters.**

AMERICAN CUSTOM MILLWORK, INC.
A variety of door and window casing assemblies are available through American Custom. A selection of hardwoods, including Appalachian poplar, walnut, oak, cherry, and mahogany, is offered. Included with

some casing designs are rosettes and base blocks. The most common form of molding used in 19th-century North American windows and door frames are fluted and have only a slight profile. There are at least five variations of this basic design in American Custom's portfolio. Other moldings are closer to an ogee or bolection form, and American Custom produces a majority of these in an embossed process.

Catalog, $5

AMERICAN CUSTOM MILLWORK, INC.
3904 Newton Rd., PO Box 3608
Albany, GA 31706
(912) 888-3303
(912) 888-6848

AMHERST WOODWORKING & SUPPLY,
   INC.
A selection of 250 molding patterns from Amherst allows almost any casing design to be made up. Stock lumber includes select pine, poplar, maple, birch, ash, red and white oak, and cherry; Douglas fir, southern yellow pine, and redwood are available on special order. Amherst is also a good source for such standard elements as doorstops and door and window jamb. For arched windows or doors, this firm will also run profiles in circle sections and ellipses.

Free catalog

AMHERST WOODWORKING & SUPPLY,
   INC.
Box 718, Hubbard Ave.
Northampton, MA 01061
(413) 584-3003
Fax (413) 585-0288

BENDIX MOULDINGS, INC.
Moldings are the focus of almost all of the Bendix output. It has been supplying carved, embossed, and plain moldings since 1924. The firm also produces a line of carved and embossed wood ornaments which can be used to highlight door and window casings. The carved moldings are of fine hardwood only; embossed and plain moldings are available in pine as well. All are sold in random lengths ranging from 3' to 15'.

Catalog, $3

BENDIX MOULDINGS, INC.
37 Ramland Rd. South

Orangeburg, NY 10962-2697
(914) 365-1111
Fax (914) 365-1218

BLUE OX MILLWORKS
Blue Ox is extremely accommodating to old-house owners seeking replacement millwork. This may mean only a 5' or 6' section and custom work, but Blue Ox will supply what is needed on a reasonable basis in prime redwood or a wood of the customer's choice. There are a number of stock window and door casing profiles to choose from if one is starting completely from scratch, including one devised solely for arched doorways. Blue Ox Millwork's customers come from as far away as the East Coast.

Pattern Book, $6

BLUE OX MILLWORKS
Foot of X St.
Eureka, CA 95501
(707) 444-3437
(800) 248-4259
Fax (707) 444-0918

SAN FRANCISCO VICTORIANA, INC.
The San Francisco area's #1 millwork fabricator has grown with the remarkable development of the restoration business. Victoriana's molding assemblies are based on historic examples found in the Bay area's 19th- and early 20th-century houses. A very basic blocked casing is illustrated here, one typical of many period interiors. Also offered are

three other corner block designs that could be used instead of the one shown. Victoriana also makes up base blocks and head blocks that can be substituted for corner blocks. Redwood is the primary material used for millwork that will be painted; poplar or fir can be substituted. For a grade suitable for stain, one can also choose from alder, ash, Honduran or Phillipine mahogany, clear pine, red oak, walnut, white oak, and a clear all-heart redwood.

Catalog, $5

SAN FRANCISCO VICTORIANA, INC.
2070 Newcomb Ave.
San Francisco, CA 94124
(415) 648-0313
Fax (415) 648-2812

SOMERSET DOOR & COLUMN CO.
This firm is one of many suppliers of doors that can also provide appropriate jambs, stops, and casings. It is convenient to be able to turn to one manufacturer when doors and the millwork to dress them up are needed. The millwork is made up on a custom basis only, but there are stock door designs to choose from.

Literature available

SOMERSET DOOR & COLUMN CO.
Box 328
Somerset, PA 15501
(814) 445-9608

Other suppliers of door and window casings are: CREATIVE WOODWORKING LTD., CUSTOM & HISTORIC MILLWORK, FOCAL POINT, THE HOUSE CARPENTERS, ORNAMENTAL MOULDINGS LTD., SHEPPARD MILLWORK, INC., SILVERTON VICTORIAN MILLWORKS, and SUNSHINE ARCHITECTURAL WOODWORKS.

Door Guards. Fortunately, security devices of this sort are only necessary in urban areas subject to high crime rates, but there are many population centers that qualify! Door guards are customarily used only for commercial establishments and public buildings to effectively block off an entrance. But they can be similarly effective for private residence entryways and sets of French doors that may open out to a garden area. ARCHITECTURAL IRON CO. has had experience in fabricating wrought- and cast-iron door guards.

In addition to being sturdily built, the guards are also well designed. One set recently made for French doors are of a bi-folding type, and all horizontal and vertical members align with the mullions in the doors. Guards are custom work for Architectural Iron, as they are for other metal fabricators.

Brochure, $4

ARCHITECTURAL IRON CO.
Box 126, Schocopee Rd.
Milford, PA 18337
(717) 296-7722
(212) 243-2664
Fax (717) 296-IRON

Another supplier of door or security guards is TENNESSEE FABRICATING CO.

Door Hardware. Included in this category are knobs, plates, latches, catches, roses, bars, and handles. Solid architectural hardware will enhance any door, interior or exterior. Blacksmiths and foundries have been producing beautiful, durable pieces for years, and continue to do so today in many different styles and designs. Each has its own function, though plates and roses are essentially decorative as they serve to frame a keyhole and a knob or handle. A great deal of antique hardware has survived over the years. When an old building is demolished, it is often only the hardware that survives to be used again. An explanation for this is hard to come by, but, clearly, well-wrought hardware has always been highly valued and prized. The same cannot be said for much of the stamped variety sold in home centers or the few remaining stores that deal exclusively in hardware. Perhaps this is why there are many speciality outlets for both antique and fine reproduction hardware. *See also* **Door Knockers, Door Locks**, and **Hinges**

THE BRASS KNOB
This Washington, D.C., outlet stocks a large supply of antique door hardware of the type illustrated. Doorknobs and plates are generally of a late-Victorian vintage and display a highly ornamental touch. The Brass Knob will help the customer find the proper fittings for knobs and plates if these are missing.

Free brochure

THE BRASS KNOB
2311 18th St., NW
Washington, DC 20009
(202) 332-3370

A CAROLINA CRAFTSMAN
Hardware of nearly every sort – architectural, furniture, cabinet, and trunk – (except bathroom and kitchen hardware) can be found at Carolina. Offered are solid-brass decorative hinges, Victorian design plates, and knobs which match the plates in ornamentation. Carolina also keeps a good supply of cast French door handles and doorknob roses which are used in place of a plate for many interior doors.

Catalog, $3 (refundable on first order)

A CAROLINA CRAFTSMAN
975 S. Avocado St.
Anaheim, CA 92805
(714) 776-7877
Fax (714) 533-0894

CIRECAST, INC.
Brass hardware from a significant period in Victorian production – 1870-1885 – serves as models for Cirecast's reproductions. The four patterns offered are "Columbia," patented in 1882 by Reading Hardware Co; "Brocade," patented in 1885 by the Sargent Lock Co; and "Lilly," patented before 1880 and attributed to Sargent. Each piece is handmade using the "cire perdue" or lost wax casting process. The result is extraordinary definition in the ornamental knobs, plates, and hinges.

Cirecast also produces roses used with some knobs. Plates are divided into those suitable for exterior and interior door use, the former being fitted for a double bit key or cylinder lock. Antiqued brass wood screws are included with all orders. Cirecast has produced hardware for many important Victorian restoration projects.

Brochure, $2.25

CIRECAST, INC.
380 7th St.
San Francisco, CA 94103
(415) 863-8319

BRIAN F. LEO
Leo handles only custom hardware orders. The demand for his services is very great as he also fabricates architectural ornaments and such cast-metal items as railings, kitchen hardware, and register grilles. Illustrated here are two plate designs and three superbly produced

doorknobs. This is but the tip of the Leo iceberg, which includes at least 80 plate designs, over 50 knobs, many hinges, roses, handles, and letter drops. Any of the items shown in his catalog can be modified to meet the customer's specifications. "I'm constantly making dimensional changes," he explains, "adding or removing things to order, or changing the metal." And he is glad to do so.

Catalog available

BRIAN F. LEO
7532 Columbus Ave. Sou
Richfield, MN 55423
(612) 861-1473

RESTORATION WORKS, INC.
This outlet offers the work of various hardware manufacturers who have recognized a need for good reproductions. Illustrated are three Victorian period pieces and matching knobs; other pieces are of an earlier style. Roses are also available. All door hardware is solid brass.

Catalog, $3

RESTORATION WORKS, INC.
PO Box 486
Buffalo, NY 14205
(800) 735-3535
Fax (716) 856-8040

SALVAGE ONE
Antique decorative hardware in brass, bronze, and iron can be found in Salvage One's enormous inventory.

One area of the 85,000 square-foot warehouse is devoted to knob sets and plates of nearly every description. Nothing, to be sure, is home-center plastic-wrapped (as the photograph indicates), but part of the delight of restoring an old house is the search for the right object, antique or reproduction.

Brochure available

SALVAGE ONE
1524 S. Snagamon St.
Chicago, IL 60608
(312) 733-0098

Other suppliers of period door hardware are: reproduction – THE ARDEN FORGE CO., BALDWIN HARDWARE CORP., BONA DECORATIVE HARDWARE, KAYNE & SON CUSTOM FORGED HARDWARE, OMNIA INDUSTRIES, INC., RENOVATOR'S SUPPLY *and* TREMONT NAIL CO., antique – GOVERNOR'S ANTIQUES, JOE LEY ANTIQUES, INC., PHILADELPHIA ARCHITECTURAL SALVAGE LTD., QUEEN CITY ARCHITECTURAL SALVAGE, WESTLAKE ARCHITECTURAL ANTIQUES, *and* WRECKING BAR OF ATLANTA, INC.

Door Heads and Window Heads/ Overdoors. A door head or window head is the topmost part of a casing or frame. The head may take the simple form of a plain wood or stone lintel, especially on a house exterior. More elaborate forms for interior and exterior use are sunbursts, pediments, crown moldings, and beaded caps. In late-Victorian interiors, a head is sometimes surmounted by a fretwork header ornament such as a scroll. Whatever type of head is employed, the purpose is the same – to dress up an opening in the wall. The head, of course, should always be in a style complementary to that of the overall architecture..

FOCAL POINT, INC.
Focal Point offers a handsome collection of "overdoors," which may be used for windows as well. Included are three rectangular plaques with Georgian, Regency, or neoclassical decoration, four pediments, and five sunburst designs. One of the sunbursts, Shell & Trellis, combines the burst with corner "trellising" to form a rectangle. The National Trust for Historic Preservation has licensed two of the sunburst designs taken from their properties Drayton Hall and Oatlands. Historic Natchez Foundation has approved the production of two pediments based on doorways found at the Banker's House and Oakland. Our experience is that all of these products, molded of a special polyurethane, are just fine for interior use and are so recommended, but they lack the depth and character of wood which is so necessary for effective exterior application.

Catalog, $3

FOCAL POINT, INC.
PO Box 93327
Atlanta, GA 30377-0327
(800) 662-5550
(404) 351-0820 (GA and AK)
Fax (404) 352-9049

SILVERTON VICTORIAN MILLWORKS
Silverton suggests the use of a cap over a plain door or window head. There are a number of profiles available for these decorative additions, any one of which would be appropriate for a late 19th- or early 20th-century residence. Rabbeting – creating a recess or groove in the edge or face of the cap – may be necessary to install the cap to the head. This Silverton will do for you if necessary.

Complete catalog package, $4

SILVERTON VICTORIAN MILLWORKS
PO Box 2987-OC7
Durango, CO 81302
(303) 259-5915
Fax (303) 259-5919

WORTHINGTON GROUP LTD.
Window or door heads termed "overdoors" or "window treatments" are featured in Worthington's literature. There are two sunburst designs, a pediment, and an Italian baroque design to choose from. Sizes range from 32" wide to 52$\frac{1}{2}$". The overdoors are made of cast reinforced plaster and can be used inside or outside a house.

Catalog, $3

WORTHINGTON GROUP LTD.
PO Box 53101
Atlanta, GA 30355
(404) 872-1608 (GA)
(800) 872-1608
Fax (404) 872-8501

Other suppliers of door and window heads or overdoors are THE BALMER ARCHITECTURAL ART STUDIOS *and* SAN FRANCISCO VICTORIANA, INC.

Doorknobs. *See* **Door Hardware.**

Door Knockers. A solid, heavy door knocker can make a surprising amount of noise, certainly enough to summon the sleeping from the dead of night. We are speaking in this regard of true hand-forged or expertly cast devices and not flimsy plated models that pass for knockers in gift shops. The knocker is considered the focal point of a main entry door and should have a substantial appearance and feel. There are a number of Colonial and Victorian designs offered by hardware manufacturers and blacksmiths. From experience we have also learned that a knocker has another practical use, as a device from which to hang Christmas or other seasonal wreaths.

HISTORIC HARDWARE LTD.
Seven different designs are offered by this firm in iron or brass. They include such traditional forms as the S-curve brass drop handle, the pineapple drop, thought to be a symbol of hospitality, an eagle design, and a Victorian shield. Illustrated is The Snug Harbor, a forged iron knocker of simple design suited for an early American setting.

Catalog, $3

HISTORIC HARDWARE LTD.
PO Box 1327
North Hampton, NH 03862
(603) 964-2280

KAYNE & SON CUSTOM FORGED
    HARDWARE
Steve Kayne includes at least a dozen knocker designs in his portfolios of cast and wrought hardware. Among the most interesting is a primitive brass ring mounted on a brass backplate, a polished brass lion head, an iron shield, and a cast eagle design. Kayne can make up just about anything desired. A door knocker can be wrought in nearly any form that would serve as a symbolic personal signature of the homeowner. A musical key, an anchor, or a star are just several forms that come to mind.

Hand-forged and cast hardware catalogs, $4

KAYNE & SON CUSTOM FORGED
    HARDWARE
76 Daniel Ridge Rd.

Candler, NC 28715
(704) 667-8868
(704) 665-1988

Door Locks. In this security-conscious age, locks are a big business. The difficulty in getting the aid of a locksmith can be very frustrating. The best means of coping with the situation is to have locks which work, especially the one used for the main entrance. Locks, it hardly needs saying, are a tricky business, but the fact that they are old or old-fashioned should not be a hindrance. Many of the hardware dealers can advise on how best to use one of various types – simple mortise locks, rim locks, dead bolts – and how to combine traditional hardware with modern locksets.

CIRECAST, INC. and BALDWIN
    HARDWARE CORP.
Locksets and latchsets from Baldwin Hardware are recommended for use with interior or exterior door hardware made by Cirecast in four Victorian designs. This is an especially valuable suggestion as Baldwin products can be found throughout North America and locksmiths everywhere can install the devices. Other makers of period hardware may make other suggestions, but it is likely that most of their pieces can also be used in conjunction with Baldwin locksets or latchsets.

Free Baldwin literature

BALDWIN HARDWARE CORP.
841 E. Wyomissing Blvd.

Reading, PA 19612
(215) 777-7811

A CAROLINA CRAFTSMAN
A Victorian-style fully mortised lock for square shaft doorknobs is one of several useful devices available through Carolina. It can be used on either right-hand or left-hand opening doors, and the bolt utilizes a key from either side.

Catalog, $3 (refundable on first order)

A CAROLINA CRAFTSMAN
975 S. Avocado St.
Anaheim, CA 92805
(714) 776-7877
Fax (714) 533-0894

RENOVATOR'S SUPPLY
As a nationally-based mail order supplier, Renovator's is a convenient source of thousands of old-house items. Colonial-style rimlocks and rimlatches in eight brass or black styles are available. Each of these sets comes with two knobs, a skeleton key, keeper, and a rose or keyhole plate. Renovator's also operates a chain of retail outlets in the Northeast.

Catalog, $3

RENOVATOR'S SUPPLY
6283 Renovator's Old Mill
Miller Falls, MA 01349
(413) 659-2211
Fax (413) 659-3796

SAMUEL B. SADTLER & CO.
Replacing a defective lock with an attractive polished cast-brass device from Sadtler will brighten up any doorway. The set comes complete

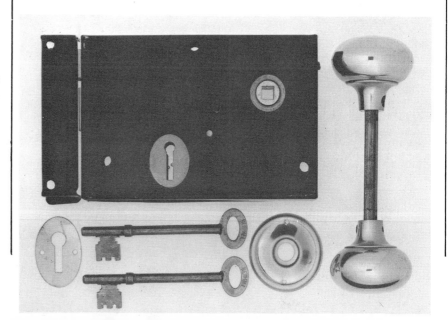

with two brass keys, six set screws, two 2" polished-brass knobs, spindle, rosette, escutcheon, and set nails. For simpler interior use, there is a flat black steel lock, as illustrated. It uses the same hardware as the brass set.

Brochure available

SAMUEL B. SADTLER & CO.
340 S. 4th St.
Philadelphia, PA 19106
(215) 923-3714

Doors. No architectural element other than windows is more important to the appearance and character of a period dwelling than interior and exterior doors. These may be of at least several types – full-length one-piece slabs, French doors, Dutch half-doors, bi-fold doors, sliding doors. In form, doors may be rectangular or arched in a rounded or Gothic fashion. Doors are remarkably consistent in style over a 250-year period, usually being divided into panels; earlier, batten doors of vertical boards without horizontal stiles on the front were commonly used. Exterior doors are most often more elaborate than interior doors and considerably thicker and heavier.

Suppliers of doors are a dime a dozen. The great majority of outlets, however, offer only flimsy slabs hardly worthy of an outhouse. During the 1950s, we lived in a new house fitted with a solid front door but featherweight interior doors. When pushed, they would fly out of the hand; trying to lock them was nearly impossible. The problem was that they had a hollow core and were assembly-line produced. In no way could they be pulled tight in the door jamb. Production of such doors is still common, and for this very reason there are now a number of millwork firms throughout North America fabricating solid traditional doors. Even several nationally-distributed door and window manufacturers can provide a door of real substance and design. *See also* **Screen and Storm Doors.**

ANDERSEN CORP.
Andersen's "patio" doors are French doors, and the principal traditional design offered is called The Frenchwood. It is the result of much research into such problems as weathering and security which particularly plague multi-pane

exterior doors. Each set of double-opening doors can be supplied with solid-maple light grilles. The basic material used for the frame and panels is solid wood with aluminum and vinyl. The glass used is either a highly efficient insulating glass or an equally effective softly tinted version. The hardware is solid brass, and a three-point locking system is provided. The weatherstripping is of one piece and wraps around the outer edge of the door panels. Sizes available are 6'8" and 8' heights and widths of 5' and 6'.

Window and Patio Door Factboook, free

ANDERSEN CORP.
Bayport, MN 55003
(800) 426-4261

ARCHITECTURAL ANTIQUES EXCHANGE
In addition to doors which have been salvaged, the Exchange offers brand-new doors in traditional styles. Some of these feature beveled or etched glass panels and are suitable for late-Victorian residences. There are matching sidelights and transoms for most of these designs. Select mahogany is the wood used. This material is also the standard for French doors in 8' or 6'8" heights. They can be ordered as a set, and may be combined with an arched transom. Sidelights to flank each side of a set can also be ordered.

Literature, $3

ARCHITECTURAL ANTIQUES EXCHANGE
709-15 N. 2nd St.
Philadelphia, PA 19123
(215) 922-3669

ELEGANT ENTRIES
Among this firm's many custom contemporary designs are some that are appropriate for period houses. Most of the models are for exterior use, but there is a small selection of interior doors to choose from. Quality is a keyword in describing Elegant Entries's work. They are not hollow core quickies or pine slabs which may warp faster then they will weather. Doors are solidly made and may involve some hand-carving. Mahogany, rosewood, teak, and red oak are the four hardwoods regularly stocked and used. Exterior doors measure $1^3/_4$" thick with panels of $1^1/_4$". Interior doors are only slightly thinner at $1^3/_8$" and with panels of $^3/_4$" thickness.

For information on the nearest dealer, call:

ELEGANT ENTRIES
240 Washington St.
Auburn, MA 01501
(800) 343-3432
(508) 832-9898 (MA)

MARVIN WINDOWS
French doors for exterior or interior use are available in the deservedly well-known Marvin line. The standard model comes with either real muntins or removable grilles. The doors are of solid-pine construction and are made with insulating two-pane or single glazing glass. Marvin is also a good source for a single terrace door in the same design as a single French door. All of the company's doors and windows are made to order, but because there are so many standard sizes offered, delivery time after placing an order is relatively short. French doors with muntins – not doors made of a single piece of glass over which grilles have been imposed – are not that easy to find these days. That Marvin offers this option is much to its credit.

Literature available

MARVIN WINDOWS
Warroad, MN 56763
(800) 346-5128

MAURER & SHEPHERD JOYNERS
When it comes to doors that will be exactly right for a Colonial property, Maurer & Shepherd can meet the requirements. Among the exterior designs routinely produced are raised panel doors clinch-nailed to beaded batten boards. The doors are $1^3/_4$" thick and are hand planed eastern white pine. Interior doors are made in $^{15}/_{16}$" thickness and can be produced in any panel combination. Maurer & Shepherd also produce barn, carriage house, and period garage doors, any of which can be equipped with electric openers. All the firm's work is by custom order.

Free brochure

MAURER & SHEPHERD JOYNERS
122 Naubuc Ave.
Glastonbury, CT 06033
(203) 633-2383

NEW ENGLAND TOOL CO. LTD.
Despite its name, this company is a source for fine metalwork, including

exterior doors. Illustrated is one of the ornamental designs called English which also features a metalwork transom. Most of the work is hand-forged in black steel. All of the work is done on a custom basis.

File of architectural metalwork design, $2

NEW ENGLAND TOOL CO. LTD.
PO Box 30
Chester, NY 10918
(914) 782-5332
(914) 651-7550

SHEPPARD MILLWORK, INC.
A great variety of doors in stock designs are offered by Sheppard in exterior and interior sizes. Among the models are paneled doors with as few as one or as many as fifteen panels, louvered doors, bi-fold paneled doors, and bi-fold louvered doors. Sheppard can also supply complementary side lights. Shown are three paneled designs – from left to right, S-110, S-111, and S-112.

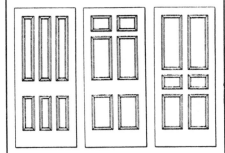

Free brochure

SHEPPARD MILLWORK, INC.
21020 70th Ave. W.
Edmonds, WA 98020-6701

(206) 771-4645
(206) 283-7549
Fax (206) 672-1622

SPANISH PUEBLO DOORS
Handsomely designed and crafted entrance and interior doors appropriate for Spanish Colonial houses are a specialty of Pueblo. The standard size of these custom-made doors is 6'8" high, 3' wide, and a very solid $1^3/_4$" in thickness. Since each door is made to order, the dimensions can vary considerably. There are two basic types of designs – paneled and the rustic Knotty Pine series. The latter is particularly suited to the simple lines of many Spanish Colonial houses; finishing options available deepen the appearance of weathering.

Literature available

SPANISH PUEBLO DOORS
PO Box 2517
Santa Fe, NM 87504-2517
(505) 473-0464

STUART INTERIORS
A firm with experience in North America, Stuart is called upon for its expertise in paneling and doors. All the material used is solid English oak. Arched and paneled slab doors are produced in traditional British styles most suitable for English Tudor

houses of the early 1900s. Shown is a heavy arched interior doorway and Gothic screen. All work is custom.

Literature available

STUART INTERIORS
Barington Court
Barrington, Ilminster, Somerset
    TA19 0NQ
England

(0460) 40349
Fax (0460) 42069

SUNNINGDALE OAK
Another British supplier, Sunningdale Oak always has on hand a stock of standard oak interior and exterior doors. Two of the designs – The Runnymede and The Ascot – are

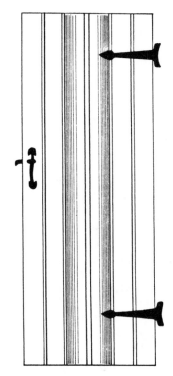

shown. The stock size is 6'6" high by 2'3" wide; other sizes will be special orders. Solid English or European oak is used for all doors, and construction

is the traditional mortise-and-tenon joinery. Sunningdale will also supply solid-oak jambs, stops, and architraves if desired.

Literature available

Sunningdale Oak
The Old Bakery
83, Chobham Rd., Sunningdale
Berkshire SL5 0HQ, England
(0990) 26504
Fax (0990) 21822

Other suppliers of new doors suitable for period houses are: Amherst Woodworking & Supply, Inc., Architectural Components, Inc., Bailey's Architectural Millwork, Inc., Creative Woodworking, Ltd., Dixon Brothers Woodworking, Early New England Rooms & Exteriors, Inc., The House Carpenters, Kentucky Millwork, Somerset Door & Column Co., *and* Wood Window Workshop.

Among architectural antiques firms offering old doors are: Architectural Antiques Exchange, Artefact Architectural Antiques, Florida Victorian Architectural Antiques, Governor's Antiques, Irreplaceable Artifacts, Queen City Architectural Salvage,. Ramase, Salvage One, United House Wrecking, Inc., Walcot Reclamation Ltd., *and* Westlake Architectural Antiques.

Doorways, Exterior. See Entryways.

Draperies. it is wise to steer away from ready-made curtains offered by direct-mail services. Curtains or draperies are relatively easy to make but measurements must be just right in each place they are used. At least draperies bought locally can be returned and exchanged for others if they are not the proper length or do not have the desired fullness. 1,001 fabric types and patterns suitable for period interiors of every type are available in fabric centers, department stores, and interior design shops for individuals who have the skill to make their own curtains or know of someone who can do it for them. For information regarding special fabrics, *see* **Fabrics.** Keep in mind, however, that draperies are sometimes not needed

or are not appropriate in a room with detailed architectural ornamentation. "Historic houses," in historian William Seales's opinion, "are usually over draped; . . . The smothering plethora of silk, damask, satin, and velvet that characterizes American restored interiors really reflects twentieth-century customs."

Drapery Hardware. The basic hardware needed to hang curtains or draperies is available from most home centers and hardware stores. It makes little differnce whether tracks, rods, or poles are used in many instances since the hardware itself is partly hidden or barely visible. Similarly, the choice of how to attach the draperies is of little consequence. The only important visual element that may be used with draperies or curtains is a tieback or a curtain pin. The deviee may be as simple as a brass hook or as ornate as a stamped brass disk.

Faneuil Furniture Hardware
A wide variety of tiebacks is offered by Faneuil. These include brass knobs, clips, and hooks. There are stamped designs featuring eagles, a rose, and thistle, and a sailing ship, cast forms such as a fleur-de-lis and a cupid, and many types of rosettes.

Catalog, $3

Faneuil Furniture Hardware
163 Main St.

Historic Hardware Ltd.
Unusual handmade tiebacks and holders for fabric swags are produced in iron, brass, and tin. These are suitable for use in an informal country interior. Illustrated are three

Salem, NH 03079
(603) 898-7733

Other suppliers of drapery or curtain tiebacks are: Kayne & Son Custom Forged Hardware, Perkowitz, *and* Renovator's Supply.

Drip Rails. See Gutters.

Drops. A drop or pendant is usually of carved or turned wood, but can also be made of plaster, stone, or metal. The device was a feature of Gothic architecture and became popular again in the Victorian era. A drop,. by definition, always hangs down and may be of simple spherical design or a highly ornate form. It can be used as part of an interior doorway spandrel, attached to a corner bracket, and, on the outside of the house, used as part of gable-end and porch ornamentation. The drop seen on the exterior of an early Colonial dwelling with a second-floor overhang is better known by the term "pendill." Today, drops are most likely to be produced by woodturners. *See also* **Finials.**

Silverton Victorian Millworks
Silverton's drops are indistinguishable from finials. In fact, they are also termed "tops" and can be so used. There are round, ball, Kent, urn, and acorn designs available. All are made from clear western hemlock and are doweled.

hand-cut tin tiebacks.

Catalog, $3

Historic Hardware Ltd.
PO Box 1327
North Hampton, NH 03862

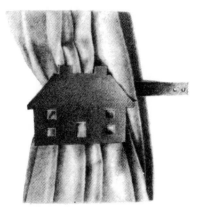

The turnings measure from $2^3/_8$" to $5^1/_4$" in diameter, the largest being the popular acorn form.

Complete catalog package, $4

SILVERTON VICTORIAN MILLWORKS
PO Box 2987-OC7
Durango, CO 81302
(303) 259-5915
Fax (303) 259-5919

GOTHOM INC.
One of Gothom's stock designs, DP101, is used in a doorway spandrel. This and six other turned drops can be made with a lap or extension for ease of installation and to conceal joints. These objects can be made even more ornamental with the addition of carving. Sizes range from 1" to 6" in diameter.

Catalog available, $5

GOTHOM INC.
110 Main St., PO Box 421
Erin, ONT N0B IT0
Canada
(519) 833-2574
Fax (519) 833-2195

CONANT CUSTOM BRASS, INC.
According to Conant, dust covers originated in the 1890s and were first made of wood. Conant makes them in brass with a standard decorative embossed surface; a smooth-surface corner is available by special order. A special steel punch is included with each order along with a supply of round-headed brass nails. One nail is needed to install a corner. A minimum order is ten pieces.

Literature available

CONANT CUSTOM BRASS, INC.
270 Pine St.
Burlington, VT 05401
(802) 658-4482

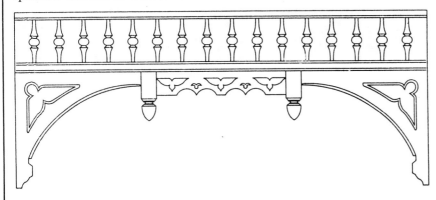

Other suppliers of wood drops are: DIXON BROTHERS WOODWORKING, MARK A. KNUDSEN, MAD RIVER WOODWORKS, PAGLIACCO TURNING AND MILLING, SHEPPARD MILLWORK, INC., *and* VINTAGE WOOD WORKS.

Dumbwaiters. A mechanism for carrying food and objects from a kitchen on one level to a dining area on another floor is a handy luxury. In the days when cooking was usually performed in the lowest level of a house, whether a country or city dwelling, there may have been servants who shuttled back and forth. Today, those who live in old houses with such split arrangements are unlikely to have a butler or serving maid. But you can install a dumbwaiter which can be hand-operated or electric-powered.

WHITCO/VINCENT WHITNEY CO.
Serving the building industry since 1929, this California-based firm manufactures a line of hand-operated dumbwaiters for commercial and residential installations. The residential models are non-geared and are manufactured in four standard sizes depending on the load capacity desired (from 65 to 500 lbs.). All dumbwaiters are furnished as complete units, including the machine with wheels, roller bearings, hardware, and, of course, the hardwood veneer car.

Literature available

WHITCO/VINCENT WHITNEY CO.
PO Box 335
Sausalito, CA 94966
(415) 332-3260

Another manufacturer of dumbwaiters is INCLINATOR CO. OF AMERICA.

Dust Corners. if housework is one of your tasks, then you will appreciate dust corners. These are triangular pieces – usually of brass – which can be nailed into hard-to-clean corners. They are usually used only on a staircase, a particularly difficult area to vacuum, but they could be used elsewhere.

Entryway, Filson Club (Ronald-Brennan House), Louisville, Kentucky. Photography by Jack E. Boucher, Historic American Buildings Survey.

Embossed Wallcoverings. *See* **Wallpapers/Wallcoverings**.

Entryways. An entryway can enhance or destroy a home's period look. It naturally draws the eye, and it must withstand more scrutiny than most other parts of a house's exterior. Georgian houses of substance

elevated the entryway to an architectural feature of considerable importance, and skilled carvers and carpenters were employed in their construction. Pediments – triangular, broken, and segmental – were frequent features, as were pillars, pilasters, fanlights, and paneled doors. Entryways were largely ornamental throughout the Victorian period, culminating in the highly decoratuve reinterpretation of Georgian architecture known variously as Colonial Revival or Neoclassial. In planning an entryway for a restored house or a new house built to traditional design, proportion and appropriateness are the key elements to be considered. An ornate

entryway on an Eastlake cottage is as absurd as a flush doorway on a Colonial Revival mansion. Happily, there are several specialists, each producing complete doorway systems and expertly knowledgeable in period styles, who can assure you of the proper entryway for your particular house.

ARCHITECTURAL COMPONENTS, INC. Architectural Components reproduces period entryways from the simplest box frame with transom to the most elaborate broken pediment entry. Employing traditional methods of joinery and construction, and reflecting a secure knowledge of Georgian, Federal, and Revival period designs and details in all their varied nuances, Architectural Components' entryways are museum-quality reproductions based on measured drawings of historic examples. All are custom-made of kiln-dried eastern pine and are

finished with a hand plane. Shown is a closed pediment entry with crossbuck doors, just one of the many authentic designs available.

Flyer available free; illustrated catalog, $3

ARCHITECTURAL COMPONENTS, INC.
26 North Leverett Rd.
Dept. OHC
Montague, MA 01351
(413) 367-9441
Fax (413) 367-9461

KENMORE INDUSTRIES, INC. Kenmore specializes in handsome entryways with delicate carving, prominent shadow lines, and classic

proportions. Each is handmade of wood, using traditional joinery, and based on authentic elements of Georgian, Federal, and Revival designs, The firm's Carved Historical Entries line owes its excellent reputation to superb doorways like the ones shown here. Model 430 features a broken pediment with a pineapple finial and a leaded glass transom. A carved panel of dolphins, a swag, or a basket or fruit may be substituted for the transom. Model 400 has an elliptical leaded fanlight,

carved capitals and pilasters, and a triangular pediment. These designs are only two of the twenty entryways (not including variations for several models) offered by Kenmore, ranging in height from 96" to 173$\frac{3}{4}$" and in width from 60" to 103$\frac{1}{2}$". Pediment depths range from 6" to 16$\frac{1}{6}$". A 15-minute video tape of Kenmore installations is available for $10 (refundable with purchase).

Brochure, $3

KENMORE INDUSTRIES
One Thompson Sq., PO Box 34
Boston, MA 02129
(617) 242-1711
Fax (617) 242-1982

KENTUCKY MILLWORK, INC. A brand-new subsidiary of Kentucky Wood Floors, Kentucky Millwork offers a broad range of standard and custom millwork and casework of uniform high quality – from doors, windows, and stairways to mantels, moldings, and cabinets. Custom designed in a variety of styles and sizes, Kentucky Millwork's complete entryway units include jambs, sidelights, transoms, pilasters, heads, and pediments, each built to your specifications and in virtually any period configuration.

Literature available, $2

KENTUCKY MILLWORK, INC.
4200 Reservoir Ave.
Louisville, KY 40213
(502) 451-3456
Fax (502) 451-6027

Other recommended suppliers of custom reproduced entryways are: ARCHITECTURAL ANTIQUES EXCHANGE, DIXON BROTHERS WOODWORKING, EARLY NEW ENGLAND ROOMS AND EXTERIORS, INC., FOCAL POINT, FYPON, INC., MAD RIVER WOODWORKS, MAURER & SHEPHERD JOYNERS, *and* SOMERSET DOOR & COLUMN CO. *Antique entryways can frequently be found at architectural antiques firms, particularly* ARTEFACT ARCHITECTURAL ANTIQUES *and* UNITED HOUSE WRECKING, INC.

Environmental Services. Buying an old house, or restoring one, sometimes brings one face to face with environmental problems, Asbestos, for example, was once commonly used in plaster, insulation, floor tiles, and linoleum, as was lead in paint and pipes. Depending upon the former use of a property, it may contain buried storage tanks. And then there is the newest scare – radon. To test for any or all of these hazards, the services of an environmental specialist is needed. But caveat emptor. The telephone directory abounds with fly-by-nighters who are more interested in selling you radon-removal systems than in accurately testing for the presence of the gas. Ask your licensed real estate broker for advice in selecting a reputable environmental services firm, or, better still, check with your local state or county environmental officer. One reliable firm – adept at working in historic buildings – is CON-TEST. For information about this New York- and New England-based company, contact William H. Parsons ar 2275 Silas Deane Hwy., Rocky Hill, CT 06067, (203) 257-4970.

Etched Glass. The Victorian era was the golden age of etched glass, even though, as in all things, the Victorians had legalistic minds in matters of taste. A new decorative style could be embraced only if it had ample historic precedents. Such was the case with etched glass, a staple of Victorian style that frequently informed entryway panels, mirrors, tableware, and other decorative objects. "Where

stained glass would obscure daylight," wrote one arbiter of domestic taste in 1894, "there are the delicate flowing forms in which the old Carthusians in their monasteries, when forbidden the use of coloi, used to enrich their clear glass and thus satisfy their sense of beauty." If the holy monks could decorate with ornamental glass, then so coould proper Victorians. Astonishing in its variety, 19th-century etched glass ranges in design from motifs and emblems adapted from the

Renaissance to configurations that are strikingly modern. Victorian glassmakers promised that "any design furnished could be reproduced on glass." Such is the case today, when the renewed interest in 19th-century arts and crafts has revitalized the production of

decorative glass. Many contemporary firms have, between them, virtually re-created the lexicon of Victorian etched-glass imagery.

ARCHITECTURAL ANTIQUES EXCHANGE
This firm offers a variety of etched glass panels in strikingly handsome designs. The majority of the designs are either botanical or figurative "exquisitely draped women" in an assortment of styles from Renaissance Revival to Art Nouveau and even Art Deco. Deep-etched on laminated safety glass, each panel measures $27^1/_2$" x $66^3/_4$" and is suitable for doors or sidelights

Literature available, $3

ARCHITECTURAL ANTIQUES EXCHANGE
715 N. Second St.
Philadelphia, PA 19123
(215) 922-3669

PHILIP BRADBURY GLASS. The preeminent supplier of Victorian-style etched glass in England is Philip Bradbury, whose door panels and transoms are exact copies of original patterned glass. So perfect is Bradbury's art that it is impossible to discern any difference between his reproductions and the antique originals. Bradbury panels, which can either be selected from an increasing library of stock designs or custom made to suit, are thus perfect for replacing broken or missing glass panels in an existing Victorian entryway. You can order clear patterns on frosted backgrounds or frosted (etched) patterns on clear glass. Bradbury recommends the former for front door panels or where privacy is desired, and the latter for transoms, conservatories, or anywhere where the view is to be preserved. Clear glass can be enhanced by beveled glass. For a detailed quote, measure the height and width of the opening into which the glass will fit and deduct $^1/_8$" (3mm) from each dimension. Decide on whether you require 4mm glass for windows, 6mm glass for doors, or 6.4mm laminated safety glass. Bradbury can also produce double-glazed sealed units. Shown are some of the firm's stock designs, although custom work is of course invited.

Literature available

PHILIP BRADBURY GLASS
83 Blackstock Rd.
London N4 2JW
England
(071) 226-2919
Fax (071) 359-6303

Other recommended suppliers of etched glass are: BACKSTROM STAINED GLASS & ANTIQUES, LYN HOVEY STUDIO, INC., MORGAN-BOCKIUS STUDIOS, INC., POMPEII & CO., J. RING GLASS STUDIO, INC., CONRAD SCHMITT STUDIOS, INC., *and* WILLIAMS ART GLASS STUDIO, INC.

Fabrics. Textiles suitable for use in curtains and draperies, for upholstery, and wallcovering are widely available in fabric centers, department stores, and decorating shops. Within the category of reproduction textiles, though, there are some which are very good, many of a so-so quality, and more than too many which are downright dreadful. The best reproduction fabrics are known as "documents"and faithfully follow the lines, color values, and textures of the originals. Since their manufacture may be more complex and costly, documents usually carry the highest price of reproduction textiles. An adaption, as the term suggests, is a reproduction design based on an historic sample but is not faithful to the original in all respects. Adaptations may be of two or three colors rather than five of six; cotton may be substituted for silk. Adaptations can be perfectly acceptable for period uses. On the other hand, one must beware of printed fabrics which attempt to simulate woven textures or which have patterns that have become distorted in the modern high-speed printing process.

Fabric manufacturers have improved the distribution of their products in recent years. The perverse system which favors the business of interior designers and which is partly closed to the general public is dying a welcome death. It must be noted, however, that the select fabric houses that still continue to restrict business to the decorating trade execute work which no one else will undertake. Many of their documentary patterns are necessarily limited in production, and can only be manufactured when sufficient orders are in hand. Included among manufacturers who continue to restrict their trade to decorators are BRUNSCHWIG & FILS, INC., and SCALAMANDRÉ. Anyone who really desires to purchase first-rate document fabrics or adaptations from either firm will find a legitimate way of doing so. Firms such as CLARENCE HOUSE, which distributes the superb COLEFAX & FOWLER line from England, the old English firm ARTHUR SANDERSON & SONS, renowned for ifs William Morris prints, and OSBORNE & LITTLE distribute widely through outlets in the United States and Canada. F. SCHUMACHER & CO. has a wide variety of reproduction adaptations in its own and subsidiary Waverly lines.

With airfares between the East Coast and London being about equal to those between New York and Cleveland, a buying trip across the Atlantic is not impractical, especially when fabric is being bought in quantity. There can be considerable savings in purchasing materials directly from the original source, and there are many firms to choose from. Reproduction English designs are often identical or very close to North American examples since fashions in fabric often originated in Europe. Among the establishments well worth visiting are: COLE & SON, DESIGNER'S GUILD, ANNA FRENCH, LIBERTY, MRS. MONRO, and WATTS & CO.

On both sides of the Atlantic there are suppliers of specialty fabrics (such as laces and brocades) and trimmings that may be able to help through the mail or to direct the customer to a distribution source.

AMAZON VINEGAR & PICKLING WORKS
    DRYGOODS
Closeouts and special-order fabrics augment Amazon's selection of stock yard goods. Most of the fabric is printed on 100 percent cotton, but dacron, acetate, and rayon are used alone and in combination. Among the hard-to-find goods stocked and available by the yard or half-yard are Osnaburg, nainsook, teal damask, jet satin, and gold "bullion" fringe. Amazon will provide price quotations on special-order fabrics as well, including slipper satin and various types of moire pattern goods.

Catalog, $2

AMAZON VINEGAR & PICKLING WORKS
    DRYGOODS
2218 E. 11th St.
Davenport, IA 52803
(319) 322-6800
Fax (319) 322-4003

J. R. BURROWS & CO.
Burrows terms itself an "historical-design merchant" and this singular designation is a fitting descrption of the service it offers. In addition to Axminster and Wilton carpets and wallpapers, Burrows is a supplier of high-quality lace and other fabrics. The Nottingham lace is 95 percent cotton and 5 percent polyester woven in Scotland on antique machinery. The panels and yard goods offered are of the authenticity called for in elegant late-Victorian interiors. The basic curtain design is called Victorian and is available in two different shades – ecru and white – one standard width (60") and six

lengths, 72", 84", 90", 102". 108", and 144". A Neo-Grec panel, a copy of a design popular in the 1870s, has the same specifications. Victorian is illustrated above; Neo-Grec , below. A cottage panel is sold in pairs and the panels are joined at the top of the

rod pocket. These come in 34" widths and lengths of 48", 54", 60", 72", 84", and 90", sizes which accommodate use on small and medium-sized windows from the top of the window to the sill. Yard goods which match the Victorian and Neo-Grec panels in the 60" width are also available; there is also a third complementary floral design. For narrow windows, 36" Cottage yardage matches the Cottage panels.

Burrows's line of other fabrics is being revised at present, and will soon include, in association with the Mark Twain Memorial in Hartford, Connecticut, reproductions of Candace Wheeler designs. For further information on this development and the historical lace collection, contact Burrows directly.

Catalog and product literature, $5

J. R. BURROWS & CO.
PO Box 1739
Jamaica Plain, Boston, MA 02130
(617) 524-1795
Fax (617) 524-5372

GREEFF FABRICS, INC./WARNER OF
    LONDON
Two well-known names in fabrics and wallcoverings have joined together in marketing quality prints and woven textiles. Illustrated is Warner's "Savoy Ribbon," which features a ribbon stripe superimposed on a trellis pattern for the wallpaper. Cabbage roses and ticking stripes are added to the complementary fabric design. This is a 100 percent cotton

print. Warner is also a good source for cotton damask weaves.

Greeff has recently introduced two fabric collections, "Bristol Channel," glazed cotton prints dating from the mid-1800s, and the "Jacobean," based on early 17th-century motifs. All are 100 percent wool upholstery fabrics, crewel, grospoint, homespun, ticking, tapestry weaves, flamestitch, velvets, petit point, sateen, damasks, and textured linen weaves.

Literature available

GREEFF FABRICS, INC./WARNER OF
    LONDON
150 Midland Ave.
Port Chester, NY 10573
(800) 223-0357
Fax (914) 939-8168

STANDARD TRIMMING CO.
This major supplier of trimmings distributes its products widely. These can be found in many fabric centers and decorating shops. Included are tassels, fringes, cords, and ropes. If assistance is needed in locating these items, contact the company directly.

STANDARD TRIMMING CO.
306 E. 61st St.
New York, NY 10021
(212) 755-3034

STUART INTERIORS
Stuart's Renaissance Textiles line includes worsted damasks, brocatelles, lampas, and double cloths. These are made in 100 percent English wool, pure silk, 100 percent cotton, and mixed yarns such as wool and silk, cotton and silk, wool and linen, and wool and cotton. Stuart is also a source for woven camblet, broadcloth, and various twills and small satins. In period, the designs date from early English and European to the Victorian period. Among the most handsome are those based on Elizabethan and Jacobean designs.

Literature available

STUART INTERIORS
Barrington Court, Barrington
Ilminster, Somerset TA19 0NQ
England
(0460) 40349
Fax (0460) 42069

Other suppliers of specialty fabrics are:
ESPECIALLY LACE, LEE JOFA, LINEN &

LACE, RUE DE FRANCE, and THE TWIGS, INC.

Fanlights. *See* **Windows.**

Faucets. *See* **Bathroom Hardware** and **Kitchen Hardware.**

Faux Finishes. *See* **Painting, Decorative.**

Fencing and Gates. Nothing so well defines a country homestead or a village house as an ornamental fence. The area which it circumscribes is called the yard, being the immediate surroundings or the setting for a residence. Fencing – and gates to go with it – has been part of the North American landscape for hundreds of years. The first enclosures were primarily of stone or wood, perhaps nothing more than palings, a form represented today by the stockade fence. In the 1700s more formal wood fencing appeared, and this continued in use throughout the 19th century when reasonably-priced cast-iron fencing also became available and very popular. Both traditional wood and cast-iron fencing and gates are made today, and there are a goodly number of craftsmen who can restore or reproduce antique examples.

CUSTOM IRONWORK, INC.
Fencing and gates are the sole concern of the Custom ironworkers. Styles range from simple and functional to ornate high-Victorian designs. The company's huge collection of patterns allows for an exact match with most fencing requests, but, if this is not possible, custom fence or gate fabricating is an option.

Literature available

CUSTOM IRONWORK, INC.
PO Box 180
Union, KY 41091
(606) 384-4122
Fax (606) 384-4848

NED JAMES, WROUGHT METALS
Absolutely superb hand-wrought iron fencing and gates are among James's masterworks. All of his work is custom, and included among his customers have been Colonial Williamsburg, Old Sturbridge Village, Sleepy Hollow Restorations, and the National Park Service. Although hammerwork is his specialty, James can also make up small castings and machine parts. Copper, brass, and bronze are also metals with which he works.

Literature available

NED JAMES, WROUGHT METALS
65 Canal St.
Turners Falls, MA 01376
(413) 863-8388

MARMION PLANTATION CO.
Using a 17th-century picket fence design, Marmion reproduces the wood Diamondtop picket that will fit many architectural settings. The pales feature a diamond pattern which creates an interesting visual effect. At $3/4$" thick, $4^1/_2$" wide, and 57" tall, these pickets will form a 5'-high fence when set 3" above the ground, high enough to keep pets and children within the yard. It is recommended that the pickets be spaced every 2", a division that will require 15 pickets for each 8'

span. Marmion also offers a 72" picket in the same design which can be placed edge-to-edge to form stockade fencing.

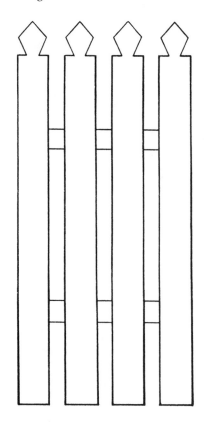

Literature available

MARMION PLANTATION CO.
RD 2, Box 458
Fredericksburg, VA 22405
(703) 775-3480

NEW ENGLAND TOOL CO.
Forged metalwork gates and fencing in classic European designs form the heart of New England's business. All of the work is undertaken on a custom basis. The company recognizes the necessity of making adaptations for automatic opening devices as well as special security locks. New England will work with the customer's drawings or blueprints, if available, or will provide design services. Illustrated is the English-model driveway gate.

File of architectural metalwork design, $2

NEW ENGLAND TOOL CO. LTD.
PO Box 30
Chester, NY 10918
(914) 782-5332
Fax (914) 783-2554

SALVAGE ONE
A supplier of architectural antiques, Salvage One is said to have miles of wrought- and cast-iron fencing and gates in its 85,000-square-foot warehouse. It is a pity to think of all this fine ornament being stripped from homes and businesses across the land, but at least the material has been saved for future generations by Salvage One and not melted down for some hapless American military adventure. For information regarding Salvage One's current inventory, call or write directly.

SALVAGE ONE
1524 S. Sangamon St.
Chicago, IL 60608
(312) 733-0098

LAWLER MACHINE & FOUNDRY CO., INC.
This is one of several Southern manufacturers of cast-iron fencing and gates in business since early this century or the late 1800s. In addition to the traditional floral designs used mainly for porches and stairway railings, Lawler offers castings appropriate for fence panels. There is also a good selection of pickets and posts, decorative spears, balls, caps,

and finials. Illustrated is just one of the many scroll designs for a gate.

Catalog, $8

American customers, contact:
LAWLER MACHINE & FOUNDRY CO., INC.
PO Box 320069
Birmingham, AL 35232
(205) 595-0596

Canadian customers, contact:
STEPTOE & WIFE ANTIQUES LTD.
322 Geary Ave.
Toronto, ONT M6H 2C7
(416) 530-4200
Fax (416) 530-4666

STEWART IRON WORKS
Stewart fabricates all sorts of work in cast and wrought iron, but specializes in fence and gate designs which are extensive in variety and size. The same attention to detail is present in the firm's newel posts, pickets, and finials. For simple, handsome iron picket fencing, Stewart is hard to beat. This type of fencing can range in heights from 37" to 72", with the size of the pickets varying from $3/_8$" square or round to $3/_4$". Illustrated is a three-rail square picket fence with

matching gate.

Brochure, $2

THE STEWART IRON WORKS CO.
PO Box 2612, 20 W. 18th St.
Covington, KY 41012
(606) 431-1985

TENNESSEE FABRICATING CO.
The selection of Victorian iron casting designs for porches, stair railings, fencing, and gates is unmatched elsewhere. A wide assortment of spears and finials complements the ornamental castings. Tennessee also stocks traditional cast porch panels, brackets, and railings in the well-known floral patterns seen in New Orleans and other areas of the Deep South.

Catalog, $5

TENNESSEE FABRICATING CO.
1822 Latham St.
Memphis, TN 38106
(901) 948-3354
Fax (901) 948-3356

Other suppliers of ornamental fencing and gates are: antique – ARCHITECTURAL ANTIQUE CO. *and* ARCHITECTURAL ANTIQUES EXCHANGE; *reproduction –* ARCHITECTURAL IRON CO., HICKSVILLE WOODWORKS CO., KENNETH LYNCH AND SONS, OUTDOOR DESIGNS & SERVICE, *and* SPANISH PUEBLO DOORS (gates only).

Fenders. *See* **Fireplace Accessories.**

Festoons. The term "festoon" is used to describe two very different things: a fabric swag used over a window or a representation of a semi-loop design in plaster or wood which may be used as a decorative element on mantels, over doors and windows, and in wall panels. Fabric festoons are described elsewhere (*see* **Swags**). The wall decorations are available in various period styles ranging from the chaste neoclassical to florid Renaissance Revival motifs. Traditionally worked in ornamental plaster, they are now available as well in fibrous materials, synthetics, and metal.

THE BALMER ARCHITECTURAL ART STUDIOS
Balmer refers to its gypsum plaster festoons as "flower swags." This may be a reflection of the firm's English

roots dating back to 1835. The founder's great-great grandsons, Wilfred and Ronald Balmer, now direct the business. Whatever the terms, these plaster decorations are an important part of Balmer's output. Over fifty designs are shown in the Master Selection Guide, along with drops which may be used with the looping forms.

Full catalog, $20

THE BALMER ARCHITECTURAL ART STUDIOS
9 Codeco Ct.
Don Mills, ONT M3A 1B6
Canada
(416) 449-2155
Fax (416) 449-3018

SAN FRANCISCO VICTORIANA, INC.
Two of Victoriana's five stock festoon designs are illustrated. Each is

intended for interior use and is therefore supplied in gypsum plaster. If such an ornament were to be needed for a house exterior, as it might for an ornate Federal period dwelling, the ornament casting would be hydrocal. Victoriana also molds a festoon superimposed on a rectangular plaque.

Catalog, $5

SAN FRANCISCO VICTORIANA, INC.
2070 Newcomb Ave.
San Francisco, CA 94124
(415) 648-0313
Fax (415) 648-2812

Other suppliers of festoon ornaments are: DECORATORS SUPPLY CORP., FOCAL POINT, *and* W. F. NORMAN CORP.

Finials. These crowning elements are used for fences, railings, posts, gable ornaments, roofs, and weather vanes. They are manufactured in wood, stone, plaster, iron, and other metals.

A ball is sometimes also termed a finial; *see* **Balls**. A drop is an upside-down finial; *see* **Drops**. *See also* **Fencing and Gates** for suppliers of fence picket tops. Finials,. of course, are also used on pieces of case furniture such as highboys and secretaries. For carvers and turners also capable of creating architectural wood finials, *see* **Desks/Secretaries**.

HICKSVILLE WOODWORKS CO. Hicksville is one general millwork company of several that include wood finials among its stock items. Finials are usually produced of solid clear white pine, poplar, or red oak, and may take the form of points, balls, or acorns. Since all items are custom made, just about any form can be ordered.

Catalog, $2

HICKSVILLE WOODWORKS CO.
265 Jerusalem Ave.
Hicksville, NY 11801
(516) 938-0171

KENNETH LYNCH AND SONS, INC. A wonderful selection of finials in cast stone has been made by Lynch for years. The finials take the form of urns, vases, obelisks, and pineapples. They are as small as 12" in height and as monumental as 47". Lynch can also produce some designs in lead with a stone base.

The Book of Garden Ornament, $9.50

KENNETH LYNCH AND SONS, INC
78 Danbury Rd., Box 488
Wilton, CT 06897-0488
(203) 762-8363
Fax (203) 762-2999

W. F. NORMAN CORP.
In addition to ceilings, roofs, and wall panels, Norman specializes in the production of stamped sheet-metal ornaments and statuary. Pictured are two custom-designed copper roof

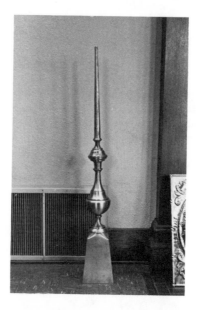

finials. Each was produced using a combination of metal stamping and metal turning. Finial sizes usually range from 3' to 6'. A finial of this type is certainly appropriate to crown the tower of a Queen Anne house.

Catalog available, $5

American customers contact:
W. F. NORMAN CORP.
214 N. Cedar, PO Box 323
Nevada, MO 64772-0323

(800) 641-4038
(417) 667-5552 (MO)

Canadian customers contact:
STEPTOE & WIFE ANTIQUES LTD.
322 Geary Ave.
Toronto, ONT M6H 2C7
(416) 530-4200
Fax (416) 530-4666

Other suppliers of finials are: cast-iron – ARCHITECTURAL IRON CO., LAWLER MACHINE & FOUNDRY CO., INC., and TENNESSEE FABRICATING CO.; *plaster –* THE BALMER ARCHITECTURAL ART STUDIOS and WORTHINGTON GROUP LTD.; *wood –* MARK A. KNUDSEN and VINTAGE WOOD WORKS.

Firebacks. At least as early as the 16th century, European ironmasters were producing firebacks. Generally rectangular in shape and usually taller than wide, they were used to protect the stonework or brickwork behind the fire. They were usually made of white iron which had been molded by being poured into boards held in sand. The decoration of firebacks remained constant for almost three centuries, consisting of coats of arms, animal and flower motifs, and topical and allegorical subjects. The date and the owner's name or initials were also common. In America, the first firebacks were of necessity plain, but it was not long before they progressed from simple decoration to often complex whimsy. Every owner of a Colonial-style house should consider the merits of installing either a freestanding or an anchored reproduction cast-iron fireback. Not only will it protect the fireplace wall from deterioration, but it will also reflect heat from the fire into the room.

NEW ENGLAND FIREBACKS
A division of Woodbury Blacksmith & Forge, New England Firebacks casts one-piece firebacks from molds made from original 18th-century "chimney backs." The firm's offerings range from unornamented firebacks in two sizes (20" high x 17" wide and 20" high x 24" wide) to the gorgeously ornate Keeping Room Fireback that celebrates in scene and symbol the planting and harvesting seasons that were fundamental to colonial life. In-between are models decorated with a single folk-art heart or the whimsical

Aetna Rooster, so-called because the proud cock was originally cast c. 1775 at New Jersey's Aetna Furnace. Shown here is the Cavalier Fireback, taken from a c. 1740 original. It measures 22" high x 18" wide and weighs about 50 lbs.

Brochure available

NEW ENGLAND FIREBACKS
PO Box 268, 161 Main St. South
Woodbury, CT 06798
(203) 263-5737

HELEN WILLIAMS/RARE TILES
Renowned for her selection of original 17th- and 18th-century Dutch tiles, Helen Williams has drawn on her three-and-a-half decades of experience in importing *objects d'art* from Holland to introduce a selection of *original* 17th-century Dutch iron firebacks, each in excellent condition and preservation. The selection includes various sizes and designs, and each antique fireback, of course, is one of a kind. Write or call for information on availability of stock.

Literature available with SASE

HELEN WILLIAMS/RARE TILES
12643 Hortense St.
Studio City, CA 91604
(918) 761-2756

Other recommended suppliers of firebacks include: THE CANOPY CO., THE COUNTRY IRON FOUNDRY, LEMEE'S FIREPLACE EQUIPMENT, and PENNSYLVANIA FIREBACKS, INC.

Firedogs. *See* **Andirons.**

Fireplace Accessories. Included in this category are items such as screens, inserts and grates, fenders, fender seats, and various tools and devices that can be used for open-hearth heating or cooking. Almost anything used in or around the fireplace is of cast or forged iron; brass, however, may be utilized for decorative handles or finials and on objects, such as fenders, which are at a remove from the fire. *See also* **Andirons, Canopies,** and **Firebacks.**

FOURTH BAY
From complete Victorian fireplace set-ups to incidental tools, Fourth Bay can provide what is needed for the hearth through 300 outlets in North America. All of the products are English, and while our brethren overseas tend to bedeck the hearth unnecessarily, they are past masters at insuring that it operates efficiently. This is especially helpful in those homes where central heating is minimally effective or, perhaps, non-existent. Fireplace inserts, for example, are very useful in collecting and distributing heat. Fourth Bay imports two types – the cast-iron Adelaide and the Hob Grate. Both will require some sort of hood and a surround to fit the average fireplace opening. Hoods are offered in solid cast iron as well as with tile insets (*see* **Tiles, Ceramic**). Surrounds are produced in poplar or oak. Several styles of American pine mantels are also available as part of a complete fireplace package which includes all the above-mentioned items. Fenders are offered in two cast-iron and two brass designs. A four-piece tool set in brass with stand comes with or without porcelain handles.

Contact Fourth Bay for a list of suppliers

FOURTH BAY
Box 287, 10500 Industrial Dr.
Garrettsville, OH 44231
(800) 321-9614
Fax (216) 527-4346

HISTORIC HARDWARE LTD.
Four tools – shovel, ash rake, broom, and poker – in hand-forged iron make up Historic Hardware's Brattleboro fireplace set. There are three handle designs to choose from. A complementary fire tool stand is also produced in the same three designs. If a stand is not wanted, the company can supply a three- or four-hook tool bar.

Catalog, $3

HISTORIC HARDWARE LTD.
PO Box 1327
North Hampton, NH 03862
(603) 964-2280

KAYNE & SON CUSTOM FORGED
    HARDWARE
Steve Kayne is a superb provider of such wrought-iron items as tool sets, trivets (illustrated is the Moravian Heart pattern), cooking utensils,

broilers, and even a Dutch oven door with or without a pre-hung frame. He is the man to turn to for special custom work as his knowledge, especially of Colonial and early 19th-century cooking practices and equipment, is extensive.

Hand Forged Hardware catalog, $2

KAYNE & SON CUSTOM FORGED
    HARDWARE
76 Daniel Ridge Rd.
Candler, NC 28715
(704) 667-8868
(704) 665-1988

LEMEE'S FIREPLACE EQUIPMENT
As a general supplier of fireplace paraphernalia, Lemee simply cannot be beat for variety or price. A customer will find here such items as wood baskets, various types of screens, tool sets, and cast-iron grates

in several models. Here, too, are hand-tied brooms and two styles of handmade bellows, each in two sizes. Illustrated is the TB model.

Catalog, $2

LEMEE'S FIREPLACE EQUIPMENT
815 Bedford St.
Bridgewater, MA 02324
(508) 697-2672

ROCKINGHAM FENDER SEATS
Leave it to the English to cling to such a quaint appurtenance as a fender seat. Can you think, however, of a more sensible arrangement? Why not *sit* at the fire in winter and not have to huddle over it when cold. Rockingham custom makes seats in three basic designs – with a curved

dip, as illustrated, a square dip, or a straight-across seat. Material options include brushed steel, brass, and satin black steel. Other alternatives include round, square, twisted, rope or reed twisted uprights; brass or steel upright collars; and wrought-iron scrollwork. Seats are usually made of leather, but a fabric of the customer's choice may be substituted. For potential North American customers who are concerned about the cost of shipping such a contrivance, there is a self-assembly fender seat, Manor House, which is flatpacked for easy export. Instructions for assembly (probably about twenty minutes time) are included with the shipment. This model is offered in two styles, either a stove-black enamel finish or brass coated in a polished and lacquered finish. The type of seat – hand-dyed red or green leather, simulated calf, brass-studded – is left for the customer to choose. Rockingham is also a source of low-level fenders in brass, brushed or burnished steel, or satin black. These are made to order.

Brochure available

ROCKINGHAM FENDER SEATS
Grange Farm, Thorney
Peterborough PE6 0PJ
England
(0733) 270233
Fax (0733) 270512

Other suppliers of fireplace accessories are: general – THE ADAMS CO., SCHWARTZ'S FORGE & METALWORKS, INC., *and* VIRGINIA METALCRAFTERS;

inserts – BUCKLEY-RUMFORD FIREPLACE CO., screens – NEW ENGLAND TOOL CO., LTD.

Fireplace/Hearth Facing. *See* **Stone; Tiles, Ceramic**

Fire Screens. *See* **Fireplace Accessories.**

Floorcloths. If it were not for the fact that canvas floorcloths have captured the public's imagination in recent years, it would be possible to categorize them under rugs and carpets. But these quite singular items require a spot of their own. Ten years ago use of the term "floorcloth" would have been met with silence in most circles. Few knew what they were, remembering, perhaps, only the successor to the floorcloth, sheets of linoleum. Use of a floorcloth, especially for a hall or dining room, died out by the mid-1800s, having enjoyed at least 100 years of popularity. Painters produced these painted and varnished canvasses, and there were manufactured versions as well. For the most part, they were a substitute for more expensive woven floor coverings, stone, or ceramic tile. It is for this reason that historians of furnishings suggest that the best reproductions made today have simple patterns imitative of natural flooring materials or geometric-design rugs. An unfortunate number of the designs on the market now reflect a current infatuation with "country" or folk motifs and have no historical basis whatsoever.

GOOD AND COMPANY,
   FLOORCLOTHMAKERS
Nancy and Philip Cayford cut their own heavy cotton duck canvas, treat it, and hand-stencil each design individually. Standard colors include soldier blue, brick red, light green, and gray. Other colors and a variety of sizes can be special-ordered. The floorcloths require little care and serve well as small area rugs and runners. The Diamonds pattern is excellent for a front hall, bath, or kitchen. Imitation of expensive marble flooring was the original purpose behind the design. With custom designs a specialty, Good and Company has worked for a variety of museums and historical societies,

including Old Sturbridge Village and the Abraham Lincoln Homestead in Springfield, Illinois.

Catalog, $2

GOOD AND COMPANY,
   FLOORCLOTHMAKERS
Salzburg Sq., Rte. 101
Amherst, NH 03031
(603) 672-0490

WALCOT RECLAMATION LTD.
In England floorcloths are called "oilcloths," a term which recalls the later Victorian use of an oiled cotton for tablecloths and shelf lining. Walcot, a large-scale architectural antiques firm as well as a center for restoration and reproduction work, is fortunate to have a talented decorative painter, Jane Taylor, among its craftspeople. She designs and produces 18th-century-style canvas floorcloths for museums and private houses. Since floorcloths are not much heavier than other fine floorcoverings, much of which is imported to North America, shipping should not be a cost impediment in approaching Walcot. Almost all the designs used in the 18th century in the Colonies, of course, would have originated in the British Isles.

Brochure available

WALCOT RECLAMATION LTD.
108 Walcot St.
Bath BAI 5BG
England
(0225) 444404
Fax (0225) 448163

Other suppliers of traditional floorcloths include FLOORCLOTHS, INC., *and* PEMAQUID FLOORCLOTHS.

Floor Coverings. *See* **Rugs and Carpets.**

Flooring. Much of the commercially-available wood flooring sold today is not fitting for an old house or a traditional new one. And old-house owners who seek only to patch or replace sections of old flooring have a particular problem on their hands. Whether it is a complete floor or merely a small section, a local lumberyard or home center is unlikely to be of help. There are, however, specialty dealers who can assist in various ways. One group of companies deals in re-milled antique lumber of various types and has the know-how and machinery to mill it in a proper fashion. A second type of supplier works with new, well-seasoned timber and reproduces both narrow and wide planks. And, thirdly, there are several national manufacturers of flooring that, while not faithful in every respect, and not true reproductions, still come reasonably close to the old-fashioned.

For suppliers of non-wood flooring, *see* **Brick, Linoleum, Stone,** and **Tile, Ceramic.**

AGED WOODS, INC.
The abused term "authentic" is one that can be honestly used in reference to the woods supplied by Aged Woods. The majority of the re-milled planks are from 100 to 200 years old and have a natural color, texture, and distressed appearance. Hemlock, cypress, chestnut, oak, and pine are the species stocked. Most planks are available in thicknesses of $3/4$" and in random widths between 3" to 9". The flooring is supplied ready for a light sanding and application of a clear finish. Stains are not necessary unless the lumber is being used for patching.

Literature available

AGED WOODS, INC.
147 W. Philadelphia St.
York, PA 17403
(800) 233-9307
(717) 843-8104 (PA)

AMHERST WOODWORKING
Primarily a millwork supplier,

Amherst also carries new strip and plank flooring; the plank flooring is milled on the premises. The company also provides plugs in the same woods for wide boards. Available in both strip and plank flooring are red oak, white oak, cherry, maple, ash, genuine mahogany, walnut, and Brazilian cherry. Birch is another strip flooring option. Yellow pine may be specified for plank flooring.

Literature available

AMHERST WOODWORKING & SUPPLY, INC.
Box 718, Hubbard Ave.
Northhampton, MA 01061
(413) 574-3003
Fax (413) 585-0288

CARLISLE RESTORATION LUMBER
As the name implies, this is a firm that takes traditional flooring seriously. Carlisle's re-milled lumber is especially good for Colonial homes as the primary wood, pine, is milled to a thickness of $^{15}/_{16}$". The firm also offers truly wide plank flooring ranging from 12" to 21". This better suits the joists of 17th- and 18th-century post and beam houses that were usually 20" to 36" on center rather than 16". If narrower planks are wanted, Carlisle produces them in eastern white pine, and these range from 8" to 12" wide. Other species that are stocked include southern yellow pine in widths from 6" to 10" and wide oak boards in the same widths. Customers can also avail themselves of Carlisle's installation services from coast to coast.

Free brochure

CARLISLE RESTORATION LUMBER
HCR 32, Box 679
Stoddard, NH 03464-9712
(603) 446-3937

CONKLIN'S AUTHENTIC ANTIQUE
 BARNWOOD AND HAND HEWN
 BEAMS
Leo Conklin has been supplying re-milled chestnut, heart pine, and hemlock from old barns for a number of years. Random lengths and widths are available.

Free flyer

CONKLIN'S AUTHENTIC ANTIQUE
 BARNWOOD AND HAND HEWN
 BEAMS
RD 1, Box 70
Susquehanna, PA 18847
(717) 465-3832

CRAFTSMAN LUMBER CO.
Proprietor Charles E. Thibeau is an expert on traditional flooring of the type seen in many Colonial houses. Literature from his firm is extremely instructive and clear-headed. The flooring stock is of high quality and is offered in eastern white pine and red oak. Generally the thickness of the pine boards is $^{3}/_{4}$", the boards having been planed $^{1}/_{4}$" to make installation easier. Widths usually fall between 12" to 18", although they are available up to 32". Lengths are from 8' to 16'. In wide oak flooring, widths are usually 4" to 10"; up to 16" is possible. The average thickness of the oak boards is 1". Craftsman Lumber is also a source for wood plugs used

when boards are screwed down and for cut nails for most pine flooring.

Literature, 50¢

CRAFTSMAN LUMBER CO.
Box 222
Groton, MA 01450
(508) 448-6336

KENTUCKY WOOD FLOORS
Custom Classics are geometric designs in wood flooring which Kentucky makes up in various-size squares. The thickness of these is $^{3}/_{4}$". Although these patterns are made only to order, they do not take long to produce as all the necessary ingredients are on hand. Among the most common woods used are oak, ash, walnut, and cherry. Burl and figured walnut may be chosen for decorative centers in several designs, including Monticello, a geometric used in the Charlottesville, Virginia, home of Thomas Jefferson. Patterned or parquet hardwood floors did not really come into popular use until the second half of the 19th-century, although some earlier grand residences would have had at least plain hardwood flooring of cherry or ash. Certainly not *all* early American homes had floors of random-width pine boards. By the late 1800s, strip flooring in oak had become popular and, in some cases, was laid right over the old pine boards. Kentucky Wood Floors also offers narrow plank and strip flooring in oak, quartered oak, walnut, and cherry. The best of the narrow plank is called Solid and is available in random or specified widths. This is tongue-and-grooved for nail-down installation; all strip flooring ($2^{1}/_{4}$" pieces) is nailed down as well. A soft finish – *not* a laminated one – is the right option for all period wood flooring, and Kentucky Wood can advise on this.

Catalog, $2

KENTUCKY WOOD FLOORS INC.
PO Box 33276
Louisville, KY 40232
(503) 451-6024
Fax (502) 451-6027

TARKETT HARDWOOD DIVISION OF
 NORTH AMERICA
The successor firm to the well-known Harris Manufacturing operation still produces some unlaminated wood flooring. Tarkett is understandably proud of its easy-to-care-for synthetic

Carlisle Restoration Lumber

finishes, but a high-shine surface is inappropriate for a period room. Turn, instead, to the prefinished solid hardware floors such as Marathon Plank, Valley Forge Plank, and Frontier Plank. The first two types are produced in red and white oak; the third in red oak only. All three call for nail-down installation, are $3/_4$" thick, and are made in 3", 5", and, with the exception of Marathon Plank, 7" widths.

Literature available

TARKETT HARDWOOD DIVISION OF
  NORTH AMERICA
PO Box 300, Rte. 9, Riverview Rd.
Johnson City, TN 37605-0300
(615) 928-3122

TIRESIAS, INC.
A major supplier of re-milled southern yellow or heart pine, Tiresias has been a source of flooring for many restorations. The pine comes in $3/_4$" thickness and is tongue-and-grooved or shiplapped. Widths are 3', 4", 6", 8", 10", and 12". The planks are available in lengths from 8' to 16'. This is #1 grade lumber. New heart pine is also available.

Free brochure

TIRESIAS, INC.
PO Box 1864
Orangeburg, SC 29116
(800) 553-8003
Fax (803) 533-0051

Other suppliers of wood flooring are: DIAMOND K. CO., INC., FLORIDA VICTORIAN ARCHITECTURAL ANTIQUES, MAURER & SHEPHERD JOYNERS, RAMASE, SILVERTON VICTORIAN MILLWORKS, *and* TRADITIONAL LINE ARCHITECTURAL RESTORATION LTD.

Floor Lamps. Although most contemporary lighting fixtures look out of place in a period interior, the floor lamp, far more suitable for comfortable reading than a table lamp, actually has historic antecedents still manufactured today, easily solving a major lighting problem for people living with Colonial- or Federal-style furnishings. An electricified candlestand, with a harp that moves up and down and swivels a full 360⁰, makes a perfect reading lamp – and is reproduced in many versions. Until the reproduction lighting industry turns

its attention to Victorian floor lamps, those living with late 19th-century furnishings will have to depend on antique shops for ornate metal originals and specialized lampshade makers for the elaborate shades they require. For those whose tastes run to the 1920s and '30s, the recent revival of interest in Art Deco has resulted in handsome reproductions of modernistic lighting fixtures, including the stylish torchière. *See also* **Candlestands, Lampshades.**

CLASSIC ILLUMINATION INC.
Classic Illumination offers nine different models of torchières – three of them illustrated here – ranging in size from a base width of 10" to a base width of 19" and an almost uniform height of 62" (not including shade). Exact reproductions of the stylish fixtures made in the 1930s, the torchières have dome, flat, stepped, or marble bases and are finished in polished brass, lightly darkened brass, chrome, verdigris bronze, or verdigris green. Each is available with either a dimmer or a touchtronic switch.

Catalog, $5

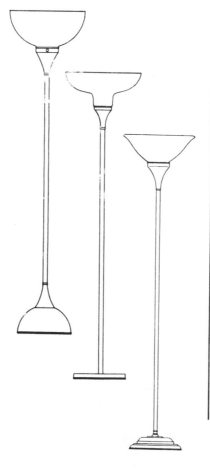

CLASSIC ILLUMINATION INC.
2743 Ninth St.
Berkeley, CA 94710
(415) 849-1842
Fax (415) 849-2328

THE VILLAGE FORGE
Michael D. Sutton of The Village Forge handcrafts a line of heavy iron lighting fixtures, including at least five different types of reading lamps based on early candleholders and each with burlap or linen shades.

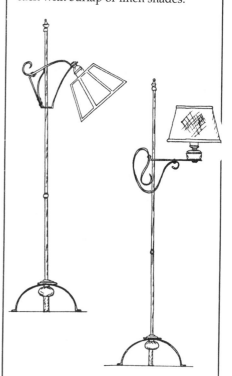

These are the authentically old-fashioned floor lamps that make one want to curl up in an easy chair with a good book. Shown are two of the models, each 54" high.

Brochure available, $1.50

THE VILLAGE FORGE
Country Club Rd., Rte. 4, Box 124
Smithfield, NC 27577
(919) 934-2581
Fax (919) 934-3298

Other suppliers of reproduction floor lamps include: COHASSET COLONIALS, LEMEE'S FIREPLACE EQUIPMENT, RENAISSANCE MARKETING, INC., *and* RENOVATOR'S SUPPLY. *A good source of antique floor lamps is* BRASS 'N BOUNTY.

Flues, Chimney. A majority of old houses have at least one chimney and herein lies what is often a problem –

the flue that ventilates the fire and carries off smoke. Sometimes the trouble is lack of a proper draft; at other times, creosote build-up can lead to a fire in the chimney itself, a very dangerous occurrence that can threaten the whole house. Flues deteriorate over time and must be maintained on a regular basis. Until the oil crisis of the 1970s and the widespread adoption of wood stoves and fireplace insets, it was difficult to find anyone who could either clean or rebuild a chimney flue. Now there are franchise operations from coast to coast that specialize in flue maintenance and rebuilding. New types of flues or linings have also been developed which can be inserted in an old chimney without having to rebuild the wall. If the problem can be cured simply be cleaning, a chimney sweep should by called. They are found in every community. On the other hand, if a new lining or other restoration work is necessary, any of the following companies is recommended: AHRENS CHIMNEY TECHNIQUE INC., HOMESTEAD CHIMNEY, NATIONAL SUPAFLUE SYSTEMS, INC., *and* PROTECH SYSTEMS, INC.

Folding Doors. *See* **Doors.**

Footscrapers. Some practical devices of the past can't be improved upon, and the footscraper, also known as a boot scraper, is one of them. Usually an edged metal strip (or strips) on decorative supports either set in the ground or freestanding in an ornate metal tray, the device is placed by an outside doorway to scrape mud from the soles of shoes. While the "H"-shaped footscraper is the most common, other styles, including a "pad" of intersecting metal strips resembling a steel doormat, are still produced today.

HURLEY PATENTEE MANOR
Best known for its superb reproductions of Colonial lighting fixtures, Hurley Patentee Manor offers other handcrafted period reproductions as well, including an elaborately ornamented iron footscraper that is a work of folk art in itself. Measuring 15" high by 8" wide, it comes equipped with bolts or can be secured in cement.

Catalog, $3

HURLEY PATENTEE MANOR
R.D. 7, Box 98A
Kingston, NY 12401
(914) 331-5414

KAYNE & SON CUSTOM FORGED
    HARDWARE
Steve Kayne's handcrafted ironwork is as close to the the original as one is likely to get, and his Moravian Heart boot scraper is an authentic design

both practical and charming. The Moravian Heart boot scraper (BS4) is one of five stock footscraper designs, but Kayne & Son will also custom make footscrapers to your specifications or duplicate one you may already have.

Hand Forged Hardware catalog, $2

KAYNE & SON CUSTOM FORGED
    HARDWARE
76 Daniel Ridge Rd.
Candler, NC 28715
(704) 667-8868 or 665-1988

Other suppliers of footscrapers include: THE ARDEN FORGE CO., LEHMAN'S HARDWARE, *and* LEMEE'S FIREPLACE EQUIPMENT.

Fountains. Although fountains have a long and colorful history, their place in American domestic landscaping was limited to the estates of the very rich until the widespread development of cast-iron brought them within the means of the Victorian middle class. Even then an

ornamental fountain would have been considered in poor taste unless one had a substantial house to go with it. Those who could afford a fountain, and the suitable setting for it, usually placed it in the center of the lawn, with a planting of low-growing shrubs, flowers, or ground cover around its base. Sometimes, but not as frequently, it was placed at the center of a garden area. If one is attempting, today, to re-create an historic garden, a fountain would still be largely out of place in all but the most stately country seats. For the many, however, who simply want a handsome garden for their period-style house, and who love the siren song of water playing on stone or iron, a fascinating variety of fountains – large and small – is available in a multitude of traditional designs and styles. Strictly speaking, such aquatic devices as rain trees, wall fountains, piped masks, and pool fountains may never have graced the property at any time in its past, but their tasteful presence in the present garden can readily enhance the enjoyment of a period house.

ARCHITECTURAL IRON COMPANY
This distinguished firm, justly famed for its restoration of historic ironwork throughout North America, won't supply you with a stock garden fountain, but if you already have a 19th-century iron fountain in need of restoration, it will refinish it to its original appearance and period perfection. For a full description of Architectural Iron's museum-quality services, *see* **Ironwork.**

Catalog available, $4

ARCHITECTURAL IRON COMPANY
Box 126, Schocopee Rd.
Milford, PA 18337
(717) 296-7722
(212) 243-2664
Fax (717) 296-IRON

KENNETH LYNCH & SONS
This venerable firm offers the widest selection of garden fountains in North America. Lynch's *Book of Garden Ornament* lists over 100 pages of fountains and fountain components in every conceivable shape and size, from massive structures suitable for public buildings and parks to simple fountains in scale with even the smallest garden. As well as full-scale

figurative fountains, Lynch offers a cornucopia of rain trees, urn fountains, shells and bowls, wall fountains, and masks piped for water. Among the hundreds of fountain components are pools, curbing, statuary, recirculating pumps, pedestals, pump cases, and stone adaptors – in short, every element needed to design a fountain for your garden. If you can't find what you're looking for in Lynch's stock selection of stone, lead, and bronze fountains and can't design your own from the many, many components, Lynch will be glad to work with you in creating one to your satisfaction. Illustrated are one of the many bronze espalier rain trees, a stone fountain from stock components, and a simple wall fountain.

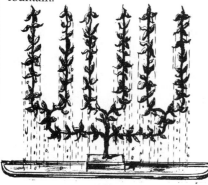

Book of Garden Ornament, $9.50

KENNETH LYNCH AND SONS
78 Danbury Rd., Box 488
Wilton, CT 06897
(203) 762-8363
Fax (203) 762-2999

Suppliers of high-quality reproduction cast-iron Victorian fountains include: ARCHITECTURAL ANTIQUES EXCHANGE, LAWLER MACHINE & FOUNDRY CO., INC., ROBINSON IRON CORP., *and* TENNESSEE FABRICATING CO. *Architectural antiques dealers, particularly* UNITED HOUSE WRECKING, INC., *are a good source of antique originals.*

Frames, Picture. Antique picture frames are undeniably charming, so delightful in fact that they have recently become relatively scarce as more and more people collect them, hoarding them against the day when they might have just the right-sized 19th-century portrait or print to fit them. A wide variety of wooden frames were handcrafted in the past, the majority of them basic moldings of varying complexity. While there is no questioning the art of the modern framer, finding one sensitive to period decor is not always easy. Old pictures were frequently framed with tiger maple or other ornamental woods, or painted or grained to simulate fine wood, materials and technique not always to be found in the modern frame shop. Two good solutions to framing period art are commissioning frames from a cabinetmaker specializing in custom reproductions or having them made up by a supplier of millwork handling picture molding. One cabinetmaker who specializes in painted and grained furniture, including handsome frames, is RICHARD A. BRUNKUS. A manufacturer of period millwork that includes frames in its catalog is ANDERSON-McQUAID CO., INC.

French Doors. *See* **Doors.**

Friezes . A frieze is an ornamental horizontal band used most commonly under a ceiling cornice. Classically, a frieze was one of the elements in an entablature appearing on the exterior of a building. A frieze of this sort is still used for monumental buildings,

but is rarely found on a private residence. Friezes for interior use are often of plaster, although stamped metal and synthetics may be substituted. Frieze papers are another form of a decorative border below the ceiling and became popular in the Victorian period as an inexpensive alternative to plasterwork. *See* **Wallpapers.**

THE BALMER ARCHITECTURAL ART STUDIOS
The largest collection of frieze designs in plaster offered in North America is from Balmer. The ornamentation is largely a series of traditional running motifs such as vines, fleurs-de-lis, and classical elements. There are also figural designs. Narrow bands called "enrichments" are very similar in style to friezes and can be used with a simple cornice molding to create the effect of a frieze. Hundreds of enrichment designs are included in Balmer's repertoire of molded gypsum plaster ornaments.

Full catalog, $20

THE BALMER ARCHITECTURAL ART STUDIOS
9 Codeco Ct.
Don Mills, ONT M3A 1B6
Canada
(416) 449-2155
Fax (416) 449-3018

FOCAL POINT, INC.
Cornice moldings which incorporate frieze designs or enrichments and accessory frieze patterns are molded by Focal Point in Endure-All, an exclusive polyurethane formula. A limited number of these designs are also produced in Contour-All, a highly flexible synthetic which allows for easier installation in curved or irregular areas. The advantage of using a one-piece cornice and frieze design is self-evident. Sometimes, however, an additional or accessory band is called for. Among the most interesting of these supplementary designs are Trellis, Greek Key, Brighton, French Scroll, and Peachtree. In height these designs range from 3" to 5".

Catalog, $3

FOCAL POINT, INC.
PO Box 93327
Atlanta, GA 30377-0327
(800) 662-5550
(404) 351-0820 (AK and GA)
Fax (404) 352-9049

W. F. NORMAN CORP.
Handsome frieze designs in stamped metal have been used for exterior and interior purposes for many years. Norman, producer of steel ceilings as well as ornaments, can supply frieze bands which match ceiling panels or which will stand by themselves. The friezes vary in size from as little as 3" or 4" to over 20" wide. Sheet sinc is the material usually used, although many can be produced in copper or stamped from aluminum.

Catalog, $5

American customers contact:
W. F. NORMAN CORP.
214 N. Cedar, PO Box 323
Nevada, MO 64772-0323
(800) 641-4038
(417) 667-5552 (MO)

Canadian customers contact:
STEPTOE & WIFE ANTIQUES LTD.
322 Geary Ave.
Toronto , ONT M6H 2C7
(416) 530-4200
Fax (416) 530-4666

Other suppliers of friezes include:
plaster – J. P. WEAVER CO.,
composition – DECORATORS SUPPLY CORP.

Fringe. *See* **Fabrics.**

Furniture. *See* **Beds, Benches, Chairs, Chests, Cradles, Cupboards and Cabinets, Desk/Secretaries, Garden Furniture, Sofas and Setees, Tables.**

Opposite page: Dormer window fanlight, Mount Custis, near Accomac, Virginia. Historic American Buildings Survey.

A pair of stone finials among the architectural artifacts at Salvage One, Chicago, Illinois.

Elias Hasket Derby Garden House (1793-94), Danvers, Massachusetts. Photograph by Cervin Robinson, Historic American Buildings Survey.

Gable-End Ornaments. *See* **Bargeboards.**

Garage Doors. *See* **Doors.**

Garden Furniture. Demand for solid, well-designed lawn and garden furnishings has increased dramatically in recent years. Polyvinyl chairs and settees are an improvement over the rickety tubular metal models of the 1950s and '60s, but nothing can replace pieces made according to old-fashioned methods and using authentic designs. Happily, a number of enterprising firms have come forward to produce handsomely crafted reproductions of wooden garden furniture from the recent and not-so-recent past. Because of the high cost of cast iron, however, most reproductions of Victorian iron lawn furniture are fashioned from cast aluminum, but this material can be given sufficient strength in the manufacturing process to approximate the solidity, but not the weight, of iron. *See also* **Benches.**

BLAKE INDUSTRIES
Dennis Blake carries a full line of old-fashioned park benches in solid cast iron or cast iron with wooden slats, including models B16 and 670, perfect replicas of Victorian "street furniture." Inasmuch as Blake Industries lists among its offerings a masterful reproduction of the handsome 1910 lamp posts of New York's Central Park, it is only natural that period park benches would also be offered.

Literature available

BLAKE INDUSTRIES
PO Box 155

Abington, MA 02351
(617) 337-8772
Fax (617) 335-3004

BRANDYWINE GARDEN FURNITURE
The English are noted not only for their magnificant gardens, but for the graceful lines of their wooden garden furniture. Brandywine offers a line of handsome benches, chairs, tables, chaises, deck chairs, tea carts, and planters, all modeled on English originals and made from teak (which won't take paint) or white-painted tropical hardwoods. Of particular interest is a reproduction of a spectacular garden bench designed by the architect Sir Edwin Lutyens early in the century. Brandywine garden furniture uses mortise-and-tenon construction and is made for permanence.

Catalog available

BRANDYWINE GARDEN FURNITURE
24 Phoenixville Pike
Malvern, PA 19355
(800) 725-5434

GLOSTER LEISURE FURNITURE
With England a nation of gardeners, it's no wonder that this English company produces outdoor furniture that suits the garden as readily as a new pair of English sècateurs. Solid teak is used exclusively in the Gloster range of seats, benches, tables, chairs, and planters, and the company ensures that timber supplies come only from well-managed plantation stock and not from endangered rain forests. Several suites of outdoor furniture are offered, each design more handsome than the other. Illustrated is the Bristol table, available in 5' and 6' versions, and a set of Thornbury dining chairs and

armchairs. Gloster is a winner of a 1990 Queen's Award for Export Achievement and its furniture is, accordingly, readily available in the United States and Canada.

American customers, contact:
UNIVERSAL GLOSTER INC.
1555-57 Carmen Dr.
Elk Grove Village, IL 60007
(708) 362-9400
Fax (708) 362-9430

Canadian customers, contact:
STEPTOE AND WIFE ANTIQUES, LTD.
322 Geary Ave.
Toronto, ONT M6H 2C7
(414) 530-4200
Fax (414) 530-4666

GREEN ENTERPRISES
The respect that Dwight Green and his associates have for Victorian design and architecture is reflected not only in the line of Victorian furniture they so skillfully reproduce, but in their involvement in the restoration of historic Victorian landmarks. (In addition to its line of stock furniture, Green Enterprises specializes in custom building and duplicating any fine Victorian furniture or architectural detail.) Shown here is one of the delights of the Victorian pleasure garden, a glider that enabled 19th-century maidens or courting couples the pleasure of swinging without ever leaving terra firma. Green's handsome reproduction, available in natural oak or white enamel finishes and in 4' or 5' models, is equipped with brass and nylon pivot bushings for smooth, quiet action. Naturally enough, Green Enterprises also offers Victorian porch swings and other outdoor furniture.

Catalog, $1.50

GREEN ENTERPRISES
43 South Rogers St.
Hamilton, VA 22068
(703) 338-3606

THE OLD WAGON FACTORY
As our English cousins were the first to recognize, Chippendale motifs lend themselves beautifully to the garden. But Chippendale was an imposing influence in colonial America as well, and the master's light and open patterns equally complement the gardens of England's lost colonies. A well-established Virginia firm, The Old Wagon Factory is a prime supplier of classic porch and garden furnishings incorporating Chippendale details. Handcrafted in wood and finished in white enamel, the line includes benches, armchairs, tables, and planters – and even Chinese Chippendale porch railing and a garden gate. The firm also invites custom work.

Catalog, $2

THE OLD WAGON FACTORY
103 Russell St., PO Box 1427
Clarksville, VA 23927
(804) 374-5787
Fax (804) 374-4646

TENNESSEE FABRICATING COMPANY
One of America's foremost metal suppliers, Tennesse Fabricating lists page after page of ornamental outdoor furniture, replicated from Victorian originals. Offered are settees, tables, benches, chairs, planters, flower boxes, and even a tree bench that provides decorative seating around a favorite shade tree. Many pieces are made of cast iron; others of cast aluminum. The variety of lacy, airy Victorian patterns displayed is imposing.

Catalogs, $5 (ask for garden furniture catalog as well as regular catalog)

TENNESSEE FABRICATING COMPANY
1822 Latham St.
Memphis, TN 38106
(901) 948-3354
Fax (901) 948-3356

Other suppliers of garden furniture include: ARCHITECTURAL ANTIQUES EXCHANGE, IRREPLACEABLE ARTIFACTS, and LAWLER MACHINE & FOUNDRY CO., INC.

Garden Houses. A gazebo may be a garden house, but not every garden house is a gazebo. Confusing? Not really. What today is called a garden house is a functionally useless structure sited in a landscaped garden for visual interest. Usually modeled on classical forms, sometimes a fake ruin, a garden house exists simply to be charming and beautiful, to provide a private respite from the world, to highlight a view, to delight the visitor with its "ancient" demeanor. In the 18th and 19th centuries such garden houses were called "follies," because money spent merely for the sake of beauty alone was considered foolish. But they were also called "eye-catchers," a name perhaps more suited to the structures' "function." Garden houses have a long and distinguished history in America, and a renewed interest in their place in the landscape can be noted today. *See also* **Gazebos.**

STICKNEY'S GARDEN HOUSES AND
 FOLLIES
Arthur E. Stickney offers the widest
selection of classical garden houses
available in North America and
Europe. The fourteen original
designs, all based on architectural
work of the 17th and 18th centuries,
range from a full triangular
pedimented temple looking very
much like a minature Parthenon to an
18' high 18th-century folly, complete
with a cupola that has two glass
fanlights and a 2' carved pineapple at
the peak. Believing that garden
houses must be attractive from all
approaches, no detail is spared in
exterior finishing. Equal care is given
to interiors, where paneled walls,
chair rails, recessed ceilings, and
barrel vaults are the rule and not the
exception. Shown is The Palladian,

with barrel-vaulted pediment and
roof supported by eight tapered
columns and hand-carved capitals. It
is 13'4" wide, 8'8" deep, and 10'10½"
high at the peak. A VHS video of
Stickney's garden houses is available
for $15.

Brochure available

STICKNEY'S GARDEN HOUSES AND
 FOLLIES
1 Thompson Sq., PO Box 34
Boston, MA 02129
(617) 242-1711
Fax (617) 242-1982

Garden Ornaments. *See* **Birdbaths,
Houses, and Feeders; Fountains;
Planters; Sundials;** and **Urns.**

**Gardens, Old-Fashioned Plants and
Seeds.** In *Green Thoughts: A Writer in
the Garden,* Eleanor Perenyi spurns
the marigold-zinnia-petunia
gardening habits of most Americans.
She considers that their "ready-made
air is a sad advertisement of the fact
that ours is a throwaway culture . . .
as temporary as a plastic pool and can
be abandoned without a qualm when
the owner moves on." "These mass-
produced, over-hybridized plants,"
adds the proprietor of THE FRAGRANT
PATH, whose beautifully written
catalog *(see below)* reveals an abiding
love for the old-fashioned garden,
"lack the grace and charm and
individuality that nature bestowed
upon them. This is not to say that the
breeder's art is without merit, for
surely in the field of vegetables and
many flowers, tremendous advances
have been made. However, when that
'art' leads to the loss of identity as in
the mop-headed dwarfs, midgets,
pygmies, and giants of current
fashion, then perhaps it has over-
stepped its bounds in creating such
monstrosities." Fortunately for those
of us who love the fragrance and
color of the old-fashioned garden, a
few firms like The Fragrant Path can
provide us with seed and plant
material of documented historic
varieties long dropped by
contemporary nurserymen in favor of
the new and scentless hybrids.

THE ANTIQUE ROSE EMPORIUM
If an "emporium" is a place selling a
great variety of goods, then The
Antique Rose Emporium is both
accurately and aptly named, for here
will be found an amazing collection
of extremely long-lived, healthy and
disease resistant, fragrant old-
fashioned roses of every type. The
current catalog, handsomely
illustrated in color and filled to
bursting with practical information

about growing antique roses, lists
species roses, China roses, noisette
roses, old European roses, Bourbon
roses, tea roses, multifloras,
perpetuals, polyanthas, rugosas,
floribundas, and shrub roses – to
name just a few types. Each of the
hundreds of varieties is documented
with the year the rose was first
introduced. No old-house garden
should be without roses from this
wonderful catalog.

Catalog, $3

THE ANTIQUE ROSE EMPORIUM
Rte. 5, Box 143
Brenham, TX 77833
(409) 836-9051

THE FRAGRANT PATH
No old-house gardener can afford to
be without this catalog, whose
subtitle is succinct and accurate:
"Seeds for Fragrant, Rare, and Old-
Fashioned Plants." There's not a
glossy color photograph anywhere in
its pages, but its wealth of garden lore
and history – not to mention its
listings of hundreds of fragrant
garden plants – create mental pictures
that entice one to create an old-
fashioned garden with seeds from
The Fragrant Path. Almost all the
plant varieties for which seed is
offered are not to be found in
ordinary mail-order seed catalogs.

Catalog, $1

THE FRAGRANT PATH
PO Box 328
Fort Calhoun, NE 68023

SELECT SEEDS
"The old-fashioned 'pleasure garden,'
brimming with flowers in a profusion
of colors and forms, and scenting the
air with unforgettable fragrances, is
experiencing a welcome revival." So
writes Marilyn Barlow, proprietor of
Select Seeds, whose catalog, "Fine
Seeds for Old-Fashioned Flowers," is
a third source of antique plant
material indispensable for old-house
gardeners. The seeds offered through
this lovely catalog are all documented
historic annual and perennial
varieties found in gardens of the 18th
and 19th centuries. Antique names
and dates of garden introduction are
given, fragrant flowers as well as
exceptional cut flowers noted, and
native plants designated. Barlow's
seeds are indeed "select" - and choice.

Catalog, $2

Other suppliers of old-fashioned plant materials and seeds include: D. LANDRETH SEED CO., ROSES OF YESTERDAY AND TODAY, INC., and SMITH & HAWKEN LTD.

Gasoliers. *See* **Chandeliers.**

Gates. *See* **Fencing and Gates.**

Gazebos. Of all outdoor living spaces none possesses more charm than the gazebo, known in the 18th and early 19th centuries as a summerhouse, in the Victorian period as a gazebo, and, concurrently, as a pavilion or arbor. Although this generally freestanding garden structure serves a practical purpose – providing shelter from the sun and rain as well as useful storage space – its principal reason for being is the visual delight it conveys to the domestic landscape. Many old-house properties would be enhanced by the addition of a gazebo, regardless of whether such a building existed there in the past. Several firms, in fact, supply architects' plans for such summerhouses, while others supply prefabricated components for DIY construction. Usually simple in plan, gazebos provide not only an interesting decorative accent to the grounds, but a practical and graceful retreat from the noise and demands of modern living.

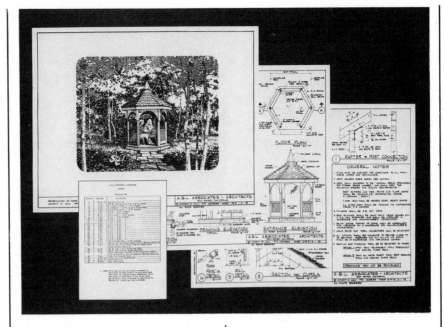

A.S.L. ASSOCIATES
Consulting architect Anthony Lalli, A.I.A., provides complete plans for a modest but architecturally handsome gazebo, the beauty of which is that one can afford to have a traditional summerhouse without in the least appearing pretentious or ostentatious. The gazebo is six-sided with posts on an 8' diameter and an inside clear height of 7'4". Plans call for wood construction with a raised, patterned deck, latticed sides, and a cedar shake roof. Architects' plans consist of three drawings, each 17" x 22", which contain all details and information required for a contractor's estimate and construction. A materials list is also included. As the designer writes, "if you're handy and can read blueprints, you can build it yourself."

Literature and photograph free

KENNETH LYNCH AND SONS
Count on this venerable firm to offer not only the traditional, but the unique as well. Illustrated is only one of Lynch's gazebos. Constructed of wrought iron, with stone column bases and stone seats, it measures 10' in diameter, 8' to the top of the

columns, and 16' high overall. As with almost all Lynch offerings, the dimensions may be varied to suit the customer.

Book of Garden Ornament, $9.50

KENNETH LYNCH AND SONS
78 Danbury Rd., Box 488
Wilton, CT 06897
(203) 762-8363
Fax (203) 762-2999

OUTDOOR DESIGNS
Outdoor Designs, a small group of craftsmen particularly skilled in exceptional wood finishing, offers a line of six different gazebos, each with variations. Shown is the Archwood model, available in 13' and 16' heights. Like all of the firm's gazebos, the Archwood is made of western red cedar, and its handcrafted parts, many pre-assembled, make self-installation relatively simple. Outdoor Designs' gazebos are fitted with charcoal-colored fiberglass screens. Options include a pre-assembled tongue-and-groove cedar floor (in place of the standard floor), a sectional perimeter bench, and several custom finishes. In addition to its standard designs, the firm will also custom build gazebos to the customer's specifications.

Color brochure, $2

OUTDOOR DESIGNS
197 George St.
Excelsior, MN 55331
(612) 474-8328
Fax (612) 474-6088

VINTAGE WOOD WORKS
"Ingenious" is the word for Vintage's prefabricated "Dolly Bryan" Victorian gazebo. Each 11' high x 11' wide wooden gazebo includes a king post, with finial; eight completely assembled side panels, two of which omit bottom rail sections for doorways; all hardware; and straightforward instructions explaining the few simple steps from uncrating to finished gazebo. Complete erection requires only a wrench, a step ladder, and two people for a freestanding, sturdy gazebo with handcrafted and lacy brackets, intricate ball and dowel work, fancy rail sections, and a bell-shaped roof.

Catalog, $2

VINTAGE WOOD WORKS
513 S. Adams
Fredericksburg, TX 78624
(512) 997-9513

Gilding/Gold Leaf. To gild an object or surface is to apply a thin coating of gold leaf, gold flakes, or bronze over it. Used sparingly because of expense, gilding is limited only to those areas which *should* stand out, perhaps elements in a ceiling cornice or frieze, details in a column capital, or an ornate picture frame. Gilded frames are widely available, but artisans who gild architectural details are relatively few. Gold leaf is available from several mail-order houses as are bronzing supplies. In addition, there are substitutes for gold leaf which can be effectively used. *See* also **Painting, Decorative** and **Paints.**

CONRAD SCHMITT STUDIOS INC.
With years of experience in theater and church restoration, the craftsmen at Schmitt are exceptionally adept at gilding. Recent major projects which have required the restoration of gilded surfaces include the Marquette County Courthouse, Marquette, Michigan; the Old Courthouse, Jefferson National Expansion Memorial, St. Louis, Missouri; and the Pabst Theatre, Milwaukee, Wisconsin.

Brochures available

CONRAD SCHMITT STUDIOS INC.
2405 S. 162nd St.
New Berlin, WI 53151
(414) 786-3030
Fax (414) 786-9036

SKYLINE ENGINEERS OF MARYLAND, INC.
Projects involving the application of new gold leaf and restoration are a specialty of Skyline Engineers. As the name implies, these gentlemen will climb the highest peaks – church steeples, towers, domes. At the same time, they are also prepared to undertake smaller projects such as a weather vane or outdoor clock face. Work takes them from coast to coast.

SKYLINE ENGINEERS OF MARYLAND, INC.
5405 Beall Dr.
Frederick, MD 21701-6839
(301) 831-8800

M. SWIFT & SONS, INC.
Professional gilders turn to Swift for their supplies as this firm is the world's largest manufacturer of gold leaf. It is also a source for silver leaf, aluminum foil, and bronzing materials.

Literature available

M. SWIFT & SONS, INC.
10 Love Ln.
Hartford, CT 06141
(203) 522-1181

Other firms involved in the art of gilding are: EVERGREENE PAINTING STUDIOS, INC., GRAMMAR OF ORNAMENT, *and* RAMBUSCH.

Glass. See **Beveled Glass; Etched Glass; Glass, Restoration;** and **Stained Glass.**

Glass, Restoration. Glass for windows and panels of all types is now available in old-fashioned form – that is, with some imperfections and a slight rippling. This has become known as "restoration glass" in recent years to differentiate it from the panes of smooth, crystal-clear glass available commercially. Restoration glass requires handwork and is, therefore, more expensive than commercial sheet glass. Anyone who appreciates old windows, however, will be willing to pay the price for replacement panes that will blend in with the old. *See also* **Bull's-Eye Panes.**

HISTORIC HARDWARE LTD.
Historic Hardware underlines the moderate distortion that its historically accurate restoration glass causes when looked through. This

Grates, Grilles, and Registers. All three objects involve the use of iron or brass and are similar if not identical in form. The grates described under this heading are not used for fireplaces, but serve as covers for openings in the floor or pavement. Registers are used in the same manner as grates but may also have a louver device that allows them to be closed. Grilles are either partial or full coverings for doors and windows; not included in this category are interior wood grilles which are a form of cabinetwork. All three types have been used for centuries, the importance and adoption of grates and registers having grown in importance with the introduction of central hot-air systems in the late 1800s. It was at the same time that casting of iron ornament became a

will not, however, cause headaches; it is a natural and rather pleasant visual effect. Seven sizes are stocked – 6" square, 6" x 8", 8" square, 8" x 10", 10" square, 10" x 12", and 12" square. Custom-size panes can also be cut.

Catalog, $3

HISTORIC HARDWARE LTD.
PO Box 1327
North Hampton, NH 03862
(603) 964-2280

KRAATZ RUSSELL GLASS
Bull's-eye panes have made this firm's reputation, but Kraatz Russell is also a source for leaded glass and restoration glass. In 1980 the two-person shop was commissioned by the Museum of Fine Arts, Boston, to reproduce leaded diamond-pane casement windows for the reconstructed 1636 Fairbanks House, considered America's oldest dwelling.

KRAATZ RUSSELL GLASS
Grist Mill Hill, RFD 1, Box 320C
Canaan, NH 03741
(603) 523-4289

Other suppliers of restoration window glass are BLENKO GLASS CO., INC. *and* S. A. BENDHEIM CO., INC.

Gliders. *See* **Garden Furniture.**

Globes. *See* **Lamp Parts/Fittings.**

very big business. Grilles for windows and doors have always been used for security as well as decoration. Basement and attic windows in mid- to late-Victorian houses are sometimes covered with decorative iron grilles. Much grillework is of forged, rather than cast, iron.

A. BALL PLUMBING SUPPLY
As illustrated on the opposite page, this company is well equipped to supply wall and floor grates of steel. Brass-plated steel is used for more conventional louvered registers. The grates are as small as $7\frac{1}{2}$" by $9\frac{1}{2}$" and as large as 30" square.

Free catalog

A. BALL PLUMBING SUPPLY
1703 W. Burnside St.
Portland, OR 97209
(503) 228-0026
Fax (503) 228-0030

NED JAMES, WROUGHT METALS
For exquisitely worked wrought-iron window grilles, look no further. All the hand-forgings are done by special order. James works in a variety of metals, including iron, copper, brass, and bronze. He recently provided decorative grilles for the renovations of the U.S. Secretary of State's office and the department's diplomatic waiting and reception rooms.

Literature available

NED JAMES, WROUGHT METALS
65 Canal St.
Turners Falls, MA 01376
(413) 863-8388

LAWLER MACHINE & FOUNDRY CO., INC.
Castings appropriate for grates, grilles, or ventilators (as Lawler terms them) are readily produced by this firm. Illustrated is a Victorian foundation grille which is now produced in aluminum only. Lawler produces many Victorian-style iron castings which could be appropriately used as window grilles.

Catalog, $8

American customers contact
LAWLER MACHINE & FOUNDRY CO., INC.
PO Box 320069
Birmingham, AL 35232
(205) 595-0596

Canadian customers contact:
STEPTOE & WIFE ANTIQUES LTD.
322 Geary Ave.
Toronto, ONT M6H 2C7
(414) 530-4200
Fax (414) 530-4666

THE REGGIO REGISTER CO.
Rugged cast iron makes the floor registers available from Reggio virtually indestructible; careful design makes them attractive as well as utilitarian adjuncts to forced hot-air heating systems or woodburning stoves. These registers are available in various sizes, and any one of them would be a handsome alternative to the plain, stamped metal types commonly utilized with such heating systems.

Catalog, $1

THE REGGIO REGISTER CO.
PO Box 511
Ayer, MA 01432
(508) 772-3493

Other suppliers of new grilles, grates, or registers are: ARCHITECTURAL IRON CO., BRIAN F. LEO, LEHMAN HARDWARE, RENOVATOR'S SUPPLY, *and* TENNESSEE FABRICATING CO. *Suppliers of antique grilles, grates, and registers include:* IRREPLACEABLE ARTIFACTS *and* QUEEN CITY ARCHITECTURAL SALVAGE.

Greenhouses. Also called conservatories in upmarket circles, these freestanding or attached structures captured the imagination of the public in the 1980s. Until that time there were only a few specialty manufacturers in North America, Lord and Burnham being the preeminent firm producing utilitarian greenhouses. Joining its ranks have been manufacturers of models best suited to a contemporary suburban house and not a traditional residence. The need for greenhouses that will suit period buildings was recognized by English firms, and they have set up shop in North America; in turn,

the English have been imitated by new American firms. All of this is predictable, and welcome. If at all possible, the design of a greenhouse, especially an attached structure, should reflect the general architecture of a house in line and color. For this reason, some of the more inconspicuous contemporary lean-to greenhouses fit better with a Colonial building than do the graceful Victorian models so widely admired today. But, above all, a greenhouse must be well-made, strong enough to resist strong wind, easy to ventilate, and arranged for ease of cleaning.

AMDEGA CONSERVATORIES
An English company, Amdega has been a leader in providing energy-efficient, well-designed greenhouses in the Victorian style. Canadian red cedar is used for all frames, which come in either of two basic modular designs – octagonal or rectangular (lean-to). Double-glazing is standard. A brick or stone base must be constructed prior to the erection of the structure itself. Once an order is received, the base plans are sent ahead so that a local builder can begin this preparatory step.

Literature available.

AMDEGA CONSERVATORIES
Boston Design Center
1 Design Center Plaza, Suite 624
Boston, MA 02210
(617) 951-2755

SUN ROOM COMPANY, INC.
An American firm, Sun Room provides two style options – an adaptation of an English Victorian greenhouse such as The Donegal illustrated here or what the firm calls a standard lean-to solarium. The simple, sturdy lines of the solarium recommend it for use with a Colonial-style building. These are stock options and do not preclude the drawing up of a custom design by Sun Room's own service. California redwood is used for framing in all models. Two-light insulated glass is a standard, with three-light as an option along with reflective and Low E glass.

Literature available

Sun Room Co., Inc.
322 E. Main St., PO Box 301
Leola, PA 17540
(800) 426-2737
Fax (717) 656-0843

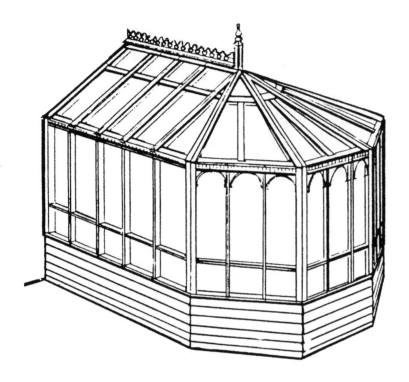

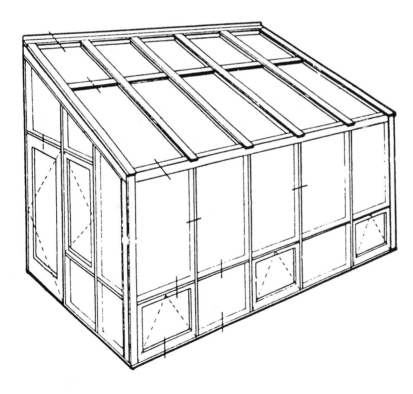

Grilles. *See* **Grates, Grilles, and Registers.**

Gutters. Even the most disinterested homeowner knows that a gutter is generally a small trough fixed under the eaves of a roof to carry off rainwater. Even if he is paying someone else to do the job, he knows vaguely that gutters, particularly wooden gutters, have to be cleaned of debris periodically to aid the flow of water to the downspouts in order to retard the primary enemy of gutters – rot caused by standing water. It is usually that same disinterested homeowner who allows himself to be talked into replacing his wooden gutters with plastic ones, at the cost of sacrificing the original profile of his old house in the name of "convenience." Wooden gutters can and should be replaced, if must needs be, with new wooden gutters modeled on the profile of the old. Most millwork shops can make up new gutters to match the old, although some (*see* Blue Ox Millworks below) are more dedicated to the task than others. *See also* **Conductor Heads.**

Blue Ox Millworks
Using antique woodworking equipment, Eric Hollenbeck and his crew of artisans specialize in historical reproductions and custom millwork with a dedication that makes the spirit soar. Instead of offering only stock patterns, Blue Ox can match any existing pattern from a sample piece, a drawing, or even a photograph. "If you can draw it," Hollenbeck says, "we can make it." And that dictum applies to gutters and gutter coves as well. Defying the popular wisdom that wooden gutters are a thing of the past, Blue Ox has been a prime supplier of redwood gutters for many years. "As with all moldings, we can match your gutter design, thereby allowing continuity and authenticity in your existing structure. Advisable is the running of a few extra pieces to store for future use." Blue Ox also crafts drip rail, which, like gutter, is designed to protect the structure from the ravages of water and decay. Fitting under the lap of the first piece of siding, drip rail directs water runoff from the wall and away from the skirting and foundation.

Pattern book, $6

BLUE OX MILLWORKS
Foot of X St.
Eureka, CA 95501
(707) 444-3437
Fax (707) 444-0918

DIXON BROTHERS WOODWORKING
This New England firm specializes in the reproduction of Federal and Victorian period architectural millwork and will custom build woodwork to the homeowner's needs and specifications. Recognizing a very real need for the replacing and matching of original wooden gutters, Dixon Brothers has the interest and ability to duplicate and properly seal gutter molding.

DIXON BROTHERS WOODWORKING
72 Northampton St.
Boston, MA 02118
(617) 445-9884
Fax (617) 445-4214

Another supplier of gutters is CONKLIN METAL INDUSTRIES.

Stair hall hanging fixture, Pendleton-Coles House, Lexington, Virginia. Historic American Buildings Survey.

Hall Trees. *See* **Stands.**

Hanging Fixtures. Any lighting device that hangs from the ceiling is, by dictionary definition, a "chandelier." But common usage and dictionary definitions are not always one and the same. Most people would feel comfortable placing a chandlier in a dining room or a very large living room. But they would recoil at the thought of a chandelier in a small hallway, despite the fact that the proportionately small hanging fixture suspended from that hallway ceiling is still technically a chandelier. By ordinary usage, then, a large hanging fixture is a chandelier, and a small hanging fixture is a hall light or just, simply, a hanging fixture. Whatever the terminology, small hanging fixtures, sometimes known in the lighting trade as "pendants," are returning to popularity. A renewed interest in the Victorian, Arts and Crafts, and Art Deco periods has brought about the reproduction of lighting devices from those periods, including many handsome hanging fixtures. Years before these current revivals, a corresponding interest in the Colonial period encouraged the rediscovery of the 18th-century lantern, which, suspended from the ceiling, became for generations the quintessential American hall light. *See also* **Chandeliers** and **Lanterns.** For flush hall lights, *see* **Ceiling Fixtures.**

GATES MOORE
Gates Moore has been making lighting fixtures by hand since 1938. Dealing specifically in early American lighting designs, the company molds each part, whether it is wood or metal, and then paints the finished piece with custom-made paints. Moore's hanging lights are excellent additions to period rooms, but they are also excellent decorative devices when standing alone in a hallway or stairwell. Primarily lanterns in various sizes and configurations, all of the firm's hanging fixtures come supplied with matching ceiling canopy, hook, and handmade chain, and each is ready for immediate installation.

Catalog, $2

GATES MOORE
River Rd., Silvermine
Norwalk, CT 06850
(203) 847-3231

THE ORIGINAL CAST LIGHTING
Just a few years back we would have been wary of recommending reproduction Deco fixtures. Most on the market exploited decorative devices of the '20s and '30s – a sunburst here, a ziggurat there – without the faintest idea of how they came together in a lighting fixture. Many of the hanging fixtures offered by The Original Cast, however, really do evoke the spirit of the jazz age. Like the company's name, these fixtures are theatrical and would not be out of place in the vestibules of the hotel suites that make up the sets of most Astaire and Rogers musicals. The Gemini spun-aluminum pendant, for example, could easily be at home in an anteroom of Radio City Music Hall. Other less grandiose models tell you in a glance why the style, before the term "Art Deco" was invented, was called "modernistic." All Original Cast lighting components are crafted of non-ferrous materials, including solid brass, copper, and aluminum.

Catalog, $2

THE ORIGINAL CAST LIGHTING
6120 Delmar Blvd.
St. Louis, MO 63112-1204
(314) 863-1895
Fax (314) 863-3278

REJUVENATION LAMP & FIXTURE CO.
Specializing in turn-of-the-century lighting fixtures of all types and designs, but concentrating in Arts and Crafts and Victorian fixtures, Rejuvenation Lamp & Fixture forms all its pieces from solid brass, which may be polished, brushed, or given an antique finish. Polished nickel, polished copper, and japanned copper are also available as finishes, with or without lacquer. Glass fittings for most fixtures are made from molds originally owned and used by the Gleason-Tiebout Glass Co. of Brooklyn, New York, and are unavailable from any other lighting supplier. The firm's reproductions of Arts and Crafts fixtures have proved so popular that the line has been expanded and a separate Craftsman Collection catalog issued. Shown are just two of the many Craftsman

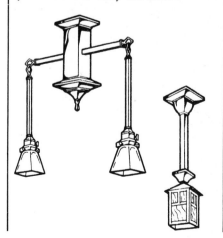

hanging fixtures that so evocatively capture the spirit of the Arts and Crafts movement. Both (CYX2E-P and CXL1C) are Mission-style pendants with art-glass shades.

Turn of the Century catalog and Craftsman Collection catalog, free

REJUVENATION LAMP & FIXTURE CO.
901 N. Skidmore
Portland, OR 97217
(503) 249-0774
Fax (503) 281-7948

ROY ELECTRIC CO.
Roy Electric began as specialists in the restoration and modernization of antique lighting fixtures in New York City brownstones, townhouses, and other old buildings. The company's current collection of first-rate reproduction lighting fixtures is based on that restoration and preservation experience and on careful research into a means of inexpensively producing quality devices in historically-accurate antique styles.

All of Roy Electric's work is in solid polished brass with lacquered or unlacquered finishes. The company's selection of hanging lamps from the Victorian period and the early years of the 20th-century is remarkable for its diversity of shape, style, and size. Illustrated are just four of the many hall pendants offered. All of the

firm's fixtures come with a choice of plain, reeded, or roped tubing, and the type of shade must also be specified from a huge selection of clear, opaque, etched, and colored-glass styles. Roy Electric welcomes custom orders and offers a free design

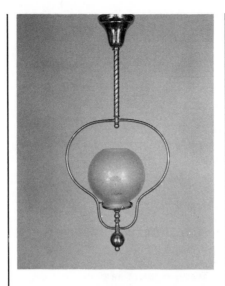

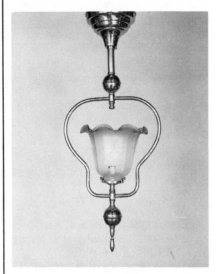

service for those who need help creating unique fixtures.

Lighting catalog, $5

ROY ELECTRIC CO., INC.
1054 Coney Island Ave.

Brooklyn, NY 11230
(718) 434-7002
Fax (718) 421-4678

Other suppliers of hanging fixtures include: AUTHENTIC DESIGNS, CLASSIC ILLUMINATION, INC., COHASSET COLONIALS, CUMBERLAND GENERAL STORE, THE COPPERSMITH, A. J. P. COPPERSMITH & CO., HISTORIC HARDWARE LTD., HURLEY PATENTEE MANOR, VICTORIAN LIGHTCRAFTERS LTD., and THE VILLAGE FORGE.

Head Blocks. *See* **Door Casings and Window Casings.**

Headers. *See* **Door Heads and Window Heads/Overdoors.**

Hinges. A hinge is the simplest of mechanisms and consists of two plates and a pin on which the pieces swivel. Used primarily for doors, shutters, and cabinets, this architectural hardware is most often iron but is sometimes brass or brass-plated. The type of hinge used is determined primarily by the nature and weight of the object being attached. For a massive (entrance or interior) door, strap hinges which extend across part of the door itself may be required. Lighter doors may need only H or HL hinges or a decorative butt hinge. There are also stylistic distinctions to be considered. Early forms of hardware such as strap and H and HL hinges would not have been used in a Victorian-period dwelling. Here would be found brass or brass-plated butt hinges, some of a strength which can carry considerable weight. *See also* **Door Hardware, Shutter Hardware.**

FORGERIES
Forgeries, in the best sense of the word, are what reproductions are all about. The craftsmen at this British firm are among the better practitioners of the ancient art of hand-forging and imitating the past. Strap, butterfly, and H and HL hinges are the standard types regularly produced. Illustrated are the butterfly hinges – each wing approximately 1" wide – which are recommended for use on cabinet or cupboard doors. The strap hinges, also shown, come in large (15" long) and small (8½" long) sizes.

is also a good source of very heavy brass H and HL hinges. Yet another type offered is a Dutch Colonial hinge in brass.

Cast and Forged Iron catalogs, $4

KAYNE & SON CUSTOM FORGED
    HARDWARE
76 Daniel Ridge Rd.
Candler, NC 28715-9434
(704) 667-8868
(704) 665-1988

BRIAN F. LEO
A Victorian-style brass hinge like the one shown here is typical of Leo's

output. There are over thirty designs to choose from, each one of which carries an ornamental motif representative of the period. The amount of detail and relief achieved on these handmade pieces is quite remarkable.

Literature available

BRIAN F. LEO
7532 Columbus Ave. S.
Richfield, MN 55423
(612) 861-1473

TREMONT NAIL CO.
All basic types of Colonial hinges are regularly stocked at Tremont, a firm

Leaflet available

FORGERIES
Old Butchery, High St.
Twyford, Hants SO21 1RF
England
(0962) 712196

KAYNE & SON CUSTOM FORGED
    HARDWARE
Hinges are a regular part of Kayne's everyday production in both cast and forged varieties. The lightweight cast-iron strap hinges are suitable for most interior doors and cabinets. These are made in a tapered style, ending in

what is called a "bean" design or a heart. The wrought-iron set shown here features a tulip design of Pennsylvania-German origin. Kayne

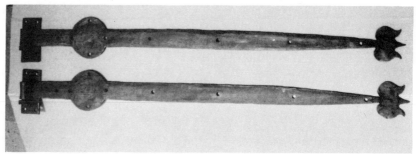

that has built its reputation on its steel cut nails. Strap hinges come in several styles and sizes. There are also dummy strap hinges, without the pintle, used for purely decorative purposes.

Brochure available

TREMONT NAIL CO.
Elm St. at Rte. 28, PO Box 111
Wareham, MA 02571
(508) 295-0038

WOODBURY BLACKSMITH & FORGE CO. Only forged hinges are made by Woodbury. The great advantage of using this supplier is that anyone outfitting or restoring a house, in Woodbury's words, "will find it possible to fill many of their hardware needs from these stock items, without the added cost of special copies." In addition to standard early American designs, originally derived from English sources, are rat-tail hinges, Queen Anne H and HL hinges made with foliated ends, Pennsylvania-German strap hinges, Dutch cusped strap hinges from the Hudson Valley, offset hinges, and ram's horn side hinges.

Catalog, $3

WOODBURY BLACKSMITH & FORGE CO.
PO Box 268
Woodbury, CT 06798
(203) 263-5737

Other suppliers of hinges include: THE ARDEN FORGE CO., A CAROLINA CRAFTSMAN, CIRECAST, EARLY NEW ENGLAND ROOMS & EXTERIORS, INC., HAMMERWORKS, HISTORIC HARDWARE LTD., LEMEE'S FIREPLACE EQUIPMENT, and RENOVATOR'S SUPPLY.

Hitching Posts. Unless you are an equine fancier, a hitching post is likely to be of little practical use. Today it exists in front of a house as a romantic reminder of slower and more gracious means of transport. Two basic designs remain available – a jockey and a horse head – the third form, what was once offensively called a pickaninny, has happily gone to its reward.

KENNETH LYNCH AND SONS
Cast stone is used for the standard model offered by Lynch. It stands 47" high and is supplied with a long

ground anchor. A hitching post can also be without a figural top, the ring instead being threaded through a ball finial. Lynch can provide this type of post – 56½" high – as well.

Book of Garden Ornaments, $9.50

KENNETH LYNCH AND SONS
78 Danbury Rd., Box 488
Wilton, CT 06897
(203) 762-8363
Fax (203) 762-2999

TENNESSEE FABRICATING CO.
A jockey boy hitching post, produced in heavy cast iron and steel, is, because of its weight, not likely to be easily carted away by an unfriendly visitor. Tennessee suggests that the model – in red or green silks – be used to hold an electric lantern or a house marker. Horse hitching posts are also available, as a standard unadorned 54" post (including horse head), and as a fluted post, 40" high, on a pediment base.

Catalog, $5

TENNESSEE FABRICATING CO.
1822 Latham St.
Memphis, TN 38106
(901) 948-3355
(901) 948-3356

Hooks. Devotees of old houses can develop odd passions, but no one we know is hung up on the subject of hooks. These simple devices, however, have more uses than is readily apparent. A hook with an eye or staple may serve as door hardware, and hooks are used to keep screens and storm windows in place. They may also be substituted for

shutter dogs. Other uses include the hanging of clothing, cooking utensils, and fireplace tools. Early chandeliers and lanterns are sometimes suspended from a ceiling hook. For hooks out of the ordinary or for examples strong enough to carry heavy objects, one can turn to a blacksmith or metalworker. Strap lengths of iron are always around the blacksmith's shop and production of utilitarian hooks is practically second-nature to the ironworker. Among those who always offer this type of hardware are KAYNE & SON CUSTOM FORGED HARDWARE, LEMEE FIREPLACE EQUIPMENT, and WOODBURY BLACKSMITH & FORGE CO. A. BALL PLUMBING SUPPLY is an excellent source of brass hooks used in the bathroom. HURLEY PATENTEE MANOR is one source of ceiling hooks for lighting fixtures.

House Plans. Use of ready-made or mail-order house plans has a long history in North America. Carpenter-builders in the early days turned to such classics as Asher Benjamin's *The American Builder's Companion* and Owen Biddle's *The Young Carpenter's Assistant* for inspiration and guidance; A. J. Downing's *The Architecture of Country Houses* and *Cottage Residences* went through many editions in the mid-1800s. Later in the century there were dozens of builder's guides available, and firms such as Sears, Roebuck even offered prefabricated buildings. The services of a trained architect were often not available in many areas until the early 1900s and, even if a professional was on call, few people could afford to

Kayne and Son Custom Forged Hardware

respond. The fact that so many houses of correct proportions, structural soundness, and some stylistic integrity were built during the Colonial and Victorian periods is testimony to the basic building skills of the average individual, and, to a lesser extent, the models presented to them for copying. The building of houses in the 20th-century, however, has become more and more a specialized business. It is not by any means clear that the presence of more professional builders and architects has improved the building scene. Developments of characterless cookie-press houses that mushroomed after World War II testify to a decline in building standards. It has been in response to this trend that old house restoration and renovation has developed in the past twenty years. And along with it has come the building of new "old" houses and the re-learning of traditional building methods on the part of both contractors and week-end builders. Publications offering advice range from the slick shelter magazines and mass-circulation house plan periodicals to compendiums of authentic designs. The plans presented by the periodicals are often only partially successful as to authenticity, but they do make provision for modern amenities such as a bathroom, a garage, and a functional kitchen. In their zeal to encompass period charm, modern convenience, and comfort, these publications can err on the side of the ersatz, coming up, for example, with a split level antebellum plantation house. The various collections of historic designs published in book form also have their limitations. They are useful, nonetheless, for illustrations of period details and how they should work together. Among the books we have found most helpful are the publications of HISTORICAL REPLICATIONS, INC., with plans which include essential modern interior features; ANTIQUITY REPRINTS; and the Main Street Old House line of paperbacks available from STERLING PUBLISHING CO., INC.

House Portraits. A portrait of a house in pen and ink is a popular way to capture its period character. Something about a drawing, as sophisticated real estate agents have learned, evokes a more positive response than a glossy photograph. STURBRIDGE STUDIO specializes in house portraits. Each drawing is executed using a photograph supplied by the homeowner in color or black-and-white. The drawings are in black ink on archival vellum paper. Each is finished with a beveled matte in one of six colors, the customer making the choice. There are three standard drawing sizes: 5 x 7, 11 x 14, 20 x 24.

Brochure available

STURBRIDGE STUDIO
114 East Hill
Brimfield, MA 01010
(413) 245-3289

Ironwork. Custom work of the highest order is available from members of the Artist-Blacksmith Association of North America who have mastered the ancient art of forging. These craftsmen may also be equally skilled in casting forms, a technique which reached a high level in the mid- to the late 1800s in the United States and Europe. Wrought iron has always been considered a higher form of ironwork, but cast iron can be as strong and durable. And there are objects such as fencing and

grilles which often combine cast and wrought elements. However well made, ornamental iron is nonetheless subject to the same degree of environmental pollution as other building materials. For this reason, a large proportion of the work undertaken by ironwork foundries or blacksmith shops consists of restoring antique structural and ornamental pieces. *See also* **Cresting; Door Guards; Door Hardware; Fencing and Gates; Fountains; Garden Furniture; Grates, Grilles, and Registers; Porches; Urns;** and **Window Guards.**

ARCHITECTURAL IRON CO.
This firm sets a high standard in both its restoration work and new work. Old ironwork must be handled with care and requires careful analysis and cleaning to determine how much of the original fabric can be saved or will need to be cast or forged anew. There are protective coatings which can be used on all ironwork assemblies to slow the effect of rust. Architectural Iron primes and paints all pieces before assembling them into what are called "field units." The company also sees to proper installation. For fencing, this often means the pouring of lead to attach the lengths into a stone base. Among the restoration projects which Architectural Iron has completed are gates, fence sections, and planters for Gramercy Park in New York City; castings for a fence at Washington's Headquarters, Newburgh, New York; and a 23'-high Florentine fountain in Mount Hope Cemetery, Rochester, New York.

Brochure, $4

ARCHITECTURAL IRON CO.
Box 126, Schocopee Rd.
Milford, PA 18337
(717) 296-7722
(212) 243-2664
Fax (717) 296-IRON

NEW ENGLAND TOOL CO.
This firm's work is primarily in wrought iron and includes such accessories as fireplace screens, table bases, and bed frames in addition to fencing, grilles, and doors. Domestic objects for interior use may require the same type of careful repair or restoration as exterior features. All of New England's work is handled on a custom basis.

File of architectural metalwork design, $2

NEW ENGLAND TOOL CO. LTD.
PO Box 30
Chester, NY 10918
(914) 782-5332
(914) 651-7550

Other firms handling new and restoration cast or wrought ironwork are: THE ARDEN FORGE CO.; NED JAMES, WROUGHT METALS; KAYNE AND SON CUSTOM FORGED HARDWARE; LAWLER MACHINE & FOUNDRY CO. INC.; SCHWARTZ'S FORGE & METALWORKS, INC.; STEWART IRON WORKS CO.; TENNESSEE FABRICATING CO.; and WALLIN FORGE.

Ironwork grille, west porch, Chateau-sur-Mer, Newport, Rhode Island. Photograph by Jack E. Boucher, Historic American Buildings Survey.

Kitchen, Van Spankeren House, Pella, Iowa. Photograph by Robert Thall, Historic American Buildings Survey.

Joists. *See* **Beams.**

Keystones. Traditionally this topmost member of an arch is made, as the word suggests, of cut or cast stone. A keystone most often appears as part of an entryway surround or is used in a window lintel. Inside a house, keystones are made of the same material as door and window casings, usually wood or plaster, and have only a decorative function. Due to the revival of neoclassical decoration in the 1980s, carved wood keystones are again available as well as molded versions in composition and synthetic materials. Keystones are usually only supplied as part of an overall framing or casing assembly but can be purchased separately.

FOCAL POINT INC.
Four different styles of keystones are included in Focal Point's collection of molded polyurethane ornaments. The four models are the Rider House, Longleaf, Fleur-de-lis, and Grand Paces, and these range from as small as $4^1/_2$" wide and 6" high to $9^7/_8$" wide and $14^1/_8$" high. Each can be used with a Focal Point arch or independently.

Catalog, $3

FOCAL POINT INC.
PO Box 93327
Atlanta, GA 30377-0327
(800) 662-5550
(404) 352-9049 (AK and GA)
Fax (404) 352-9049

SILVERTON VICTORIAN MILLWORKS
Silverton's keystones are wood blocks not unlike head or corner blocks used in late-Victorian door and window casings. As illustrated, there are eight designs, most of which feature a bull's-eye or rosette. All are 1" deep and vary from $3^1/_2$" x $4^1/_2$" to $5^1/_2$" x 7".

They are available in common poplar or pine, premium pine, oak, or premium oak.

Complete catalog package, $4 (refundable with first order)

SILVERTON VICTORIAN MILLWORKS
PO Box 2987-OC7
Durango, CO 81302
(303) 259-5915
Fax (303) 259-5919

Other suppliers of keystones are: THE BALMER ARCHITECTURAL ART STUDIOS, DECORATOR'S SUPPLY CORP., W. F. NORMAN CORP., and SUNSHINE ARCHITECTURAL WOODWORKS.

Kickplates. These are metal panels used on the bottom of a door to protect it from the assaults of daily living. Kickplates are most often found on entrance doors in public buildings, but their utility at home, especially one occupied by children, is undeniable.

BEDLAM BRASS
Bedlam is a manufacturer of standard brass kickplates in two sizes: 6" x 34" for a 36" door and 6" x 28" for a 30" door. Screws are provided and six holes are predrilled. Bedlam is also able to supply brass sheet for other size panels and will prepare

115

countersunk holes and provide screws.

Railing catalog, $2

BEDLAM BRASS
137 Rte. 4 Westbound
Paramus, NJ 07652
(201) 368-3500

RESTORATION WORKS, INC.
This firm is a general supplier of old house products and will make up solid-brass kickplates to order. All it requires are the measurements of the door's bottom panel. It is suggested that 1" clearance be left on the sides and base.

Catalog, $3

RESTORATION WORKS, INC.
810 Main St.
Buffalo, NY 14202
(800) 735-3535
Fax (716) 856-8040

Other suppliers of brass kickplates are CONANT CUSTOM BRASS, INC. *and* RENOVATOR'S SUPPLY.

Kitchen Fittings and Hardware. A kitchen in any house – modern or traditional – must be functional. The use of modern appliances will dictate to some extent how the room is laid out. Some semblance of a period feeling can be introduced in cabinets and in the materials used for counters. Lesser items as pot and towel racks, wood boxes, iron trivets, an overhead drier, metal match holders, and old-fashioned utensils will contribute to softening the practical lines of a modern kitchen. If this room is one in which meals are also taken, so much the better, for then period table and chairs can be introduced.

DOMESTIC PARAPHERNALIA CO.
A traditional ceiling-mounted clothes airer or towel drier is a staple item in many British and Irish kitchens. It is usually positioned high above the stove. The apparatus consists of four pine rails fitted into cast-iron ends. Cleat hooks, double and single pulleys, and a pulley cord raise and lower the rack. The model shown is called the "Sheila Maid." Whatever the name, the device is both a practical and attractive one, and an improvement over the type of

overhead rack at one time used in American apartment-house kitchens.

Literature available

DOMESTIC PARAPHERNALIA CO.
2a Pleasant Street
Lytham, Lancs. FY8 5JA
England
(0253) 736334

KAYNE & SON CUSTOM FORGED
    HARDWARE
An astonishing variety of objects in iron is fashioned by Kayne. Pot racks include two Dutch crowns, a half-crown design, and ornamental bars with sliding hooks to hold pots or utensils. There are also trivets and broilers in various forms. All these items are of forged or wrought iron.

Catalog, $2

KAYNE & SON CUSTOM FORGED
    HARDWARE
76 Daniel Ridge Rd.
Candler, NC 28715
(704) 667-8868
(704) 665-1988

SHAKER WORKSHOPS
The design sense of these inspired 19th-century craftspeople shines through the reproductions produced in the 1990s. Typical of the attractive and functional designs of the Shakers is the Sabbathday Lake towel rack shown here. It was used in a kitchen

or wash house and is perfect as a drier of tea towels. The rack is made of hard maple and stands 33" high, 34" wide, and 6½" deep. It is available in kit or assembled and finished form. Shaker Workshops is also a good source for such attractive items as a hanging cupboard, oval serving trays, fruit trays, oval boxes, and carriers.

Catalog, $1

SHAKER WORKSHOPS
PO Box 1028
Concord, MA 01742
(617) 646-8985

Other suppliers of kitchen paraphernalia are: COHASSET COLONIALS, CUMBERLAND GENERAL STORE, INC., LEHMAN HARDWARE, RENOVATOR'S SUPPLY, *and* SUNRISE SALVAGE CO.

Kitchens. It is often said that the kitchen is the area of the house which profits the most from investment. There is no doubt that a well-equipped and designed kitchen is a drawing card when a house is up for sale; whether this truism applies equally to an old-house kitchen is hypothetical. Old-fashioned appliances, if they still work properly, can actually have a cachet. A wood or kerosene-burning stove may be considered a plus by some; others find anything other than an electric cooktop and microwave oven an anachronism. It is certain, however, that well-built cabinets or cupboards are always admired and that the use of quality natural materials such as pine and oak, ceramic tile, and metals rather than synthetic substitutes measurably enhance the value of a

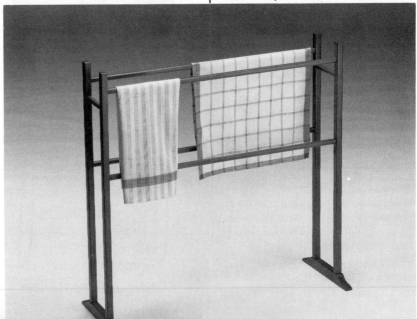

house. The kitchen can also be a pleasant environment in which to live and work if laid out with care and imagination. Kitchen design is a specialized field, and a remake of the whole space may not be in the cards for most people, despite the entreaties of shelter magazines and home centers. Where to turn for advice on a kitchen for a traditional house is not as clear as that for a contemporary home. Kitchen design, nevertheless, has begun to move beyond the lines of the past and to assume a more traditional form. This is especially true of firms in Europe and Great Britain such as POGGENPOHL, GASSENAU, SIEMATIC, and a host of design and fabrication workshops. Some of these European cabinetmakers have American distributors; others will work directly with a customer in either limited or major projects. There are, of course, American and Canadian restoration and woodworking firms of the same level of competence and imagination who can assist. *See also* **Contractors, Restoration; Cupboards and Cabinets.**

EARLY NEW ENGLAND ROOMS & EXTERIORS, INC.
Country kitchens with raised panel cabinetry is a specialty of this contractor. Each kitchen is custom-designed, in the words of the designer, to have "a character totally in keeping with the Colonial atmosphere of the main house yet completely convenient for modern use." The key to this is, of course, the cabinetwork. All of this is *solid* and does not consist of composition backs and shelves to which solid doors are attached. Early New England is also likely to introduce freestanding pieces such as a cupboard, combination bookcase and desk, or a hutch for displaying china.

Catalog, $10

EARLY NEW ENGLAND ROOMS & EXTERIORS, INC.
37 McGuire Rd.
South Windsor, CT 06074
(203) 282-0236

ROBINSON & CORNISH
The high level of design maintained by this firm is typical of up-market British and European kitchen specialists. Maximum use is made of natural materials – pine and ash for cabinets and freestanding cupboards, slate for counter tops, granite for a pastry surface, marble or glazed tiles for backsplash panels. Each kitchen differs, of course, as the illustrations show, but most have an unregimented, unfitted pleasing appearance. Preparation of food may be a domestic "science" but a laboratory-like setting – the usual modern look – is unappetizing. Robinson & Cornish can, nonetheless, provide for all the necessary appliances and fixtures, and will make up half-carousel trays, pull-out shelves on runners, pull-out single and double pan drawers, pull-out

vegetable baskets, towel rails, and a variety of concealed bins. Although projects were previously limited to the United Kingdom, the same expertise and service is now also available to North American customers.

Literature on request

ROBINSON & CORNISH
The Old Tannery
Hannaford Lane, Swimbridge
Devon EX32 0PL
(0271) 830732

Other specialists in old house kitchens include: ANTIQUE BATHS & KITCHENS,

JON EKLUND RESTORATIONS, RESTORATIONS UNLIMITED, VINTAGE INC., and WINANS CONSTRUCTION INC.

Kitchen Utensils. There's no use romanticizing the Victorian kitchen. Thornton Wilder might have been nostalgic for all those apple-pie smells emanating from the kitchens of *Our Town*, but he never saw the kitchen hearth from a woman's point of view. The Victorian housewife walked hundreds of miles annually just tending the appliances of her obstacle-course kitchen. A coal or wood stove was often four to five feet wide, and even taller if furnished with a high shelf. Feeding it broke the back; its heat, the spirit. A wooden icebox could measure two or three feet across; an iron sink fitted with a drying rack and a force pump to draw water from the cistern could take up nearly a whole wall. In 1879 one expert on "household management" wrote that "the kitchen is a family laboratory, and a good cook should be a chemist." In actuality, the family chemist was a combination marathon runner, workhorse, and mechanic, and we would not willingly change places with her. While we modern old-house lovers would think twice about relinquishing the convenience of gas or electricity in the kitchen, we've no quarrel, however, with the wisdom of using old-fashioned kitchen utensils. For one thing, they're handsome in

their many nostalgic shapes, and in appearance can do much to warm the modern "scientific" kitchen. For another, they're frequently better built than their contemporary counterparts. And, finally, they frequently work as well, if not better, than much of our modern gimcrackery and are often more practical and energy-saving. What's the use of running the food processor to chop a single onion if *five* appliance parts thereby require washing? Anyone who doesn't know the old-house sound of an old-fashioned stainless chopper striking against the scarred pit of a wooden chopping bowl doesn't know what a "user-friendly" kitchen really is.

CUMBERLAND GENERAL STORE
Whoever came up with the expression "everything but the kitchen sink" would have had to modify it to *include* the kitchen sink after perusing the mail-order catalog of the Cumberland General Store. Cumberland offers old-fashioned farm and household devices from adzes and axes to zink laundry tubs. The old-fashioned kitchen utensil section runs for pages and includes among its nostalgic treasures cast-iron corn-stick pans (and every other kind of cast-iron utensil), blue-speckled graniteware, blue-striped stoneware mixing bowls, and a cast-iron sausage stuffer that you'd swear was manufactured in 1886.

Catalog, $3

CUMBERLAND GENERAL STORE
Rte. 3
Crossville, TN 38555
(615) 484-8481

LEHMAN HARDWARE & APPLIANCES, INC.
Lehman's was founded many years ago to supply the farm and household needs of America's largest Amish community, which it does to this day. As a result, it can rightly claim that the items it stocks "are not found in the world at large." Browsing through the Lehman catalog is like a visit to the last century, although nothing is listed that does not "retain a valid usefulness." The kitchen utensils section runs for pages and includes a pasta dryer that looks like a miniature indoor clothes dryer, a grain mill that might very well have come out of an 1895 grocery store, and everything in-between.

Catalog, $2

LEHMAN HARDWARE & APPLIANCES, INC.
PO Box 41, 4779 Kidron Rd.
Kidron, OH 44636
(216) 857-5441
Fax (216) 857-5785

THE TINNER
For over twenty years Jim Barnett has provided expertise in restoration projects throughout America. A master tinsmith, blacksmith, and coppersmith, working in traditional metal crafts, Barnett brings a strong sense of history to his trade. He works in a restored 19th-century tinshop where visitors are welcome. He produces a wide range of 18th- and 19th-century styles in lighting and other accessories, but also provides fine custom designs for the needs of individual projects. Typical of the Tinner's art are these handsome domestic devices that could find a place in every old-house

kitchen. The original of the large colander shown (12" in diameter, 10" high) was found in Connecticut; the small colander shown ($6^1/_2$" in diameter, $4^1/_2$" high) is based on one from Lancaster County, Pennsylvania. The fine sculptural dust pan is modeled on a 19th-century Pennsylvania original. It comes with a handmade broomcorn brush. Both dust pan and brush are sufficiently attractive to hang on a kitchen wall.

Catalog, $1.50

THE TINNER
PO Box 353
Spencer, NC 28159
(704) 637-5149

Other suppliers of old-fashioned kitchen utensils include KAYNE & SON CUSTOM FORGED HARDWARE *and* SHAKER WORKSHOPS.

Front hall, showing lantern on wall and iron door latch, Nathaniel Macy House, Nantucket, Massachusetts. Historic American Buildings Survey.

Lace. *See* **Fabrics.**

Lamp Parts/Fittings. Antique light fixtures often need replacement parts or special fittings to adapt them for modern use. If the fixture requires detailed work, it may be best to entrust it to a specialist (*see* **Lamp Repair/Restoration**), but if it is only a minor change that is needed, you can order a part from one of several direct mail sources. For suppliers of shades and globes, *see* **Lampshades.**

LEHMAN'S HARDWARE
Since this is an outlet serving the Amish community in eastern Ohio, parts for non-electric, old-time fixtures are routinely stocked and offered. For ordinary kerosene-burning lamps, there are burners, cotton wicks, and chimneys. Since Aladdin kerosene lamps are among the most popular models made today, Lehman carries a good stock of Aladdin chimneys, tripods, mantles, wicks, and burners, and such devices as a flame spreader, wick cleaner, wick raiser, and bug screen to protect the mantle.

Catalog available, $2

LEHMAN'S HARDWARE
4779 Kidron Rd., PO Box 41
Kidron, OH 44636
(216) 857-5441

PAXTON HARDWARE LTD.
The lamp fittings index of Paxton's catalog includes an astonishing sixty-six entries. Included are such items as cord, cord bushings, wire connectors, plugs and switches, sockets of various types, fixture arms and cluster parts, nipples, pipe, tubing, couplings, canopies, ceiling hooks, link chain, vase caps, brass lamp bases, finials and spindles, shade and chimney holders and harps, oil burners, smoke bells, electric converters, and such decorative items as prisms, bobeches, and pendalogs. A full line of Aladdin kerosene lamp fixtures is also offered.

Catalog, $4

PAXTON HARDWARE LTD.
7818 Bradshaw Rd., PO Box 256
Upper Falls, MD 21156
(301) 592-8505
Fax (301) 592-2224

E. W. PYFER
In addition to its main repair service, Pyfer supplies parts for pre-1925 gas, kerosene, and electric fixtures. What cannot be drawn from stock will be custom-produced. In this regard, Pyfer's forty years of experience are of considerable value. The number of fixtures he has rebuilt is in the thousands.

Literature available

E. W. PYFER
218 N. Foley Ave.
Freeport, IL 61032-3943
(815) 232-8968

Other suppliers of lamp parts/fittings include: CENTURY HOUSE ANTIQUE LAMP EMPORIUM AND REPAIR, BRADFORD CONSULTANTS, and LAMP GLASS.

Lampposts. *See* **Lanterns** and **Posts.**

Lamp Repair/Restoration. Antique fixtures are more than likely to show their age in an unattractive manner. Almost any device, however, can be brought back to useful life and attractiveness in the hands of an expert restorer. The problem may be as minor as refurbishing the brass or other metal. The most common need is to adapt a fixture for electrical use. A converter is an easy do-it-yourself solution for some types of table lamps. Hanging fixtures, however, often need more complicated work such as threading wires through the hub and arms.

CENTURY HOUSE ANTIQUE LAMP EMPORIUM AND REPAIR
The only kind of work not undertaken by Marilyn and Hal McKnight is the repair of glass. Everything else to do with old fixtures can be done, including metal stripping, polishing, lacquering, and wiring. Because the McKnights carry hundreds of antique lamps in their inventory, most of which have required some type of repair or change, they know how to handle both the usual and the unusual type of assignment.

Literature available, SASE for inquiries

CENTURY HOUSE ANTIQUE LAMP EMPORIUM AND REPAIR
46785 Rte. 18 West
Wellington, OH 44090
(216) 647-4092

OLD LAMPLIGHTER SHOP
Located in The Musical Musuem, with its collection of restored pump organs, nickelodeons, grind organs, and other musical antiques, the Old Lamplighter antique workshop focuses on the repair and restoration of lighting fixtures and on replacement parts. This is a particularly good source of glass chimneys. Like many other restorers, the shop also trades in antique fixtures.

Brochure available

OLD LAMPLIGHTER SHOP
The Musical Museum
Deansboro, NY 13328
(315) 841-8774

Other sources for lamp repair and restoration are: KAYNE & SON CUSTOM FORGED HARDWARE, E. W. PYFER, ROY ELECTRIC ANTIQUE LIGHTING CO., WATERTOWER PINES, and YANKEE CRAFTSMAN.

Lamps, Antique and Reproduction. See **Ceiling Fixtures, Chandeliers, Floor Lamps, Hanging Fixtures, Lanterns, Sconces,** and **Table Lamps.**

Lampshades. What makes a lighting fixture pleasing to the eye is not merely the outline of its shape or the materials from which it is made, but the play of light against the surface of its decorated shades, whether parchment, silk, or glass. The design of lampshades first came into its own during the 19th-century. Victorian glassmakers became masters of the art of creating and decorating chimneys, globes, and shades as fixtures of every lighting mode were introduced and improved upon. Working with parchment, and particularly silk and other delicate fabrics, Victorian lampshade makers created imaginative shades that rivaled the elaborate hats of the period in shape, size, fashion, and workmanship. The current revival of interest in Victoriania has brought about a corresponding renascence of later 19th- and early 20th-century fixtures and the concomitant need for reproduction period lampshades. Glass shades, many from original molds, are readily available in a profusion of designs that rival the contents of early lighting catalogs. Fabric shades in fanciful shapes and rainbow hues, once ubiquitous at the beginning of the century and out of vogue for at least seventy years, are now made by a handful of entrepreneurs who can rightly be called fabric artists.

LAMP GLASS
With well over 100 different styles and sizes in stock, and many more available by special order, these specialists in replacement glass lampshades offer a wide and comprehensive selection. Included in the firm's stock are shades for gas and early electric fixtures, German student lamps, "Gone with the Wind" lamps, billiard lights, bankers' lamps, gooseneck lamps, 1930s torchières, and every other conceivable type of

fixture. Although Lamp Glass's small catalog lists only a fraction of the shades it carries in its Massachusetts shop, it welcomes inquiries about particular items sought – and is more than likely to replicate what you have in mind. Illustrated are just a few of the gas shades and student-lamp shades available.

Catalog, $1

LAMP GLASS
2230 Massachusetts Ave.
Cambridge, MA 02140
(617) 497-0770

LAMPSHADES OF ANTIQUE
Dorothy Primo, who designs lushly beautiful Victorian fabric lampshades, writes that "because of the unique materials and dyes we use, no two lampshades are ever created alike; rather each is a signed piece of art." Working with a wide variety of materials, including new and vintage brocades, damasks, tapestries, silks, laces, and velvets, she will either use a frame you supply or create the frame for your lamp herself. And she will either design the lamp by using her own fabrics and following your suggested color scheme or by employing the fabrics you send her. Either way the result is the same – a custom-made

shade that is elegant and surprisingly inexpensive.

Catalog, $4

LAMPSHADES OF ANTIQUE
PO Box 2
Medford, OR 97501
(503) 826-9737

PAXTON HARDWARE LTD.
Anyone who has ever searched for a parchment or fabric shade for an old-fashioned reading lamp knows how fruitless such a search can be. Here, finally, is a reliable source. Not only do Paxton's parchment and fabric shades come in a variety of tasteful period patterns, but they are available

with the proper hardware to fit even the most hard-to-fit lamp assemblies, be they clip-on, chimney, UNO, or washer types. In addition, Paxton carries a complete line of glass shades for most Victorian lighting fixtures as well as shades for 1930s torchières.

Catalog, $4

PAXTON HARDWARE LTD.
7818 Bradshaw Rd.
Upper Falls, MD 21156
(301) 592-8505
Fax (301) 592-2224

ROY ELECTRIC CO.
Among Roy Electric's huge collection of reproduction lighting fixtures and accessories is an enormous stock of glass shades in over 100 designs, only a few of which are shown here. Made for normal-size gas and electric fixtures, with some also for larger pendants and chandeliers, these shades are available in acid-etched, ribbed, pressed, swirled, fluted, dotted, frosted, colored, or clear-blown designs. Fitter sizes for standard electric fixtures are 2$\frac{1}{2}$" or 3$\frac{1}{4}$"; those for gas are 3$\frac{1}{4}$" or 4". Shades for unusually large fixtures vary in fitter sizes as well as in overall dimensions, and there is again a broad choice available. For any lighting fixture or accessory needs, Roy Electric is well worth contacting.

Lighting Catalog, $5

ROY ELECTRIC CO., INC.
1054 Coney Island Ave.
Brooklyn, NY 11230
(718) 434-7002
Fax (718) 421-4678

SHADY LADY
Marilynn Pinney is the shady lady in question, but aside from the pleasant nostalgic glow her delightful period lampshades provide, there's nothing remotely "shady" about the service she offers. Only color photographs could do justice to the multi-hued fabric shades she designs, and her many varieties of shades can be ordered either from stock or on a custom basis. Shown are just a few of the many frame shapes available. If

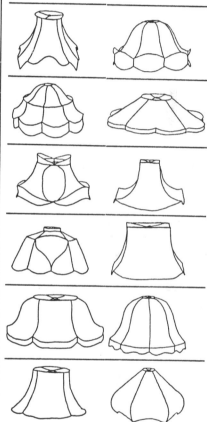

you have an antique shade in need of restoration, the Shady Lady will be glad to do the job for you. And, if you admire her period shades, but don't have the antique lamp base to go with them, she'll be pleased to offer you a variety of reproductions to select from.

Catalog, $4.50

SHADY LADY
418 East Second St.
Loveland, CO 80537
(303) 669-1080

YESTERSHADES

Esther Rister pioneered in the rediscovery of antique lampshades in 1978 and is the undisputed doyenne of the few now proficient in the craft. Her shades are arguably unique works of needlecraft art. "I usually use laces to decorate my shades," she says, "but sometimes I make a 'rosette,' an old tucking and pleating technique which features a sculptured flower in the center of the design." Her choice of materials is both liberal and original, and her combinations of needlecraft techniques and her unique color sense make her shades unlike those of any other maker.

Shown are only two of the many Yestershades in stock. Custom work is also welcome.

Catalog, $3.50

YESTERSHADES
3824 SE Stark
Portland, OR 97214
(503) 235-5645

Additional suppliers of period shades are CENTURY HOUSE ANTIQUE LAMP EMPORIUM AND REPAIR *and* RENOVATOR'S SUPPLY.

Lanterns. Lighting devices which are enclosed and protected from the elements have been especially valued in North America for hundreds of years. In rural areas lanterns have been indispensable for carrying out work in barns, stables, and other out-buildings. Wherever light is needed outside the house, in town or country, a lantern is a good solution. It may be mounted on a post or bracket, hung from a ceiling, set on a table, or carried by hand if a portable source of fuel such as kerosene is used. Lanterns have been increasingly used inside the house as well, particularly as an entrance hall or foyer light; it may also find a place in a country kitchen. These are appropriate areas for a lantern in a Colonial, early 19th-century, or a Craftsman-style dwelling of the 1900s. The practice of using a lantern purely as a decorative accessory in other interior spaces is not rooted in history but, rather, is an expression of the modern tendency to kitsch. *See also* **Hanging Fixtures** and **Posts.**

BLAKE INDUSTRIES
Post lanterns and luminaires for street lighting are among the products manufactured and distributed by Blake. Several different lantern designs are available for use with a reproduction of the lamppost from New York's Central Park originally designed by architect Henry Bacon in 1910. This type of post lantern is unlikely to be used on the grounds of a modest home, but it could be appropriate for an estate property. Post heights range from 9'3" to 12'6". Blake also produces other light posts in cast aluminum, cast iron, and wood along with lanterns or luminaires in cast aluminum.

Literature available

BLAKE INDUSTRIES
PO Box 155
Abington, MA 02351-0155

(617) 337-8772
Fax (617) 335-3004

A. J. P. COPPERSMITH & CO.
Over thirty lantern models are produced by this firm, in business since 1940. Nearly every regional New England type is available, including reproductions of Paul Revere's famous light, a copy of the Dietz globe lantern which achieved fame in steam railroading days, and a narrow doctor's-lantern carried when visiting the sick. Most of the models are offered in several sizes and are finished in antique copper, antique brass, pewter, or verdigris. And nearly all the lanterns can be fitted with a bracket for a post or with a chain for hanging. There are ten lanterns designated specifically for outdoor post use; one of them, the Wilshire model, is shown here. It is

40" high by 16" wide and has a double finial. A wrought-iron or a solid-brass cradle support is available. Each post lantern comes with a 3" diameter post fitter; other sizes can be specified.

Catalog, $3

A. J. P. COPPERSMITH & CO.
20 Industrial Pkwy.
Woburn, MA 01801
(800) 545-1776
(617) 932-3700 (MA)
Fax (617) 932-3704

HAMMERWORKS
Lanterns of all types comprise more than half of Hammerwork's production. All are made with solid antique copper or antique brass. Most, as the model illustrated, can be fitted with a two-light cluster, or used

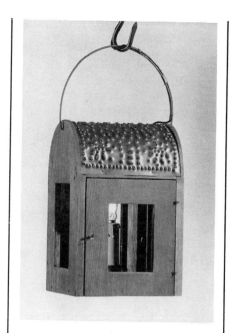

simply with one light. Hammerworks recommends that any fixture that is to be wall-mounted be one-quarter to one-third the height of the doorway it is to adjoin.

Catalog, $3

HAMMERWORKS
6 FREMONT ST.
WORCESTER, MA 01603
(508) 755-3434
    or
798 Boston Post Rd., Rte. 20
Metro-West Plaza
Marlboro, MA 01752
(508) 485-6721

HISTORIC HARDWARE LTD.
The proprietors of this enterprising firm are well acquainted with the history of lighting design. Their lanterns are based on solid Colonial American and English models. Each one of them can be fitted with restoration glass if desired, an attractive option when a lantern is being used on an old building.

Pictured are two wall-mounted models – The Barn Lantern, available with either a two-light cluster or a chimney, and The Old Chatham, a three-sided light with a three-light cluster. These and all other lanterns are made of either copper or brass and can be finished in the same shades or in verdigris. Historic Hardware also produces five post light models.

Catalog, $3

HISTORIC HARDWARE LTD.
PO Box 1327
North Hampton, NH 03862
(603) 964-2280

HURLEY PATENTEE MANOR
Each of Hurley's many lighting fixtures is virtually unique. The form and detailing of the historic lantern models are no exception; each lantern is handmade and modern *only* in that

it has been wired for electricity. Illustrated, in order of appearance, are: a wall-mounted barn lantern with a side hinged door, smoke chimney, and reflector back; a wood and pierced-tin lantern, a very early Colonial design; and the Welcome lantern, a wall-mounted model with a shaped apron and front and side piercing. The barn lantern is useful for an area that needs to be especially well-lit. The wood-and-tin model would be best hung or wall-mounted indoors where it would be protected from the elements.

Catalog, $3

HURLEY PATENTEE MANOR
RD 7, Box 98A,
Kingston, NY 12401
(914) 331-5414

LEHMAN'S HARDWARE

Dietz lanterns have been stamped from terne plate and sold for generations. The Dietz model is the practical type of kerosene lantern used today on the typical Amish farm and not a reproduction. Each is finished in blue enamel and has a heavy crossed-wire globe guard. All models are exclusively handled by Lehman, and these include the D-Lite, Blizzard, Little Wizard, and Monarch. Illustrated is the Monarch,

which holds one pint and is guaranteed to burn for twenty-three hours. Genuine Dietz parts are also available through Lehman.

Catalog, $2

LEHMAN'S HARDWARE
PO Box 41, 4779 Kidron Rd.
Kidron, OH 44636
(215) 857-5441
Fax (216) 857-5785

SALVAGE ONE

As the photograph shows, there is a plentiful supply of original lanterns available in Chicago! Just about every type of wall-mounted and hanging fixture can be found. Most of the fixtures are already wired for electricity, but may require new fittings and refinishing.

Literature available
SALVAGE ONE
1524 S. Sangamon St.
Chicago, IL 60608
(312) 733-0098

Other suppliers of reproduction lanterns include: COHASSET COLONIALS, THE COPPERSMITH, GATES MOORE, NED JAMES, WROUGHT METALS, NEWSTAMP LIGHTING CO., THE SALTBOX, SHAKER WORKSHOPS, and THE TINNER.

Latches. Within this small category of reproduction architectural hardware are many forms and designs to choose from. The best of these are wrought iron and not cast, although much of the door hardware used from the early 1800s was cast. Forged hardware is especially recommended for exterior doors which are heavier than interior doors and are subject to weathering. In addition to the common thumb latch of the Suffolk and later Norfolk types, there are also spring latches and bar latches, the latter designed primarily for use on cabinets or cupboards. *See also* **Door Hardware.**

HAMMERWORKS

Reasonably priced forged thumb latches in eleven designs are available through Hammerworks, seven of which are recommended for exterior doors. They range in style from the simple bean latch to the fancy moon cusp and pineapple designs; lengths vary from a minimum of 9" to a

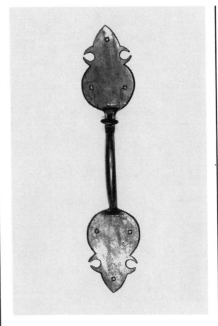

maximum of 17". Illustrated, above, is the moon cusp exterior latch; below is the pierced cusp arrow.

Catalog, $3

HAMMERWORKS
6 Fremont St.
Worcester, MA 01603
(508) 755-3434
        or
798 Boston Post Rd., Rte. 20
Metro-West Plaza
Marlboro, MA 01752
(508) 485-6721

KAYNE & SON CUSTOM FORGED HARDWARE

Kayne offers both cast and wrought latches, the former suggested for cabinet use. His wrought thumb latches of various 18th-century designs are available in sets, each set including a handle, thumb piece, keeper, plain catch, and latch bar. Illustrated is a pigtail latch set. Kayne can also produce longer than usual thumb pieces for thicker than

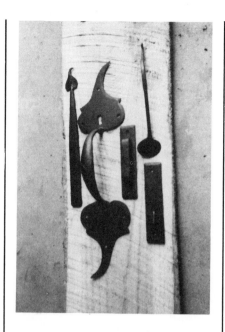

standard doors, and locks which will operate with thumb latch handles.

Catalog, $2

KAYNE & SON CUSTOM FORGED
    HARDWARE
76 Daniel Ridge Rd.
Candler, NC 28715
(704) 667-8868
(704) 685-1988

WOODBURY BLACKSMITH & FORGE CO. It would be very difficult for an antique hardware expert to distinguish between an antique latch and the same design produced by Woodbury. The company's selection of Colonial latches is unrivaled. The majority of these are Suffolk thumb latches for exterior or interior doors, as is the pierced cusp design shown.

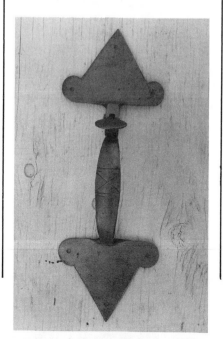

The designs are drawn from English, Dutch, New England, and Pennsylvania sources. All are hand forged of pure wrought iron, or, if the supply of this material is scarce, soft steel. The Norfolk latch designs, dating from the early 19th-century, incorporate a back plate, the bar assembly thereby mounted on the plate. All latches include a bar assembly; even the earlier Suffolk type can be mounted on a plate if desired. A third form of latch available exclusively with Woodbury is the spring latch, each exact copy of which comes with two forged brass knobs, rose, and shaft.

Catalog, $3

WOODBURY BLACKSMITH & FORGE CO.
PO Box 268
Woodbury, CT 06798
(203) 263-5737

Other suppliers of latches include: THE ARDEN FORGE CO., EARLY NEW ENGLAND ROOMS & EXTERIORS, INC., FORGERIES, HISTORIC HARDWARE LTD., LEMEE'S FIREPLACE EQUIPMENT, OMNIA INDUSTRIES, INC., RENOVATOR'S SUPPLY and TREMONT NAIL CO.

Leaves. *See* **Ornaments.**

Letter Drops. If you are fortunate enough to have mail delivered directly to your house, a letter drop in the entrance door or next to it is a handsome addition. During the Victorian era when the post might arrive twice a day, a letter drop cast in iron or brass was commonly used. Today brass letter drops are produced in the same manner in plain or ornamental designs. Two sizes – large, to accommodate magazines, and small, for letters – are usually offered. Unfortunately, these drops or boxes will not eliminate your junk mail. Suppliers of these useful devices include: BRIAN F. LEO, THE OLD WAGON FACTORY, and RENOVATOR'S SUPPLY.

Light Bulbs, Period. In 1879, after months of fruitless experiments, Thomas Alva Edison succeeded in making an incandescent lamp in which a loop of carbonized cotton thread glowed in a vacuum for over

forty hours. Thus began a lighting revolution that led eventually to the wiring of the world. The benefits of electric light were immediately recognized – illumination at the turn of a knob, with no fuel fonts to fill, no wicks to clean, no smoke to soil draperies and walls – and for the first time in history, the source of light could be directed downward as well as up. As a result, many early electric fixtures, taking full advantage of this dramatic novelty, looked like nothing that had come before them. The soft glow of early incandescent bulbs through the glass shades of the new fixtures was remarkably like gaslight, but without the flickering and guttering. But, as new improved light bulbs appeared in rapid succession, with the earliest types disappearing from the marketplace, early electric lighting fixtures began to appear harsh and outdated as new bulbs replaced the old. With early fixtures reproduced for today's homeowners, it's nice to report that period incandescent bulbs are once again available so that the authentic "glow of the past" that glass shades require to look their best is now easily achieved. Most retail outlets, however, do not stock these old-fashioned bulbs, leaving the field open to the two excellent firms listed below. *See also* **Candles, Electric.**

BRADFORD CONSULTANTS
Bradford stocks the complete line of Phoenix Historic Light Bulbs, consisting of four different models: The Century, The Majestic, The Imperial, and The Eureka P. The Century dates from the 1890s and was the first type of bulb produced in quantity for the burgeoning electric light industry. At 12 candlepower (40 watts), it contains the original

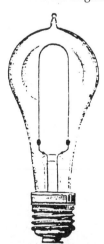

"hairpin" single-loop carbon filament of early clear glass bulbs and is an imposing 6" tall. The Majestic, which emits a soft golden light from its 3"-diameter clear globe, was often incorporated into the design of Art Nouveau fixtures. The 8 candlepower (30 watts) bulb with a twin-loop carbon filament is perfect for Art Nouveau, Mission, and similar period lamps. The Imperial, a 12 candlepower (60 watts) twin-loop carbon flament bulb which comes to a characteristic point, is the bulb that most people think of as the traditional old-style incandescent bulb. As such, it is recommended for most wall and ceiling fixtures in any period setting.

The Eureka P was originally marketed as the Mazda by its developer, General Electric. A 60-watt straight-sided bulb with a zigzag filament, it employs a tungsten wire filament to produce a bright white light. This is the classic bulb that lit the ill-fated *Titanic*. Bradford, a scrupulously unsinkable lighting source, can supply any or all of these period light bulbs by mail order.

Brochure, free

BRADFORD CONSULTANTS
PO Box 4020
Alameda, CA 94501
(415) 523-1968

KYP-GO
Kyp-Go has offered these old-style incandescent bulbs for more than a quarter of a century. First developed in the late 19th century, they emit a soft, warm, mellow glow absent in modern bulbs. Exceptionally attractive with the etched-glass shades used with most early fixtures,

Kyp-Go's bulb is perfect for turn-of-the-century lighting fixtures of all types.

Literature available

KYP-GO, INC.
PO Box 247, 20 N. 17th St.
St. Charles, IL 60174
(312) 584-8181

Lighting Fixtures. *See* **Ceiling Fixtures, Chandeliers, Floor Lamps, Hanging Fixtures, Lanterns, Sconces,** and **Table Lamps.**

Lincrusta. *See* **Wallcoverings.**

Linoleum. If you've spent too many of your days in the past removing old layers of linoleum in a kitchen or bathroom, you will rightly wonder why anyone would want to replace this scabrous material. But it, too, is now a period material with a respectable pedigree. Linoleum was first introduced in the mid-1800s in England by Frederick Walton. What he called "oiled-linen" was made with a coating of oxidized linseed oil. Adopted in North America with a passion in the late 1800s, linoleum was manufactured in vast quantities and brought an end to the use of floorcloths. To this day, sheet flooring is often called linoleum even when it is vinyl or some other synthetic. Two suppliers of true linoleum are BANGOR CORK CO. and LINOLEUM CITY.

Locks/Locksets. *See* **Door Hardware.**

Looking Glasses. *See* **Mirrors.**

Louvers. *See* **Grilles, Ventilators.**

Luminaires. *See* **Lanterns.**

Mailboxes. You would think that something as simple as a mailbox would present few problems. Yet there are few mailbox designs which are pleasing in a local hardware store, the usual models being either too lumpen or, at the other extreme, loaded with inappropriate ornament. It's too bad the Shakers weren't concerned with wordly mail. One of their well-designed wood boxes with a lid could have served nicely for a mailbox. There *are* antique mailboxes, but these are generally of the type used by official agencies and are as inappropriate for home use as one of Her Majesty's scarlet post bins of which more than a few have drifted across the Atlantic. For a box that is by the front door, one can sometimes find a brass or iron bin with a lid in a giftware or accessories shop. For a rural box by the side of the road, a coat of enamel paint can do wonders to a regulation model. Or, if you are truly desperate, buy one of the boxes offered by the sporting goods suppliers and paint over the flying geese or cardinals.

Mantels. The return of the fireplace to the American interior in recent years has been accompanied by the use of a mantel. Many old-house owners have had to reopen fireplaces and replace mantels which had been torn out in the frenzy of installing central heating or a freestanding heating stove during the late 1800s. An amazing number of mantels of all types have survived to be recycled in the 1900s and are stock items with many architectural antiques firms. Sometimes, however, an entirely new mantel must be installed. There are a goodly number of woodworkers and other craftspeople who can help out as well as importers of traditional British and European designs. In general, the style of a mantel follows that of the architectural decoration of a room. If of wood, the mantel should blend in with the lines of the moldings. This is especially important in Colonial interiors where all the wood trimmings – doors and window casings, any paneling or wainscoting, and other moldings – should appear to be the work of one individual. Marble, slate, or iron mantels are more likely to be found in Victorian houses of a mixed or eclectic style. These mantels should not blend in as inconspicuously as the earlier wood models. In fact, the use of mantels in more expensive materials – or, in the case of slate, in imitation of marble – was intended to impress, to underline the fashionable taste of the homeowner. Victorian mantels of any material should be prominently displayed as the central focus of a room. The most elaborate Victorian mantels build level upon level, towering high above the fireplace *(see* **Chimney Breasts/Overmantels)**, and often incorporate shelves and a mirror. Only the most important rooms in a house, such as a parlor or dining room, are likely, however, to have any sort of elaborate mantelpiece. The mantels used in private areas such as bedrooms tend to be much simpler, whether the dwelling is of Colonial or Victorian vintage.

In the pursuit of a proper fireplace treatment, it is well to keep in mind that many early Colonial homes had no mantels at all. A shelf above the opening was all that time or money could afford. This is often the case with a cooking fireplace in the kitchen or keeping room, an all-purpose space where food was prepared and served and various chores were performed. In time, however, even this room might have been fitted with a mantel. Appointments change from generation to generation. Wood mantels took the place of shelves, and one hundred years later there may have been yet another switch to slate or marble. Only when the fireplace seemed to have lost its practical function did the art of the mantel decline. Even then, many remained to define a blank space on the wall.

The variety of mantels available today – antique and reproduction – is probably greater than at any time in the past.

ARTEFACT ARCHITECTURAL ANTIQUES
Architectural antiques from the late

1700s to the 1920s fill the quarters of Artefact in the former Doylestown Agricultural Works in central Bucks County, Pennsylvania. Fireplace mantels are among the prizes in wood. The carved ornamental mantel illustrated probably dates from the late 1800s.

Profile sheets and photos of inventory available

ARTEFACT ARCHITECTURAL ANTIQUES
130 S. Main St.
Doylestown, PA 18901
(215) 340-1213

THE BRASS KNOB
One of the largest suppliers of architectural antiques, The Brass Knob always had a good stock of fireplace mantels on hand. A very late Victorian mantel with overmantel is shown here. It includes side vent units which probably also served as stands for vases. China and knicknacks may have occupied the upper shelves.

Brochure available

THE BRASS KNOB
2311 18th St., NW
Washington, DC 20009
(202) 332-3370

HERITAGE MANTELS INC.
The most expensive and exclusive fireplace mantels were made of marble. Until the mid-19th century, their use in North America was limited by expense to the homes of the very wealthy. Of the limited number of marble mantels in use, most were imported as skilled craftsmen were not usually available to carve in stone. As Americans became more affluent, marble works were established to supply domestic needs. The marble composition mantels made today by Heritage are molded copies of traditional designs and are of a pulverized quarry marble and fillers held together with a binding agent. There is a wide range of styles, as illustrated, which encompasses the neoclassical and various Victorian revivals. The first model, no. 132, is of a white marble with green inserts. Following that is model no. 128, in a shade the manufacturers call Italian bianco or white; the third mantel, no. 125, is in the same shade. Heritage also offers a very handsome green neoclassical mantel and a very simple frame of moldings in black and white.

Catalog, $3

HERITAGE MANTELS, INC.
PO Box 240
Southport, CT 06490
(203) 335-0552

figured burls and inlays is in the development stage. About 50 percent of Maizefield's business is done on a custom basis, and the firm can reproduce just about any design submitted to it.

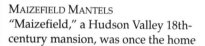

MAIZEFIELD MANTELS
"Maizefield," a Hudson Valley 18th-century mansion, was once the home

Victorian interior, although a new line of late 19th-century mantels with shelving, beveled mirrors, and highly

of Sebastian Eggert, proprietor of Maizefield Mantels. With eight working fireplaces, each with a different mantel, Eggert had all the inspiration he needed to produce traditional designs. These are now fabricated on the other side of the continent, in Washington state, of kiln-dried hemlock. Illustrated, in order of appearance, are three stock models: Revere, Franklin, and Astor. The last of these designs includes applied ornamentation and would be most appropriate for a Colonial Revival dwelling. This is the only stock Maizefield model suitable for a

Catalog, $3

MAIZEFIELD MANTELS
PO Box 336
Port Townsend, WA 98368
(206) 385-6789

FRANCIS J. PURCELL II
Extraordinary carved antique mantels make up Purcell's collection of more than 100 examples. The detail shown would be very difficult for a craftsman to capture today. Both mantels illustrated date from the early 1800s and were made in the Philadelphia area. The first is gouge carved of pine; the second is an intricately carved mantel carrying, on the central panel, a view of the Battle of Lake Erie and the motto "WE HAVE MET THE ENEMY AND THEY ARE OURS." To possess such a mantel as this commemorative one would be a privilege. For an updated list of antique inventory, contact:

FRANCIS J. PURCELL II
88 N. Main St.
New Hope, PA 18938
(215) 862-9100

QUEEN CITY ARCHITECTURAL SALVAGE
Antique mantels form an important part of Queen City's regular inventory. Owner Tom Sundheim has been dismantling and saving old buildings and objects of art for eighteen years. Unfortunately his place of business, Denver, has suffered measurably from the rush to renew in the 1960s and '70s. The carved wood mantel shown may

have come out of one of Denver's late 19th-century houses. Happily or unhappily, depending on your perspective, there are others like it at Queen City.

Photos available, $1 and SASE

QUEEN CITY ARCHITECTURAL SALVAGE
PO Box 16541
Denver, CO 80216
(303) 296-0925

SUNSHINE ARCHITECTURAL WOODWORKS
As explained earlier in this book (*see* **Chimney Breasts/Overmantels**), Sunshine Architectural Woodworks is a prime supplier of reproduction Colonial chimney breasts and paneled room ends. Standard size mantels without an upper section are also produced, most in kiln-dried poplar in a paint or stain grade. They can also be manufactured in walnut, cherry, mahogany, or oak. Many of the designs feature a raised center panel or a carved oval panel.

Catalog, $5

SUNSHINE ARCHITECTURAL WOODWORKS
2169 Sunshine Dr., Dept. C
Fayetteville, AR 72703
(800) 628-8004
Fax (501) 521-8863

Other suppliers of antique mantels are:
ARCHITECTURAL ANTIQUE CO.,
ARCHITECTURAL ANTIQUES EXCHANGE,
FLORIDA VICTORIAN ARCHITECTURAL

ANTIQUES, GOVERNOR'S ANTIQUES, IRREPLACEABLE ARTIFACTS, SALVAGE ONE, and WESTLAKE ARCHITECTURAL ANTIQUES.

Other suppliers of reproduction mantels are: ARCHITECTURAL ANTIQUES EXCHANGE, BAILEY'S ARCHITECTURAL MILLWORK INC., THE BALMER ARCHITECTURAL ART STUDIOS, MARION H. CAMPBELL, CABINETMAKER, CREATIVE WOODWORKING LTD., EARLY NEW ENGLAND ROOMS & EXTERIORS, INC., FOURTH BAY, KENTUCKY MILLWORK, SHEPPARD MILLWORK, INC., SOMERSET DOOR & COLUMN CO., TRADITIONAL LINE ARCHITECTURAL RESTORATION LTD., FREDERICK WILBUR, WOODCARVER, and WORTHINGTON GROUP LTD.

Masonry Restoration. *See* **Contractors, Restoration.**

Medallions, Rosettes, Centerpieces. Decorations for the center of a ceiling are among the most popular interior ornaments used today in traditional homes. They are most commonly known as "medallions," but the terms "rosette" and "centerpiece" are sometimes substituted. The latter term aptly describes the function of these circles, squares, or oval forms. "Rosette" is a misnomer and more properly describes a small circular decoration used together with moldings. Traditionally cast in plaster, medallions are now more frequently molded of a polyurethane formula. A limited selection of lightweight polyurethane medallions can be found in many home centers. Very few of these designs, however, have the quality of relief work that makes for an effective ornament, one that has the look of being cast and not stamped out. A medallion is sometimes used in combination with other ceiling decorations, but most commonly it appears alone, a lighting fixture being hung from its center. For this reason, most designs are made with a hole through which a chain or rod carrying the wiring is threaded. A canopy may be used to cover up the opening.

Medallions have been used for many hundreds of years in formal areas such as front halls, dining rooms, parlors and libraries. There are designs appropriate for almost all periods of historic design. Medallions are most fitting for high-style

interiors. It would be rare to find a medallion in an early Colonial house, a vernacular farmhouse of the 19th-century, or an Arts and Crafts bungalow. Determining the proper size of a medallion is one common problem that every homeowner faces. A fabricator of fibrous gypsum medallions, THE BALMER ARCHITECTURAL ART STUDIOS, recommends the following formula: "For a rough guide to the diameter, calculate the area of the room and divide by 7, e.g. 14' x 16' = 224/7 = 32". You may safely add or substract several inches."

THE BALMER ARCHITECTURAL ART
   STUDIOS
Very traditional European centerpieces comprise Balmer's inventory. Over eighty designs are featured in the firm's catalog, most of which can only be described as extremely ornate. The relief work is first-rate, and it helps that the ornaments are cast of fibrous gypsum which takes detail exceptionally well. All but twelve medallions include a $3^3/_4$" center hole. The diameters of the pieces range from 10" to 96".

Full catalog, $20

THE BALMER ARCHITECTURAL ART
   STUDIOS
9 Codeco Ct.
Don Mills, ONT M3A 1B6
Canada
(416) 449-2155
Fax (416) 449-3018

FOCAL POINT
The leading manufacturer of polyurethane moldings and ornaments, Focal Point has contributed greatly to the new popularity of medallions in interior design. Each of the designs is remarkably articulated with projections varying from under an inch to nearly 3". All medallions come with a center hole, the usual size being 15/16". Diameters or widths (in the ovals and squares) range from under 7" to more than to 39". In addition to traditional neoclassic, rococo, and Renaissance revival designs, Focal Point features the Victorian Society in America collection of 19th-century medallions and the new Historic Natchez collection of Greek Revival or antebellum designs. Focal Point also offers a small selection of rosettes

which can be used with a medallion to cover a center hole or as door and window casing ornaments.

Catalog, $3

FOCAL POINT
PO Box 93327
Atlanta, GA 30377-0327
(800) 662-5550
(404) 351-0820 (GA and AK)
Fax (404) 352-9049

GIANNETTI'S STUDIO, INC.
Medallions that are cast in plaster with fiber reinforcement have been made by Giannetti for many years. Most of the designs are circular with a few ovals available on a custom basis. Diameters vary from 15" to 30".

Ceiling medallions brochure available, $3

GIANNETTI'S STUDIO, INC.
3806 38th St.
Brentwood, MD 20722
(301) 927-0033
Fax (301) 779-5193

SAN FRANCISCO VICTORIANA, INC.
Medallions appear in many Bay area houses and it is difficult to determine now whether they are originals or copies from Victoriana. Because these centerpieces are so well cast in gypsum plaster, it really does not matter which is which. There are thirty-eight stock designs in round or oval form, and the relief projects at least 1" and may reach 6". Victoriana suggests that a room ceiling height be used to determine the amount of decorative relief selected, with lower ceilings (8' to 9') accepting less decoration, and higher ceilings (12' to 14'), more. There are, however, stylistic considerations as well. Many of the Victoriana designs are taken from antique examples found in San Francisco's late 19th-century interiors. Those illustrated here are of that

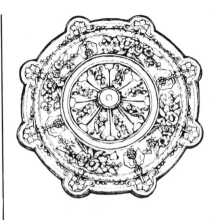

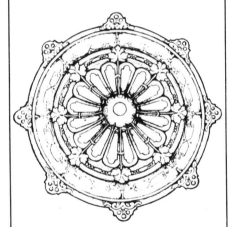

variety and carry names familiar to Bay area residents. This does not exclude their use elsewhere, but it does mean that most of these designs are not appropriate for Colonial or early 19th-century interiors. Victoriana also offers a selection of cast rosettes, or what are also termed "buttons," as well as two types of canopies which function in the same manner as medallions.

Catalog, $5

SAN FRANCISCO VICTORIANA, INC.
2070 Newcomb Ave.

San Francisco, CA 94124
(415) 648-0313
Fax (415) 648-2812

WORTHINGTON GROUP LTD.
A small selection of neoclassic medallions cast in plaster are offered by Worthington. Illustrated is the Adams design, 45" in diameter, which would enhance the interior of any late 18th- or early 19th-century home.

Catalog, $3

WORTHINGTON GROUP LTD.
PO Box 53101
Atlanta, GA 30355
(800) 872-1608
(404) 872-1608
Fax (404) 872-8501

Other suppliers of ceiling medallions are: DECORATOR'S SUPPLY CORP., FELBER STUDIOS, INC., MARK A. KNUDSEN, NOSTALGIA, INC., RENOVATOR'S SUPPLY, RESTORATION WORKS, INC., and J. P. WEAVER CO.

Metalwork, Custom. Work in special metals such as copper, brass, and bronze is usually done on a custom basis only. The skills necessary are not widely available, and the demand for decorative objects in such metals is not great except in the field of lighting devices. There are, however, several individuals who pride themselves in their fine metalsmithing and hammerwork skills and have successfully undertaken major restoration or replication work for public agencies, including the National Park Service, museums, antique dealers, and individual homeowners. Among these are NED JAMES, WROUGHT METALS, BRIAN F. LEO, and the craftspeople of the NEW ENGLAND TOOL CO. See also **Chandeliers, Fencing and Gates, Ironwork, Lanterns, Sconces.**

Mirrors. Since almost any smooth surface will reflect light, mirrors have been known since antiquity, but mirrors made from glass, surprisingly, did not appear until the 16th century – in Venice, center of European glassmaking. Not until the 1670s was glass for mirrors made in England, and it was clearly the close of the 18th century before even a small amount was produced in the United States. Looking glasses, as mirrors were then called, were expensive and, consequently, prized possessions, and because of the dearness of mirror glass (then produced in small sheets), mirrors were quite small. As a result, mirror *frames* took on increased importance as they enhanced the small areas of glass. Mirrors, then, utilize the work of two different artisans – glassmaker and cabinetmaker – and their ever-changing styles reflect the march of fashion in both arts. Every new style in furniture – from Chippendale to Art Deco and beyond – has had its corresponding style in mirrors. For this reason, most cabinetmakers who reproduce fine period furniture will also custom make mirrors, as will picture framers, particularly those sensitive to period design. One cabinetmaker listed in this book, RICHARD A. BRUNKUS, makes particularly beautiful mirrors in the style of primitive American painted furniture. More formal 18th- and 19th-century looking glasses are precisely crafted by the cabinetmaker GERALD CURRY. And then, of course, there are still antique mirrors to be found in such architectural antiques establishments as ARCHITECTURAL ANTIQUES EXCHANGE and in hundreds of antiques shops from coast to coast.

ARTEFACT PICTURE FRAMERS LTD.
Enjoying a distinguished reputation as one of England's leading specialist mirror makers, Artefact offers a wide selection of custom crafted mirrors in traditional styles from Regency to Victorian. With good reason Artefact calls itself a firm of "perfectionists," a designation the accompanying photograph can only support. Shown are the classic lines of Regency mirrors, several styles of Victorian dome mirrors, and a unique Portico mirror. Artefact mirrors are available in a choice of standard or custom finishes.

Literature available

ARTEFACT PICTURE FRAMERS LTD.
353 Upper St.
Islington, London N1 8EA
England
(071) 226-8867

EAGLE EYE TRADING CO.
This enterprising firm retails and manufactures quality reproductions of antique looking glasses dating back as far as the 17th century. Eagle Eye's catalog includes a wide variety of looking glasses, each handmade to exacting specifications and none available from any other source. Eagle Eye also cleans, repairs, gilds, re-silvers, and rebuilds antique looking glasses from any period. The company will provide a free estimate if it is supplied with a good 8" x 10" color photograph of the mirror together with a detailed description of the damage.

Catalog, $6

EAGLE EYE TRADING CO.
PO Box 17900
Milwaukee, WI 53217
(414) 374-1984

RAVENGLASS PTY. LTD.
Ravenglass specializes in Victorian and Art Nouveau mirrors and cabinets, many of which incorporate stained glass and leaded glass in their design. Handcrafted of solid oak, these handsome pieces feature elaborate scrolled wood in a choice of stains, although other woods are available upon request. While Ravenglass includes many mirrors in varied shapes and sizes in its catalog of stock designs, it welcomes custom orders. Shown is the Coventry mirror, a graceful scrollwork piece with inlaid stained glass in several shades

of blue.

Catalog, free

RAVENGLASS PTY. LTD.
PO Box 612
Goodland, KS 67735
(913) 899-2297

An additional supplier of period looking glasses is THE COUNTRY BED SHOP.

Mitres. *See* **Ornaments.**

Modillons. *See* **Brackets.**

Molder Knives. Molder knives and shaper knives are the tools that make it possible for woodworkers to replicate period molding and are, of course, indispensable for accurate restoration of old houses. Unfortunately, most local millwork suppliers carry a few stock molding profiles and are incapable of

reproducing non-stock profiles because they lack the proper equipment to do so. The next time your neighborhood supplier cannot replicate the exact profile of a molding sample you bring him, refer him to F. A. Compton III, president of COUNSELOR PROFILES, manufacturers of shaper and molder knives used in furniture, cabinet, and molding restorations. Counselor specializes in custom designs (non-stock profiles) for all molder machines, including Williams & Hussey, Foley-Belsaw, Wilke-Bridgewood, SCMI, Wadkin, Weinig, and, of course, all shaper collar/knife systems. Although Counselor Profiles is a commercial woodwork tooling establishment serving the molding, shaping, and tenoning needs of some of North America's largest furniture and window manufacturers, the company believes that local cabinet and millwork shops can have the same technology and expertise as industrial firms – and at a moderate cost. For further information about Counselor molder and shaping knives, contact Mr. Compton at COUNSELOR PROFILES, 40 Lawlins Park, Wyckoff, NJ 07481, (800) 635-6285, Fax (201) 848-9867.

Moldings. Moldings are used in almost every old house, plain or high-style. Even Spanish Colonial adobe dwellings may contain wood profiles around doors and windows. The basic purpose of a molding is to hide a seam, a place where two walls come together or where the ceiling, floor, window, or door meets a wall. The extent and the type of moldings used are indicators of a building's style or lack thereof. A Queen Anne Victorian parlor, for example, might contain examples of crown moldings, complex door and window casings, a picture rail, a chair rail, baseboard moldings, corner beads, and panel moldings. At the other extreme, a parlor in an early New England Colonial often displays nothing more than door and window casing moldings with only a slight beaded profile. In a Georgian Colonial or high-Victorian interior, moldings may also be used simply for their decorative effect, much as a frame defines a picture on the wall.

Our concern here is with crown or cornice moldings and panel mold-

ings, the former used at the meeting of ceiling and wall, and the latter intended to define wall space. These are the most decorative of all moldings and are available in wood, composition, metal, plaster, and polyurethane. A small selection of both these moldings may be available locally, but most must be ordered from specialty outlets. For information on other molding types, *see* the entries for **Baseboards, Chair Rails, Door Casings and Window Casings, Friezes, Picture Rails,** and **Plate Rails.**

AMERICAN CUSTOM MILLWORK INC. A great variety of moldings suitable for cornices are available through American Custom. The design illustrated – cornice assembly CC400 – is representative of the firm's elegant

millwork. A cornice molding actually may be a series or assembly of moldings which can include, as does the example illustrated, embossed elements. Any embossed molding design, however, is also available plain. Appalachian poplar is used for all American Custom moldings unless another wood is specified. Particularly complex cornice assemblies with a considerable profile may require furring out. Boards for this purpose can be supplied.

Catalog, $5

AMERICAN CUSTOM MILLWORK INC.
3904 Newton Rd., PO Box 3608
Albany, GA 31706
(912) 888-3303
Fax (912) 888-9245

AMHERST WOODWORKING & SUPPLY, INC.
Highly ornamental cornice and panel moldings are stock items with Amherst. Reflecting a New England background, the designs are primarily Colonial. From Amherst's 250 moldings, however, just about any style, design, or assembly can be put together. Any special molding knife needed for creating a new profile can be machined right in the shop. Stock woods at Amherst are cedar, butternut, cherry, mahogany, red and white oak, black walnut, ash, birch, maple, poplar, select pine, and teak.

Literature available

AMHERST WOODWORKING & SUPPLY, INC.
Box 718, Hubbard Ave.
Northampton, MA 01061
(413) 584-3003
Fax (413) 585-0288

BENDIX MOULDINGS, INC.
One of the best names in decorative wood moldings, Bendix specializes in carved as well as embossed designs. Almost all are one-piece moldings and, therefore, not quite as complex as those by some other suppliers. The carved crown moldings are unornamented; the embossed designs feature traditional ornamentation such

as dentils, egg-and-dart, and acanthus leaves. Bendix also has a small but select group of panel moldings for use on walls.

Catalog, $3

BENDIX MOULDINGS, INC.
37 Ramland Rd. South
Orangeburg, NY 10962-2697
(914) 365-1111
Fax (914) 365-1218

FOCAL POINT, INC.
Along with medallions, one-piece cornice moldings have established Focal Point's reputation. All are molded in a special polyurethane formula. The relief work is very fine with most projections being those of more traditional plaster or wood moldings. A number of the cornice moldings have been modeled directly on historic examples. Included in this category are the Colonial Williamsburg, Historic Natchez, The American 19th Century, and the National Trust for Historic Preservation collections. The Victorian designs, licensed by the Victorian Society in America, are particularly good to have as many millwork firms do not as yet offer distinctive late 19th-century patterns featuring a combination of blocks and liner moldings. Many moldings in all styles can be provided in Contour-All material in addition to the standard Endure-All formula. As the name suggests, Contour-All is a formula with special elasticity which lends itself to curved or very irregular surfaces.

Catalog, $3

FOCAL POINT, INC.
(800) 662-5550
(404) 351-0820 (GA and AK)
Fax (404) 352-9049

GIANNETTI'S STUDIO, INC.
Giannetti's plaster crown moldings are like those found in elegant Colonial Maryland and Virginia interiors. They are beautifully defined ornaments molded in one solid piece and do not require furring or angling. Appropriately, the designs, some of which reach a height of 9" to 11", are almost uniformly neoclassical in inspiration. If assistance is needed in installation, Giannetti will quote on this phase of the work as well.

Crown Mouldings brochure, $3

GIANNETTI'S STUDIO, INC.
3806 38th St.
Brentwood, MD 20722
(301) 927-0033
Fax (301) 779-5193

KENTUCKY MILLWORK INC.
Custom moldings suitable for ceilings will be made by Kentucky in just about any hardwood or softwood. A subsidiary of Kentucky Wood Floors, the millwork unit prides itself in providing decoration that matches the parent firm's flooring in grain and color. Although most crown moldings are painted, there are instances where a wood finish would be more appropriate, thus bringing the firm's expertise to full play. Any of the moldings it supplies, of course, can be painted as long as a paint grade wood is specified.

Literature available

KENTUCKY MILLWORK INC.
4200 Reservoir Ave.
Louisville, KY 40213
(502) 451-3456
Fax (502) 451-6027

NOSTALGIA, INC.
This is a firm that has made its reputation in architectural antiques. It recently became the distributor of plaster ornaments, including cornice moldings, produced by Sort & Chasle of Nantes, France. Illustrated is one of thirty crown moldings offered. Like others in plaster, it is molded in one piece and does not require furring or special angling in installation. The

design shown is a classic acanthus leaf pattern. Although the designs are French, they are very similar to the neoclassical patterns which were used in Colonial North America during the 18th and early 19th centuries.

Catalog available at no charge

NOSTALGIA, INC.
307 Stiles Ave.
Savannah, GA 31401
(912) 232-2324
(800) 874-0015
Fax (912) 234-5746

W. F. NORMAN CORP.
Noted for its metal ceilings, Norman manufactures many matching or complementary metal cornices. Some of these are assemblies comprised of a crown and a frieze molding. The stamped moldings of sheet zinc have a most impressive depth of relief and projection. They are especially suitable for exterior use and have been widely utilized over the years for marquees and other decorative embellishments. The moldings can be stamped from other materials, including copper, bronze, and aluminum. The molds used were developed by Norman in the very early 1900s.

Ceiling catalog, $5

American customers contact:
W. F. NORMAN CORP.
214 N. Cedar
Nevada, MO 64772
(800) 641-4038
(471) 667-5552 (MO)

Canadian customers contact:
STEPTOE & WIFE ANTIQUES LTD.
322 Geary Ave.
Toronto, ONT M6H 2C7
Canada
(416) 530-4200

ORNAMENTAL MOULDINGS LTD.
Ornamental specializes in embossed
moldings available in either one-piece
units or assemblies. Illustrated is a
graceful dentil crown molding, one of
nine stock designs in this category.
Kiln-dried poplar is standard, but
some designs are also made in oak or

a white hardwood.

Brochure available

American customers contact:
ORNAMENTAL MOULDINGS LTD.
PO Box 7123
High Point, NC 27264

Canadian customers contact:
ORNAMENTAL MOULDINGS LTD.
289 Marsland Dr., PO Box 336
Waterloo, ONT N2J 4A4
Canada
(519) 884-4080
Fax (519) 884-9692

SAN FRANCISCO VICTORIANA, INC.
Victoriana is unique in offering both
wood *and* plaster cornice moldings.
The selection in wood is, understandably, much greater and includes
embossed designs as well as plain.
Illustrated are two of the plaster
moldings, a simple dentil and a more
complex acanthus leaf design. Plaster
moldings are cast in one piece,
whereas many of the wood designs
must be assembled. Of special interest
in the wood category are several sizes

of cove molding, one of the most frequently encountered profile patterns
in a ceiling cornice. The simplest of
these cove profiles require no furring
or special angling, making installation relatively easy.

Catalog, $5

SAN FRANCISCO VICTORIANA, INC.
2070 Newcomb Ave.
San Francisco, CA 94124
(415) 648-0313
Fax (415) 648-2812

SILVERTON VICTORIAN MILLWORKS
No category of architectural millwork
would be complete without the inclusion of Silverton. This is a firm that
has provided countless homeowners
with the essential elements of late
19th-century decoration. Stock cornice assemblies may serve most purposes. Silverton also provides outside
and inside corner blocks and drops
that can be used with the moldings, a
common late-Victorian arrangement.
Silverton calls these additions "crown
corners" and offers two stock designs.
Custom-order crown moldings are
also regularly produced by the millworks.

Complete catalog package, $4

SILVERTON VICTORIAN MILLWORKS
PO Box 2987-OC7
Durango, CO 81302
(303) 259-5915
Fax (303) 259-5919

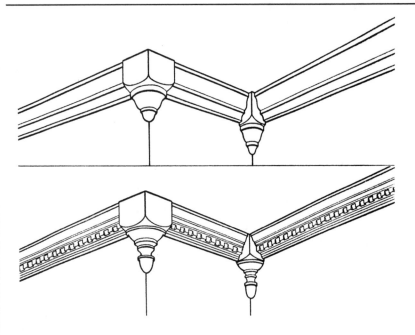

*Other suppliers of crown moldings
include:* ARCHITECTURAL COMPONENTS,
INC., ARTISTIC WOODWORKING
PRODUCTS, BALMER ARCHITECTURAL
ART STUDIOS, BLUE OX MILLWORKS,
CRAFTSMAN LUMBER CO., CREATIVE
WOODWORKING LTD., DECORATORS
SUPPLY CORP., EARLY NEW ENGLAND
ROOMS & EXTERIORS, INC., FELBER
STUDIOS, INC., FRANK J. MANGIONE,
SHEPPARD MILLWORK, INC., SOMERSET
DOOR & COLUMN CO., SUNSHINE
ARCHITECTURAL WOODWORKS, J. P.
WEAVER CO., FREDERICK WILBUR,
WOODCARVER, and WORTHINGTON
GROUP, LTD.

*Double dentil crown molding, front
drawing room, Benjamin Dulaney
House, Alexandria, Virginia. Photograph
by Victor Amato, Historic American
Buildings Survey.*

Panel ornament, dining room, Morse-Libby House, Portland, Maine. Historic American Buildings Survey.

Nails, Old-Style. Nails have been in use since iron came into general use eons ago. And for centuries they have been seen as a symbol of care and security. "For want of a nail the shoe was lost; for want of a shoe the horse was lost; and for want of a horse the rider was lost." Or so Benjamin Franklin wrote. (Or did he? Actually, he lifted this bit of wisdom, word for word, from English poet George Herbert who had already been dead for three-quarters of a century when Franklin was born.) Many old-house dwellers don't have to worry about shoeing their horses, but they should worry about the slates on their roofs, the millwork on their floors, the siding on their walls. If these are held in place by old-style nails, then most of their worry can be put to rest, for cut nails are extremely durable. They are tougher then today's wire nails, which pull out easily, because wood fibers are pushed downward when old-style nails are used, thus wedging the nail in place and preventing loosening. In the late 18th century, the first nail-making machine was invented by Ezekiel Reed of Bridgewater, Massachusetts. Although improved machines in the following century ultimately replaced handmade nails, these early machines still produced nails in the old style and in several variations and sizes. But soon the 20th-century wire nail became the norm, even though what's new is not necessarily better. Fortunately, there are still firms, and even individual craftsmen, producing old-style nails, thus ensuring old-house owners of the structural security their antecedents enjoyed and a small degree of added old-house beauty. (Flooring and wainscoting look particularly dreadful with *new* nails.) After all, as

FORGERIES (*See below*) writes, "When the woodwork looks good," make certain to "ensure it isn't spoiled with ironwork that looks better on rabbit hutches."

FORGERIES
This English firm of ironmongers is as swift with the pen as it is with the anvil. Its old-fashioned ironwork is "not *like* the real thing, it *is* the real

thing." And this includes nails. "Handmade nails, like handmade needles, really are a thing of the past," they write. "Even ours are machine-made . . . but on machines dating back to the industrial revolution. They aren't smooth like new wires. And they do have a proper 'rose' head, not like a modern nail. The most useful are the 40mm

door nails with a head 7mm across or rose heads twice the size. They come in packets of 20 or by the kilo. We also have limited quantities of smaller nails suitable for our latches. Other sizes are available to order – natural color or galvanized, clasps, cuts, or studs." These evocative photographs testify that Forgeries' forgeries don't look like forgeries at all.

Free brochure

FORGERIES
Old Butchery
High Street
Twyford, Hants SO21 1RF
England
Tel. and Fax (0962) 712196

CRAFTSMAN LUMBER COMPANY
Charles E. Thibeau owns the Craftsman Lumber Company, which specializes in supplying kiln-dried pine and custom millwork for restoration and reproduction work. As one might expect, his work has made him an expert in many areas of construction, including the use of nails in flooring and wainscoting. "If you're using pine," he writes, "the traditional approach is to face-nail with cut-steel nails. Use 10d nails, or 8d if you're going into 2x sleepers. Nail about 1 inch from either edge and about 5 inches apart in the field. At the ends of the boards, nail about an inch in, angled to catch the joist. Because of the blunt nail heads, you should not have to predrill any holes. Set the nails about $^1/_{16}$ inch below the surface before lightly sanding." Because of the difficulty in locating traditional old-style nails, Craftsman Lumber stocks two of the most essential types for millwork, both

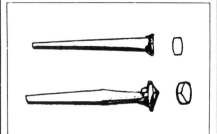

illustrated here. For pine flooring, use common cut-steel nails (top). A wrought head (bottom) is used for pine paneling or wainscoting. Craftsman sells these nails by the pound.

Literature, 50¢

CRAFTSMAN LUMBER COMPANY
Box 222, 436 Main St.
Groton, MA 01450
(508) 448-6336

TREMONT NAIL COMPANY
For over 170 years, Tremont Nail Company has enjoyed a reputation for the production of cut nails of the highest quality and remains the only producer of old-style nails making as many as twenty different patterns. Although the company traces its origins back to 1819, it has been making nails in the same building since 1848. As America's oldest nail manufacturer, Tremont is able not only to offer nails appropriate to almost any period restoration being undertaken, but it can also provide historical information to help the restorer in determining what types of nails would be authentic to the period of the house. Among the old-style nails offered (and in as many sizes as sixteen) are common, floor, masonry, shingle, slating, sheathing, brads, common siding, hinge, clinch rosehead, common rosehead, wrought head, and eight other types of nails. In addition to a standard finish, several types are also galvanized or mechanically zinc plated. Tremont Nail Company may also be the only place in the world to go for jewelry made from old-style cut nails! Men's tie tacs and cuff links and women's stick pins, incorporating old-style nails, are made on a 125-year-old nail-making machine.

Literature available; sample set of twenty nail patterns, $4.50

TREMONT NAIL COMPANY
8 Elm St., PO Box 111
Wareham, MA 02571
(508) 295-0038

Other suppliers of old-style nails are: EARLY NEW ENGLAND ROOMS & EXTERIORS, INC., KAYNE & SON CUSTOM FORGED HARDWARE, and THE WOODBURY BLACKSMITH & FORGE CO.

Newel Posts. See Posts.

Niche Caps and Units. A niche is a wall recess, and the cap which often fits at the top is dome-shaped. Traditionally, a niche would be used to display sculpture or an ornamental object such as an urn. It is rare to find a niche used in a North American interior, but they are occasionally found in Georgian Colonial and Federal interiors, especially in dining rooms and stair landings. A niche opening may be as small as several feet in height, but most are of a size similar to interior doors.

THE BALMER ARCHITECTURAL ART
STUDIOS
The long experience of this firm in plaster ornamentation holds them in good stead when it comes to such specialty items as niches. All of the niche shafts feature shell caps. Shaft and shell are available attached and ready for installation. Shafts run from 48" to 61" in height, and to this must be added the shell or cap height which may range from $11^3/_4$" to 19". Seven shell designs are offered in widths from $16^1/_2$" to 43"; a depth to accommodate the shaft is taken into consideration.

Balmer suggests that a shell can be used in an opening without a niche shaft. This may be only a square rather than a rounded space in the wall containing shelves. The effect is that of a cupboard without doors which has been set into the wall. Square or rounded, a niche will still require side moldings and blocks which match the shell cap. Balmer can provide these additional elements which are used very much like a door or window casing. The usual design is a fluted pediment molding.

Full catalog, $20

THE BALMER ARCHITECTURAL ART
STUDIOS
9 Codeco Ct.
Don Mills, ONT M3A 1B6
Canada
(416) 449-2155
Fax (416) 449-3018

FOCAL POINT, INC.
The desire for such an elegant feature as a niche is being met by Focal Point in one-piece units as well as combinations of shaft, shell, casing, and shelf bracket. All of the Focal Point designs are suggested for use with either a simple shelf or one with a tapered bottom like a basin. There are six integral niche unit designs which run from 3' to nearly 5' high overall. Widths overall range from

16⅞" to 32⅞". The rough opening needed for these units will be slightly larger. Niche shells or caps, moldings for the caps, and side moldings for an opening are also sold separately from the one-piece integral units. A special polyurethane formula is used for all the products.

Catalog, $3

FOCAL POINT, INC.
PO Box 93327
Atlanta, GA 30377-0327
(800) 662-5550
(404) 351-0820 (GA and AK)
Fax (404) 352-9049

WORTHINGTON GROUP LTD.
As illustrated, integral niches are offered by Worthington. These are cast in England in a dense, reinforced plaster. Although not shown here, bases in a basin form can be ordered as well. The niche farthest back in the photo has outside dimensions of 53" high and 33" wide; the middle design is 43½" high and 22" wide. The plain niche model in front may be made in almost any size.

Catalog, $3

WORTHINGTON GROUP LTD.
PO Box 53101
Atlanta, GA 30355
(800) 872-1608
(404) 872-1608
Fax (404) 872-8501

Other suppliers of niche units and caps are: FELBER STUDIOS, INC., FRANK J. MANGIONE, and NOSTALGIA, INC.

Notions, Sewing. Decorative items such as braid, tassels, gimp, and other trimmings for draperies, tiebacks, cushions, lampshades, and period clothing can be found in the furnishings section of most quality department stores. STANDARD TRIMMING CO. is one of the primary suppliers of these materials;

BRUNSCHWIG & FILS, SCALAMANDRÉ, and F. SCHUMACHER & CO. are other sources of both European and American-made trimmings. Notions for period clothing is a specialty of AMAZON VINEGAR & PICKLING WORKS DRYGOODS. Only here will you find such arcane materials as metal boning stays, hoop wire, maribou banding, vest buckles, and hook-and-eye tape. *See also* **Fabrics.**

Ornaments. This is a useful designation for all those infrequently used and highly decorative wall and ceiling motifs such as garlands, leaves, scrolls, shells, shields, sunbursts, and wreaths. They serve no practical purpose, but are embellishments or, as plasterers often term them, enrichments. The rich vocabulary of medieval and renaissance European design is virtually unknown in North America except in old-fashioned hotel lobbies and dining rooms, places of worship, and the baronial residences of the late 19th and early 20th centuries. Putti, heraldic shields, and baroque scrollwork are usually considered somewhat inappropriate for the American scene. More commonly used ornaments are garlands, leaves, and wreaths associated with ancient Greek democracy. This identification became well established in the early years of the new republic. Federal, Greek Revival, and Italianate house exteriors and interiors sometimes display these ancient motifs, although the American eagle remains numeri-

cally superior in its use. *See also* **Cartouches; Festoons;** and **Medallions, Rosettes, Centerpieces.**

ARCHITECTURAL IRON CO.
This firm deals primarily in fencing and gates, but is perfectly well equipped to supply other forms of metal ornamentation from stock or custom designs. Offered are simple forms such as stars and flowers and more elaborate shields, griffins, and gargoyles. Patterns for these elements are on hand.

Catalog, $4

ARCHITECTURAL IRON CO.
Box 126, Schocopee Rd.
Milford, PA 18337
(717) 296-7722
(212) 243-2664
Fax (717) 296-IRON

ARTISTIC WOODWORKING PRODUCTS
Embossed ornaments, also known as carvings, enjoyed a great vogue early in this century. They were used primarily for furniture, but also were applied architecturally on walls and mantels. Artistic Woodworking produces over 300 stamped designs from original hand-tooled brass dies. For architectural uses it is best to have these embossed on a specialty wood such as oak, walnut, mahogany, cherry, and redwood.

Catalog, $4

ARTISTIC WOODWORKING PRODUCTS
PO Box 4625
Englewood, CO 80155
(303) 721-6514

DECORATORS SUPPLY CORP.
The largest selection in North America of plaster, wood fiber, and composition ornaments comes from Decorators. The plaster decorations are to be preferred for architectural work either inside or outside the house. In stock are dozens of shields, wreaths, shells, urns, and eagles, as well as many other decorative motifs. Stucco plaster is used for exterior application and plaster of Paris for interior use.

Catalog #130, Plaster Ornaments, $3

DECORATORS SUPPLY CORP.
3610-12 S. Morgan St.
Chicago, IL 60609
(312) 847-6300
Fax (312) 847-6357

W. F. NORMAN CORP.
Sheet-metal ornaments in high relief are Norman's stock in trade. Most are intended for exterior use and are stamped in sheet zinc. Shells, shields, wreaths, shell and leaf mitres, rosettes, garlands, gargoyles and caryatids, lion heads, urns, and eagles are included among the forms offered.

Sheet Metal Ornaments catalog, $5

American customers contact:
W. F. NORMAN CORP.
214 N. Cedar
Nevada, MO 64772-0323
(800) 641-4038
(417) 667-5552 (MO)

Canadian customers contact:
STEPTOE & WIFE ANTIQUES LTD.
322 Geary Ave.
Toronto, ONT M6H 2C7
Canada
(416) 530-4200
Fax (416) 530-4666

FREDERICK WILBUR, WOODCARVER
The finest ornaments have always been hand-carved, and Wilbur is extremely adept with a gouge, mallet, and plane. Floral rosettes and garlands are part of his repertoire as are moldings and acanthus brackets. Manufacturers of embossed ornamentation often use the term "carvings"; Wilbur's handiwork is the real thing and not a stamped or cast version. He can work in practically any wood.

Brochure available

FREDERICK WILBUR, WOODCARVER
PO Box 425
Lovingston, VA 22949
(804) 263-4827 (telephone and fax)

Other suppliers of ornaments include:
THE BALMER ARCHITECTURAL ART STUDIOS, BENDIX MOULDINGS, INC., FRANK J. MANGIONE, and J. P. WEAVER CO.

Outdoor Furniture. *See* **Garden Furniture.**

Outdoor Lighting. *See* **Lanterns** and **Posts.**

Ovens. This is one of those appliances which should be modern, fast, and easy. Although we are not great fans of microwave models, we are not about to give up our standard electric oven or the English kerosene-fired stove with oven which serves as a backup. Cooking in an old Dutch wall oven or in the fireplace is not for us, though they may be possible options for others. If you are fortunate to have an oven built into the fireplace wall – a common enough feature in many Colonial cooking fireplaces – you may want to give hearth baking a try. If the oven needs refurbishing, Steve Kayne of KAYNE AND SON CUSTOM FORGED HARDWARE can produce a new iron door with or without a pre-

hung frame. In some early American households, reflector ovens were used directly in the fireplace. HAMMERWORKS makes an exact reproduction of an early model in bright tin. Each oven comes with spit and two skewers, and measures 20" high, 20" wide, and 14" deep. The company claims that "these ovens will roast meat in approximately the same time as conventional ovens." Don't depend on it for Thanksgiving, but, for a less important occasion, it is surely worth a try. *See also* **Stoves.**

Round and hexagonal staircase ornaments, Women's City Club (Daniel P. Parker House), Boston, Massachusetts. Photograph by Stanley P. Mixon, Historic American Buildings Survey.

Paneling, Pusey House, near Chatham, Pennsylvania. Photograph by Ned Goode, Historic American Buildings Survey.

Painting, Decorative. Painted ornamentation is too much with us. The rage since the early '80s, there is not an effect or a method that has not been explained to death in the popular press and in countless books by British and American experts. Perhaps because painted effects are seemingly so easy to obtain, everyone wants to try his or her hand at it. In these days of ever higher household costs, this attitude is most understandable. Decorative painting, however, is an art and requires artists with an understanding of period design and architecture. There is no doubt that an amateur can acquire the basic skills and knowledge necessary to successfully grain a door, stencil a wall or floor, or marbleize a panel, but the most authentic work is likely to be produced by a professional who has dedicated his life to it. Trompe l'oeil, the creation of an illusion of space, for example, is a tricky visual conceit to achieve. Successful painted decoration of even simple types, however, should have an illusionary quality. The art is one of imitation – of rich fabrics such as watered silk, of an expensive stone like marble, of a fine-grained wood such as cherry or tiger maple. Decorative painting has developed over the centuries as an alternative and cheaper means of achieving luxurious or colorful effects. The ways in which artists have captured these elements is by sponging, graining, stenciling, glazing, gilding, and many other techniques. What is essentially fake takes on an appearance all its own, qualities of artistic merit nearly as valuable as the real thing. Painted finishes, artist and teacher JoAnne Day has explained, are meant "to fool the eye and yet still look faux, a trick that requires skill and imagination." See also **Contractors, Restoration; Gilding.**

Day Studio-Workshop, Inc. Workshops on the East and West coasts each year provide the eager amateur an excellent opportunity to learn professional skills of decorative painting. Stenciling, gilding, glazing, graining, marbleizing, and trompe l'oeil techniques are the primary subjects of these hands-on sessions. JoAnne Day and her colleagues continue to undertake decorating projects for private and commercial clients. For information regarding the current workshop schedules, contact the studio directly.

Literature available

Day Studio-Workshop, Inc.
1504 Bryant St.
San Francisco, CA 94103
(415) 626-9300

EverGreene Painting Studios, Inc. Decorative painters tend to be a rather anarchic lot, preferring to express themselves in their own way and pace. Jeff Greene, the Greene in EverGreene, has gained the approval of other painters and succeeded in welding together what is a most resourceful and enterprising crew. EverGreene has completed projects throughout the United States for commercial, public, and private clients, including the U.S. Department of State, the Vice-President's office, Bergdorf Goodman, and The Limited. EverGreene has achieved an enviable reputation for its dramatic and whimsical trompe l'oeil murals and painstakingly correct historic restoration work.

Literature available

EverGreene Painting Studios, Inc.
635 W. 23rd St.
New York, NY 10011
(212) 727-9500

Metropolis
Guenter de Vincent and his two colleagues are European-trained decorative painters who have found their skills highly valued in the preservation-conscious San Francisco area. These gentlemen are particularly adept with special paint finishes, varnishes, and lacquers, very intricate stenciling work, and texturizing.

Metropolis
1210 46th Ave.
San Francisco, CA 94122
(415) 564-5776

Monarch Painting
Victor and Guy Demasi make up Monarch, specialists in decorative painted finishes for architectural surfaces and furniture. Among their special skills are pickling, antiquing, sponging, and the creation of porphyry, marble, and tortoise finishes. One of the recent commissions, the Elias Unger House at the Johnstown Flood Memorial, Johnstown, Pennsylvania, was executed for the National Park Service.

Monarch Painting
W. Redding, CT 06896
(203) 938-9016
(203) 322-7853

THE STENCIL LIBRARY
Proper stencils are one of the most essential elements in the successful stenciling of designs. Over 200 stock designs, and any custom pattern required, are available in precise, clear polyester form from The Stencil Library. The patterns are offered in either cut or uncut forms, the latter being less expensive. Almost all sten-

cils are simple one-layer designs in which color changes are effected through the one stencil. Included in the stock portfolio are basic geometric and floral patterns, neoclassical motifs, and figural ornaments.

Catalog available, $5

STENCILWORKS
1723 Tilghman St.
Allentown, PA 18104

TROMPLOY STUDIO AND GALLERY, INC.
Despite its name, a play on the term for a painted illusion, this artists' cooperative will undertake a wide variety of work, including faux finish-

es and murals. The naive wall painting shown is an example of work for a private client. Other customers have included the New York Public Library, the Los Angeles Museum of Science and Industry, and various hotels and restaurants.

Free brochure

TROMPLOY STUDIO AND GALLERY, INC.
400 Lafayette St.
New York, NY 10003
(212) 420-1639 (telephone and fax)

Other firms undertaking decorative painting include: JOHN CANNING & CO., GRAMMAR OF ORNAMENT, RAMBUSCH, CONRAD SCHMITT STUDIOS, INC., and WIGGINS BROTHERS INTERIORS.

Paints. The variety of colors suitable for old-house interiors and facades increases each year as paint companies recognize a need for historic shades. Colonial Williamsburg, in association with MARTIN-SENOUR, pio-

TRADITIONAL LINE ARCHITECTURAL
    RESTORATION LTD.
One of Traditional Line's craftsmen is shown finishing new woodwork in a private library located in White Plains, New York. From hand-rubbed varnishes to shellac and oil finishes, Traditional Line uses 18th- and 19th-century formulas and recipes to re-create brillant and permanent coloration and effects. The firm is also experienced in cleaning and restoring original wood finishes.

TRADITIONAL LINE ARCHITECTURAL
    RESTORATION LTD.
143 W. 21st St.
New York, NY 10011
(212) 627-3555

neered in the production of traditional colors. This and other well-established paint lines based on regional
color types are always being revised
in the light of new research. There are
also smaller paint companies that
have put together carefully conceived
period paint collections. The reader is
further advised to consider the use of
custom-mixed colors. There is almost
always at least one paint merchant in
any area who enjoys the challenge of
matching one shade with another. It
costs more, of course, to have this
done, but if you plan to live with the
color for at least a few years, it should
be done right. For advice on choosing
exterior colors, there are several
guides, one of which – *Old House
Colors* by Lawrence Schwin – covers
all periods of architectural style. It is
available through STERLING
PUBLISHING CO.

CALIFORNIA PRODUCTS CORP.
Contrary to its name, the firm is New
England-based and includes an
Historic Newport line of colors. All
are for exterior use in an acrylic or
alkyd-linseed oil base. Newport
buildings of the 18th and 19th centuries are noted for their handsome
colors – soft blues, yellows, and rose
shades. There are also very strong
reds, greens, and browns. California's
standard color line of house and trim
paints features colors common
throughout Colonial New England.
Two finishes – gloss and satin – are
available. California Paints are distributed only in the Northeast; contact the company for other avenues of
supply.

CALIFORNIA PRODUCTS CORP.
169 Waverly St.
Cambridge, MA 02139
(617) 547-5300

CHROMATIC PAINT CORP.
Japan colors, so-called because they
originated in Japan, are very strong
pure-paste pigments. Used primarily
indoors, they are ideal for tinting
clear lacquers, oil-based paints, or
varnishes and are therefore often
used in decorative painting for
glazes, stenciling, staining, and other
faux finishes. Chromatic offers twenty
colors and white in a highly concen-
trated formula. Any of the colors can
be reduced in mineral spirits.

Brochure available

CHROMATIC PAINT CORP.
PO Box 690
Stony Point, NY 10980
(800) 431-7001
(914) 947-3210
Fax (914) 947-3546

COHASSET COLONIALS
Stains and a selection of oil-based
paints in traditional Colonial colors
are offered to Cohasset's customers.
Since many of the company's furniture products are sold in kit form and
require finishing, the paints have a
ready use. Cohasset advises that they
are also suitable for use on interior
walls and woodwork and will usually
cover a surface in one coat and dry to
a hard, durable finish. The company
will supply accurate paint samples.

Catalog available, $3

COHASSET COLONIALS
Cohasset, MA 02025
(800) 288-2389

COOK & DUNN PAINT CORP.
This excellent line of exterior and
interior paints needs more recognition. Because it is not based on a
particular town or region's traditional
color palette, the Cook & Dunn line
has a broad applicability. And,
because someone has done his historical research very well, there are suitable colors for all types of Colonial,
Victorian, and early 20th-century

buildings. Illustrated is a drawing
shown in one of the company's
brochures which accurately details
the use of paints on the facade of a
Queen Anne residence of the late
1800s.

COOK & DUNN PAINT CORP.
Box 117
Newark, NJ 07101
(201) 589-5580

DEVOE & RAYNOLDS CO.
"Traditions" is the name of Devoe's
historical color collection including
sixty shades. Although there are some
shades appropriate for Colonial interiors or exteriors, most of the colors
better suit a mid- to late-19th century
house. One of the oldest ready-made
paint companies in America, Devoe
has based its period collection on a
book they first issued in the 1880s,
*Exterior Decoration, Victorian Colors for
Victorian Homes*. Both this book,
which shows the homes painted in
various combinations, and actual
color chips for true color matching
are available from Devoe.

DEVOE & RAYNOLDS CO.
4000 Dupont Circle
Louisville, KY 40207
(800) 654-2616
(502) 897-9861

FINNAREN & HALEY
Meticulous paint research is behind

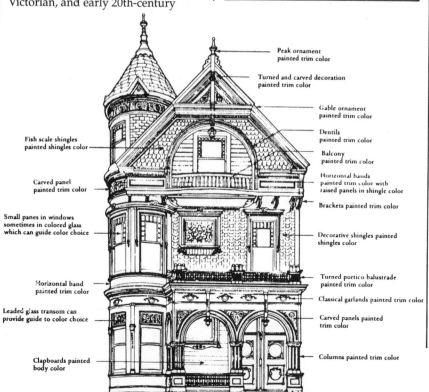

Peak ornament
painted trim color

Turned and carved decoration
painted trim color

Gable ornament
painted trim color

Dentils
painted trim color

Balcony
painted trim color

Horizontal bands
painted trim color with
raised panels in shingle color

Brackets painted trim color

Decorative shingles painted
shingles color

Turned portico balustrade
painted trim color

Classical garlands painted trim color

Carved panels painted
trim color

Columns painted trim color

Fish scale shingles
painted shingles color

Carved panel
painted trim color

Small panes in windows
sometimes in colored glass
which can guide color choice

Horizontal band
painted trim color

Leaded glass transom can
provide guide to color choice

Clapboards painted
body color

both of this company's collections - "Victorian Colors" and "Authentic Colors of Historic Philadelphia." Based in the Delaware Valley, the firm has carefully studied the rich historical record available at Independence National Historical Park and examples of Victorian architecture in such localities as Cape May, New Jersey, and south Jersey. Many of the thirty-one Philadelphia colors have been authenticated by the National Park Service and are known to have been used widely during the Colonial period.

FINNAREN & HALEY
2320 Haverford Rd.
Ardmore, PA 19003
(215) 649-5000

THE MARTIN-SENOUR CO.
Paint research has gone on uninterrupted at Colonial Williamsburg since its founding in the 1920s. For years, Martin-Senour has been designated to produce the foundation's documented colors. Forty-five interior and thirty-five exterior paints make up the line and each is named for a building in the museum complex. Interior paints are available in flat latex and satin gloss latex enamel; exterior, in a satin gloss latex. Those who prefer to work with an oil-based formula will have to try and match these colors elsewhere. Martin-Senour does, however, offer simulated whitewash in an alkyd flat blend for interior use.

THE MARTIN-SENOUR CO.
PO Box 6709
Cleveland, OH 44101
(800) 542-8468

BENJAMIN MOORE & CO.
Moore offers one of the largest selections of historical colors on the market today. The paints are presented in two collections, one for interior and the other for exterior use. Selections have been based on a wide range of architectural and decorating styles and are representative of many parts of the North American continent during the 18th and 19th centuries. Emphasis is given, however, to the earlier Colonial shades of the East Coast and South. Both latex and alkyd formula paints are available.

BENJAMIN MOORE & CO.
51 Chestnut Ridge Rd.
Montvale, NJ 07645
(201) 573-9600

THE MURALO CO., INC.
With plants in Bayonne, New Jersey, Chicago, Los Angeles, and Atlanta, Muralo is equipped to supply customers on a nationwide basis. It describes its line of restoration interior and exterior colors as being, "Early American," but a majority of the paints have a richness just as suitable for use on or in a Victorian house. All paints except the floor trim enamels are latex rather than oil-based.

THE MURALO CO., INC.
148 E. 5th St.
Bayonne, NJ 07002
(201) 437-0770

THE OLD-FASHIONED MILK PAINT CO.
Years ago Charles Thibeau, also proprietor of Craftsman Lumber Co., developed his own formula for a milk paint similar to that used in the Colonial period. This was intended for use on furniture, but it has also been successfully applied to interior walls and trim. Eight colors are available in powder form to which water is added.

Brochure and color card, three first-class stamps

THE OLD-FASHIONED MILK PAINT CO.
PO Box 222
Groton, MA 01450
(508) 448-6336

PITTSBURGH PAINTS
Pittsburgh's "Historic Colors" are made up in various latex and oil-based formulas for interiors and exteriors. A number of colors are as appropriate for use in the Far West, but others are common to the Midwest or Northeast. The western colors reflect a more natural palette, dusty shades of brown, the pink of sandstone, the light blue of bluebells. Fifty-six colors are featured in the Pittsburgh collection.

PITTSBURGH PAINTS
1 PPG Plaza
Pittsburgh, PA 15272
(412) 434-2400

PRATT & LAMBERT PAINTS
In association with Henry Ford Museum & Greenfield Village in Dearborn, Michigan, Pratt & Lambert launched its Early Americana Colours collection some years ago. It remains a rich treasury of authentic shades, many of which are based on the colors used for buildings at the museum complex. The term "early American" is somewhat of a misnomer, however, since a majority of the colors were not popularly used until the 19th century. The line includes thirty-six colors, all of which are available for both interior or exterior use in oil or latex finishes.

PRATT & LAMBERT PAINTS
PO Box 22, Dept. GV
Buffalo, NY 14240
(716) 873-6000

THE STULB CO.
Stulb is a fairly new name on the paint scene, and recently acquired the Allentown Paint Co., the oldest ready-mix paint firm in America, dating from 1855. In addition to the Allentown line, which includes the very fine Pennsylvania-Dutch colors first commercially introduced in 1867, Stulb also offers what it calls buttermilk paint colors for furniture and interior use and the Old Village paint colors for interior or exterior application. The buttermilk paint line, licensed by The Colonial Williamsburg Foundation and The Abby Aldrich Rockefeller Folk Art Center, is a water-based formula which simulates a flat, matte finish. The colors were selected from objects in the Folk Art Center's collection. Another line of colors based on buttermilk shades of the Colonial period is included under the Old Village rubric. Perhaps the most useful paints of all are the Old Village oil-based paints in a soft-sheen finish. These are divided into two categories – those from Old Sturbridge Village in Massachusetts, which have an early 19th-century appearance to them; and Stulb's Old Village colors, more reflective of the 18th century. Stulb offers so many different paints that only a careful reading of its literature can lead to a proper choice.

Literature available, $1

THE STULB CO.
PO Box 597, E. Allen and Graham Sts.
Allentown, PA 18105
(800) 221-8444

Other suppliers of period paint colors include: FINE PAINTS OF FRANCE, FLETCHER'S PAINT WORKS, and THE GLIDDEN CO.

Paneling. Fine wood paneling has been prized for hundreds of years. In North America, where wood has been so plentiful, finishing walls in this manner was, until recently, not an expensive proposition unless it involved very rare species or complex joinery. The early colonists may have chosen wall boards for many rooms because installation was easier and cheaper to do than plastering. Unlike later paneling, however, these walls were not often prized for their texture or fine grain. In fact, many such wood-paneled walls were painted. This practice also persisted later in the Colonial period when high-style Georgian elements were introduced. As criminal as it may seem to some, the proper way to treat early Colonial paneling might be to give it a soft paint finish. Similarly, Georgian paneling might be pickled, a bleaching process. Only in the Victorian era did it become common to prize wood as wood, and if pine had to be substituted for a fine hardwood such as cherry or chestnut, then the lesser wood was grained in imitation. The use of gleaming woods in Victorian paneling and wainscoting was matched in furniture. Ceilings were sometimes paneled as well, especially in kitchens and bathrooms, but cheaper woods such as pine and cypress were used for this purpose and paint was substituted for graining. *See also* **Wainscoting.**

AGED WOODS, INC.
Hemlock, pine, poplar, cypress, oak, and chestnut are the principal wood species available through Aged Woods. The planks, used also for flooring, are cut from old beams, and therefore can qualify as being "aged" or antique. Because it is newly milled, the planks will not have the distressed appearance favored by many old-house purists. Nonetheless, as Aged Woods explains, "As with most things in nature, no two are the same and this applies to our wood as well. There will be a variation from board to board in color, grain pattern, nail, knot, and worm holes, etc. No two installations will ever be the same. This is not unfortunate, but is part of the appeal." Of the woods available, cypress is especially recommended for paneling in rooms with a high moisture level such as kitchens and bathrooms. It is practically impervious to water. The average thickness for a plank is $3/4$"; $5/8$" may be available and suitable for paneling purposes. As with Aged Woods's flooring, the planks are available in random widths. The company will provide installation guidelines if these are needed.

Brochure available

AGED WOODS, INC.
147 W. Philadelphia St.
York, PA 17403
(800) 233-9307
(717) 843-8104 (PA)

ARCHITECTURAL COMPONENTS, INC.
The owner of this millwork firm, Charles Bellinger, enjoys custom work such as raised paneling and hand-planed wide board sheathing with either a beaded or a feather edge. Most of the firm's business is in stock items such as window sash and frames, doors, and moldings patterned after examples found in the Connecticut Valley. The paneling – in milled, dried, and selected eastern white pine – is of the same early New England tradition. Entire room ends are also produced with fluted pilasters, dentil cornices, and hidden doors. All joinery is mortise and tenon. Illustrated is a raised panel room end or fireplace wall of $15/16$" pine; such hardwoods as cherry, poplar, or oak may be substituted.

Catalog, $3

ARCHITECTURAL COMPONENTS, INC.
26 N. Leverett Rd.
Montague, MA 01351
(413) 367-9441
Fax (413) 367-9461

CRAFTSMAN LUMBER CO.
Wide boards in pine or oak are a specialty of Craftsman for both paneling and flooring. The boards are available in random widths, and one or both faces can be planed and edges finished in one of several ways – shiplapped, featheredged, or tongue-and-grooved. One or both edges can be beaded or molded. The minimum order is 100', and delivery, anywhere in the continental United States, will usually occur within four to six weeks.

Brochure, 50¢

CRAFTSMAN LUMBER CO.
PO Box 222
Groton, MA 01450
(508) 448-6336

EARLY NEW ENGLAND ROOMS & EXTERIORS, INC.
Paneled chimney breasts, sheathing, and entire room ends with raised paneling are standard items with Early New England. So fine is the firm's reputation that the Henry Francis du Pont Winterthur Museum has licensed it to reproduce an exclusive line of Winterthur millwork, including paneling. Existing exam-

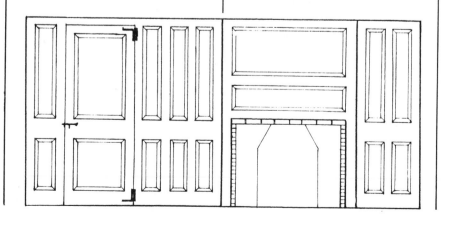

ples of early work are faithfully copied with the correct proportion of stiles and rails to panels. Simple featheredge or beaded paneling may be used in place of raised panels if that seems more appropriate for the interior.

Catalog available, $10

EARLY NEW ENGLAND ROOMS & EXTERIORS, INC.
37 McGuire Rd.
South Windsor, CT 06074
(203) 282-0236

MAURER & SHEPHERD JOYNERS, INC. Eighteenth-century paneled room ends are made to order by hand throughout. Featheredge and beaded board paneling is also available. Eastern white pine is usually used for these traditional types of wall boards. If you are looking for someone to undertake paneling of an even earlier vintage, say the 17th century, Maurer & Shepherd should be able to help. They are masters of imitation and will ferret out the right examples to follow.

Brochure available

MAURER & SHEPHERD JOYNERS, INC.
122 Naubuc Ave.
Glastonbury, CT 06033
(203) 633-2383

STUART INTERIORS
There was a time when antique wood paneling was imported from Europe and Great Britain. In fact, whole rooms were moved lock, stock, and barrel to the New World. Ancient paneling can still be found in the architectural antiques warehouses of England, and with container shipping arrangements possible, the client with deep pockets may wish to indulge his fancy. We'll all be better for it as long as the antique lumber is not being ripped out of a national architectural treasure. Another and less expensive alternative is to import new oak paneling. Stuart Interiors is expert at producing traditional 17th-century work. Among its recent projects has been the complete restoration of the screen and stalls at Lambeth Palace Chapel, London, the installation of plank and muntin paneling and stairs in several small 17th-century houses, and the re-creation of a large paneled library for

a 16th-century-style estate in California. Solid English oak is used for all paneling.

Literature available

STUART INTERIORS
Barrington Court, Barrington
Ilminster, Somerset TA19 0NQ
England
(0460) 40349
Fax (0460) 42069

Other suppliers of wood paneling include: woods – CARLISLE RESTORATION LUMBER, CONKLIN'S AUTHENTIC ANTIQUE BARNWOOD AND HAND HEWN BEAMS, DIAMOND K CO.,INC., *and* TIRESIAS, INC.; *new paneled walls –* AMHERST WOODWORKING & SUPPLY, INC., BAILEY'S ARCHITECTURAL MILLWORK, INC., SOMERSET DOOR & COLUMN CO., *and* TRADITIONAL LINE ARCHITECTURAL RESTORATION LTD.; *antique paneling –* ARCHITECTURAL ANTIQUES EXCHANGE, IRREPLACEABLE ARTIFACTS, RAMASE, *and* SALVAGE ONE.

Parquet Flooring. *See* **Flooring.**

Pedestals. Another name for a column base, a pedestal is also used for the display of vases, garden ornaments, or sculpture. Pedestals in the form of neoclassic columns have recently been introduced by interior designers smitten with postmodernism. A capital, of course, belongs at the top of a column; either way around, a capital pedestal has no historical meaning. A. J. Downing, America's leading 19th-century architect, explained in 1842, "It should always be remembered that all vases, urns, or other sculptured ornaments for gardens and grounds, should be placed on proper pedestals, plinths, or bases, to serve as a firm support . . . it gives a dignity and importance to the vase as a work of art." The proper display of a fine object was then the intent, and since few Americans possessed such treasures, use of a pedestal was quite limited. Besides use in a garden or on a terrace, a pedestal might appear in a dining room or stairway niche supporting a piece of sculpture or vase. One of the few producers of old-fashioned pedestals is KENNETH LYNCH AND SONS. These are made of cast stone and take many forms – square, round,

columnar, octagonal, vase-like, and rectangular. Illustrated is a fluted column pedestal suitable as a sundial base. Lynch also produces what are

called wall pedestals in cast stone, the form being that of a giant corbel or bracket with a shelf.

Pediments. Formally a pediment is the triangular section at the gable end of a building formed at the base by the upper part of a classical entablature. It is seen most often in Greek Revival temple-form buildings of the early 19th century. The same term is often used to describe the topmost member of a formal entryway as well as the caps or heads which ornament windows and interior doors. Used in these ways, a pediment needn't be triangular, but may be rectangular or curved. Pediments may be made of plaster, wood, stone, metal, or in that most modern of materials, polyurethane. Pediments are usually made up as part of other units such as entryway systems or door and window casings. *See also* **Door Heads and Window Heads/Overdoors; Entryways.**

Pendants. *See* **Hanging Fixtures.**

Pickets. *See* **Fencing and Gates.**

Picket Tops. *See* **Fencing and Gates.**

Picture Rails. A picture rail is a molding which may form the bottom part of a cornice or be positioned by itself a foot or so below the cornice. The molding has a slight lip to which hooks can be attached for hanging pictures. So accumstoned are we today to pounding nails in wherever we want that use of a picture rail and wires trailing down the wall seem slightly bizarre. The practice, which probably originated in private galleries or salons, becomes a little more understandable if you have ever tried to sink a hole into a solid stone wall. Now we have the use of electric drills with very fine masonry bits; in the 1800s it would have taken a sledgehammer to sufficiently pierce the same surface. Modern plasterboard walls absorb nails like putty, and, if a stud can be found, the nail will be anchored securely. Old true plastered or paneled walls, like stone walls, present more difficult problems when it comes to pictures. In this light, the old practice of using a picture rail makes a great deal of sense. The wire or rope used to hang a picture was sometimes wrapped in a fabric to make it less objectionable. The chief advantage in hanging pictures by this method, however, is the ability to change their position at will by merely adjusting the wires up or down or by shifting them from one section of the room to another.

BLUE OX MILLWORKS

Five picture molding designs are produced by Blue Ox. Each has a rounded element to receive an S-hook. Prime redwood is used for all moldings. Other designs will be made on a custom basis. Blue Ox grinds its own molding knives for special order items.

Pattern book, $6

BLUE OX MILLWORKS
Foot of X St.
Eureka, CA 95501
(707) 444-3437

SAN FRANCISCO VICTORIANA, INC.
Fourteen picture rail designs in wood and four in plaster make up the largest selection offered by any firm. Two of the wood profiles contain plaster insets, as illustrated. Both are attractive options, one for a late-Victorian interior and the other for a room in the Anglo-Japanese style of the 1880s.

Catalog, $5

SAN FRANCISCO VICTORIANA, INC.
2070 Newcomb Ave.
San Francisco, CA 94124
(415) 648-0313
Fax (415) 648-2812

Another supplier of picture rails is
SILVERTON VICTORIAN MILLWORKS.

Pilasters. The etymology of the word "pilaster" is, with one key omission, its virtual definition. The word consits of two roots: "pile," a now-obsolete word for "pillar"; and "aster," a suffix noting something that imperfectly resembles or merely apes the real thing. A pilaster, then, is a pillar that isn't quite the real thing. The element missing from the etymology is the fact that this imperfect pillar is also "engaged," meaning that it is attached, or apparently attached, to a wall by being partly embedded in it or bonded to it. While some pilasters are actually supporting structures, only part of which is visible, the rest being embedded in the wall, most pilasters are purely decorative features that imitate engaged pillars but are not themselves supporting structures. Pilasters may be rectangular or semicircular, and, like the classical columns they imitate, often contain a base, shaft, and capital. These "half pillars" are most frequently used as simulated columns in entryways and

other door openings and in fireplace mantels. Almost all decorative pilasters are bonded, flat, to the wall. All suppliers of columns and pillars also supply pilasters. *See also* **Columns and Capitals** *and* **Entryways.**

THE BALMER ARCHITECTURAL ART STUDIOS
As with its columns, Balmer's pilasters are available in most of the classic orders and in a variety of widths and diameters, with the lengths being custom sized to the customer's requirements. Although reflecting numerous neoclassical designs, Balmer pediments are particularly rich in the Adam style, and several stock sizes are available. Many Bulmer pediments are offered with the margin moldings matching the accompanying capitals. The firm's pilasters are produced in a very hard and dense gypsum cement, three times as hard as plaster.

Catalog, $20

THE BALMER ARCHITECTURAL ART STUDIOS
9 Codeco Court
Don Mills, ONT M3A 1B6
Canada
(416) 449-2155
Fax (416) 449-3018

SAN FRANCISCO VICTORIANA, INC.
San Francisco Victoriana is famous for its fidelity to the molding profiles used in the Bay Area during the last half of the nineteenth century. As such, it offers several profiles of wood molding intended for simple Victorian fluted pilasters. As illustrated, four of the profiles are for round-

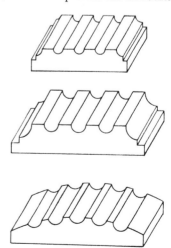

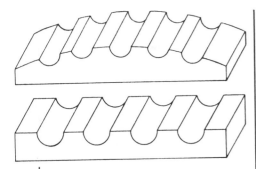

ed pilasters, and one for a rectangular pilaster. A variety of capitals for the pilasters is also offered. As with its many other types of molding, the firm's pilasters are available in a wide selection of woods.

Book of Architectural Building Materials, $5

SAN FRANCISCO VICTORIANA, INC.
2070 Newcomb Ave.
San Francisco, CA 94124
(415) 648-0313
Fax (415) 648-2812

SILVERTON VICTORIAN MILLWORKS
Suitable for mid- to late 19th-century interiors, Silverton's decorative pilasters have vertical flutes on a rounded profile, offering a columnar appearance. They are particularly effective used in entryways and mantels. The illustration shows the firm's pilasters used with corner blocks, base blocks, and a cap. Silverton's

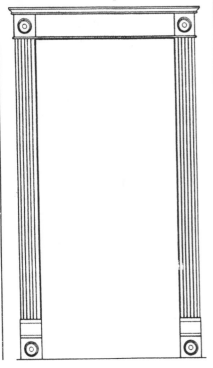

pilasters are not split sections of columns, but are instead manufactured as moldings and are available up to 16' in length. Three different rounded profiles are offered in a wide variety of woods, but the company will also replicate any profile of your choice.

Complete catalog package, $4

SILVERTON VICTORIAN MILLWORKS
PO Box 2987-OC7
Durango, CO 81302
(303) 259-5915
Fax (303) 259-5919

Other suppliers of pilasters include:
CHADSWORTH INC., THE DECORATORS SUPPLY CORP., EARLY NEW ENGLAND ROOMS & EXTERIORS, INC., A. F. SCHWERD MANUFACTURING CO., SOMERSET DOOR & COLUMN CO., and WORTHINGTON GROUP LTD.

Planters. Finding suitable planters for the garden of a period or traditional house is hardly one of the major priorities of old-house ownership. Yet, like most minor acquisitions that make a house a home, locating taste-

ful garden planters is sometimes more frustrating than, say, selecting period lighting fixtures or finding just the perfect chair rail profile for the dining room. The problem is that few specialty suppliers have turned their attention to the humble garden planter, assuming, incorrectly, that the local garden center satisfies such needs. There was a time when terra cotta and stone were the materials of choice for North American garden

planters. In *Cottage Residences* (1842) the great American landscape architect Andrew Jackson Downing recommended these materials "as suited to our economical habits in this country" and would undoubtedly have approved of cast iron for planters once that material became popular later in the century. But democratic as he was, Downing would have despaired at plastic, the modern garden center curse. If you can't ferret out terra-cotta, stone, iron, or wooden planters of good design locally, there are several reputable suppliers that can aid you in your quest. *See also* **Urns.**

KENNETH LYNCH AND SONS
This inimitable firm lists about 50 different stone planters in its massive *Book of Garden Ornament.* The planters come in every conceivable shape, from rectangular to curvilinear; in every possible size, from minuscule to models 3' high or even 6' long; in every tasteful decorative motif, from garland and Greek key and shell to perfectly plain. Most Lynch planters are made of cast stone, a process developed by the firm a century ago. Some are available as well in lead or Armorstone, a fiberglass-like material that the company endorses to the fullest.

Book of Garden Ornament, $9.50

KENNETH LYNCH AND SONS
78 Danbury Rd., Box 488
Wilton, CT 06897-0488
(203) 762-8363
Fax (203) 762-2999

THE OLD WAGON FACTORY
Four different planters – each 16" wide, 16" long, and 18" high – are offered as units in The Old Wagon Factory's line of Classic Chippendale porch furniture. Handmade from a variety of hardwoods, each is finished in high-gloss white enamel and completely lined with a removable galvanized metal insert to protect floors or carpets if used on a porch or solarium. They may be used as well on the patio or in the garden. Two different Chinese Chippendale patterns are complemented by a cross-panel model and a raised-panel model.

Catalog, $2

THE OLD WAGON FACTORY
103 Russell St., PO Box 1427
Clarksville, VA 23927
(804) 374-5787
Fax (804) 374-4646

SMITH & HAWKEN
Well known as a purveyor of beautifully designed garden implements, Smith & Hawken offers two lines of teak planters that share the same solid construction and durability as the firm's teak garden furniture. Because teakwood will not warp, buckle, or rot, it is admirably suited to the moist condition of planters and will weather to a rich silver-gray. The Classic Planter line features bevelled slat sides; the Versailles Planter line carries round finials atop each corner. Each line comes in three sizes, approximately 15", 17", and 23" square; heights vary from 18" to 26". Smith & Hawken is also a good source for ornamental terra-cotta pots and a lovely teak window box.

Literature available

SMITH & HAWKEN
25 Corte Madera
Mill Valley, CA 94941
(415) 383-2000

TENNESSEE FABRICATING COMPANY
This well-known producer of cast-iron and cast-aluminum objects replicates several Victorian planters that would be equally at home in the garden, on the porch, or in the parlor. Employing classic lacy iron patterns of the 19th century, they are elevated on scroll legs that incorporate the same cast-iron patterns, and range in height from 12½" to 21" and in length from 21" to 32".

Catalogs, $5

TENNESSEE FABRICATING COMPANY
1822 Latham St.
Memphis, TN 38106
(901) 948-3354
Fax (901) 948-3356

Other suppliers of planters include: BLAKE INDUSTRIES, BRANDYWINE GARDEN FURNITURE, LAWLER MACHINE & FOUNDRY CO., INC., NEW ENGLAND TOOL CO., and ROBINSON IRON CORP.

Plaques. *See* **Ornaments.**

Plaster Restoration. Don't believe that your everyday plasterer can be entrusted with the repair or restoration of ornamental plasterwork of another era. This type of decoration calls first for a very careful analysis of the composition content, something which can vary greatly from a brittle plaster of Paris mixture to an almost rock-like concrete. Fibrous elements are often used to strengthen the formula and these, too, must be analyzed. We recently learned of a ceiling repair project which necessitated the re-creation of an ancient recipe for wattle. Every type of modern material had been tried without success before twigs were mixed together with gypsum plaster. Coloration is also an element to be considered. The new work must blend in with the old. Once the formula is set, castings of original motifs most probably will be performed so that the new work will match the old in line and form. Ornamental ceilings are, of course, the most difficult elements in a room to repair or restore. Cornice moldings, door and window casings and heads, and brackets are, however, only slightly less difficult if the restoration work is to appear seamless. Among the experts undertaking this specialized work are THE BALMER ARCHITECTURAL ART STUDIOS, FELBER STUDIOS, DAVID FLAHERTY, SCULPTOR, HAMPTON DECOR & PLASTERING, and FRANK J. MANGIONE.

Plate Rails. A plate rail is a narrow band – either a molding or shelf – affixed to the wall several feet below the ceiling. It is used for displaying plates and other ornamental objects. Popular in Victorian interiors, it continued to be used in early 20th-century bungalows in the Arts and Crafts style. Very few millwork suppliers carry such an item, and one alternative is to have very narrow shelving fabricated. Blue Ox Millworks is one of the only firms to suggest plate rails as an option. The top of its bracket-like rail contains two grooves in which to position plates.

Plates. Metal plates are used on doors in various ways. The most common are the brass or iron plates which make up a lockset and are used in place of a rose. Kickplates or escutcheons and pushplates are less common forms, but are more useful than the decorative escutcheons. For suppliers of brass pushplates, *see* **Kickplates.** For escutcheons, *see* **Door Hardware.**

Player Pianos. The golden age of the player piano was the 1910s and 1920s, before the widespread popularity of radio in the early '30s changed the pattern of family musical entertainment for all time. Family and friends would gather 'round the piano as the "player" inserted a selected piano roll, engaged the starting mechanism, and pumped the treadle for all it was worth to keep the music flowing. As Sears, Roebuck advertised its 1927 Beckwith "New Era" player piano, "This latest, improved model in the new apartment size is thoroughly equipped to give you the greatest pleasure. A transposing device enables anyone to change the key instantly, an indispensable aid to singing. The automatic sustaining pedal removes the dampers from the strings at just the right moment to give that full, loud pedal effect so noticeable in hand playing, while an automatic tracking device keeps the music roll running evenly over the tracking bar at all times." Music rolls were available in "orchestral" versions for polite listening, or in "word

rolls" with the lyrics of popular songs printed on the right side of the roll for sing-alongs. For a country that was still a nation of immigrants, the word rolls were available in English, German, Italian, Polish, and Bohemian versions. What "Yes, We Have No Bananas" sounded like in Bohemian is anybody's guess. Restored player pianos are in demand today as the pleasures of the recent past are once again discovered. Most areas of North America boast a piano restorer with an interest in old-style players. One we can confidently recommend is BRYANT STOVES AND MUSIC, INC., Box 2048, Rich Rd., Thorndike, ME 04986, (207) 568-3665. Aside from its "antique mechanical music rental service," Bryant buys, sells, and repairs player pianos.

the veranda gives to a dwelling the very expression of hospitality so far as any one feature of a dwelling can do it." The veranda remains the *ne plus ultra* of porches, the full expression of a romantic building style. Many millwork and ironwork suppliers can provide the necessary elements for the restoration or addition of such a graceful structure. *See also* **Balusters, Brackets,** *and* **Posts.**

ARCHITECTURAL IRON CO.
If restoration of porch ironwork is your aim, you could not turn to a better supplier than Architectural Iron. The company is dedicated to the careful disassembly of iron ornament, cleaning, casting of new parts, and proper reassembly. Both cast and wrought ironwork are treated and produced. New parts such as panels and posts may be available in stock already on hand.

Catalog, $4

ARCHITECTURAL IRON CO.
Box 126, Schocopee Rd.
Milford, PA 18337
(717) 296-7722
(212) 243-2664
Fax (717) 296-IRON

GOTHOM, INC.
Victorian wood fretwork or gingerbread ornamentation is Gothom's rea-

Porches. A porch was as commonplace a feature of the Victorian house as the deck is of a 1980s contemporary. Popularity of the porch lasted well into the 1930s, some houses having front, side, and back porches. Bungalows often incorporated a front porch under the sloping roof line, and a screened upper-story sleeping porch was an addition to many residences before World War II. The Victorian veranda is a type of porch, but, rather than occupying one corner of a building, it often runs across the whole facade and may wrap around one or both sides of the building. It is frequently overladen with decorative ironwork or gingerbread. Lewis Allen, an architect of the mid-1800s, observed of the veranda: "Many southern people almost live under the shade of their verandas. It is a delightful place to take their meals, to receive their visitors and friends; and

son for being. Hand-turned posts of almost any design can be produced so that they will blend with the secondary decorative porch elements. Gothom's selection of brackets, perhaps used with or in place of spandrels at the top between the posts, spans the Victorian decades in style. The same is true of the balusters which are used below with railings. The firm suggests the use of square rather than turned balusters, arguing that "all turned components . . . can sometimes appear overwhelming." Flat sawn balusters can also be supplied (see also **Balusters**) and these give a pronounced cutout or gingerbread effect. Completely useless but whimsical elements such as drops and pendants can enliven the whole structure.

Catalog, $5

GOTHOM, INC.
110 Main St., PO Box 421
Erin, ONT N0B 1T0
Canada
(519) 833-2574
Fax (519) 833-2195

TENNESSEE FABRICATING CO.
Cast-iron porch components are Tennessee's primary products. These are almost all of a traditional design known since the early to mid-19th century, especially in the South. The elements consist of posts, brackets, valances or friezes, and railing panels. Included in the traditional floral designs are California Oak, Curly Oak, Vineyard, Pontalba, Rose, Morning Glory, Bird of Paradise, Ivy Leaf, Passion Flower, Dogwood, and Magnolia. Tennessee also makes up highly ornamental late-Victorian designs.

Catalog, $5

TENNESSEE FABRICATING CO.
1822 Latham St.
Memphis, TN 38106
(901) 948-3354
Fax (901) 948-3356

VINTAGE WOOD WORKS
Posts, balustrades, brackets, spandrels, and running trim or friezes are produced for outdoor use. The most important elements, the posts, are carried in stock and in three thick-nesses, 4", 5", and 6", the 5" being recommended for most purposes. Each post is square and Vintage recommends that it be fitted into a steel base mounting plate to protect it from moisture. Most of the posts average $8\frac{1}{2}$" in height, but length can be adjusted to any requirement. Vintage has also given special thought to the bottom rail of a balustrade, and offers a special "Sloped Top" rail which provides proper water drainage. You may decide to use Vintage's corbels rather than the standard brackets since the former are 3" or more thick rather than $\frac{3}{4}$" or $1\frac{1}{2}$".

Catalog, $2

VINTAGE WOOD WORKS
513 S. Adams
Fredericksburg, TX 78624
(512) 997-9513

Other suppliers of porch components are: wood – BLUE OX MILLWORKS, CUMBERLAND WOODCRAFT CO., INC., GAZEBO & PORCHWORKS, MAD RIVER WOODWORKS, PAGLIACCO TURNING AND MILLING, SILVERTON VICTORIAN MILLWORKS, and TURNCRAFT; *cast iron –* THE ARDEN FORGE CO., LAWLER MACHINE & FOUNDRY CO., INC., NEW ENGLAND TOOL CO., SCHWARTZ'S FORGE & METALWORKS, INC., and STEWART IRON WORKS CO.

Porch Ceiling. *See* **Wainscoting.**

Porch Swings. Swinging on the porch during good weather is one of the most pleasant of sedentary experiences. Not long after porches became a feature of American houses in the mid-1800s, furniture for them was adopted. A swing hung from ceiling hooks by chain became as common a feature as porch rockers.

CANDLERTOWN CHAIRWORKS
A very handsome red oak swing is one of the latest additions to the Candlertown handmade furniture line. It measures 50" wide and has a gently bowed seat and back. All sharp edges are chamfered, and brass-plated screws, not nails or staples, are used. Each swing, shipped fully assembled, is finished in a Danish oil that brings out the natural beauty of the oak.

Catalog, $2

CANDLERTOWN CHAIRWORKS
PO Box 1630
Candler, NC 28715
(704) 667-4844

LAWLER MACHINE & FOUNDRY CO., INC.
Lawler's porch swing is a much simpler device than that made by Candlertown. Cast-iron ends, black primed, secure seat and back wood slats and provide places to attach chain for hanging. All necessary hardware and the chain are supplied with the unit, which is shipped unassembled. The assembled size is 48" wide, 19" deep, and 21" high.

Catalog, U.S., $5; Canada, $8

American customers contact:
LAWLER MACHINE & FOUNDRY CO., INC.

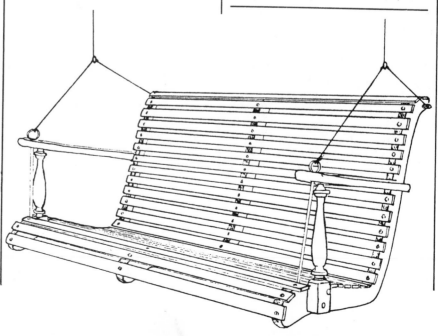

PO Box 320069
Birmingham, AL 35232
(205) 595-0596

Canadian customers contact:
STEPTOE & WIFE ANTIQUE LTD.
322 Geary Ave.
Toronto, ONT M6H 2C7
(416) 530-4200
Fax (416) 530-4666

Another supplier of porch swings is
GREEN ENTERPRISES.

Post Lights. *See* **Lanterns** *and* **Posts.**

Posts. Besides their use for porches (*see* **Porches**) and fencing (*see* **Fencing and Gates**), posts are used in stairways and for outdoor lights. Lighting companies sometimes stock posts for outdoor lanterns, but most must be supplied separately. Newel posts for stairways are a stock item with many millwork firms as well as specialty stairbuilders. Posts can be square or turned in any number of Colonial and Victorian designs; those used indoors as newel posts are more than likely to be capped in some fashion. The cap may be integral to the piece or a separate element fitted into place. An important consideration for outdoor posts is their proper anchorage and protection from rot. You can, of course, use a metal standard, different models being available from many lighting outlets.

NEW ENGLAND WOODTURNERS
Turned posts and half-posts (used for inside porch corners) in very handsome designs are custom produced by New England. Newel posts with appropriate caps are hand-sanded in both directions and are finished suitable for paint or stain. Information on size, type of wood to be used, design, and number of pieces will be needed before a job can be quoted. New England Woodturners is relied on by many architects, restoration contractors, and cabinetmakers for elegant turnings.

Brochure available

NEW ENGLAND WOODTURNERS
75 Daggett St., PO Box 7242
New Haven, CT 06519
(203) 776-1880

PAGLIACCO TURNING AND MILLING
Eighteen different turned newel post designs, each one available with complementary balusters, are produced in the best of American woods, California redwood. Each post assembly includes the post itself, a cap, and a dowel screw for attaching the cap. Illustrated are two of the designs. The posts come in two standard lengths,

48" and 53". Newel caps are offered in five styles; and each of these in three sizes. The caps are also sold separately, and if you wish to use one different from that ordinarily specified for a post, Pagliacco will be glad to oblige.

Catalog, $6

PAGLIACCO TURNING AND MILLING
PO Box 225
Woodacre, CA 94973
(415) 488-4333
Fax (415) 488-9372

SACO MANUFACTURING &
    WOODWORKING
Lamp and newel posts are custom manufactured by this well-established New England firm. Standard

trimmings are of eastern pine, but Saco is prepared to work in poplar, basswood, oak, or other woods. Each turned piece is produced by hand. In additon to custom posts, Saco also offers a line of stock designs as well as balltops, urns, and drops for 3½" and 4½" square posts. Illustrated is the firm's selection of hand-turned lampposts, each of which is turned to accept a standard 3" lamp base. The post is center-bored to allow for easy wiring. To prevent wood rot, the bottom of the base may be factory treated with a preservative. The standard lamppost is 8' long and 4½" square at the base.

Brochure available

SACO MANUFACTURING &
    WOODWORKING
39 Lincoln St.
Saco, ME 04072
(207) 284-6613

Other suppliers of wood newel posts and lampposts are: BLUE OX MILLWORKS, GOTOM INC., MARK A. KNUDSEN, SAN FRANCISCO VICTORIANA, INC., *and* SILVERTON VICTORIAN MILLWORKS. *Several architectural antiques outlets can supply old newel posts,* ARCHITECTURAL ANTIQUE CO. *and* ARTEFACT ARCHITECTURAL ANTIQUES *among them.*

Post Racks. *See* **Kitchen Fittings and Hardware.**

Pottery. As Ellen and Bert Denker write in *The Main Street Pocket Guide to North American Pottery and Porcelain,* "In our daily lives we are surrounded by objects made of clay. From the ceramic tile and sanitary fixtures of the bath to the plates on the table, we are constantly in contact with the potter's craft, although often in highly mechanical forms. In the past, too, ceramics of all kinds were in regular use. They included the finest porcelain teacups, as well as the cheapest redware chamber pot. Although Americans during the last 300 years have continued to enjoy ceramic wares of foreign manufacture, much of what we have consumed has been made on this continent." North American pottery has enjoyed a long and distinguished history, relevant to the furnishing and decorating of the period house but largely outside the scope of this book. Still, it is good to hint through the inclusion of two contemporary potters that the old ways and wares of the craft have survived to the present and that pottery forms centuries old are still being produced today for the utility and beauty of our homes.

HEPHAESTUS POTTERY

Hephaestus was, of course, the ancient Greek god of fire and handicrafts, and Jeff White, by naming his kiln-fired reproductions of Pennsylvania-German redware after Hephaestus, neatly combines both attributes of the god. White first began throwing pots in 1966, and three years later he set up his own working pottery for making Colonial-style stoneware and salt-glaze pieces. He now produces redware exclusively. Redware has been made in America since the Colonial period and was particularly popular through

the 1850s. White's specialty is the hand-decorating of each piece. Two forms of decoration are used. Slipware is made by painting or trailing yellow slip over red clay; sgrafitto ware is made by covering red clay with yellow slip and then carving through to expose the red clay underneath. Manganese black and copper green are then added for highlights. Each piece is glazed in the last stage to set the design. White produces pitchers, crocks, bowls, banks, steins, jugs, vases, plates, and other household wares, but welcomes commission work in addition to his stock pieces. Since his redware contains no lead, it is completely safe for eating and drinking. Illustrated is a sgrafitto jar, 10" tall.

Catalog, $2

HEPHAESTUS POTTERY
2012 Penn St.
Lebanon, PA 17042
(717) 272-0806

WESTMOORE POTTERY

Although Westmoore Pottery offers a number of reproductions of antique redware and salt-glazed stoneware, most of the designs are uniquely those of David and Mary Farrell, Westmoore's potters. Both new and old-style pieces, however, have the look and feel of antiques. Designs range from simple to very fancy. Slip is used to decorate plates, crocks, and jugs in various colors. Each piece is finished with a clear glaze to enable the true clay colors to show through. Since the pieces are handmade, natural variations will occur in each. These differences are also the result of firing and salt-glazing stoneware in an old-style wood-burning groundhog kiln, as did earlier potters. Illustrated are just a few of the hundreds of beautiful items that are on display at the Farrells' shop.

Literature available, 25¢

WESTMOORE POTTERY
Rte. 2, Box 494
Seagrove, NC 27341
(919) 464-3700

Prisms and Pendalogs. *See* **Lamp Parts/Fittings.**

Pulls. Pulls are handy wherever a door is not fitted with a latch or lockset. Most commonly, storm and screen doors, garage doors, and closet doors are left without a locking mechanism with a handle. Rather, the door may have a sliding bolt or simple eye and hook. Pulls are also used for cabinet or cupboard doors and furniture. Cabinet hardware in wood, iron, and brass is not difficult to find in a wide variety of designs. If you are seeking something with a marked period character, however, you may need to apply to a specialty manufacturer. FANEUIL FURNITURE HARDWARE is highly recommended for this purpose. It is also a source of hard-to-find architectural hardware suitable for exterior and interior doors. Blacksmiths who produce hand-forged pulls are other excellent suppliers.

HISTORIC HARDWARE LTD.
Norfolk and Suffolk latches made without thumbpieces are ideal for

door pulls. Illustrated is a model called the Spade Barn Pull based on an exterior Suffolk latch design. This is a big and heavy piece of hardware as suits a barn or garage door. It measures 3" wide by 12" high. Historic

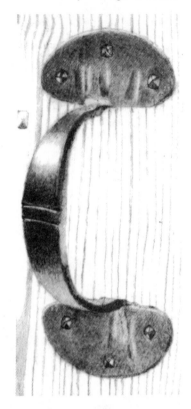

Hardware also makes small interior Suffolk pulls; these are offered in 3" and 6" lengths. They are suitable for cabinets and furniture as well as closet doors.

Catalog, $3

HISTORIC HARDWARE LTD.
PO Box 1327
North Hampton, NH 03862
(603) 964-2280

KAYNE & SON CUSTOM FORGED
    HARDWARE
Steve Kayne custom forges even the most limited production items, including, as illustrated, reproduc-

tions of Gustav Stickley furniture pulls in copper. They suggest that the same type of design, with or without a keyhole, might be appropriate for closet doors in an early 1900s bungalow or Craftsman house. Kayne is just as capable of forging the most medieval style of iron door pulls for a Tudor mansion.

Custom forged hardware catalog, $2

KAYNE & SON CUSTOM FORGED
    HARDWARE
76 Daniel Ridge Rd.
Candler, NC 28715
(704) 667-8868
(704) 665-1988

Pumps. At one time a force pump could be found in every country kitchen. Positioned next to the sink, it supplied most cooking and washing-up needs. Today, with the water table dropping in many areas and the purity of water supplies under siege, a force pump is unlikely to have a practical use. Use of a force pump requires not only a ready supply of water but a strong arm. Presumably, the Amish still have the strength, if not also the wisdom, to draw water manually as well as by wind power. LEHMAN'S HARDWARE still supplies several pitcher pump models, including the turn-of-the-century, one-piece cast-iron model shown. It can be used

only with a cistern or shallow well with less than a 20' vertical drop to the water supply. Lehman also carries deep well pump heads, cylinders,

drop pipe, and rods. If you are truly ambitious (and courageous), Lehman can supply you with an Aermotor Water Lift Windmill or a hydraulic ram.

Quarter-Rounds. *See* **Moldings.**

Quoins. Pronounced like the word "coin," quoins are the corner pieces which reinforce an exterior wall. Quoins are usually thought of as being stone, but in North America they have also been fashioned of brick and of wood, the wood being only an imitation of masonry. Stone quoins are usually blocks of cut and dressed material. This is as true for rubble or fieldstone houses as for structures of quarried cut stone. For suppliers of stone suitable for this use, *see* **Stone.** Any other material would have to be custom-produced by a woodworker or brickmaker.

Newel post, Elliot House, Petersburg, Virginia. Photograph by George Eisenman, Historic American Buildings Survey.

Carpeting, Old Merchant's House, New York, New York. Photograph, courtesy of Patterson, Flynn, & Martin, Inc.

Racks. *See* **Kitchen Fittings and Hardware.**

Radiators. Although several central heating systems were patented in America by 1850, only the well-to-do could afford such luxury at first. By the 1880s, however, the mechanics of heating had been so improved, and the prices so reduced, that central heating began to appear regularly in the houses of the middle class. Given the choice between ducts for a hot-air system or pipes for a radiator system, most people chose pipes because they were easier and cheaper to install. As a result, hot-air registers, beautifully ornamented and discreetly hidden, appeared in Victorian homes far less frequently than radiators that had to be displayed as prominently as furniture. Early radiators were pleasantly ornamented and featured scrolled

legs and what one advertiser called "artistic designs" – decorative motifs that were embossed on the metal. These designs were repeated in the semiattached covers that were sold together with the heating units. Although almost everyone today seems to paint old radiators a shiny silver color, these devices were usually painted much more vibrantly, with a ground in one color and the raised pattern in another, the whole intended to harmonize with the essential colors of the room.While some people continue to denigrate the hulking presence of these cast-iron pieces, others, insisting on their considerable charm, maintain that a late-Victorian room without a radiator's friendly hiss is as empty as a period house without the ticking of a clock. Old radiators are surprisingly difficult to come by today, the Victorian models

having been replaced by later compact ones in the 1920s and then hauled out to the barn to rust. Many were sacrificed as scrap metal during World War II. The best source for locating old radiators would seem to be architectural antiques warehouses or even old-fashioned junk shops.

Railings. Rails for stairways, porches, and balconies are among the most frequently replaced or restored items in an old house. As structural elements, it is important that they not be rickety. For suppliers of structural railings, *see* **Balconies, Balustrades, Porches,** and **Stairs/Stairways.** Other types of railings such as chair, plate, and picture rails do have a practical function as well, but their use is not structural. *See* **Chair Rails, Picture Rails,** and **Plate Rails.**

Railroad Siding. *See* **Wainscoting.**

Registers. *See* **Grates, Grilles, and Registers.**

Restoration Workshops and Courses. *See* **Workshops/Courses.**

Rocking Chairs. No one knows who first came up with the idea of mounting a chair on rockers – pieces of wood with curved undersides – but whoever it was is an unsung American genius who ushered in a new era of seating comfort for a people who had hitherto been too busy clearing the land to take the time to sit down. Perhaps the most democratic piece of furniture of the 19th century – its popularity was shared by rich

and poor alike – the rocking chair borrowed a principle from infancy (that a gentle rocking motion can soothe and calm) and applied it to the adults of the species. First the old were given the luxury of rocking ("from the cradle to the grave") and then nursing women. Eventually, in a society where old-line puritanism was beginning to soften, even men were allowed the leisure to rock, even if it took the medical men of the day to endorse the health-giving benefits of rocking before some men would succumb to such temptation. Although rocking chairs were exported to Europe, they never achieved the popularity attained in its native land. At the height of its glory during the Victorian age, the rocking chair existed in hundreds of models, many of them bizarre. Patent records show that the rocker was a favorite tinkering ground for putative inventors. One inventor came up with a model that cooled the person rocking by blowing air in his face each time he rocked. Other models were even sillier. (Not for nothing is someone deranged called "off his rocker.") Happily, only the simple, conservative design of the basic rocking chair succeeded with the public, giving us several classic models along the way – the Boston rocker, the Salem rocker, the Bentwood (Thonet) rocket, the Shaker rocker – all of which are still made today.

CANDLERTOWN CHAIRWORKS
Susan and Rick Steingress specialize in chairs and painted country furniture designed to imitate hard-to-find or prohibitively expensive originals. Proprietors of Candlertown

Chairworks, they aim to fashion furniture that can be easily mixed with antique originals. Candlertown chairs are crafted of hickory, maple, or red oak and feature hand-woven split seats. Each is finished with the company's worn milk paint in red, blue, green, black, gray, mustard, or pumpkin. Many styles, shapes, and sizes are available, including this children's rocker, based on an old original, and made of maple. It is 31" high, with a seat height of 12".

Catalog, $2

CANDLERTOWN CHAIRWORKS
PO Box 1630
Candler, NC 28715
(704) 667-4844

NORTH WOODS CHAIR SHOP
The aesthetic ideals of the Shakers, a small religious sect that lived and worked in nineteen communities from Maine to Kentucky, are much admired today and are being upheld by a small body of skilled contemporary craftsmen. Among them are Lenore Howe and Brian Braskie, proprietors of North Woods Chair Shop, named by Constance Stapleton in her book *Crafts of America* "the best Shaker chairmakers in the country

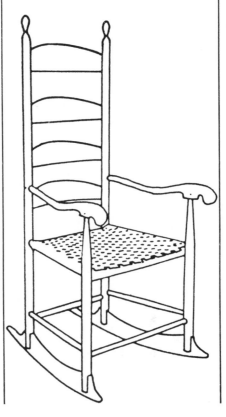

today." North Woods Chair Shop copies only original Shaker designs, incorporating classic lines, elegant curves, and restrained ornamentation. All North Woods furniture is handmade of cherry, although any type of wood may be used for a custom project. Customers can choose a natural oil finish or any number of custom-blended stains. Chair seats can be caned or woven with fabric in a wide range of authentic colors – from black to red and green stripes to beige and white – and patterns similar to those used by the Shakers themselves. Several types of Shaker rocking chairs are offered, including the Canterbury Rocker illustrated. (The original is on display at the Shaker meetinghouse in Canterbury, New Hampshire.) The Canterbury Rocker is 47" high, 23" wide and $15\frac{1}{2}$" deep, with a seat height of $16\frac{1}{2}$". Other Shaker rocking chairs offered are 3-slat and 4-slat versions of the famous Enfield ladder-back rockers and an armless rocker ideal for a small space.

Catalog, photographs, and tape samples, $3

NORTH WOODS CHAIR SHOP
237 Old Tilton Rd.
Canterbury, NH 03224
(603) 783-4595

Another supplier of rocking chairs is SHAKER WORKSHOPS.

Roof Drains. Clogged gutters and downspouts can cause a great deal of grief. Old houses were often built to great heights, and mounting an extension ladder even once or twice a year to pick the gutters free of debris is not our idea of a pleasant Sunday afternoon. Every owner of a house, new or old, would be pleased to have some automatic device installed that would sweep gutters free of leaves before saplings start to sprout along the roof line, but no such luck. It does help to cover gutters with fine screening, but this material can also become swamped in leaf mold. The wiry traps sold in hardware stores for placement in downspouts are also useful – if they stay in place or do not turn to rust. Another aid is suggested by THE COPPERSMITH. It is called a roof drain, and as illustrated, consists of a perforated copper cone that is tack

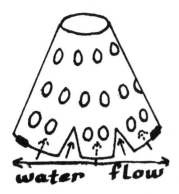

water flow

soldered over the drain hole. For further details, contact the inventor.

Roofing.

A sound, moisture-resistant roof is a must for any structure. Roofs with only very minor troubles may require only partial replacement, the addition of flashing, or, with luck, sealing with pitch or creosote. Flat roof sections are notoriously troublesome since water has no place to run off. Unless you live in the sunny and dry Southwest, you will probably want to give any flat roof area some slight pitch. Gable roofs, however, also have their drawbacks. The valleys formed by intersecting gables are where problems are likely to occur. Any good roofer or builder knows that these sections should be fitted or coated with flashing that will contract with cold and expand with heat, and that whatever roofing material selected must be laid in a way which allows for proper run-off. Any openings in a roof such as a dormer or skylight must be carefully sealed and protected by flashing. The same treatment is accorded chimney stacks or ventilators.

Many different types of materials have been used for roofing buildings over the past three hundred years. Thatch is one of the most ancient, but its use has never been widespread in the New World as it was in Europe. The art of thatching, however, is still alive and is being practiced in North America. The ideal roof is usually considered to be of slate since this stone – if properly applied – can serve effectively for at least 50 to 75 years. A slate roof, however, is likely to be an expensive proposition in the short run. One must also be cautious of roofing contractors who claim the ability of slating a roof but who do not even possess the right tools.

Slating a roof is not a D.I.Y. proposition. The same is true for clay tile roofs, another very resilient form. Other types of roofing materials are concrete tiles, a fiber cement substitute, galvanized and tin sheathing, wood shingles, and asphalt shingles. Try, if at all possible, to avoid the last-named and most common roofing material. It has little or none of the appearance of age and, ironically, may last for only ten years or less. Wood shingles will give a much better appearance and, if properly treated and laid, will require little maintenance for fifteen to twenty years.

CONKLIN METAL INDUSTRIES
Metal roof tiles or shingles have been in use since the late 1800s. Conklin is one of several firms still making the pieces in galvanized, copper, terne or tin, and terne-coated stainless. Various patterns are offered.

Brochure, $3

CONKLIN METAL INDUSTRIES
PO Box 1858
Atlanta, GA 30301
(404) 688-4510

EVERGREEN SLATE CO., INC.
Southern Vermont and upper New York State are areas rich in slate. It comes as a surprise to some people considering a slate roof that such a wide variety of colors is available. Evergreen, for example, quarries and finishes roofing stock in a gray green, purple, red, gray, and black. In 1989 the company opened up a new quarry yielding a black slate, the traditional color used for most roofs. Slate is produced in various thicknesses, the standard being $3/16$" to $1/4$". The standard slate is smooth, but one can choose a rough textured surface as well. All slates are shipped with punched nail holes.

Brochure available

EVERGREEN SLATE CO., INC.
PO Box 248, 68 Potter Ave.
Granville, NY 12832
(518) 642-2530
Fax (518) 642-9313

LUDOWICI-CELADON, INC.
True clay roofing tiles are still made by this esteemed manufacturer in Ohio's historic tile producing region. There are a number of forms available, including the well-known Spanish and barrel styles. Ludowici-Celadon tiles have been used to roof many important public buildings over the past century and are the choice of many owners of grand houses in the Spanish Colonial style. For information regarding distributors, contact the company directly.

LUDOWICI-CELADON, INC.
4757 Tile Plant Rd.
New Lexington, OH 43764
(614) 342-1995
Fax (614) 342-5175

OAK CREST MANUFACTURING, INC.
White oak shingles are Oak Crest's specialty and these are available either split sawn or smooth sawn. Characteristic of white oak shingles is a consistent thickness and grain structure which make installation relatively easy. The product is guaranteed for twenty years against any defects in workmanship and quality.

Literature available

OAK CREST MANUFACTURING, INC.
6732 E. Emory Rd.
Knoxville, TN 37938
(615) 922-1311

PENN·BIG BED SLATE CO., INC.
Big Bed is one of several major suppliers of roofing slate quarried in Pennsylvania's northeast slate belt. Quarrying of this material has been a tradition of the past 150 years, many of the miners and slaters having come from Wales to work in America. The principal product is of a rich black color.

PENN BIG BED SLATE CO., INC.
PO Box 184
Slatington, PA 18080-0184
(215) 767-4601
Fax (215) 767-9252

RISING & NELSON SLATE CO., INC.
The motto of this firm of miners and manufacturers is "The Roof That Never Wears Out." Rising & Nelson has been around since 1869 and has the experience to back up its claim. Vermont colored slate is the principal product, although the company also handles solid black from Pennsylvania and Virginia. With the use of softly colored slate, various effects can be produced – in green

and gray, reddish purple, gray green, and tones of red. Thicknesses range from the standard $3/16$" to 1". The company is prepared to cut any kind of butt that might be required – pointed, fishscale, clipped corner, and others – for special roof treatments. Any person seeking to patch an old slate roof is advised to send Rising & Nelson a color picture to aid in proper matching.

Literature available

RISING & NELSON SLATE CO., INC.
West Pawlet, VT 05775
(802) 645-0150

SUPRADUR MANUFACTURING CORP.
Cement shingles with fiber reinforcement have the appearance of slate but are considerably less expensive. The standard size is a 9.35" by 16" rectangle; hexagonal shapes can also be supplied. With six-sided shingles, it is possible to duplicate a multicolor Victorian mansard roof. Contact the company for information on distributors.

SUPRADUR MANUFACTURING CORP.
Box 908
Rye, NY 10580
(800) 223-1948
(914) 967-8230 (NY)

THATCHING ADVISORY SERVICE
Proprietor Robert West has helped spark a revival of the art of thatching in England and North America. Over the past several years he and his colleagues have provided traditional natural fiber roofing for reconstructed early American buildings. West has found a plentiful supply of water reed for his jobs on the East Coast. Thanks to modern formulas, thatching materials can be treated so that they are as fire-resistant as concrete or slate. West is the author of a useful and informative book, *Thatch, A Complete Guide to the Ancient Craft of Thatching* (STERLING PUBLISHING CO.) which includes information on all the various traditional forms.

THATCHING ADVISORY SERVICE
Rose Tree Farm, 29 Nine Mile Ride
Finchampstead, Berks RG11 4QD
England

VANDE HEY-RALEIGH ARCHITECTURAL
   ROOF TILE
Tiles in concrete which approximate

clay tiles are this firm's specialty. Various forms are produced, including barrel, coping, and flat shapes. Nearly all colors can be reproduced, which greatly enlarges the possibilities when a polychrome effect is desired. Contact the company regarding materials and installation.

Catalog available

VANDE HEY-RALEIGH ARCHITECTURAL
   ROOF TILE
1665 Bohm Dr.
Little Chute, WI 54140
(414) 766-1181

Other suppliers of roofing materials are: slate – BUCKINGHAM-VIRGINIA SLATE CORP. *and* STRUCTURAL SLATE CO.; *metal –* W. F. NORMAN CORP.

Room Ends. *See* **Paneling.**

Rosettes. *See* **Medallions, Rosettes, Centerpieces.**

Rugs and Carpets. Not too long ago a braided rug for informal areas and an oriental carpet for more formal rooms seemed the only alternatives in a sea of historically inappropriate floor coverings. Almost everyone knew that shag or tufted broadloom had no place in a Colonial or Victorian dwelling. Braided or hooked rugs and orientals still remain valid options today, but there are other choices which now can be explored. Thanks to the encouragement of private individuals and restoration groups, the weaving of traditional Axminster and Wilton carpeting has been given a new life, and Scotch ingrain is also being produced on a limited basis. Flat woven rugs, including striped Venetian runners, are again being manufactured in a wide range of colors and patterns. Wall-to-wall carpeting made its appearance in American interiors by the mid-19th century, but it was of a somewhat different variety from that purveyed today. It was without a tufted texture and was made in narrower strips. A border was often incorporated in the design or added to it around the perimeters of the room. As mentioned, carpeting of this type is once again available, but, because of limited production, it is expensive to produce. The average

old-house owner may find that area rugs or carpets better serve his purpose and pocketbook. *See also* **Floorcloths.**

AMS IMPORTS
Linen rugs from Sweden come close to traditional Venetian designs popular in the 19th century. AMS is a distributor of all-natural fiber floor coverings which vary in size from 2' by 4' to 6' by 9'. Pieces can be seamed together to produce larger area rugs. AMS is also a source of United States-produced handwoven cotton fabric rugs in simple geometric patterns. The floor coverings can be custom colored if desired.

Literature available

AMS IMPORTS
23 Ash Lane
Amherst, MA 01002
(413) 253-2644
(800) 648-1816

J. R. BURROWS & CO.
Anyone interested in floor coverings of the 19th and early 20th centuries should consider the extraordinary reproduction textiles produced in England for Burrows. Any of the room-size carpeting patterns can also be cut and sewn for area rugs. All are Wilton and Brussels weaves. An 80 percent *worsted* wool/20 percent nylon blend is used for extra definition and strength of design. A narrow-gauge loom is used to produce a pile count of almost 100 tufts per square inch rather than today's industry standard of 64 per square inch. Carpets are produced in 27"-wide strips which are then sewn together unless they are to be used as runners. Borders may be woven separately in 18"-wide strips.

Among the newest offerings from Burrows's English manufacturer, Woodward Grosvenor & Co. Ltd., are two William Morris designs from the 1870s in an Axminster weave. "Poppy" and "Acanthus" are available in three different color combinations in body and border widths. A complete set of 9" by 12" samples (twenty-four items) is available for $100. The same samples can be loaned for thirty days at a charge of $20 for the first item, and $10 for each additional item.

The regular Woodward Grosvenor Wilton and Brussels weaves range in style from the Regency and Federal periods through the Victorian and Edwardian eras. Shown first is an 1878 Anglo-Japanese border design, #12/6480; it is available with a complementary overall floral motif body.

Illustrated next is a runner, 36" wide, in the "Ivy Leaves" pattern (#14/6645). "Tropical Leaves and Flowers" is a third design (#26/6791), dates from 1875, and is shown with its border attached. Last is a rococo design dated to 1822 (#14/6987), swirling with bright bouquets of roses.

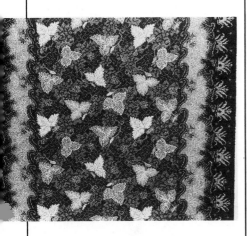

All of these designs and other production textiles can be woven as either a Brussels or Wilton. There are three grades of Wilton available, classed according to cut-pile height, from low to high: super, extra-super, and luxury. Brussels weaves are available in only one loop-pile height.

In addition to these designs from regular production, Burrows & Co. can provide examples from its archives which can be produced on a custom basis. The firm will also supply information on installation and qualified installers.

Literature available

J. R. BURROWS & CO.
PO Box 1739, Jamaica Plain
Boston, MA 02130
(617) 524-1795
Fax (617) 524-5372

COUNTRY BRAID HOUSE
Braided rugs which are hand-laced will not unravel after several weeks of use, an experience we once had with a "store-bought" variety. And, also, because the braids are hand-laced, the rugs are completely reversible. Country Braid House wouldn't have it any other way and uses *only* high-quality wool in four layers. You can select from two sizes of braid – the traditional 3/4" New England style or the 1"-wide Continental. Over 200 colors of wool are available for use in various combinations. All rugs are custom-produced.

Brochure available

COUNTRY BRAID HOUSE
RFD #2, Box 29, Clark Rd.
Tilton, NH 03276
(603) 286-4511

FAMILY HEIR-LOOM WEAVERS

David and Carole Kline should receive a medal for their contribution to reproduction textiles. Until they began producing flat woven ingrain carpet in the 1980s, little or none was available. Today their well-researched and beautifully woven designs appear in such important restorations as the Abraham Lincoln Home, Springfield, Illinois; the Noah Webster House at the Henry Ford Museum and Greenfield Village; and Wheatland, the Lancaster, Pennsylvania, home of President James Buchanan. The 90 percent

worsted wool and 10 percent nylon blend is woven in 36"-wide strips. The Klines will arrange the hand-seaming of strips to form room-size carpets, if that is desired. Two runner patterns are also produced in 22½" strips.

Two of the larger carpet designs are illustrated first: "Maple Leaf," dated to the 1850s, and "Ballestone," c. 1870-1910. These illustrations are

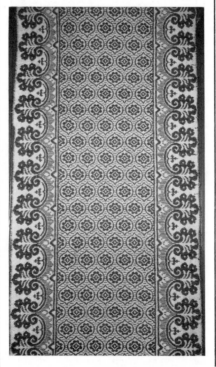

followed by the two runner patterns: "Victorian Rose" and "Goldy Paley."

Literature, $1

FAMILY HEIR-LOOM WEAVERS
RD #3, Box 59E
Red Lion, PA 17356
(717) 244-5921
(717) 246-2431

HERITAGE RUGS

Woven flat area rugs in 100 percent wool are custom produced by this firm. No one rug is like another. Any size up to 15' wide by 35' long can be woven on an antique loom. Colors, too, are selected by the client. For a Colonial or early 19th-century country house, this kind of design might be just right.

Brochure available

HERITAGE RUGS
Lahaska, PA 18931
(215) 343-5196

PAT HORNAFIUS

Delightful hooked rugs with folk motifs have made Pat Hornafius's reputation. She is a native of Lancaster County, Pennsylvania, and fortunately has not become a victim of latter-day Pennsylvania-Dutch kitsch. Her designs, as the photo illustrates, are refreshingly original. All

rugs are handmade of wool, hand-dyed, and hand-cut to ¼" strips. These are then hooked on a burlap base and finished with a rug yarn binding and dyed-to-match rug tape.

Literature available with SASE

PAT HORNAFIUS
113 Meadowbrook Lane
Elizabethtown, PA 17022
(717) 367-7706

The Royal Brighton Pavilion Collection has been introduced recently. There are eleven rugs, including the 27"-wide Wilton, "The King's Suite," shown as used in the P. T. Barnum Museum, Bridgeport, Connecticut. Also displayed at this museum is the Wheeler Drawing Room carpet, a 27"-wide Wilton weave, and illustrated on the following page.

A very traditional French design is "Salle de Fete," a cut pile carpet woven in France. The motifs are richly colored and rendered in wool.

Designs suitable for Art Deco interiors are woven in 36"-wide Wilton wool cut piles in Austria. The collection is named after the original designer, Josef Hoffmann, an architect and craftsman who founded the Wiener Werkstätte in 1903.

Venetian and list carpeting in varied stripes or herringbone patterns from

PATTERSON, FLYNN & MARTIN, INC.
This well-known supplier of quality carpeting has very carefully and intelligently enlarged its selection of textiles suitable for period buildings. In addition to its own line, the company now also distributes some thirty 18th- and 19th-century carpet designs from Colefax and Fowler and the Roger Oates Design Associates collection of list and Venetian flat woven carpeting.

The first photograph shows Patterson, Flynn & Martin's design for The Old Merchant's House, an 1832 New York City landmark. All wool 27" Wilton carpeting is used in both parlors. This is an exact reproduction of material first installed in 1867.

The Colefax and Fowler Line of English country house designs is shown next. Each is a Brussels loop

pile 27"-wide carpet. Borders are available for use with the carpeting.

Literature available.

PATTERSON, FLYNN & MARTIN, INC.
979 Third Ave.
New York, NY 10022
(212) 688-7700
Fax (212) 826-6740

RASTETTER WOOLEN MILL
Cotton or wool rag rugs and carpeting can be produced by Rastetter in 27" and 36" widths. One of the favorite designs, "Brick and Block,"

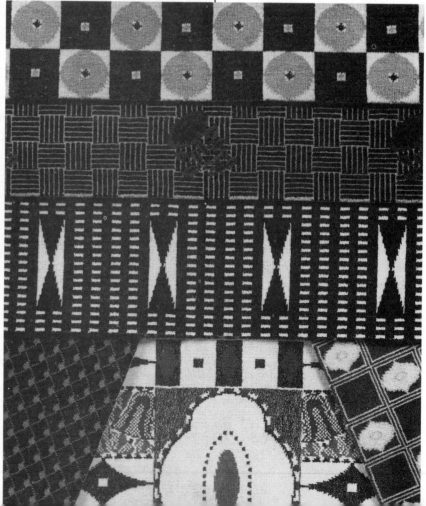

the Oates collection are especially useful for Colonial and early 19th-century interiors. Flat woven in 27" widths, these may be used as runners, area rugs, or sewn together to form large-scale carpeting. All are of pure new wool, and larger rugs are bound with wide linen tape.

was woven at a demonstration held for the Smithsonian Institution in 1971. It can be made in rug sizes and custom carpet lengths. There are many other patterns to choose from, many of which are available in stock. Rastetter is also a good source for wool runners. They can be woven with a heavy duty black warp or an even tougher linen warp.

Brochure available

RASTETTER WOOLEN MILL
State Rte. 39 and 62
Millersburg, OH 44654
(216) 674-2103

THOS. K. WOODARD AMERICAN
    ANTIQUES & QUILTS
Long experience serving the needs of folk art collectors convinced Woodard and his partner, Blanche Greenstein, that simple flat-woven floor coverings were badly needed. Long before other suppliers had emerged, the Woodard Weave line was introduced. It is based on the plain but very colorful cotton textiles of Pennsylvania-German craftsmen. The rugs are especially effective as stair or hall runners. Each is supplied in a 27" width. Area rugs in various widths and lengths up to 31' can also be supplied. The rugs are hand-knotted with fringed ends. At a small additional cost, the edges may be bound. As illustrated, there is a wide variety of stripes and checks to choose from. Woodard

Weave textiles are distributed nationally. For a list of distributors, contact the New York gallery.

Catalog, $5

THOS. K. WOODARD AMERICAN
    ANTIQUES & QUILTS
835 Madison Ave.
New York, NY 10021
(800) 332-7847
(212) 988-2906 (NY)

Other suppliers of period rugs and carpeting include: LANGHORNE CARPET CO., SCALAMANDRÉ, *and* STARK CARPET CORP.

Runners. *See* **Rugs and Carpets.**

Shutters on a house in Princeton, New Jersey. Photograph by Jack E. Boucher, Historic American Buildings Survey.

Sash. *See* **Windows.**

Sconces. Few forms of early lighting were more simple – or more varied in design – than the sconce. With candles a scarce and expensive commodity in 18th-century North America, a way was needed to provide both a fixed place for a candleholder and a means to protect the candle from tallow-wasting drafts. A primitive metal candleholder mounted on a wall removed from drafts was both functional and decorative. Moreover, the metal often reflected candlelight, thereby increasing the illumination in a room. From the simple ornamentation of these first sconces developed more creative and elaborate designs. The variety of sconces crafted in the century before gaslight eventually eclipsed the candle is nothing short of astonishing, and the number of designs expertly reproduced by modern lighting artisans is an almost equal source of wonder and delight. In the 19th century, the advent of gaslight and, later, electric light, produced sconces and wall fixtures in imaginative designs reflecting the various revival styles of the day. These, too, are reproduced today.

AUTHENTIC DESIGNS
Authentic Designs is one of those rare firms sufficiently ethical to use the rarely-seen word "adaptation" in its literature. Its handsome catalog is entitled "Catalogue of Hand Crafted Re-creations & Adaptations of Early American Lighting Fixtures," clearly delineating a difference between a "re-creation" – a reproduction, down to the smallest detail, of an object from the past – and an "adaptation" -

an *interpretation* of a style from the past. Too frequently modern suppliers adapt the past but label their goods "reproductions" when in fact they are not. Authentic Designs knows the difference and we applaud their honest approach to producing period lighting fixtures. Over thirty different sconce designs are offered, most reproductions, some adaptations. All are made of brass and available in a variety of finishes.

The sconces can be had electrified or fitted for candles. Shown are SC2-228, a two-candle model 12" high, 9" wide, and 4$\frac{1}{2}$" deep; and SC1-139, a one-candle model 9$\frac{3}{4}$" high, 4$\frac{1}{2}$" wide, and 6$\frac{3}{4}$" deep.

Catalog, $3

AUTHENTIC DESIGNS
42 The Mill Rd.
West Rupert, VT 05776
(802) 394-7713
Fax (802) 394-2422

THE BRASS KNOB
Antique lighting fixtures like this handsome turn-of-the-century gas and electric sconce are among The Brass Knob's specialties. Emphasizing Victorian pieces, but featuring many

other styles as well, including Art Nouveau and Art Deco, The Brass Knob warehouses an exclusive collection of architectural antiques. Much of the company's stock is one of a kind, so the selection is ever changing. No catalog can keep up with the stock's turnover, but written inquiries are welcome. Since the firm is one of the best sources of antique lighting fixtures on the East Coast, a visit to the shop is highly recommended.

Brochure, free

THE BRASS KNOB
2311 18th St., NW
Washington, DC 20009
(202) 332-3370

CLASSIC ILLUMINATION INC.
Particularly rich in reproduction lighting fixtures of the Victorian and early 20th century, Classic Illumination is a fundamental source for sconces in the Mission and Art Deco styles. Deco, in particular, is difficult to reproduce convincingly, but Classic Illumination has succeeded in doing so, especially in its Art Deco "wall shield" model, which would require color photography to do it half justice. In the decades immediately preceding American Deco, the Mission style was popular in some sections of the country, including California, so it is only appropriate that a Berkeley supplier should carry an entire line of Mission fixtures. Shown are two models of sconces in a simple

reduction of the Mission aesthetic. They are available in a number of finishes and in a wide choice of shades.

Catalog, $5

CLASSIC ILLUMINATION INC.
2743 Ninth St.
Berkeley, CA 94710
(415) 849-1842
Fax (415) 849-2328

CONANT CUSTOM BRASS
This firm of metal fabricators, skilled in every area of the trade from welding to metal spinning, entered the decorative lighting field over a decade ago and has been involved in all aspects of the business from restoration and design to custom manufacturing and production. Although the company offers a line of stock fixtures, including sconces, almost all of which are refreshingly simple and functional, it is particularly interested in custom design and is willing and able to build any conceivable type of fixture. What's more, it maintains a restoration division providing complete refinishing services as well as complex repair and rewiring. It also keeps a large and ever-changing inventory of restored antique fixtures, including sconces, in its Vermont showrooms. If it's sconces you want, you can find them new, antique, restored, or custom made at Conant.

Catalog, $2

CONANT CUSTOM BRASS, INC.
270 Pine St.
Burlington, VT 05401
(802) 658-4482

HURLEY PATENTEE MANOR
Handcrafted lighting fixtures modeled after museum pieces and items in private collections comprise the attractive offerings from Hurley Patentee Manor. Each is a faithful copy of an outstanding 17th- or 18th-century fixture; many have been electrified and use fifteen-watt candle bulbs set in sleeves made to resemble aged, dripped candles, while most are also available in candle-burning models. Hurley's collection of reproduction sconces is more extensive than any other supplier's and incorporates a variety of styles from primitive to sophisticated Colonial decor. The firm's catalog is a virtual illustrated history of 18th-century lighting. Space allows us to show only one of the sixty or so sconces in the Hurley catalog. The oval mirror sconce measures 16" high,

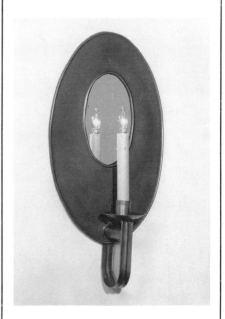

9" wide, and 4 1/2" deep, and is a quaint and unique early tin fixture.

Catalog, $3

HURLEY PATENTEE MANOR
R.D. 7, Box 98A
Kingston, NY 12401
(914) 331-5414

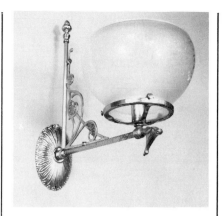

NOWELL'S, INC.

Nowell's, Inc. opened in Sausalito almost four decades ago. As the shop evolved, antique lighting became the most important part of the business, and repair, restoration, and maintenance of light fixtures became the shop's most important service. For years, the firm planned the production of a collection of top-quality reproductions of antique lighting fixtures, and, encouraged by a growing national interest in architectural preservation, began to produce them in the mid-'70s. Nowell's is a good source of Victorian and turn-of-the-century fixtures, including a broad spectrum of sconces, only two of which are shown here. The North Beach (left) and the Russian Hill (right) are *simple*, functional fixtures from an age of opulence. Reflecting the early 20th-century Colonial Revival style, the North Beach would be perfectly at home in any traditional room. In addition to its catalog of stock fixtures, Nowell's continues to sell antique fixtures, including sconces, in its showroom.

Catalog, $3.50

NOWELL'S INC.
PO Box 295, 490 Gate 5 Rd.
Sausalito, CA 94966
(415) 332-4933

fixtures of the day. Victorian extravagance is notoriously difficult to reproduce, but, as these sconces demonstrate, Roy succeeds where others have failed.

Lighting catalog, $5

ROY ELECTRIC CO., INC.
1054 Coney Island Ave.
Brooklyn, NY 11230
(718) 434-7002
Fax (718) 421-4678

THE TINNER

Tinsmith Jim Barnett reproduces almost a score of 18th-century tin sconces. The quality of his handmade reproductions is such that it is difficult to detect them from the originals, housed in museums and private collections. The sconces, primitive in design and justly deserving of the overused designation "Early American," are exact replicas of sconces from Pennsylvania, Virginia, North Carolina, and New England. Most are available electrified or fitted for candles.

Catalog, $1.50

THE TINNER
PO Box 353
Spencer, NC 28159
(704) 637-5149

ROY ELECTRIC CO.

The virtues of this fine supplier of reproduction lighting fixtures are well-known to readers of *The Old House Catalogue* and are enumerated elsewhere in this book *(see* **Chandeliers** and **Hanging Fixtures**).

Suffice it to say regarding Victorian and early 20th-century sconces that Roy offers a selection unrivalled in scope, with particular attention paid to the more elaborate and fanciful

VICTORIAN LIGHTCRAFTERS

The Stansfield family began restoring and selling Victorian lighting fixtures in 1971. In 1979, their company, Victorian Lightcrafters, expanded and began making its own reproduction fixtures, basing its designs on original models. All of the company's products are soldered and assembled by hand, using the same techniques as those used more than a century

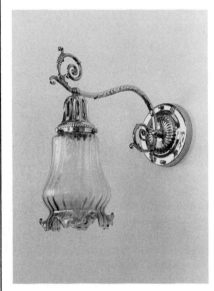

ago. Victorian Lightcrafter's lights are made of solid brass, and all the components are cast, spun, or stamped. Various finishes and a choice of shades are available. About thirty different Victorian wall fixtures are included in the firm's catalog, all of them unique to the company. Two are illustrated here: W-610, an electrified gas fixture, and W-851, an early electric fixture.

Catalog, $3

VICTORIAN LIGHTCRAFTERS, LTD.
PO Box 350
Slate Hill, NY 10973
(914) 355-1300

Other suppliers of sconces and wall fixtures include: antique – CITY LIGHTS, QUEEN CITY ARCHITECTURAL SALVAGE, SALVAGE ONE, *and* WATERTOWER PINES; *reproduction –* COHASSET COLONIALS, THE COPPERSMITH, A. J. P. COPPERSMITH & CO., GATES MOORE, HAMMERWORKS, HISTORIC HARDWARE LTD., KING'S CHANDELIER CO., LEMEE'S FIREPLACE EQUIPMENT, THE ORIGINAL CAST LIGHTING, RENAISSANCE MARKETING, INC., REJUVENATION LAMP & FIXTURE CO., RENOVATOR'S SUPPLY, ROBERTS LIGHTING CRAFT, SHAKER WORKSHOPS, *and* THE VILLAGE FORGE.

Screen Doors and Storm Doors.
Screening was available in America as early as the 1700s, but it was not until the years following the Civil War that screen doors and window screens became common. The sound of a screen door being opened and then slamming shut has a familiar ring to many older Americans. It is a sound that one identifies with an old house and a screen door that is wood and not aluminum. In recent years it has become difficult to buy a decent screen door. Consequently, special manufacturers of decorative wooden doors have appeared on the scene to challenge the mediocrity of our age. Window screens may be made up by some of these millwork firms, but doors are their bread and butter. For simple wood window screens, the only kind that were made in the past, a local carpenter usually can be called upon. Storm doors and windows are also without ornamentation, and there are only a handful of firms that supply custom wood models. Once again, a local craftsman probably can be relied upon. Most of the aluminum models are not appropriate for an old house of any age or style. With both screens and storm windows, however, it is important for any muntins to be fixed in the same position they assume in the windows that are covered. One-piece screening or glass, of course, will work perfectly well for small or medium-sized windows.

COPPA WOODWORKING INC.
A wood screen door may not be a necessity, but Ciro C. Coppa felt that an aluminum model "wasn't right." "Friends and neighbors started asking me to do it for them. I made up the screen designs in my head to go along with the design of the house." That was ten years ago and now Coppa Woodworking offers at least fifty stock screen-door designs as well as the fabrication of custom designs. These are made in ³/₄" sugar pine or solid oak. The standard sizes are 30" by 81", 32" by 81", and 36" by 81". At an additional cost, Coppa will make up a door with a 1¹/₈"-thick frame and in just about any size. The doors may be left unfinished or given

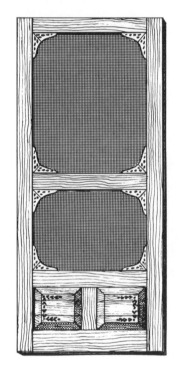

a Spanish oak (light) or American walnut (dark) finish. Hardware is included with each order. Coppa Woodworking is also a good source of arch-top doors and pine screens for regular windows and sidelights. Only fiberglass screening is used.

Free catalog

COPPA WOODWORKING INC.
1231 Paraiso Ave.
San Pedro, CA 90731
(213) 548-4142
Fax (213) 548-6740

CREATIVE OPENINGS
Hardwood screen doors suitable for Victorian and later houses have been produced by Creative Openings for a dozen years on a custom basis. The firm claims to have the largest selection of designs in the country.

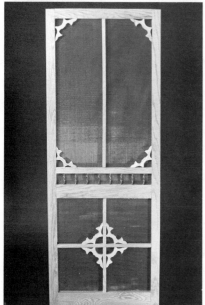

Only mortise and tenon construction is used and no portion of a joint is left exposed to the elements. For this reason, Creative Openings also uses brass screening. Doors can be supplied unfinished or with a white, black, or clear lacquer, three coats of which are applied. Glass or plexiglass storm inserts can be supplied for winter use. They are wood-framed. Illustrated are three of Creative Opening's imaginative designs.

Literature available

CREATIVE OPENINGS
PO Box 4204
Bellingham, WA 98227
(206) 671-6420 (WA)
(800) 677-7420

THE OLD WAGON FACTORY
Combination wood storm and screen doors for almost any style house can be made up by The Old Wagon Factory. Models may feature Victorian gingerbread trim, Colonial raised panels, or multi-lights. One model,

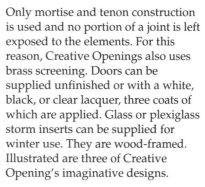

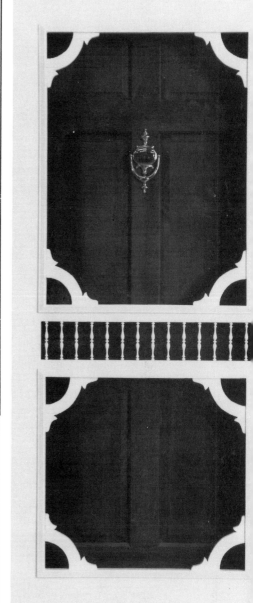

the six panel door #108, has panels which correspond with those on a popular-style Colonial entrance door. Poplar is used for most work, but other woods can be specified. All doors are custom made and fall into two categories – standard or special – depending on size. Standard doors are 32" by 80" or 81", and 36" by 80" or 81"; all other sizes are considered special. Illustrated are two Victorian designs incorporating spindles and brackets. Construction is mortise and tenon.

Catalog, $2

THE OLD WAGON FACTORY
PO Box 1427, OC91

Clarksville, VA 23927
(804) 374-5787
Fax (804) 374-4646

*Other suppliers of combination wood
screen and storm doors are:* GOTHOM,
INC. and SILVERTON VICTORIAN
MILLWORKS.

Scrolls. *See* **Ornaments.**

Sculpture. Sculpture in North
America is displayed primarily
outdoors. Most interiors do not have
the space or the proportions
necessary for this type of fine or
decorative art. As to period styles,
good art of any age is appropriate.
Certain motifs, however, have been
popular at various times. Sets of cast-
iron or stone dogs, for example, were
sometimes stationed on a porch or
flanked a garden path. Eagles may
have been positioned on gateposts.
Figural art in cast lead or stone, such
as a neoclassical nymph or Pan, was
also once considered appropriate.
Gnomes, burros with carts, and
composition deer have not yet
achieved a sufficient historical patina
for erstwhile reproducers! Cast-iron
deer, however, were used as lawn
ornaments in the Victorian period.

Sources of good sculptural pieces are
few and far between. KENNETH LYNCH
AND SONS stands out from all others
for quality and variety. Several
representative pieces from the vast
Lynch collection are shown.
CHILSTONE is a recognized English
manufacturer of garden sculpture.
Architectural antiques firms are
sometimes good sources, and among
the best for sculpture are
IRREPLACEABLE ARTIFACTS and UNITED
HOUSE WRECKING.

Seeds. *See* **Gardens, Old Fashioned
Plants and Seeds.**

Settees and Sofas. Before there were
settees, there were settles. The first
North American settles were long,
high-backed, heavy wooden benches,
usually made of pine, which
provided little in the way of comfort,
but did offer seating for three or four
persons. Occasionally these massive
pieces were permanently fixed; more
often they were positioned near the
fire in a sitting room, where their
solid backs afforded some protection
from cold winter drafts. Usually such
pieces provided extra storage space in
boxes beneath the seats. A more
popular and lasting derivative of the
settle was the settee, which could
usually accommodate two people in
relative comfort. While some settees,
like low-backed Windsors, continued
to be made entirely of wood, it
became more common for upholstery
to be added. Frames were beautifully
carved of walnut, mahogany, or
beechwood; seats (and sometimes
backs) were padded and covered in
fine fabrics, or sometimes painted
and gilded to elegant effect. While the
terms "sofa" and "settee" are
sometimes confused, the former
generally applies to a later, larger, and
more generously upholstered piece of
furniture. The words "sofa" and
"couch" are now used
interchangeably to define a
generously-proportioned upholstered
seating unit for two or more persons.
A couch, however, was originally a

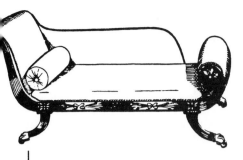

long, half-backed lounge with a headrest, meant for solitary reclining, and is now more commonly referred to as a day bed or chaise longue. The word "sofa" comes from the Turkish word for a pile of carpets used for reclining in comfort. The term was not in general use before the 18th century; early sofas are difficult to differentiate from settees, but usually they are larger, more generously upholstered, and less formal pieces.

During the early 19th century, sofas became increasingly fashionable, and it was *de rigueur* to have at least one (or preferably two) large ones in the drawing room to facilitate conversation or aid relaxation, as they were frequently used for lounging. Over the centuries sofas, like other furniture, reflected changing modes and styles, but they remained essentially the same in form. Most 18th- and 19th-century sofas, however, had in common their wedding of beautiful woods to fine upholstery: the frame and supports were as important as the stuffing. Modern imitators too often hide inferior legs and framing beneath billows of fabric.

Almost any homeowner considers the acquisition of a sofa or settee a major investment, with selection governed by taste, quality, style and cost. Given these considerations, the choices are many. Antique? Commercial reproduction? Handcrafted reproduction? Antique 18th- and early 19th-century sofas and settees are expensive and relatively difficult to find, but Victorian pieces, particularly if in need of reupholstering, are less pricey than one might think, especially if they have sat for some time in an antique

shop and the proprietor is eager to make room for new stock. If the frame is in reasonably good condition, it's well worth the additional investment of reupholstery, or even restoration, since to our mind no commercial reproductions of Victorian furniture successfully replicate the exuberant and elegant workmanship of the originals. Reproductions of 18th- and early 19th-century furniture, however, are something else again.

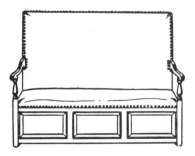

Several well-known lines of 18th-century reproductions, including sofas and settees, are well made and faithful to original pieces in design and finish. The Seraph Country Collection, available through SERAPH EAST and SERAPH WEST, is well worth considering since it is particularly rich in very successful adaptations of

period sofas. Seraph's Chippendale Camelback sofa, upholstered in a lovely flamestitch fabric, is particularly recommended, as is the firm's late 17th-century-inspired William and Mary sofa. Both sofas, and their companion wing chairs, would be handsome additions to period rooms.

Finally, in the quest for the right sofa, one should seriously consider the many woodworkers listed in this book who use antique tools and follow traditional methods of cabinetmaking. Their reproductions are more costly than those produced by manufacturers, but they are in every respect "antiques of the future" and works to be treasured. A handcrafted settee, for example, is more than likely to be worth the extra

investment. It will have been made from a carefully selected hardwood, hand assembled, and hand carved or turned. The finish alone will be of museum quality. GERALD CURRY'S hand-carved reproduction of a rare Queen Anne transitional settee, for example, is a work of art, and he is more than capable of reproducing other high-style settees or sofas on a custom basis. Every aspect of Curry's work is authentic, and it would take an expert to differentiate his finished pieces from their antique originals. Another cabinetmaker worth considering is E. RUMSEY, who specializes in sack-back and bow-back Windsor settees.

Settles. *See* **Settees and Sofas.**

Shakes and Shingles. In addition to serving as a roofing material (*see* **Roofing**), wood shingles are also used to cover exterior walls. Shakes are a special form of shingle first introduced in the Pacific Northwest. They are split and usually given a

special edge profile. Oak, cedar, and redwood are common materials for shakes and shingles. The term "shingle style" refers to those buildings of the late 19th century which have facades ornamented with shingles. Henry Hobson Richardson and the firm of McKim, Mead and White are generally credited with popularizing the style in seaside houses for wealthy clients in the Northeast. The inspiration for these late-Victorian designs is thought to be the one-and-a-half-story shingle-clad Cape Cod house of the Colonial period. Cladding in shingles was a protective measure against the elements, and the shingles were allowed to gray with weathering. Shingles, solely for ornamental purposes, can also be used in modest ways in late-Victorian and Colonial Revival houses for facade panels and gables. The wood shingles may often be combined with brickwork or clapboards.

SHAKERTOWN CORPORATION
Western red cedar shingles are Shakertown's principal product. As illustrated, these are offered in even forms as well as what the company calls "fancy cuts." There are nine of these patterns – square, arrow, diamond, diagonal, round, octagonal, half cove, hexagonal, and fishscale. The even shingles are sold in 8' single or double courses; fancy cuts may be purchased individually or in a single 8' course. Panels are permanently laminated to exterior-type waterproof

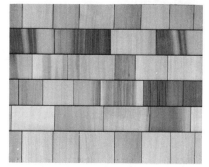

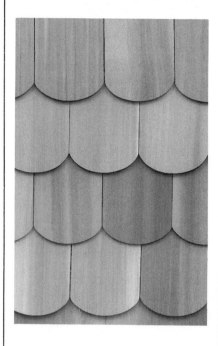

plywood. Shakertown products are available nationally. Contact the company for the name of your nearest distributor.

Literature available

SHAKERTOWN CORPORATION
1200 Kerron St., PO Box 400
Winlock, WA 98596
(800) 426-8970
(206) 785-3501 (WA)

OAK CREST MANUFACTURING, INC.
In addition to roofing shingles, Oak Crest is a supplier of oak shakes for walls. Unlike the roofing shingles, these are not tapered and are available in only one uneven form. Consequently, they have a rough, rustic appearance. They will soon weather to a traditional soft gray.

Literature available

OAK CREST MANUFACTURING, INC.
6732 E. Emory Rd.
Knoxville, TN 37938
(615) 922-1311

Other suppliers of wood shingles are:
CEDAR VALLEY SHINGLE SYSTEMS and MAD RIVER WOODWORKS.

Shaper Knives. *See* **Molder Knives.**

Shells. *See* **Niche Caps and Units; Ornaments.**

Shields. *See* **Ornaments.**

Shingles. *See* **Shakes and Shingles.**

Shower Units/Fittings. *See* **Bath Hardware.**

Shutter Hardware. The principal items required especially for shutters are fasteners or dogs. Other types of hardware such as hinges and latches are the same or similar to those used for doors. Shutter dogs are used only with exterior shutters which can be easily blown to and fro by the wind. Some say that the sound of a banging shutter is evocative, but it is also damaging and soon becomes a nuisance.

BEECH RIVER MILL CO.
Greg Dales has recently added a new line of New England-style shutter hardware to his main output of louvered and paneled shutters. Not satisfied with the usual hinges and hooks, he supplies one to fasten the

shutter edge to the side of a window. This mounting hardware consists of a one-side flat hinge that will receive a hook. Two sets of hinges and hooks are installed for each shutter, the hinge being mounted on the back edge of the shutter, and the hook being driven into the window casing. Fasteners to hold the shutters against the wall are also available.

Catalog, $3

BEECH RIVER MILL CO.
Old Rte. 16
Centre Ossipee, NH 03814
(603) 539-2636 (telephone and Fax)

HISTORIC HARDWARE LTD.
Three styles of shutter dogs or

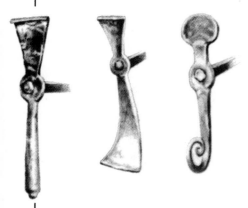

holdbacks are hand-forged at Historic Hardware. The designs are based on antiques used in St. Augustine, Florida; Charleston, South Carolina; and Germantown, Pennsylvania. Each is supplied with a forged pintel that can be driven into a frame wall. If walls are of stone or brick, the company will provide another type of pintel.

Catalog, $3

HISTORIC HARDWARE LTD.
PO Box 1327
North Hampton, NH 03862
(603) 964-2280

WOODBURY BLACKSMITH & FORGE CO.
Extremely attractive Colonial-period wrought-iron shutter dog designs have been selected by Woodbury from its own reference library of historic designs. Each is mounted with a pintel so that the fastener can be turned in a horizontal position to allow the shutter to swing free; a

counterweight will cause the shutter dog to return to the vertical. A New Jersey design has a whimsical rat-tail counterweight, and one from New York state is tapered with a flared counterweight. Each of the shutter dogs is, in essence, sculpted on the forge. Unfortunately, as Woodbury notes, it is impossible for them to duplicate later Victorian cast-iron designs.

Catalog, $3

WOODBURY BLACKSMITH & FORGE CO.
PO Box 268
Woodbury, CT 06798
(203) 263-5737

Other suppliers of shutter hardware are:
THE ARDEN FORGE CO.,
HAMMERWORKS, KAYNE AND SON
CUSTOM FORGED HARDWARE,
RENOVATOR'S SUPPLY, SHUTTERCRAFT,
and TREMONT NAIL CO.

Shutters. The fashion of shuttering windows is now very much with us. Only ten years ago it was possible to locate old shutters in a salvage yard, but the supply has practically disappeared. Consequently, the manufacture of new shutters has had a rebirth. To be avoided at all cost are vinyl and other cheap imitations which have neither the weight nor the profile necessary for exterior or interior use, and frequently are not even sized properly for the space they are intended to cover when closed. While decorative and enhancing most facades as well as interior spaces, shutters are meant to be used – to seal off the cold, and to block out light, and perhaps even noise, from the street. Houses that have been fitted with exterior shutters in the past are unlikely to have interior shutters as well, and vice versa, but both types might be used in the same building. Interior shutters are frequently bi-fold and, when open, are folded back against the window reveal. Yet another special type of shutter is a wood panel fitted on a track so that the shutter can be used like a sliding door. The most common design, however, for both exterior and interior use, is a set of two frames which may contain raised panels, louvers, or board-and-batten sheathing.

ARCHITECTURAL COMPONENTS, INC. Eighteenth-century interior and exterior shutters are produced in various designs by this firm. All are custom made to fit properly. Clear kiln-dried eastern white pine is the usual material used for either raised panel or louvered designs. Louvered shutters can be made with either fixed or movable components. Architectural Components is also a good source for board-and-batten shutters as well as those which may require a special applied or incised design. Illustrated is the traditional Deerfield shutter.

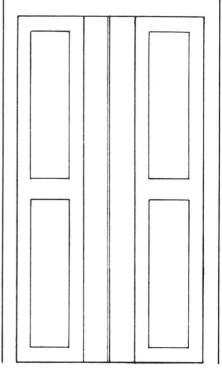

Catalog, $3

ARCHITECTURAL COMPONENTS, INC.
26 N. Leverett Rd.
Montague, MA 01351
(413) 367-9441
Fax (413) 367-9461

BEECH RIVER MILL CO.
It is fitting that the window shutters
and doors made by Beech River in
various traditional styles are
produced on Victorian-era machinery.
In 1982 Greg Dales bought a late
1800s shutter mill and the similarly
aged equipment in use since the turn
of the century. As shown, the shutters
are available in various styles; all are
made to order. For outside use, one
can choose from raised panel,
louvered, and combinations of the
two styles. Use of a decorative cutout
in a top raised panel is one of the
options offered. Beech River provides
a selection of simple but effective
cutout designs. Louvers can be fixed
in place or made moveable; if the
latter, a center control bar is
recommended. Shutters for interior
use are either louvered (stationary or

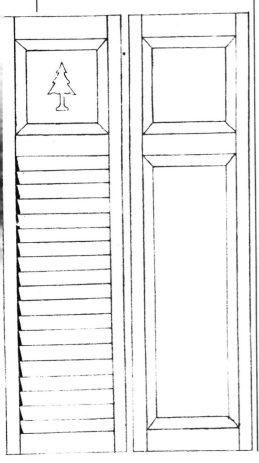

moveable) or of a raised-panel
design. Exterior shutters are 1$\frac{1}{8}$" or
1$\frac{3}{4}$" thick pine; inside shutters $\frac{3}{4}$"
thick. Cherry, mahogany, cypress,
oak, or ash may be substituted for
pine. Beech River is also an excellent
source for louvered and/or paneled
folding doors.

Catalog, $3

BEECH RIVER MILL CO.
Old Rte. 16
Centre Ossipee, NH 03814
(603) 539-2636 (telephone and Fax)

PERKOWITZ
Louvered interior shutters are carried
by this long-established firm in
several stock designs. Louvers may
be horizontal or vertical. Ponderosa
pine in a $\frac{3}{4}$" thickness is used for
complete shutters and for frames
which may carry fabric inserts rather
than louvers. Full-length and half-
length window units are available in
two- to eight-panel sections. Shutters
are shipped ready for the customer to
finish or will be stained at the factory.
At extra cost, Perkowitz can also
provide raised panels and hanging
hardware. Each two panels in an
assembly come already hinged
together.

Catalog, $1

PERKOWITZ
135 Green Bay Rd.
Wilmette, IL 60091-3375
(708) 251-7700

REM INDUSTRIES
Russell Uppstrom has been in
business for thirty-six years and has
watched the rebirth of a national
industry from his small town New
England outpost. All of his shutters
are custom made from the best
available pine. Shutters may be of
plain beaded boards, raised panels, or
louvered with movable or fixed
louvers. Both interior and exterior
types are made up. Open frame
interior shutters designed for fabric
or wallpaper-covered inserts are also
available.

Literature, $2

REM INDUSTRIES
Box 504
Northboro, MA 01532
(508) 393-8424

SHUTTERCRAFT
One of the largest producers in North
America of solid-pine shutters,
Shuttercraft offers many different
options. Each of the company's
products is correctly sealed;
galvanized yoke pins are used for
durability. Shuttercraft is also a
source for louvered doors. Just about
anything a customer could want is
available in stock and won't require
custom work.

Brochure available

SHUTTERCRAFT
282 Stepstone Hill Rd.
Guilford, CT 06437
(203) 453-1973

Other suppliers of shutters include:
AMHERST WOODWORKING & SUPPLY,
INC., BAILEY'S ARCHITECTURAL
MILLWORK, INC., THE BANK
ARCHITECTURAL ANTIQUES, ISLAND CITY
SHUTTERS, MAURER & SHEPHERD
JOYNERS, MICHAEL'S FINE COLONIAL
PRODUCTS and SUNSHINE
ARCHITECTURAL WOODWORKS.

Sidelights. *See* **Windows.**

Siding. Replacing sections of wood
siding is sometimes necessary;
hopefully, the problem will not
require complete residing. In either
case, millwork firms should be able to
help out if a local lumberyard does
not have a proper pattern on hand or
can not make one up. Siding for
Colonial houses is often clapboard
(*see* **Clapboards**); Victorian and later
buildings may require other forms of
siding. BLUE OX MILLWORKS and
DOVETAIL WOODWORKING are two
millwork firms with a well-developed
appreciation for 19th- and early 20th-
century buildings. *See also* **Shakes
and Shingles.**

Sills. A lamentable old house disease
is sill rot. Next to wormy beams,
nothing causes as much distress as
discovering that door or window sills
have started to disintegrate. The
problem may be simply one of old
age. Sills are among the most exposed
of building elements and can catch
water like a roof. Inside the house,
sills are unlikely to leak water, but

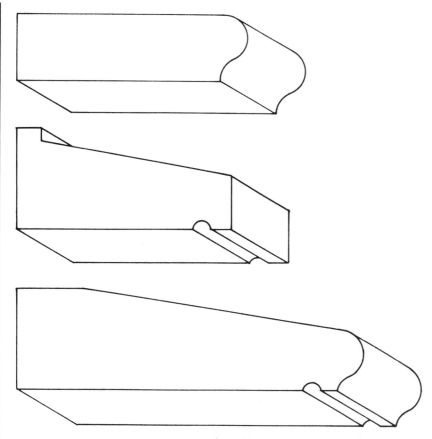

they can sweat, a condition caused by moisture absorption through the outside projection. It is a problem that has led many builders to recommend masonry sills and, if this is not possible, the use of as strong a hardwood as possible. A facade may contain a belt course or band of stone or brick above the window and door line which will serve to divert rain from the sills below. If your house, like most in North America, is of frame construction, a belt course is probably out of the question. Sills will simply have to be replaced when they cannot take any more abuse. If good materials have been used, this procedure may only occur once or twice in 100 years. If your time is now, consult one of the general millwork suppliers with a good stock of wood sills on hand such as SAN FRANCISCO VICTORIANA, three of whose designs are shown, or contact a supplier of cut stone (see **Stone**).

Sinks. Anyone aged forty-five or older will remember the day in the years following World War II when the kitchen and bathroom were "modernized." That would have been the day when the "unsightly" kitchen sink, bracketed to the wall and resting on clumsy porcelain forelegs, would have been carted away together with the "wretched" bathroom sink, a hopelessly out-of-date rectangular lavatory atop a fluted pedestal. The kitchen sink would have been replaced by a sink "unit," a single building block in a functional and expressive unit of cabinet-blocks arranged contiguously around the room. The new bathroom lavatory might have rested on gleaming stainless-steel legs, or, if it resembled the one down the street, it might already have been a porcelain basin set into a cabinet as the bathroom sink began its forward march towards becoming a "vanity." Everything, they say, comes full circle – or almost everything. As contemporary shoddiness makes us more and more nostalgic for the solidity of the past, the old-fashioned bathroom sink has been rediscovered. The pedestal sink, recalled from exile, is in demand once more, its lines peculiarly postmodern, its stark negation of the vanity-look an implicit rebellion against suburbia. Besides, some see the absence of storage space beneath an old-style

pedestal sink a hygienic blessing: there is no enclosed moisture-ridden space to clean. As to the "unsightly" kitchen sink on rickety poreclain legs, it remains in designer purgatory, despairing of its resurrection, unpopular as ever.

A. BALL PLUMBING SUPPLY
This fine company calls itself "the definitive supplier of nostalgic, European, and contemporary plumbing supplies," and, if you're nostalgic for any of the various styles of pedestal sink between the turn-of-the-century and, say, 1927, A. Ball will be able to oblige. The company's pedestal sinks are high-quality reproductions, six in all, of styles featuring round or rectangular pedestals (both fluted or plain) and basins in several period shapes.

Catalog, free

A. BALL PLUMBING SUPPLY
1703 W. Burnside St.
Portland, OR 97209
(503) 228-0026
Fax (503) 228-0030

KOHLER
Kohler has long been known as an innovative producer of durable kitchen and bathroom fixtures. In response to the demand from home renovators and those looking to incorporate old-fashioned charm into modern homes, Kohler has introduced a line of fixtures modeled after antiques, including bathroom sinks. Part of Kohler's Vintage line (including high-tank toilet,

freestanding bath, and other late-Victorian-inspired fixtures), the Vintage pedestal lavatory is a handsome melding of Victorian flavor and modern flair. An updated version of Kohler's original turn-of-the-century pedestal sink, the cast-iron lavatory features a rolled rim and stands 31" high. Shown with a faucet set from the company's Antique faucet line, the Vintage pedestal lavatory is available in a selection of colors. Another modern adaptation of the period pedestal sink is Kohler's Portrait pedestal lavatory. At 34" tall,

the lavatory features a graceful backsplash that tapers into a sculptured, tiered rim and a pedestal with strong vertical lines, resting on a tiered base. For those who want the convenience of a cabinet sink without the suburban home-center look of the conventional vanity, Kohler's furniture-quality Vintage vanity will prove an unexpected godsend.

Created by Baker Furniture for Kohler, its design is based on an original 18th-century French Provincial bow-front commode in the Baker Museum collection. Crafted of ash wood solids and veneers, it is offered in a choice of three finishes – natural ash, golden oak, and dark walnut. A large drawer, two smaller

ones, and a cane pull-out shelf are hidden behind curved and paneled doors.

Contact Kohler for the name of a distributor in your vicinity

KOHLER CO.
Kohler, WI 53044
(414) 457-4441

SALVAGE ONE

No, this wonderfully evocative photograph was not taken in the lavatory of a superannuated boarding school. It is, rather, one corner of one room of one floor of the five-floor old Chicago warehouse bulging with the architectural treasures of Salvage One, the Midwest's largest source for architectural artifacts. This veritable supermarket of antique interior house fittings houses 85,000 square feet of mantels, doors, hardware, light fixtures, millwork, columns, paneling, garden statuary, stairway parts, bar fixtures, claw-foot bathtubs, and, of course, pedestal sinks.

Brochure available

SALVAGE ONE
1524 S. Sangamon St.
Chicago, IL 60608
(312) 733-0098

VERMONT SOAPSTONE CO.

Soapstone is one of nature's wonder materials. It is soft enough to carve and yet amazingly durable. In addition, it is easy to maintain and is uniquely capable of absorbing and retaining heat. Vermont Soapstone Co. produces everything appropriate to the material from griddles to bedwarmers. Soapstone sinks are in a class by themselves. Prized for their natural beauty, these custom-made items are handmade by the craftsmen at Vermont Soapstone, a company that has been mining and manufacturing the material since 1850. The sinks are suitable for bath, kitchen, and greenhouse, and can be made with or without a drainboard and backsplash. The firm will work with you in designing a soapstone sink to your specifications.

Brochure available

Vermont Soapstone Co.
PO Box 168, Stoughton Pond Rd.
Perkinsville, VT 05151-0168
(802) 263-5404
Fax (802) 263-9451

Other suppliers of sinks and lavatories include: antique – The Brass Knob, Florida Victorian Architectural Antiques, Irreplaceable Artifacts, and Vintage Plumbing & Sanitary Specialists; *reproductions and adaptations –* Antique Baths and Kitchens, Crawford's Old House Store, Renovator's Supply, Restoration Works, Inc., Roy Electric Co., Watercolors, and West Hartford Lock.

Slate. *See* **Stone.**

Slide Bolts. *See* **Bolts.**

Snow Guards. A snow guard is a device, usually metal, that projects from the roof slope to prevent, or at least hinder, snow slides, thereby protecting people and pets from possible injury and foundation plantings from damage. These devices are usually placed across the roof in several alternating rows for maximum effect. Depending upon the size of the house, it may take thirty or more guards to protect a single side of the building. Snow guards are sometimes simple projecting wires, but in the past were made of iron in fanciful shapes. Snow guards in the shape of eagles are sometimes called snow birds. Another synonym for snow guard is snow iron.

Kenneth Lynch and Sons
Lynch's most notable snow guard is a replica of the famous Philadelphia

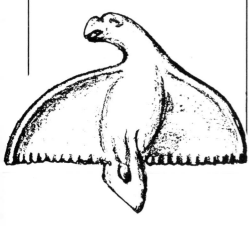

eagle snow guards that first appeared on Philadelphia buildings more than 200 years ago. Originally, these eagles were made of cast iron and fastened to slates with wrought-iron straps. Lynch's replicas are available in cast brass, cast bronze, cast lead, and stamped copper – all with copper or stainless-steel straps. The firm will advise how many guards are necessary for your particular roof and reminds you "that these eagles, in order to be effective, must be properly distributed over the roof. Too few will result in no effect at all." Other Lynch snow guards are an additional antique eagle, a fleur-de-lis, and a practical geometric-looking

device that hooks over slate and asbestos shingles without nailing.

Book of Garden Ornament, $9.50

Kenneth Lynch and Sons
78 Danbury Rd., Box 488
Wilton, CT 06897
(203) 762-8363
Fax (203) 762-2999

M. J. Mullane Co.
Cast in bronze for enduring wear, M. J. Mullane's snow guards replicate two classic versions of 18th- and 19th-century designs. The standard guard is T-shaped and was popular in the 19th century; an eagle model is similar to guards installed on townhouses, estates, and government buildings in the 18th and 19th centuries. The guards are easy to install and do not require removal of slates. Instead, using a special tool or two flat bars, adjoining slates are raised and the guard is slid into place between them until it hooks fast. To test whether the guard is firmly attached, the installer pulls it until the hook can be felt engaging the head of the slate. To be effective, snow guards

must be installed in sufficient quantity, about twenty to twenty-five per one hundred square feet of roof area. Mullane's snow guards can be installed on copper, metal, shingle, and shake roofs, too, by other methods.

Brochure available

M. J. Mullane Co.
PO Box 108, 17 Mason St.
Hudson, MA 01749
(508) 568-0597

Windy Hill Forge
For those who prefer figurative snow guards to geometric, Windy Hill Forge offers a variety of iron guards shaped like fans, leaves, acorns, eagles, or flowers. Steel bolts, brackets, and castings accompany all guards.

Brochure available

Windy Hill Forge
3824 Schroeder Ave.
Perry Hall, MD 21128-9783
(301) 256-5890

Soapstone. *See* **Sinks and Stone.**

Sofas. *See* **Settees and Sofas.**

Solariums. *See* **Greenhouses.**

Spandrels. Spandrels are common in medieval architecture. Used in an arched door opening, a spandrel fills the two upper corner spaces and forms, with the arch, a rectangle. These corners are usually very ornamental. Today the term "spandrel" has taken on a much broader meaning. It is a word that may be applied to a straight or arched band of ornamentation at the top of an opening in a wall. And rather than there being two spandrels, one on each side, there is one component which may be made up of brackets, drops, spindles, and rails. Fancy gingerbread spandrels are often used for porches and very wide openings in Victorian parlors where doors are not desired or needed. The passion to ornament passageways from one room to another reached its height in the late 19th century. Some interiors do, indeed, look almost if they were infested with gingerbread-spinning spiders. A little bit of this kind of decoration can go a very long way. *See also* **Arches, Brackets,** and **Porches.**

GOTHOM INC.
Elaborate spandrels are produced in pine or birch for interior use, and slightly simpler compositions are recommended by Gothom for porches where a harder wood may be needed. Many of the designs consist of spindles and balls and may also include drops, brackets, pendants, or running trim. Illustrated are two interior arrangements: the Classic (INTO6) and the Cupid (INTO2). Gothom frames out most of its designs so that they are ready for installation.

Catalog, $5

GOTHOM INC.
Box 421
Erin, ONT N0B 1T0
Canada
(519) 833-2574
Fax (519) 833-9751

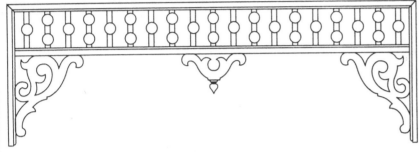

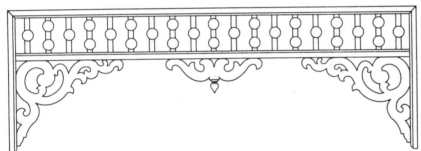

HICKSVILLE WOODWORKS CO.
White pine, poplar, or red oak can be used for the highly decorative spandrels made by Hicksville for interior and exterior purposes.

Illustrated are designs FS-3 and FS-5. All are ³/₄" thick with 1¹/₂" by ³/₄" frames. All work is custom. As the drawings show, the spandrels require lacy, intricate fretwork. Hicksville

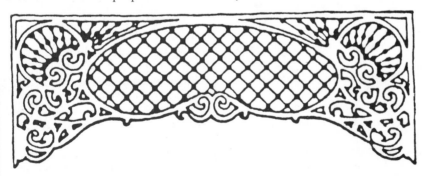

also offers a selection of much simpler ball spandrels.

Catalog and quarterly newsletter, $2

HICKSVILLE WOODWORKS CO.
265 Jerusalem Ave.
Hicksville, NY 11801
(516) 938-0171

VINTAGE WOOD WORKS
Vintage calls its gingerbread "Victorian" and "country." Victorian it certainly is. Offered are traditional spandrels with spindles or balls and dowels, and more ambitious compositions with names such as Jenny Lind, Lisa, Eloise, Mary Elizabeth, Anna Marie, and Lily Langtry. Undoubtedly, each design has a singular pedigree and story behind it. Pine is used for all of the work.

Catalog, $2

VINTAGE WOOD WORKS
513 S. Adams
Fredericksburg, TX 78624
(512) 997-9513

Other suppliers of spandrels include: CUMBERLAND WOODCRAFT CO., INC., W. F. NORMAN CORP., and THE OLD WAGON FACTORY.

Spindles. *See* **Balusters.**

Spiral Stairs. *See* **Stairs/Stairways.**

Stained Glass. Stained glass, which so suggests luxury and wealth to the modern eye, was commonly used in houses built in the late 1800s. By no means was the decorative use of multicolored glass confined to the wealthy. So popular was its use, in fact, that examples still abound in the residences of the middle class, especially in dining room and bathroom windows, front-door transoms and side-lights, and, particularly, staircase windows. "So valuable is stained glass in a hall," the author of a book on house decoration wrote in 1896, "that, whenever possible, windows are introduced above the landings or following the turn of the stairs." The area being pointed out could have been dark and gloomy, as were many stairhalls in Colonial Revival houses. Stained glass was a perfect medium for suffusing the staircase with light. Used in doors and upper sections of windows, stained glass guarantees privacy while at the same time providing a dash of color and the semblance of light. Panels from the last decades of the 1800s are widely available from architectural antiques dealers, although the great treasures of the period have probably disappeared forever. There are a number of artists in stained glass who are accomplished at producing reproductions as well as contemporary work of considerable merit.

GOLDEN AGE GLASSWORKS
Barbara Arrindell of Golden Age displays skill and ingenuity in everything she undertakes – from the restoration of a 3$^1/_2$' by 4$^1/_2$' window with a classical theme to the creation of a vivid yellow lampshade bordered with scarlet flowers and foliage in several shades of green. Although she excels at re-creating many styles, Arrindell is at her best when tackling natural subjects – vines, trees, flowers, or entire pastoral scenes. She is very much in the tradition of Louis Comfort Tiffany. She also manages Nottingham Gallery, which specializes in the sale of English, American, and Canadian antique windows.

Sets of slides or photographs, $2 each

GOLDEN AGE GLASSWORKS
339 Bellvale Rd.
Warwick, NY 10990
(914) 986-1487

POMPEI & CO.
The dogwood motifs expressed in stained glass are exactly like the naturalistic designs which so

enthralled the late Victorians. Joe and Ivy Pompei are expert at capturing the form and the spirit of design during the 1880s and '90s. As with most stained glass artists, all their work is custom.

POMPEI & CO.
454 High St.
Medford, MA 02155
(617) 395-8867

WALCOT RECLAMATION ARCHITECTURAL ANTIQUES
England is still an excellent source of antique stained glass. Stained glass was as widely used in Great Britain and neighboring Ireland as it was in North America during the late 19th century. Many of the examples found in salvage warehouses such as Walcot's were originally used in commercial structures such as hotels, bars, and even industrial buildings, but they can also be suitable for domestic use. Walcot always has a selection of panels and windows in stained glass on hand. Among the craftspeople associated with Walcot are Tony Bristow and David Bonham who create new designs in stained glass as well as restoring old pieces. They can skillfully match glass panels.

Brochure available

WALCOT RECLAMATION ARCHITECTURAL ANTIQUES
108 Walcot St.
Bath BA1 5BG
England
(0225) 444404
Fax (0225) 448163

Suppliers of antique stained glass are: ARCHITECTURAL ANTIQUE CO., ARCHITECTURAL ANTIQUES EXCHANGE, ARTEFACT ARCHITECTURAL ANTIQUES, THE BRASS KNOB, FLORIDA VICTORIAN

ARCHITECTURAL ANTIQUES, IRREPLACEABLE ARTIFACTS, SALVAGE ONE, and WESTLAKE ARCHITECTURAL ANTIQUES.

Other suppliers of new stained glass panels and windows are: BACKSTROM STAINED GLASS & ANTIQUES, LYN HOVEY STUDIO, INC., J. & R. LAMB STUDIOS, INC., MORGAN-BOCKIUS STUDIOS, INC., RAMBUSCH, SUNFLOWER GLASS STUDIO, and WILLIAMS ART GLASS STUDIO, INC.

Stairs/Stairways. This writer confesses to being in love with well-designed residential staircases even if, in old age, he will be reduced to contemplating them from ground level. A stairway can be the most interesting architectural feature of

any house, new or old. Chances are, however, that most main stairways were better designed and built in the old days than they are now. The art of stairbuilding is far from dead, and the elements needed for a successful treatment are still being produced. Most new homeowners, however, simply will not invest either the time

or the money in good design or allocate the space necessary for more than a straight shot up the wall. Considering the fact that even stairs not seen or used by visitors in old houses, such as back stairs and cellar stairs, were often handsomely built, it should not come as a surprise that today's principal staircases are so uninteresting. If you are determined to recapture something of the romantic past in a stairway or are attempting to restore, repair, or rebuild a period flight of stairs in or outside the house, there are traditional designs to copy or to be consulted for details, and craftsmen who can aid you. *See also* **Balusters, Posts,** and **Railings.**

AMERICAN CUSTOM MILLWORK, INC.
One of the specialties of this millwork firm is wood spiral and circular stairs. Treads, risers, posts, rails, balusters, handrails, and brackets are coordinated to create flowing, dramatic designs in proportion to the space allowed and in keeping with the other architectural appointments. A number of different radius designs are available and are sufficient to satisfy most space requirements. The firm has its own custom design service which will provide preliminary sketches as well as detailed technical drawings. Just about any fine wood can be specified.

Catalog, $5

AMERICAN CUSTOM MILLWORK, INC.
3904 Newton Rd., PO Box 3608
Albany, GA 31706
(912) 888-3303
Fax (912) 888-9245

THE DAHLKE STAIR CO.
Tom Dahlke ranks among the best stairbuilders today. He delves deep with his research, and when he uncovers suitable historical precedents, he uses them imaginatively to produce pieces that cleave to the period without plagiarizing its motifs. Using laminations of wood slivered to thicknesses of $^3/_{32}$", Dahlke bends and glues dozens of layers, with a resulting curved piece that looks like a twist of solid wood. Even his 180° Colonial winding stair for a simple saltbox has grace and authenticity. Dahlke knows how to put myriad

pieces together in a smooth, convincing manner. He is also skilled at repairing and restoring both high-style and rather commonplace old house stairways.

Brochure, $2

THE DAHLKE STAIR CO.
Box 418
Hadlyme, CT 06439
(203) 434-3589

THE IRON SHOP
Spiral staircases can be used effectively in some areas of old houses. They are especially useful when one wants to provide access to an upper level without destroying the structural integrity of a space, blocking out windows or doors, for example. Despite its name, The Iron Shop produces very handsome oak spiral stair kits as well as an oak straight stair kit. You may not want or have the ability to put it together

yourself, but a builder can certainly do so in no time at all. Kit form makes sense since the unit would have to be knocked down in any case for shipping. The kit includes all the basic ingredients needed for normal installation – top landing, landing rail, all hardware, treads, spindles, curved rail, etc. Various extras such as a solid oak handrail and different style posts and spindles can be successfully incorporated to provide a more distinctive design. The Iron Shop also continues to manufacture iron spiral stairs that are appropriate for outdoor use. They are at work on a new Victorian-style spiral stair kit in cast aluminum that will be suitable for either indoor or outdoor use.

Brochure available

THE IRON SHOP
Dept. HC, PO Box 547, 400 Reed Rd.
Broomall, PA 19008
(800) 523-7429
(215) 544-7100 (PA)

STAIR SPECIALIST
Very elegant stair systems in traditional curved designs have been produced by this firm for more than twenty-five years. The stairways are built as a single unit for easy installation along with railings, parts,

nosing, curved nosing, cove, etc. Oak, cherry, walnut, rosewood, teak, and mahogany are some of the woods that are used. Balusters are always made of a hardwood, especially maple or beech. Stringers make use of sugar pine instead of the plywood used by

many builders. Risers are always of hardwood composition. There are some standard handrail, tread bracket, and baluster patterns to choose from, but these are offered as ideas only, the customer making the final determination as to whether yet another option should be considered. Carved tread brackets, newel posts, and balusters can be custom created.

Catalog, $4

STAIR SPECIALIST
2257 W. Columbia Ave., Rte. 7
Battle Creek, MI 49017
(616) 964-2351

STEPTOE & WIFE ANTIQUES LTD.
Thanks to Steptoe, the cast-iron staircase has made a triumphant return to the old-house scene. Shown is the Barclay spiral staircase which has won many endorsements for its good construction, detailing, and authenticity. The model illustrated has the addition of a polished brass handrail. The Barclay is 60" in

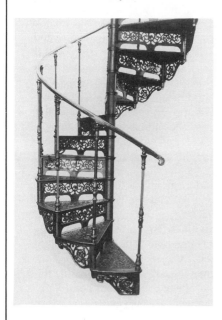

diameter and modular in form, with each complete riser consisting of three separate castings. The bolt-together system provides convenient packing, shipping, and on-site assembly.

Also available from Steptoe is a straight cast-iron staircase, the Kensington. It is especially suited for outdoor use and is of 36"-wide modular construction. Larger widths can be made on a custom basis. Each

complete riser consists of four castings.

Catalog, U.S. or Canadian customers, $3

STEPTOE & WIFE ANTIQUES LTD.
322 Geary Ave.
Toronto, ONT M6H 2C7
Canada
(416) 530-4200
Fax (416) 530-4666

Other builders of new stairs/stairways are: BAILEY'S ARCHITECTURAL MILLWORK, INC., DIXON BROTHERS WOODWORKING, KENTUCKY MILLWORK, and NEW ENGLAND WOODTURNERS.

A number of architectural antiques dealers stock parts as well as complete stairway systems. These include: ARCHITECTURAL ANTIQUE CO., ARCHITECTURAL ANTIQUES EXCHANGE, THE BRASS KNOB, FLORIDA VICTORIAN ARCHITECTURAL ANTIQUES, QUEEN CITY ARCHITECTURAL SALVAGE, and SALVAGE ONE.

Stands. The objects included in this category are special pieces of household furniture with a Victorian flavor such as hall stands, fern stands, and umbrella stands. They are by no means essential items, but they are practical and decorative. There are no similar Colonial pieces, the artifacts of this period being more Spartan and conventional, at least in comparison with the Victorian. Houses and their furnishings became more and more complex during the 19th century.

ARCHITECTURAL ANTIQUES EXCHANGE. A delicate fern stand in cast aluminum is a very close copy of a Victorian piece. The stand is a suitable pedestal for the display of a luxuriant plant anywhere in the house. Addressing the floral needs of

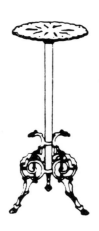

a Victorian household, one commentator wrote in the 1870s: "There are niches and corners in mansions where symmetry rather than colour is wanted; where a noble palm or graceful fern judiciously placed seems to harmonise so thoroughly with the architecture and other permanent ornaments that to remove the plant seems to leave an almost irremediable blank." What kind of fern? Probably asparagus. They were easy to cultivate 125 years ago and remain so today.

Literature available, $3

ARCHITECTURAL ANTIQUES EXCHANGE
715 N. Second St.
Philadelphia, PA 19123
(215) 922-3669

EAGLE EYE TRADING CO.
A mirrored hall tree with a seat and storage compartment below would be a most useful item for the hall or entryway of any Victorian or early 20th-century residence. Constructed of a solid hardwood, it has a distinctive dentil molding crown, solid-brass hat hooks, a tuffed green canvas cushion, and a full-length mirror. The design is late 19th century, suitable for Queen Anne or Colonial Revival interiors. The piece measures 78" high, 24" wide, and 15" deep. It is hand finished in either natural or dark oak.

EAGLE EYE TRADING CO.
PO Box 17900
Milwaukee, WI 53217
(414) 374-1984

LAWLER MACHINE & FOUNDRY CO.
A fabricator of metal ornamentation, fencing, and decorative accessories, Lawler includes a tree stand and an umbrella stand among its products. The tree stand also incorporates a place for umbrellas. Each of the models is highly ornate and is based on a cast-iron Victorian model. These pieces are now cast in aluminum only. The tree stand with six branches for hanging hats or coats stands 75" high and is 27" wide at the base. The umbrella stand is smaller – 28" high, 15" wide, and 7" deep – and includes a removable drip pan.

Catalog available, $8

American customers contact:
LAWLER MACHINE & FOUNDRY CO., INC.
PO Box 320069

Birmingham, AL 35232
(205) 595-0596

Canadian customers contact:
STEPTOE & WIFE ANTIQUES LTD.
322 Geary Ave.
Toronto, ONT M6H 2C7
Canada
(416) 530-4200
Fax (416) 530-4666

Stenciling. *See* **Painting, Decorative.**

Stone. By the mid-18th century stone quarries had been established in North America for extracting various types of sandstone, limestone, granite, and marble – the principal building stones. Because of the abundance of wood for houses, however, building in stone was always the exception. Unless one was using only random fieldstones, unearthed when preparing land for farming, the cost of obtaining quarried and cut stone was too great for most purposes. If there was a supply of cut stone available, it was most often saved for foundations and such elements as cornerstones, lintels, sills, hearths, and thresholds. There were areas such as the Delaware Valley, Rhode Island, parts of Virginia, river towns in the Midwest, and the hill country of Texas where stone building thrived at least during the period of settlement. These are the same areas in which stone was most

often quarried and where trained masons, often of Celtic or German extraction, were available. Scottish masons were employed to construct the White House and used locally quarried Acquia sandstone. By the late 1800s, however, many quarries had been closed down. Only recently has there been any increase in quarrying activity relating to building. The Acquia quarry, for example, has been reopened along the Potomac and has supplied stone for restoration work at the White House. Slate companies in upper New York State, New England, Pennsylvania, and Virginia have been opening new pits. A Delaware Valley quarry offering sandstone, in operation since the 1750s, has had to greatly expand its operations. The reason for all this activity is not that building in stone is enjoying a renaissance, but that the use of stone for various building elements is increasing. Stone has been rediscovered for flooring, paving, garden walls, and nearly hidden uses such as window sills and lintels. The natural strength and beauty of this most natural of earth's products is being admired anew. Stone will always be expensive to use because of the cost of transporting it even a small distance, but it will always be a good long-term investment. Stone is the rock of ages.

To secure building stone, it is best to consult first with the closest supplier.

He may only have ornamental stone sufficient for a hearth or sills, but if the need is greater there is a good chance that contact can be made through him to one of the large regional distributors or even with the original supplier or quarry. Some stone producers will deal directly with a customer whether the need is small or great. A small selection of these firms is given below. Keep in mind also that very fine stone such as a European marble is regularly imported and stocked nationally. *See also* **Roofing.**

CATHEDRAL STONE CO., INC.
A considerable demand for limestone and sandstone exists in the nation's capital. Washington is a city of monumental buildings, and excepting New York City, probably the only place in America where a gigantic cathedral of stone has been built in the second half of the 20th century. Buildings such as the White House and other important edifices need repair from time to time, and Cathedral Stone Co. can supply what is needed. The company is also called upon to create as well as restore carvings of various types.

CATHEDRAL STONE CO., INC.
2505 Reed St.
Washington, DC 20018
(202) 832-1135

CONKLIN'S PENNSYLVANIA WALL STONE
In addition to recycled lumber, Conklin is also a source of what the firm calls "wall stone," a bluestone or sandstone, and flags of the same material. The flags are suitable for paving and hearths; the thicker stones could be used for foundations, fireplaces, and walls.

Brochure available

CONKLIN'S PENNSYLVANIA WALL STONE
RD 1, Box 70
Susquehanna, PA 18847
(717) 465-3832

DELAWARE QUARRIES, INC.
A quarry operation has existed along the Delaware River in the small village of Lumberville, Pennsylvania, since the mid-18th century. Old residents can explain how the area being worked has continued to expand over the years. The present

firm is a major supplier of limestone and sandstone for reproduction period stone houses as well as much simpler building projects. It can also supply granite and slate cut to the size required.

Brochure available

DELAWARE QUARRIES, INC.
River Rd.
Lumberville, PA 18933
(215) 297-5647

RISING & NELSON SLATE CO., INC.
One of the principal suppliers of slate for roofing and other purposes, Rising & Nelson is a particularly useful source because of the wide range of colors offered. A gray green and gray black or black are the basic colors, but Vermont slate is also found in red, a strong green, and purple. The slate is available in smooth and rough textures and is made up in thicknesses of approximately $1/4$" to 1".

Literature available

RISING & NELSON SLATE CO., INC.
West Pawlet, VT 05775
(802) 645-0150

THE STRUCTURAL SLATE CO.
Structural's product, dark gray or black Pennsylvania slate from the state's slate belt above Easton, is what one would regard as standard. The material, however, need not be simply a dull institutional gray. Structural can supply a variegated shade of greater interest in a natural cleft or sand-rubbed finish. A honed glossy finish is probably best only for public buildings.

THE STRUCTURAL SLATE CO.
Pen Argyl, PA 18072
(800) 67-SLATE
Fax (215) 863-7016

Stools. Stools are convenient in many ways and, if low, can be pushed out of sight when not in use. Styles range from primitive carved wood tripods, not unlike those used in the past for milking, to countertop-height models with backs.

CANDLERTOWN CHAIRWORKS
Located in western North Carolina, the chairmakers of Candlertown,

Susan and Rick Steingress, know what "country" means. It is not an easy way to describe something unsophisticated or badly made. Candlertown's chairs and stools have style, and all of the models could have been used as easily 150 years ago as they are today. Among the stools is a design originally used by a weaver, a Shaker tall stool, a tall stool with arms, and, illustrated here, a low stool in either a 25" or 30" seat height.

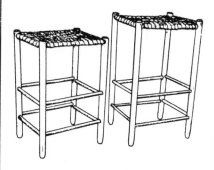

All the models are available in maple, hickory, or red oak and have hand-woven splint seats.

Catalog, $2

CANDLERTOWN CHAIRWORKS
PO Box 1630
Candler, NC 28715
(704) 667-4844

SPRING HOUSE CLASSICS
Reproductions of Pennsylvania country pieces of the 19th century began as a hobby for Dan Backenstose of Lebanon County. Assured of his ability to please others, he began producing a very wide array of furnishings. Native Pennsylvania hardwoods such as

tulip poplar, black walnut, and wild cherry are used for most of the pieces. The saddle seat stool shown is available in the three woods and is offered in 10", 18" and 24" heights; a four-legged model 30" high is also produced.

Catalog, $3 (refundable with first purchase)

SPRING HOUSE CLASSICS
Schaefferstown, PA 17088
(717) 949-3902

Other suppliers of stools are: STEPHEN P. BEDARD, COHASSET COLONIALS, and SERAPH WEST and SERAPH EAST.

Storm Doors. *See* **Screen and Storm Doors.**

Stoves. The choice of wood or coal as alternative fuel sources in recent years has rescued many an old cast-iron monster from the junkyard. But before you buy one of these originals, beware. While an antique can be equally as warming as a reproduction, make sure that it has been expertly refurbished. A stove that isn't airtight can be just as great a fuel thief as the oil burner in the basement, and a hundred times as dangerous. Many companies have capitalized on the recent demand for wood- or coal-burning stoves by mass-producing reproductions. Finding one isn't difficult; what *is* difficult is to locate one that's handsome as well as utilitarian. The suppliers listed below have not sacrificed style for the sake of utility or profit. They offer a variety of attractive models, many based on 19th-century originals, in an assortment of styles and sizes to suit every need.

BRYANT STOVE WORKS
There's a reason why so many modern stoves have been based on 19th-century patterns – old stoves work. They're efficient, and they have a beauty, some say, that modern stoves can't match. At the Bryant Stove Works, a family business located on a 100-acre farm, old stoves are appreciated. Joe and Bea Bryant sandblast and restore antique stoves, using new parts, nickling, grates, and liners. About 150 are kept in stock at

all times, and searches for particular models are undertaken willingly. One stove occasionally available in the constantly changing stock is this Ideal Maine, one of the many stoves produced by the famous Portland Foundry. Bryant also offers parlor heaters, including the majestic Ideal Clarion shown here. If you can visit the company, Joe and Bea recommend seeing their stoves in person to appreciate their beauty. If you can't, write or call. Bryant Stove Works will crate and ship stoves anywhere in the world.

Brochure, free

BRYANT STOVE WORKS
BOX 2048, RICH RD.
THORNDIKE, ME 04986
(207) 568-3665

HEARTLAND APPLIANCES, INC.
This firm is the proud new manufacturer/marketer of the

famous Elmira Oval cookstove, which has been in continuous production for almost ninety years, one model of which is shown here. The Elmira Oval features a cast-iron and firebrick-lined firebox that is 20" long, 9" wide, and 11" deep, six square feet of cooking surface, and a ten-year limited warranty. The oven, 11½" high by 18" wide by 20" deep, has a three-position rack and a door thermometer. Options include almond or black porcelain finish, a solid-copper water reservoir, coal grates, and a water jacket for heating running water. The cooktop height is 32"; overall measurements are 62" high by 41" wide by 29½" deep. Elmira stoves are also available in combination wood-electric and all-electric or all-gas models. The styling is traditional on all.

Brochure available

HEARTLAND APPLIANCES, INC.
5 Hoffman St.

Kitchener, ONT N2M 3M5
Canada
(519) 743-8111
Fax (519) 743-1665

LEHMAN HARDWARE
Modern electrical stoves and microwave ovens are certainly convenient, but they don't have the even cooking, the heating capacity, or the aesthetic appeal of wood- or coal-burning cookstoves. Lehman sells over eighty different models of stoves that heat, cook, and please the eye, including the Scandinavian-made Jotul 8 shown here. Its design is based on that of a hand-crafted Colonial cabinet, and its glass front lets you watch the fire. The flue outlet vents from the top or the rear, and, although the Jotul 8 is designed for freestanding installation, it can be adapted for most fireplaces. The Jotul 8 accommodates logs up to 20" in length (or will burn coal) and comes in four finishes – black paint, blue/black porcelain, almond porcelain, or red porcelain. Every stove sold by Lehman has its own special features. The Waterford Stanley wood cooking range, for example, has a heat control that makes it easy to keep the stove burning overnight; a convenient warming shelf is an extra bonus. (An

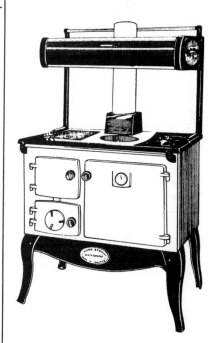

optional coal grate converts the range to a coal-burner.) The Waterford Stanley is made in Ireland, and that's an important consideration because the Irish people are experts when it comes to staying warm and dry efficiently and economically.

Catalog, $2

LEHMAN HARDWARE AND APPLIANCES, INC.

4779 Kidron Rd., PO Box 41
Kidron, OH 44636
(216) 857-5441
Fax (216) 857-5785

PORTLAND STOVE COMPANY
Portland's Queen Atlantic is billed as
the reigning majesty of household
ranges. The firm's reproduction of the
1906 model is indeed sturdy, reliable,
and stately. Constructed completely
of cast iron with no steel alloys or
sheet metal parts, its thick walls
assure uniform cooking. The Queen
Atlantic is available in either wood-
or coal-burning models. Extra long
and deep fireboxes accommodate
long burning loads and infrequent
ash cleanouts. And a lot of cooking
can be done on the six-lid top. An
elevated warming oven and high
shelf are options to make the Queen
Atlantic even more useful. The stove
is decorated with long-lasting nickel-
plated ornamentation, giving it an
accurate turn-of-the-century
appearance. The Queen Atlantic
measures $32^1/_2$" to the range top,
another 30" from range to the back of
the main top, and is 57" long. The
roomy oven is $19^3/_4$" deep, $18^1/_4$" wide,
and 11" high. Portland Stove also
manufactures a smaller Princess
Atlantic cook stove, Franklin stoves,
pot bellies, and box stoves.

Literature, $2

PORTLAND STOVE COMPANY
PO Box 37, Fickett Rd.
N. Pownal, ME 04069
(207) 688-2254

RUTLAND FIRE CLAY COMPANY
You won't be able to order a stove
from this enterprising firm, but you
won't be able to maintain the one you
do buy or already have without
stocking up on the stove and fireplace
products Rutland manufactures. A
division of Rutland Fire Clay
Company, Rutland Products offers a
line of goods, many of them
indispensable, for the care and repair
of wood-burning or coal-burning
stoves, kerosene heaters, fireplaces,
and even furnaces and barbeque
grills. Among the products are
several that attack some of the most
common problems facing stove and
fireplace users. The firm's 1200°F
Stove Paint, for example, is a specially
formulated paint that resists peeling
and blistering under high

temperatures. With this product and
Rutland's Liquid Stove & Grill Polish
or Paste Stove Polish, your stove (or
any cast-iron surface) can retain its
shiny black appearance. Fireplace
inserts and the door-glass of coal, oil
and wood-burning stoves can be kept
shining with Rutland's Hearth Glass
Conditioning Cleaner. The company's
Dry Stove Lining is a preparation for
repairing or replacing worn-out brick
stove linings. Both Rutland's Stove &
Gasket Cement and its High Heat
Silicone Sealant are resistant to the
high temperatures of heating and
cooking stoves. Other products
include stove gaskets, self-adhesive
strip insulation for fireplace inserts,
stove mortar, exterior chimney
masonry patching cement, cement for
easy re-pointing of fireplace brick,
various soot and creosote retarders,
fireproof protective gloves, and even
a fireplace and stove deodorant that
eliminates the stale odors that stove
and fireplace users know too well in
hot and humid weather.

*Write or call for the name of a distributor
in your area*

RUTLAND FIRE CLAY COMPANY
PO Box 340
Rutland, VT 05702-0340
(802) 775-5519
Fax (802) 775-5262

Sunbursts. *See* **Ornaments.**

Sundials. A sundial is an instrument
that indicates the time of day by the
shadow, cast on a surface marked to
show hours or fractions of hours, of
an object on which the sun's rays fall.
While any object whose shadow is
used to determine time is called a
gnomon, the term is usually applied
to a style, pin, metal plate, or other
shadow-casting object that is an
integral part of a sundial. Although
primitive sundials were known from
the beginning of time, the accuracy of
sundials was greatly improved in the
first century A.D. by setting gnomons
parallel to the earth's axis of rotation
so that the apparent east-to-west
motion of the sun governs the swing
of the shadow. The development of
trigonometry permitted precise
calculations for the marking of dials.
During the Renaissance sundials in a
number of elaborate forms and

surfaces were devised. Many of these
magnificent dials are reproduced
today by KENNETH LYNCH AND SONS
(see below). Although watches and
clocks came into popular use in the
18th century, sundials were long
employed for setting and checking
them. In the informative historical
introduction to the ABBEY GARDEN
SUNDIAL catalog (see below), the story
is told of an inscription on an 18th-
century dial that proudly proclaims
its superiority to mechanical time-
telling devices: "The iron bell may
wrongly tell;/I err not, if the sun
shine well." In an age such as ours,
where time is too much with us, a
sundial in an old-house garden is a
fine way to keep a check on the
exigencies of mechanical time. As
Abbey remins us, a sundial is
"handsome to look at, easy to read,
and a constant reminder of our past."

ABBEY GARDEN SUNDIALS
Sundials are this Canadian firm's sole
product and are made in Wales by
bronze founder Andrew Evans and
sculptor Christopher Tynan.
Illustrated, in order of appearance,
are the Zodiac Convoluted Round
dial, one foot in diameter; the Sun
Square, 9" square; the Cherub Scroll,
8" wide and one foot tall; and the
Lion armillary, 10" high. All models

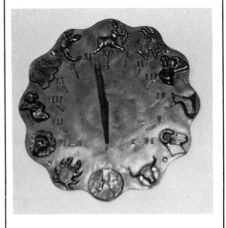

are custom made for the latitude in
which the customer lives. (The
standard for Canada, for example, is
Latitude 45° North.) The customer
must also indicate whether a model is
to be mounted horizontally or on a
wall and, for wall sundials, the
direction the wall faces. There are

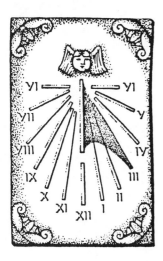

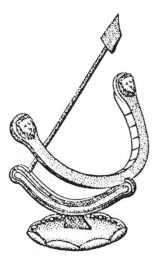

various motifs and symbols such as Cherub, Lion, Sun, Zodiac Signs, and Celtic Design, all of which are generally interchangeable among the many styles of dials. Inscriptions are a common feature of antique sundials, and Abbey will include one of your choice if requested. Cast bronze is used for all models, and each is given a satin polish finish which will weather naturally.

Catalog, $2 (refunded with purchase)

ABBEY GARDEN SUNDIALS
PO Box 102, Indian HillRd.
Pakenham, ONT K0A 2X0
Canada
(613) 256-3973

KENNETH LYNCH AND SONS
Readers of *The Old House Catalogue* are aware of the many specialized interests of this long-established firm, but may not know that sundials were a personal passion of Kenneth Lynch himself. So intense was his interest that he compiled a book about the art of sundials, past and present, complete with over 350 photographs and drawings, called *Sundials and Spheres*. (Write or phone the company for current price.) The firm's catalog of garden ornament lists almost a hundred sundials of every type, from hemispherical to wall dials. The range of styles is astonishing, as is the range of sizes. A simple garden sundial might be as small as 10" in diameter, while a hemispherical dial might be as large as 27' across! There is probably no place else in North America where one could purchase a sculpture of Atlas holding an armillary sundial or find a simple sundial incorporating the "timely" figures of the tortoise and the hare. Illustrated is Lynch's model number 4200, 48" in diameter, and available in bronze or iron. Many other sundials, more elaborate or more simple, can be had from stock or by custom order.

Book of Garden Ornament, $9.50

KENNETH LYNCH AND SONS
78 Danbury Rd., Box 488
Wilton, CT 06897
(203) 762-8363
Fax (203) 762-2999

Swags. *See* **Festoons; Ornaments.**

A stone urn and other architectural antiques. Photograph courtesy of Walcot Reclamation Ltd., Bath, England.

Table Lamps. Lamps are a relatively new category in lighting. Thomas Jefferson and other late 18th-century tinkerers played with various inventions, but it was not until the 1830s and '40s that table lamps with burners were used at all widely in the North American home. The introduction of new fuels – whale oil, and, later, kerosene – made possible the development of glass, brass, and china table lamps. Thousands of different kinds of burners and wick tubes were patented, each offering a different measure of safety and convenience. By the second half of the 19th century, even a gas table lamp was made possible by the development of a "gooseneck" connector on the lamp that enabled a six-foot-long mohair hose leading from it to be attached to a gas source – the gas chandelier above. Such "gas portable lamps" were still being offered by Sears, Roebuck in the first years of the 20th century. Among the most famous and accomplished of 19th-century lamp manufacturers was the Boston & Sandwich Glass Company. Their pressed and molded lamps have been collectors' items for many years. Competition among lamp makers, however, was fierce and healthy. By the time of the Centennial, kerosene had replaced other fuels such as whale oil and lard oil, and simple glass kerosene table lamps were being produced by the hundreds of thousands each year. It is still relatively simple to find these clear glass fixtures in antique and junk shops, for their production lasted well into the electric age. They are, in fact, still made today. And it is very easy to adapt them for use as modern lamps with the replacement of the burner (if still attached) by an electric adapter. These adapters, together with a harp and shade, are a commonplace and inexpensive solution to the problem of providing table lamps for period rooms. Well-equipped hardware stores sometimes stock them, but you're certain to find adapter kits through CUMBERLAND GENERAL STORE, LEHMAN HARDWARE and PAXTON HARDWARE LTD.

Since the first *Old House Catalogue* was published in 1976, we have recommended that readers haunt antique lighting emporiums and architectural antiques warehouses for restored lamps, and we have hoped aloud that our colleagues in the reproduction lighting field would come forward with some acceptable solutions to the problem of finding suitable table lamps for period rooms. Much of what we've seen, however, has been disappointing. "Paul Revere" lanterns with lamp shades growing out of the peaks look pretty silly to us, and we've rejected them even though they are produced by an otherwise reputable firm. A few suppliers have come up with reasonable adaptations of small candlestands for table use, of appeal to those in 18th- or early 19th-century settings; others have turned their attention, quite successfully we think, to reproducing the brilliant art-glass lamps of the early 20th century. One supplier has even reproduced the almost-impossible-to-find piano lamps that illuminated the parlor piano in the 1920s. We offer, then, a small number of the better ideas, but acknowledge that the problem of locating suitable table lamps for period rooms will be with us for some time to come.

CENTURY HOUSE ANTIQUE LAMP EMPORIUM AND REPAIR
Marilyn and Hal McKnight, proprietors of Century House, say that "if we don't have it, it's not available," and they apply this proud boast to every type of antique lamp fixture, table lamps included, from the age of candles to the age of electricity. Shown are a few of the kinds of lamps that are likely to be

found in the McKnights' ever-changing stock.

SASE for inquiries

CENTURY HOUSE ANTIQUE LAMP EMPORIUM AND REPAIR

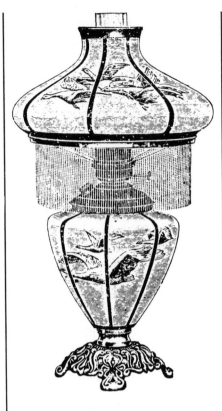

46785 Rte. 18 West
Wellington, OH 44090

CLASSIC ILLUMINATION, INC.
This well-known company offers a
number of adaptations of early 20th-
century table lamps, among the most
practical of which is this adjustable
trough-shade piano lamp. A key near
the base allows the lamp to be tilted
forward, illuminating piano scores –
or more mundane work if you choose

to use it as a desk lamp. A well-
weighted base provides stability.
Customers can choose among white,
beige, green, or brown cased-glass
shades and between a pull-chain
socket or a full-range dimmer.

Catalog, $5

CLASSIC ILLUMINATION, INC.
2743 Ninth Street
Berkeley, CA 94710
(415) 849-1842
Fax (415) 849-2328

HURLEY PATENTEE MANOR
Among this firm's several
adaptations of 18th-century
candlestands suitable for use as table
lamps is this shaded "sophisticated-
primitive" lamp of iron and tin. It is

available electrified, as shown, or for
use with candles. In the electrified
model, the shade is adjustable. In the
candle model, both shade and candle
holders are adjustable. The fixture is
32" high and 14" wide. Also
illustrated is Hurley Patentee
Manor's formal desk lamp, available
in the double model shown or with a
single lamp. Both models are
available in iron, as shown, in copper,
or in copper and iron. At 28" high and
16" wide, the fixture can be had in
electrified or candle models.

Catalog, $3

HURLEY PATENTEE MANOR
R.D. 7, Box 98A
Kingston, NY 12401
(914) 331-5414

RENAISSANCE MARKETING, INC.
The Renaissance Lily Collection is the
foremost source in North America for
first-class reproductions of Art
Nouveau lighting fixtures. (We stress
"first-class" because the lighting
market is flooded with cheap
Taiwanese imitations.) An example of
the firm's excellence is this eighteen-
stem lily lamp. A lost wax cast-bronze

edition of one of Tiffany's most
famous lamps, the lily table lamp is
re-created in exacting detail and
finished with hand-blown silver-
lustre art-glass shades. Each lamp is
signed and numbered by the makers.
Other models of the lily lamp are

available in versions with from one to twelve lilies. Matching sconces, floor lamps, and ceiling fixtures are also offered.

After years of experience reproducing some of the timeless designs of Tiffany, Quezal, Larche, Gurschner, and others, Renaissance Marketing has turned its expertise in the Art Nouveau period to the creation of original designs that successfully capture both the period look and its quality of craftsmanship. Illustrated is the firm's Sea Nymph lamp, cast in bronze by the lost wax method and hand-finished in traditional patinas of gold, brown, and green. In the mermaid's hands is a large hand-blown silver-lustre art-glass shell. Illumination from beneath the shell lights her face and form. The lamp is 22" high.

Free catalog

RENAISSANCE MARKETING, INC.
PO Box 360
Lake Orion, MI 48035
(313) 693-1109
Fax (313) 693-1118

THE VILLAGE FORGE
We've always liked Michael D. Sutton's approach to reproduction Colonial lighting. Each iron fixture is an exercise in direct, simple honesty – no frills, no flights of the historic imagination. Both of Sutton's electrified candlestands offer a practical solution to the problem of table lamps in a Colonial setting.

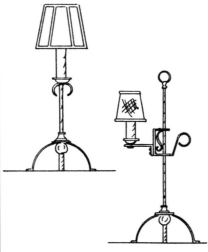

Model 2011 is 20" high and takes a 100-watt bulb; model 2021 is 23" high and takes a 75-watt bulb. Both are also available as candle-burning fixtures.

Brochure, $1.50

THE VILLAGE FORGE
Country Club Rd., Rte. 4, Box 124
Smithfield, NC 27577
(919) 934-2581
Fax (919) 934-3298

Other suppliers of table lamps include: COHASSET COLONIALS, GATES MOORE, *and* REJUVENATION LAMP & FIXTURE CO.

Tables. Small four-legged tables were common among the inventive people of ancient Egypt. Though tables of various kinds were used by the Greeks and Romans, the form faded in the Middle Ages, and the table did not return as an ordinary piece of household furniture until the Renaissance. From the 15th century on, tables became ever more specialized and were particularly popular and elaborate in upper-class households. Among the lower classes, the simplest tables – constructions of boards placed across trestles – were in use until the 19th century. Over the last three centuries tables have become an intrinsic part of everyday life. Their uses are as varied as function dictates. There is no shortage of antique tables, although the prices for the better pieces are well beyond the means of most people. But that still leaves choice examples to be claimed from antique shops and architectural salvage warehouses

from coast to coast. The high cost of new machine-made reproduction period tables should give one pause to consider the handcrafted tables made by today's talented cabinetmakers, tables that are a far more satisfying investment than those in the department store "Paul Revere Shoppe." A few samples of the many high-quality *documented* table reproductions follow.

G. R. CLIDENCE
Antique tavern tables are prohibitively expensive – if you can find them. But G. R. Clidence's reproduction of a rugged New England tavern table is the next best thing. All the lathe work is done by

hand to best duplicate the uniqueness found in each original turning, and each table is fitted with mortise-and-tenon skirts and legs and slot-and-mortise breadboard ends. G. R. Clidence's tavern tables are available in a wide range of woods, sizes, and finishes. Also available from Clidence are Queen Anne tea tables and small 18th-century tables suitable for use as nightstands in period bedrooms.

Brochure and photographs, $3

G. R. CLIDENCE
Box 386, James Trail
West Kingston, RI 02892
(401) 539-2558

GERALD CURRY, CABINETMAKER
A cabinetmaker of the first rank, Gerald Curry reproduces quality 18th-century furniture entirely by hand, and entirely alone. He is the only worker in his shop and profits from the solitude reflected in the sensitivity and harmony characterizing his work. After thorough research and investigation, Curry has learned the various methods of design and construction

that were employed by the distinct cabinetmaking regions of Colonial America. With this historical knowledge and intimate understanding of the woods used in his trade, he is able to re-create furniture of the same character as the furniture produced by the 18th-century masters – a truth illustrated by this exquisite Chippendale piecrust candlestand. Made of

mahogany, it features a piecrust top, hand-carved from a single wide board, that tips and turns on a bird-cage support; a fluted column; and ball and claw feet. Gerald Curry can custom-make other styles of tables and will work directly from photographs, books, or drawings.

Brochure, $2

GERALD CURRY, CABINETMAKER
Pound Hill Rd.
Union, ME 04862
(207) 785-4633

FIRESIDE REPRODUCTIONS
John R. Glenn, who crafts the unique 1830 Pennsylvania benchtable shown here entirely by hand, supplies the following historic background: "The original benchtable dates from about 1670 and has its origin in New England and Eastern Pennsylvania. The benchtable was most often made

completely of pine, although examples are found in other woods, including poplar, cherry, walnut, and chestnut. The versatility of the table made it very popular throughout the early days of the Colonies. When the evening meal was finished, the family members would clear the table and pivot the top up and back to make a high-backed bench (similar to a high-backed settee). The high-backed bench was positioned in front of the fireplace. The highback would act as a heat shield to retain the heat from the fire while at the same time preventing drafts from blowing on the backs of the family members as they sat before the fire." The last benchtables were made about 1840, and there are very few of the original tables still in existence. John R. Glenn's reproduction benchtable is correct in every detail, and made using the

same materials and tools as of old. All wood used is 150 to 200 years old; the pins used to hold the top to the base, for example, are hand-turned from 155-year-old beech. Even the nails used are old square nails reclaimed from the past. Several sizes are made: lengths vary from four to seven feet. A variety of techniques are employed to give the benchtable the worn and aged appearance characteristic of the original. The obvious care and craftsmanship lavished on the 1830 Pennsylvania benchtable is typical of Glenn's work in general. Other pieces include a good-looking open-top pewter cupboard and a variety of small furniture, including tables.

FIRESIDE REPRODUCTIONS
4727 Winterset Dr.
Columbus, OH 43220
(614) 451-7695

SHAKER WORKSHOPS
The great triumph of Shaker design and craftsmanship is that their furniture, conceived 150 years ago, is

just as appealing in its appearance and practical in its function today as it was then. The Shaker serving table shown, for example, was possibly

intended for the ministry's dining room, but it is also perfect for a hallway, behind a sofa, as a desk, or even as a dressing table. Note the uniquely-designed feet at the base of the gently tapered legs. The original of this table is at Hancock (Massachusetts) Shaker Village, but Shaker Workshops' reproduction is faithful in every way. Available in kit form or fully assembled, the maple table measures 50³/₄" by 20". Other Shaker tables available from this fine source are a drop-leaf table, a trestle table, and a side table.

Catalog, $1

SHAKER WORKSHOPS
PO Box 1028
Concord, MA 01742
(617) 646-8985
Fax (617) 648-8217

Among other suppliers of period tables are: THE COUNTRY BED SHOP, JEFFREY P. GREENE, FURNITUREMAKER, NORTH WOODS CHAIR SHOP, *and* SPRING HOUSE CLASSICS.

Telephone. When in 1876 Alexander Graham Bell summoned his assistant to him, uttering the first *audible* words spoken via telephone – "Watson, I want you" – he could not possibly have envisioned the plethora of telephones available to the public, particularly after the "break up" of Ma Bell's monopoly a century later. The offerings of the typical "phone store" are as bewildering, headache-producing, and hideous as those of the typical lighting fixture emporium. For readers looking for a period telephone for their old house, we recommend MAHANTANGO MANOR, INC., a company that works *with* history and not against it. The firm's reproduction period telephones are historically accurate – from the solid-hardwood case to the real bell-ringing sound of the nickel-plated brass bells. The telephone shown is the Cathedral Top model of Western Electric Company's No. 1317 wall telephone, first introduced in 1907. As Mahantango Manor informs us, "In 1907 the Western Electric Company introduced the No. 1317 wall telephone with the distinctive 'picture frame' molding on the front of the case. During 1907 and most of 1908

the 1317 was manufactured with a cathedral top. At the end of 1908 the flat-top version was introduced, and the picture frame front remained a standard feature of 1317 until 1919. The 1317 was often referred to as a 'farmers line set' because it was designed for rural party line service in areas far from the central office. Each party line customer could signal the operator or one of the neighbors on the same party line by turning the magneto crank to ring a code using long and/or short rings." But don't worry about having to make your calls by turning the crank and saying, "Hello, Central." To dial calls, just slide the shelf out to uncover a rotary dial or a modern keypad. Mahantango Manor offers other historic phones and replacement parts for all its models. For more information, call or write: MAHANTANGO MANOR, INC., Hickory Corners Rd., Dalmatia, PA 17017-0170, (717) 758-8000, Fax (717) 758-6000.

Thresholds. A threshold is sometimes known as a saddle, an apt description of a board or slab of stone which is placed under a door and covers the place where two flooring surfaces meet. The phrase "crossing the threshold," as in carrying the bride across the threshold, is usually meant to mean entering a house through its main door. Thresholds, however, can

also be used between rooms. It may be a very narrow strip of wood with a slight pitch to each side or a wide carved slab. Because it is subject to heavy wear and, if used in the main entryway, projects to the outside, a threshold must be made of the most durable material such as oak or slate. For suppliers of stone threshold, *see* **Stone.** For a wood threshold, contact a millworking firm or a company that manufactures doors (*see* **Doors**).

Tiebacks. *See* **Drapery Hardware.**

Tie Rods. *See* **Wall Ties.**

Tin Ceilings. *See* **Ceilings.**

Tiles, Ceramic. Tiling has always been an expensive propositon, except in those parts of the Southwest and West where clay products have been widely available. Southern Californians say that Mexico is still the place to go for the widest and most inexpensive assortment of glazed and unglazed tiles, but they are reluctant to give away their sources. As for other forms – Italian, Minton-style Victorian pieces, and the extraordinary art tiles used in the early years of this century – you must be willing to search high and low unless price is no object. A few of the better architectural antiques warehouses keep occasional stocks on hand of such antique tiles, but these are the exceptions and not the rule. For the most part, commercially-available American ceramic tiles are just plain ugly. The palette seems limited to the pastels, and patterns are similarly pale. If you search through the offerings of home centers you might occasionally find a modern ceramic tile which will enhance your period surroundings, but why waste your time when the suppliers below can easily suit your needs with historically-accurate tiles of high quality?

CASTELNAU TILES OF BARNES
Even if it were not for the fact that Castelnau distributes the magnificent Victorian tiles made by the Decorative Tile Works at Ironbridge (of which more later), there would be a great deal to interest the old-house

owner in this English firm's catalog. The most beautiful terra-cotta tiles we have ever seen – the San Genis floor tiles, based on examples found in historic Mediterranean buildings dating back hundreds of years – are reason enough to become acquainted with Castelnau. San Genis terra-cotta tiles are ideal for old-house kitchens, halls, patios, and greenhouses. They are particularly suitable for barn conversions and other older buildings that are being modernized, but where the need is to retain the original character of the building. In addition to Castelnau's tile murals – both stock designs and custom designs made to match the customer's fabric or wallpaper – the firm offers a new and innovative line of white limestone floor tiles. Quarried from a limestone pit known to date to the Iron Age, these tiles are suitable for indoor or outdoor use. Limestone has long been known for its insulating properties and, compared to many forms of stone, is warm underfoot. Although soft until quarried, it becomes tougher than the hardest concrete after oxidization takes place. These white limestone tiles will be available in various shapes and finishes, but initially just two are available – the first an oblong and the second a smooth octagon set with black slate infills.

THE DECORATIVE TILE WORKS AT IRONBRIDGE is an institution with which all old-house owners should be acquainted. We quote from the company's brochure: "Until recently the bustling activities of tile making in Jackfield have lain dormant, living only in the memories of those who once worked in the two great tile factories of Maw & Co. and Craven Dunnill & Co. On 17 January 1989 a new company, The Decorative Tile Works, was established, housed within the Jackfield Tile Museum, part of the highly acclaimed Ironbridge Gorge Museum. The company's aim is to recreate tiles with all the qualities of color and design to be found in the products of the best 19th-century manufacturers. With unlimited access to the Museum's collections and expertise, The Decorative Tile Works is able to rise to the challenge of rediscovering traditional manufacturing techniques.

The Museum houses the largest collection of original tiles and some 14,000 plaster patterns, reflecting the industry at its peak during the 1880s and 1890s when the tile factories of the Servern Gorge were the largest producers of decorative tiles in the world." The initial collections of tiles from The Decorative Tile Works have already been introduced, and we can guarantee you that they are dazzlingly beautiful. The black-and-white illustrations of just a few of the patterns can hardly do justice to their vibrant colors.

Literature available

CASTELNAU TILES OF BARNES

175 Church Rd.
Barnes, London SW13 9HR
England
(081) 741-2452 or 748-9042
Fax (081) 741-5316

DESIGNS IN TILE
In the late-Victorian period, when the aim of the Aesthetic Movement was "to surround the home and everyday life with objects of true beauty," the use of decorated tiles was an easy and relatively inexpensive way to introduce art into the home without seeming frivolous. Designs in Tile, contemporary producers of custom hand-decorated tiles and murals, was inspired by the philosophy and art of

the Aesthetic Movement. The firm's goal, superbly realized, is the revival of art tile – fine art rendered on ceramic tile – and, by extension, the creation of a strikingly and expertly integrated environment employing art tile. Each tile created by Designs in Tile is individually decorated by hand, using only the finest ceramic materials. All work is fired to a high temperature, making each tile extremely durable and causing the colors to vary slightly in shade from tile to tile and lot to lot. Such color variation is a desired and inherent characteristic of all handcrafted ceramic products and clearly distinguishes the firm's work from the dull uniformity of machine-made tile. In addition to its burgeoning custom-design business, Designs in Tile offers stock designs in historic

styles ranging from Victorian transfer tiles in the Anglo-Japanese style to Art Nouveau and Art Deco tiles. Current stock designs include, in addition to those already mentioned, William DeMorgan-style tiles, a hand-

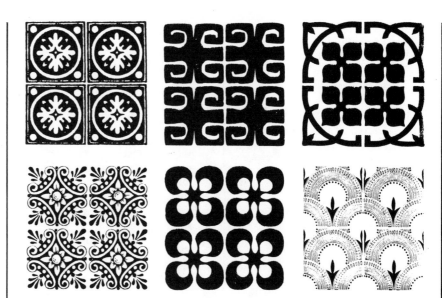

painted historic reproduction series of coordinating tile patterns and mini-murals; folk tiles hand-painted in traditional Pennsylvania-German and Northern European styles; Persian Revival tiles from the Arts and Crafts period; and spring flower tiles executed in the naturalistic style reminiscent of Art Nouveau pen and ink drawings with watercolor washes. (Shown here are several Victorian transfer tiles in the Anglo-Japanese style and two William DeMorgan-style tiles.) In addition, traditional and contemporary designs – from country motifs to children's patterns – are also available. If Designs in Tile's wide range of stock murals, border, and field tiles do not suit your needs, the firm will customize designs for you or reproduce patterns and colors from any wallpaper, fabric, or original piece of art. (Eighty percent of the firm's business is custom work.)

Catalog, $3

DESIGNS IN TILE
Box 358, Dept. G
Mt. Shasta, CA 96067
(916) 926-2629

FIREBIRD HANDMADE TILES, INC.
Handcrafted tiles and original tile murals by Firebird accent home interiors from entrance to bath. To our eye the ceramic tile murals seem particularly effective in decorating kitchens. Flat-line tiles and raised embossed tiles are fired to 1800°F., individually hand-painted, glazed, and fired again for permanence. Designs range from floral displays to entire barnyard manageries, and many are inspired by antique butter molds and other Victorian and folk art sources. Firebird ceramic tile murals and borders can be selected from stock designs or custom designed.

Brochures, $2

FIREBIRD HANDMADE TILES, INC.
335 Synder Ave.
Berkeley Heights, NJ 07922
(201) 464-4613
Fax (201) 464-4615

RYE TILES
Rye Tiles is a limited production factory catering specifically to customers who want specialized attention for tiling projects with an emphasis on color, design, and quality. The firm specializes in color toning and matching to complement any design scheme. Because the method of manufacture gives each job a specific shading and depth of color, it is important to order sufficient tiles to complete a job. If you run short and need to reorder, there is a risk of having a different shade effect in another batch of tiles. An almost innumerable number of designs are offered by Rye Tiles. In addition to overall patterns, hand-painted mural panels and many border designs are created. Shown here are just a few designs from the company's vast offerings.

Catalog, free

RYE TILES
Ceramic Consultants Ltd.
The Old Brewery
Wishward, Rye, Sussex TN31 7DH
England
(0797) 223038
Fax (0797) 224834

HELEN WILLIAMS/RARE TILES
Antique faience Delft tiles are so rare that they cannot be lavished on floors and walls. Used for a fireplace surround or as focal points of a tiled wall, they can prove spectacularly decorative. Helen Williams is North America's foremost dealer in antique Delft tiles, and, as she points out, only tiles made before 1800 are the true hand-painted, tin-glazed tiles that can legitimately be called Delft. She has an extensive collection of these, and each measures roughly 5" square. The most expensive (but still eminently affordable) are 17th-century blue-and-white designs depicting soldiers, shepherds and shepherdesses, ships, flower vases with tulips, sea animals and fish, cherubs, tradesmen, and mythological subjects. Even more affordable are 18th-century blue-and-white or manganese-and-white squares depicting biblical scenes and little animals, or in marbelized or tortoise-shell designs. Helen Williams also stocks antique English Liverpool transfer tiles and antique Spanish and Portuguese transfer tiles in blue and in polychrome. Illustrated are three 18th-century manganese-and-white Delft tiles.

Brochure for SASE

HELEN WILLIAMS/RARE TILES
12643 Hortense St.
North Hollywood, CA 91604
(213) 761-2756

Other suppliers of ceramic tiles include:
THE BRASS KNOB, CANDY TILES LTD.,
FERGENE STUDIO, MANNINGTON
CERAMIC TILE, and STEPTOE AND WIFE
ANTIQUES LTD.

Toilets. The stock of old toilets is so
large that if every person desiring one
of these loos was suddenly to satisfy
his urgings, thousands of models
would still remain unclaimed. It is
hard to think of old tank tops or floor
models as being architectural
antiques, but the architectural
antiques warehouse is where many of
the old tank tops and floor models
reside. Toilets are always being
stripped from hotels and motels,
public buildings, and commercial
establishments. A ceramic toilet is, of
course, almost impossible to destroy.
There are basically two types which
emerged in the 19th century – a high,
wall-mounted tank with a commode
below which is flushed with a pull of
a chain, and a floor commode-and-
tank combination. Seats and tanks
can be made of wood; commodes are
always porcelain. If making use of an
antique toilet doesn't move you, a
reproduction model can be purchased
from several suppliers. Make sure
that it is very sturdy. More than one
high ceiling tank has been known to
crash to the floor when being
summoned too urgently to do its
business. Among the suppliers of
reproduction toilets are ANTIQUE
BATHS & KITCHENS, A. BALL PLUMBING
SUPPLY, BESCO PLUMBING & HEATING
SALES, CRAWFORD'S OLD HOUSE STORE,
RENOVATOR'S SUPPLY, RESTORATION
WORKS, INC. and ROY ELECTRIC
ANTIQUE LIGHTING CO. If an exact
reproduction isn't necessary, the
KOHLER CO. can help. It currently
offers models in the Portrait Suite and
Vintage Suite collections which are
handsomely sculpted and have the
added advantage of being low in
water consumption. Contact Kohler
for your nearest supplier. And last,
for those who cannot abide a squishy
foam or brittle plastic toilet seat,
sturdy wood seats are now stocked in
many home centers. If this is not the

case in your area, contact DEWEESE
WOODWORKING or BUDDY FIFE & CO.

Tools. Every craft has its special tools
– planes and knives for wood-
workers; hammers and tongs for
blacksmiths and other metalworkers;
brushes of various types for
decorative painters; trowels for
plasterers and masons; the level and
saw for carpenters. Professionals of
every kind can draw on various
sources of tools, including antiques.
Restoration or reproduction work
often calls for a particular type of
instrument to achieve an authentic
effect. THE MECHANICK'S WORKBENCH
is one of the best sources for antique
woodworking tools. Suppliers of new
woodworking and carpentry tools
include FROG TOOL CO., LTD., GARRETT
WADE CO., and WOODCRAFT SUPPLY
CORP. THE MURALO CO., INC., and
WOLF PAINTS & WALLPAPER can be
relied on for special brushes and
other tools required by decorative
painters. Plastering and masonry
tools are a specialty with HYDE
MANUFACTURING CO. and
MARSHALLTOWN TROWEL CO. For the
right kind of tools used in slating a
roof, contact either EVERGREEN SLATE
CO. or LEHMAN HARDWARE AND
APPLIANCES, INC. Lehman's is also a
source for blacksmith tools, small
farm implements, logging tools,
carving knives, and whetstones.

Topiary Frames. The art of topiary
has engaged the interest of many
Americans in the past few years. The
subject of magazine articles and
books, topiary has taken on new
miniature forms in addition to the
traditional garden variety known in
the past. Gardens containing plants
sculpted in unusual forms were rarely
encountered in the North American
past. Topiary appeared in some
Colonial gardens, but as landscaping
assumed more naturalistic lines in the
19th century, sculpting was largely
forgotten. Sculpted forms can be
created without topiary frames, but
for ambitious shapes, the frames are
essential. KENNETH LYNCH AND SONS is
one of the only suppliers of such
metal structures. Illustrated are
several of Lynch's many designs.

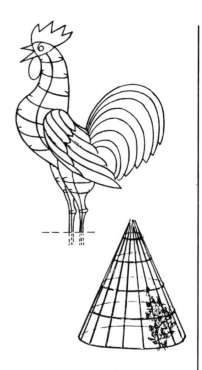

Torchières. *See* **Floor Lamps.**

Transoms. *See* **Bull's-Eye Panes** and
Windows.

Treads and Risers. *See*
Stairs/Stairways.

Tree Benches. *See* **Garden Furniture.**

Tree Grates and Guards. Although
more expensive than wood stakes,
iron tree guards are attractive and
durable. They are especially useful
for protecting new shade trees along a
city or town street. Grates are used at
the base of trees and are made in
square and round cast-iron forms.
Among suppliers of both grates and
guards is NEENAH FOUNDRY; two of its
square designs are shown. STEWART
IRON WORKS CO. supplies tree guards,
as illustrated, three pickets of which
are an extra 2" longer than the others
and have holes in them for fastening
to wood or iron stakes driven in the
ground.

Trelliswork. Trellising is an effective and attractive method of supporting climbing plants, especially vines and climber roses. Wood latticework may be applied directly to walls or formed into freestanding structures such as an arched trellis or lattice screening. Most of the trellising sold today in garden centers is flimsy and will not bear the weight of a strong vine or rose bush for long. Trellising in various patterns can be constructed quite simply of 1" square battens. If you are not up to doing it yourself, a millwork company can probably assist.

STUART GARDEN ARCHITECTURE Stuart's designs, two of which are illustrated, are executed only in a hardwood – African teak or Iroko. These can be oiled, stained, painted, or left to weather to a beautiful silver gray. The posts used for freestanding structures are also hardwood. The panels are screwed to the posts and do not require special fittings. Planters, also in teak, are available as built-in units and serve to support the latticework screening in places where posts cannot be driven into the ground, such as a paved area or roof garden.

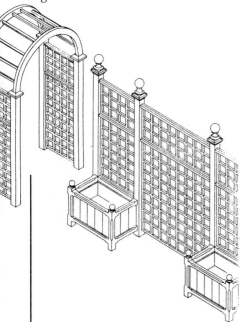

American customers, contact the firm for information about distributors:

STUART GARDEN ARCHITECTURE
Larchfield Estate, Dowlish Ford
Ilminster, Somerset TA19 0PF
England

(0460) 57862
Fax (0460) 53525

Canadian customers, contact:

STEPTOE & WIFE ANTIQUES LTD.
322 Geary Ave.
Toronto, ONT M6H 2C7
Canada
(416) 530-4200
Fax (416) 530-4666

Umbrella Stands. *See* **Stands.**

Urns. In ancient Greece, the urn was originally a memorial vessel made to contain the ashes of the dead. But centuries later, in periods marked by a revival of interest in classical times, particularly the 18th century and the eclectic Victorian era, the urn was widely adapted as a decorative shape in architecture, cabinetmaking, and garden design. In stone it was used as a finial for the facades of buildings; in wood as a finial for chests and clocks and desks and also as a container for knives; and in plaster or in bronze or other metals as a decorative element on elaborate chimneybreasts. It was also made in stone, terra cotta, or cast iron as a pivotal or focal point in formal garden design.

Urns are readily available today for all the uses to which the past has put them, including, of course, their original purpose. Architectural antiques suppliers are an obvious source for both architectural and garden urns. For architectural use, W. F. NORMAN CORPORATION is a source of metal urns and THE BALMER ARCHITECTURAL ART STUDIOS of plaster urns. Three sources of garden urns are ARCHITECTURAL ANTIQUES EXCHANGE, whose stately Victorian urn is pictured here; KENNETH LYNCH AND SONS, who list about fifty different urns in stone, lead, or bronze; and TENNESSEE FABRICATING

CO., well-known for its reproductions of Victorian cast-iron urns.

Valances. "Valance" has become a catch-all term to describe fabric hangings or a wood cornice which covers the top of a window; it may also be used to describe a type of bed hanging (*see* **Bed Hangings**).

Natural cotton "fishnet" valances in a half-dozen geometric designs are available from two sources in North Carolina: CARTER CANOPIES and VIRGINIA GOODWIN. Both firms feature hand-tied fringe. While a carpenter can supply a simple wood box valance to which paint or fabric can be applied, more elaborate fretwork cornice valances are offered by THE OLD WAGON FACTORY and VINTAGE WOOD WORKS. Vintage will also supply a curtain rod, fascia board, and fabric or wallpaper insert boards for its openwork cornices.

Vanities. *See* **Sinks.**

Venetian Blinds. Used in the 18th and early 19th centuries, Venetian blinds disappeared for a period of time when louvered shutters became commonplace to filter light. Early Venetian blinds were made of wood, and the slats were narrower than those usually seen today. Three suppliers of traditional blinds are DEVENCO PRODUCTS, INC., NANIK, and PERKOWITZ WINDOW FASHIONS, INC.

Ventilators/Vents. Made of wood, plaster, or metal, ventilators cover openings in the wall to exhaust heat (*see also* **Grates, Grilles, and Registers**). Vents may be used in the gable end of a house for the release of attic heat. THE OLD WAGON FACTORY offers a simple circular hardwood vent in 24" and 32"- diameter sizes. This could also be used in conjunction with a wall duct for a stove or fireplace. Classic ornamental plaster ventilators are a specialty of THE DECORATORS SUPPLY CORP. These are used for venting interior heating systems in walls and ceilings.

Verandahs. *See* **Porches.**

Vergeboards. *See* **Bargeboards.**

W·X·Y·Z

Wainscoting. To wainscot a wall is to cover what is usually the lower section or dado with wood boards. Wainscoting, however, can reach more than several feet in height and may, in late-Victorian houses, nearly climb to the ceiling. The ceiling is yet another area that can be wainscoted. A wainscot ceiling, however, is usually not covered with wide panels, but rather narrow strips also known as "railroad siding," after its common use in Victorian railroad stations, or "porch ceiling," a reference to a frequent outdoor practice. The wainscoted section of a wall is delineated by use of a baseboard below and a molding, such as a chair rail or cap, above. Unless a room is vary small, its appearance is often greatly improved by defining the wall space in this manner. Wainscot adds character in a space and allows for the use of colors and materials that add richness but still complement the other wall surfaces. *See also* **Paneling.**

BLUE OX MILLWORKS
The firm's vintage sawing equipment allows it to produce just about any kind of wood wainscot from narrow strips to wide panels. All is fabricated from California redwood. Several designs are often produced on a custom basis – 6" lap joint, 4" and 5" tongue and groove, and 6" V-groove. Blue Ox will also supply appropriate caps in a number of suggested patterns.

Pattern book, $6

BLUE OX MILLWORKS
Foot of X St.
Eureka, CA 95501
(707) 444-3437

CRAFTSMAN LUMBER CO.
Craftsman is a first-rate source for wide pine boards used for paneling and "railroad siding" with a beaded edge and center bead as a dual wainscoting with a V-groove on the opposite side. The narrow boards can be ordered in $5/8$"- thick by $3/4$"- wide strips in clear pine or clear oak. Random lengths of 3' to 8' are available.

Brochure, 50¢

CRAFTSMAN LUMBER CO.
Box 222
Groton, MA 01450
(508) 448-6336

SUNSHINE ARCHITECTURAL WOODWORKS
A cutaway view of the use of wainscoting, baseboard, and chair rail illustrates Sunshine's mastery of this type of wall treatment. Raised panel wainscoting in poplar or other woods such as oak, cherry, walnut, or Honduras mahogany is usually

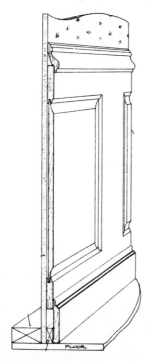

produced in 28" heights. It is most suitable for Colonial houses from the early 1700s to the mid-1800s. Sunshine is also a good source for angled staircase wainscoting, a use which requires extraordinary exactitude in cutting proper angles and in joinery.

Catalog, $4

SUNSHINE ARCHITECTURAL WOODWORKS
2169 Sunshine Dr., Dept. C
Fayetteville, AR 72703
(501) 521-4329
(800) 628-8004
Fax (501) 521-8863

Other suppliers of wainscoting include: AMHERST WOODWORKING & SUPPLY, INC., ARCHITECTURAL COMPONENTS, INC., BAILEY'S ARCHITECTURAL MILLWORK, INC., CARLISLE RESTORATION LUMBER, MAD RIVER WOODWORKS, MAURER & SHEPHERD JOYNERS, SAN FRANCISCO VICTORIANA, INC., *and* SILVERTON VICTORIAN MILLWORKS.

Wallcoverings. Papers suitable for old houses, like fabrics, are divided into those which are "documents" or exact reproductions, and "adaptations" that loosely interpret traditional designs. The finest documents are papers made on a very limited basis by such firms as SCALAMANDRÉ, BRUNSCHWIG & FILS, ARTHUR SANDERSON & SONS, COLE & SONS, and F. SCHUMACHER & CO. You may find pattern books for some of these companies at a local home center or decorating shop, but production of the papers must sometimes await sufficient orders to make a printing-run a practical option. Document papers may require five- or six-color printing with added special effects. Other sources of document papers are given below in addition to suppliers of unusual adaptations. There should be little or no problem in finding papers suitable for practically any period interior.

BENTLEY BROTHERS

A principal distributor of Anaglypta and Lincrusta wallcoverings in the United States, Bentley has achieved great success with its marketing. The new-found popularity of these late-Victorian materials for wainscoting and borders is not surprising. Produced by Crown Decorative Products Ltd. in England, the various types of embossed patterns have a definition and substance which reflect period character. The top of the line, Lincrusta, is made of a linseed-based formula bonded to paper. Akin to linoleum, it is a very durable material suitable for heavy traffic areas such as front halls and staircases. There are a number of patterns available. Angylpta is considerably less expensive than Lincrusts and may do

for less important spaces. It is an embossed paper to which cotton fibers have been added for strength and substance. These fibers allow for the embossing of strong, clear patterns. Both Lincrusts and Anaglypta wallcoverings are available in white or in ivory. The materials take paint easily. Anaglypta is also made in a vinyl which may better suit your purposes.

Lincrusta and Anglypta are offered by several old-house catalog houses, including RENOVATOR'S SUPPLY. In Canada the distributor is STEPTOE & WIFE ANTIQUES LTD. For further information regarding sources of supply, contact Bentley Brothers.

Literature available

BENTLEY BROTHERS
918 Baxter Ave.
Louisville, KY 40204
(800) 824-4777
(800) 828-0271 (KY)
Fax (502) 581-0748

William Morris; the Fenway, combining elements of the Aesthetic Movement and the Art Nouveau style; the Aesthetic Movement; the Woodland, which combines designs of Morris and Walter Crane; and In the Dresser Tradition, based on the designs of Christopher Dresser.

To illustrate the imaginative depth and versatility of these designs, patterns and elements from one roomset, The Fenway, are shown.

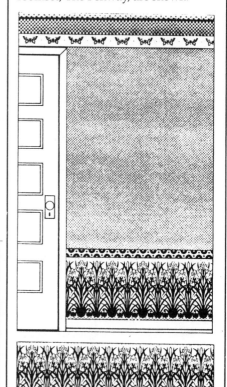

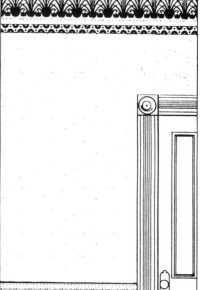

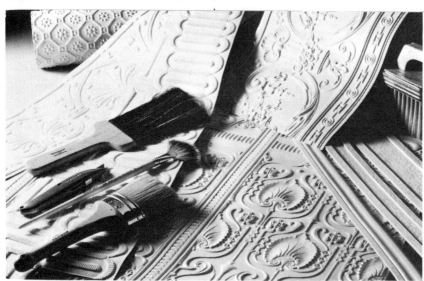

BRADBURY & BRADBURY ART
   WALLPAPERS

In their Benicia, California, studio, Bruce Bradbury and associates produce some of the best late 19th-century reproduction papers. These historic wall and ceiling coverings and coordinated elements are organized into a number of collections. In turn, each collection is subdivided into an almost endless number of patterns, accents, designs, and coordinating pieces. Bradbury's

modular approach to wallcoverings allows for the use of easily interchangeable elements so that almost any setting can be created or re-created down to the most minute detail.

What the collection includes is a series of seven "roomsets" which encompass all necessary papers. These model rooms are the Neo-Grec of the 1880s; the Anglo-Japanese, also dating from the 1880s; the Morris Tradition, based on the designs of

Bradbury provides two suggested wall treatments, one for a low ceilinged room (up to 8') and a high ceilinged space. The first arrangement, from top to bottom, is made up of a 6" border trimmed from the "Iris Frieze," a 4"-wide "Moth" border frieze, a panel paper called "Neptune," and the "Iris" frieze used above the baseboard. The second elevation, from top to bottom, shows an 18"-trimmed version of the "Irish Frieze" with the lower 3" border trimmed off and dropped down slightly below a picture molding, "Serpentine" used as the panel paper, and a full 27" "Fiddlehead Dado" used above the wide baseboard. A ceiling paper design, "Gossamer," is shown in a third drawing in use with a second pattern, "Raindrop Enrichment," as well as the "Moth" border and "Spiral Corner Block."

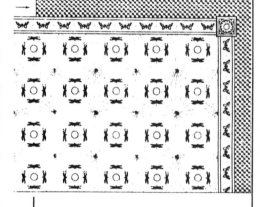

Catalog, $10

BRADBURY & BRADBURY ART
    WALLPAPERS
PO Box 155
Benicia, CA 94510
(707) 746-1900
Fax (707) 745-9417

J. R. BURROWS & CO.
The same degree of expertise and sensitivity has guided Burrows in its selection of wallpaper designs as it has its fine carpet collection discussed earlier in this book. Wallpapers are screen-printed, block-printed, or stenciled patterns printed in either England or Massachusetts. The American screen-printed papers are available in 21" rolls of a 6-yard length, an amount covering 30 square feet. Three of the designs shown, in order of appearance, are "Persis," a

c. 1990 pattern for panels; a complementary ceiling paper and a 9" frieze are also offered. The document or original color is a sage green; terra cotta, cream, and blue-gray colorings are also available.

"Chauncy Frieze," 18" high, was discovered in a mid-19th-century Italianate villa in Marshall, Michigan. The original document color is tan on an oatmeal ground.

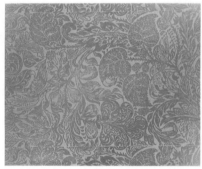

"Summer Street Demask" is, like many 19th-century patterns, reflective of a rich fabric. It has been named for a Queen Anne mansion in Kennebunk, Maine, dating from 1885.

Samples of colorings can be ordered.

Literature available

J. R. BURROWS & CO.
PO Box 418, Cathedral Station
Boston, MA 02118
(617) 451-1982
Fax (617) 524-5372

HAMILTON-WESTON WALLPAPERS LTD.
Patterns for 18th- and early 19th-century panel papers and borders

have been carefully documented and reproduced by this small and enterprising English firm. The designs are part of the "Papers of London" collection, and two are shown. "Mayfair," c. 1755, is shown with its framed original. The original coloring is blue and white, and four alternate combinations are also provided. "Bloomsbury Square"

dates from c. 1810 and is shown here with a border, "Anthemion." The

documented color of the panel design is a shade of green; six other shades are available. The border is made up in four colorings. All these papers are machine-printed.

Other collections of interest are "Old Paradise," designs from c. 1690-1840 which are hand-printed, and "Chiaroscuro," solid-color papers with a dappled effect resembling that found in early 19th-century oatmeal papers widely used for walls and ceilings.

Samples can be provided at a small cost. Hamilton-Weston is represented in the United States by three firms and in Canada by one.

American customers contact:

CHRISTOPHER HYLAND INC.
D&D Building, Suite 1714
979 Third Ave.
New York, NY 10022
(212) 688-6121
Fax (212) 688-6176
     or
THE RIST CORPORATION
Washington Design Center, Suite 338
300 D St., NW
Washington, DC 20024
(202) 646-1540
Fax (202) 646-1543
     or
CLASSIC REVIVALS INC.
1 Design Center Plaza, Suite 545
Boston, MA 02210
(617) 574-9030
Fax (617) 574-9027

Canadian customers contact:
CHARLES RUPERT
2004 Oak Bay Ave.
Victoria, BC V8R 1E4
(604) 592-4916
Fax (604) 592-4999

Other period wallpaper firms include:
BASSETT & VOLLUM WALLPAPERS, OLD STONE MILL, RICHARD E. THIBAUT, INC., *and* THE TWIGS, INC.

Wall Tie Plates. By definition, wall ties are "small pieces of metal, each end of which is built into joints in the two skins of a cavity wall, thus tying the skins together." In construction, a cavity wall, otherwise known as a "hollow wall," consists of two brick walls, two to three inches apart, held together by metal ties and secured by plates. In laymen's terms, wall tie plates are the decorative structural devices seen on the brick walls of old multistory buildings that prevent the walls from bulging and spreading.

TONY REDGWICK
Tony Redgwick is an English specialist fabricator whose wall tie plates are small pieces of art. Located in the prime beer-brewing area of Staffordshire, Redgwick has studied the old industrial buildings and

introduced not only a range of interesting wall tie plates, but has enabled various sizes to be used in combination with complementary center panels, thus adding considerably to the number of permutations available from a nucleus of design styles. A very small number of possible design combinations are shown here. Tony Redgwick's decorative wall tie plates are cast from spheroidal graphited iron and may be used as decorative centers for larger steel plates.

Literature available

TONY REDGWICK
35 Henhurst Hill
Burton upon Trent, Staffs. DE13 9TB
England
(0283) 65299 or (0831) 415707
Fax (0283) 67761

WINDY HILL FORGE
Ray Zeleny refers to his wall tie plates as "washers," which, when you think about it, is exactly the function that such decorative plates perform, placed as they are between the wall tie and a bolt. Windy Hill Forge's collection of cast-iron wall tie plates includes decorative pieces in the shapes of diamonds, flowers, or stars, ranging in size from 7" to 14". They can add distinction to otherwise dull brick walls, and can also be ordered in brass or aluminum for indoor use on through-bolts.

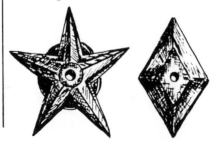

Brochures available

WINDY HILL FORGE
2824 Schroeder Ave.
Perry Hall, MD 21128
(301) 256-5890

Weather Vanes. Metal vanes that rotate and indicate wind direction have been known for centuries. Perched atop steeples, barn roofs, and cupolas, they have been widely used in North America since first settlement. Perhaps because so many Colonists were non-conformists in religion and were loathe to use what they considered Popish symbols, the vane took the place of a cross on church steeples and other public buildings. During the 19th century there were a number of vane manufacturers, and copper vanes made by the best of these firms, J. W. Fiske of Paterson, New Jersey, are valuable antiques. Fortunately, a goodly number of craftsmen in metal are still attracted to the lofty trade of making vanes.

GOOD DIRECTIONS, INC.
Copper and brass vanes are at the core of this firm's business. Each model, like the eagle illustrated,

includes a figure in copper, copper spacer balls, brass directionals, and a steel rod. Roof or eave mounts of steel or cast iron can be supplied as well. Most of the designs are of animals, and nearly all can be given either a green patina, weathered finish, or a high polish.

Catalog, $1

GOOD DIRECTIONS, INC.
24 Ardmore Rd.
Stamford, CT 06902
(203) 348-1836

MARIAN S. IVES
Quite wonderful handmade designs come from Ms. Ives, a metalsmith, jeweler, and gemologist. She makes copper as well as steel vanes. The animal figures have superb detail and modeling. She welcomes orders for custom designs and would be just right to reproduce an Elizabethan banneret or some other fanciful form not found in the repertoire of other vane manufacturers.

Brochure, 50¢

MARIAN S. IVES
Forget Rd.
Hawley, MA 01339
(413) 339-8534

TRAVIS TUCK, METAL SCULPTOR
New England is the home of weather vane artists, and Tuck lives in its deepest reaches, the island of Martha's Vineyard. It is no wonder that nautical themes crop up in his work. A recently completed reproduction of the bark "Perry" has

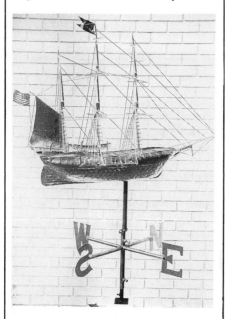

been mounted on the Edgartown town hall. Commissioned by the town's selectmen, it is 44" long, 29" wide, and is 23-karat gold-leafed over a copper body. The vane weighs twenty pounds and is weighted with lead in the bow for ballast. A copy of the painting of the early 1800s whaler from which Tuck worked is also shown. In business now for over twenty years, he is a craftsman who has successfully combined art and enterprise.

Brochure available, $1

TRAVIS TUCK, METAL SCULPTOR
Box 1832
Martha's Vineyard, MA 02568
(508) 693-3914

Other producers of weather vanes include: DENNINGER, INC., KAYNE & SON CUSTOM FORGED HARDWARE, KENNETH LYNCH AND SON, W. F. NORMAN CORP., and E. G. WASHBURNE & CO., INC.

Well Heads. A surprising number of American homesteads still have open hand-dug wells or flowing springs from which water is drawn. Whether it is a working well or just a wishing well, a well head is the appropriate superstructure and support system for a bucket and pulley arrangement.

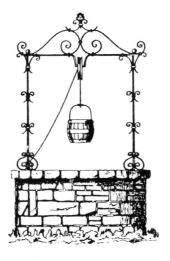

The well head shown is manufactured by THE STEWART IRON WORKS CO., a firm in business since 1886. This is just one of several styles available. A similar kind of rigging in wrought iron is available through KENNETH LYNCH & SONS.

Wickets. The only kind of wicket most people would recognize is one for croquet. The wickets used in gardening are very similar in form, but much sturdier. These, as illustrated, were used around trees

and flower beds during the Victorian period. Because they are of such solid construction, they will survive for years. LAWLER MACHINE & FOUNDRY CO., INC., is the maker of this venerable ornament. Each weighs a good eight pounds.

Window Guards. Windows may need the same protection as doors, at least at ground-floor level. Guards of cast or forged iron are the usual recommended type, since roll-down metal "shades" are neither attractive nor easy to use. Window guards stay permanently in place and may extend only half way up the sash, especially when the guard is being used as much for the safety of children as it is to deter unwanted outsiders. Most architectural iron firms can supply railings or grilles suitable for use as guards, although custom sizing may be necessary. *See also* **Door Guards,** and **Grates, Grilles, and Registers.**

Window Hardware. Specialized hardware for old windows or sash can be notoriously difficult to find. Common articles such as latches in iron or brass are still available in hardware stores and from such general old-house suppliers as RENOVATOR'S SUPPLY. A good name to keep in mind for other types is BLAINE WINDOW HARDWARE, INC. This firm will custom make whatever you need if they don't have it in stock, as also will the following metalwork firms: THE ARDEN FORGE CO., CIRECAST,

KAYNE & SON CUSTOM FORGED HARDWARE, and BRIAN F. LEO. For cast-iron sash weights in 1½- and 2-pound sizes, Architectural Iron Co. is

a superb source. These are carried in stock and can be supplied overnight.

Window Heads. *See* **Door Heads and Window Heads/Overdoors.**

Window Screens. *See* **Screen and Storm Doors.**

Window Weights. *See* **Window Hardware.**

Windows. Windows are never easy to handle. In hot weather they stick, and in cold weather they leak. Windows that are properly framed, that have sash with panes that are well puttied, and that are provided with suitable hardware shouldn't stick and won't leak. But they still occasionally do both. We don't know any complete solution to the problem, but we do know that we'd just as soon have handsome, solidly built windows that add character to the house. Most old

houses don't look right with modern sash. (An old house without its multipane windows looks as if its had all its teeth yanked out.) And there's no excuse for such desecration since there are many suppliers who will help you to maintain the old image in good shape. If you need to replace a window, remember that the architectural salvage warehouses stock old windows that are perfectly recyclable. SALVAGE ONE, whose stock is shown here, in one of them.

ARCHITECTURAL COMPONENTS
This company is typical of woodworking establishments, mainly in New England, who are expert at producing traditional double hung sash and frames in the Colonial style. Shown are overall drawings of Architectural Components' 18th-century plank window and a 19th-century window. Eastern white pine is used for all elements. The 18th-century sash measures $^{15}/_{16}$" thick, and the standard muntin width is 1" with ovolo sticking; 1½" and 1¼" muntins are also made up. Mortise and tenon joinery is used for the sash and the frames of 2½" thick pine. The upper sash is fixed and the lower operable. The units usually take 6" by 8" or 7" by 9" lights and are available in a number of upper/lower combinations.

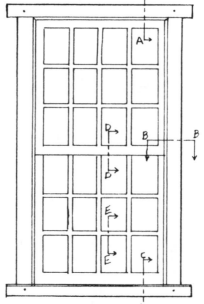

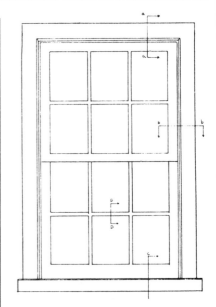

The 19th-century sash is thicker than 18th-century sash, increasing to 1⅛". The muntins, however, are much thinner and delicate at ⅝". The sashes take an extra heavy sill and 1⅛" exterior casings. Like the Colonial model, they are available with various combinations of lights in not only 6" by 8" and 7" by 9" sizes, but also in the following larger panes: 8" by 10", 8" by 12", 9" by 12", and 9" by 13".

In addition to rectangular sash windows, Architectural Components also makes up arched windows, transoms, fanlights, sidelights, and circular windows.

Brochure, $3

ARCHITECTURAL COMPONENTS
26 N. Leverett Rd.
Montague, MA 01351
(413) 367-9441

CAIN ARCHITECTURAL ART GLASS
A glass studio, Cain is fortunate in possessing 1915 equipment which allows it to hand bevel glass panels. These are used in doors, for sidelights and transoms, and regular windows. All work is custom.

Literature available

CAIN ARCHITECTURAL ART GLASS
Bremo Bluff, VA 23022
(804) 842-3984

HOFF'S CUSTOM WOODWORKING, INC.
Arched windows are Hoff's specialty. Among the forms available in quality poplar, clear white pine, or poplar with a pine veneer are Gothic, oval, round top, full round, half-round, ellipse, and quarter-round arches. True divided lights may be specified. The company can also supply framing. The glass used is a standard $^3/_4$" insulated type or a Low-E energy-efficient glass.

Brochure available

HOFF'S CUSTOM WOODWORKING, INC.
20 W. South St.
Greenfield, IN 46140
(317) 462-9522
Fax (317) 462-0776

THE HOUSE CARPENTERS
Builders of traditional timber frames, The House Carpenters know how important well-fitting and designed windows are for both practical and aesthetic reasons. All elements of their 18th-century-style sash are properly cut of clear eastern white pine and are put together with mortise-and-tenon joinery. The plank window frames or casings are made from four heavy planks and mortise-and-tenon joined. All are hand-planed. When sash is ordered separately, it is shipped slightly oversize to allow for fitting, a wise move.

Brochures, $6

THE HOUSE CARPENTERS
Box 281
Leverett, MA 01054
(413) 367-2189

KRAATZ RUSSELL GLASS
A commission from Boston's Museum of Fine Arts to make a series of casement windows for the Fairbanks House was recently executed by this firm. The dwelling in Dedham, Massachusetts, is considered America's oldest frame building. Michael Kraatz and Susan Russell had to fashion leaded diamond-pane panels that would satisfy curators and restoration experts. With their knowledge of decorated and patterned glass and a mastery of handblown techniques, Kraatz and Russell are well equipped to fashion similar types of leaded window panels. Bull's-eye panes for sidelights and transoms are their stock in trade. All lead-glass panels destined for exterior walls are double glazed with laminated glass.

Literature available

KRAATZ RUSSELL GLASS
Grist Mill Rd.
RFD 1, Box 320C
Canaan, NH 03741
(603) 523-4289

WOOD WINDOW WORKSHOP
Reproduction of correct period windows and restoration of the old are two major aspects of the Workshop's business. There is no type that the firm will not tackle, including circle head, old-fashioned bays and bows, Palladian windows, sidelights, and transoms. All wood species are used.

Brochure available

WOOD WINDOW WORKSHOP
432 Lafayette St., PO Box 310
Utica, NY 13503
(315) 732-6755
Fax (315) 732-2863

Other suppliers of windows are: EARLY NEW ENGLAND ROOMS & EXTERIORS, INC., KENMORE INDUSTRIES, KENTUCKY MILLWORK, MARK A. KNUDSEN, MARVIN WINDOWS, MAURER & SHEPHERD JOYNERS, *and* SILVERTON VICTORIAN MILLWORKS. *Sources of antique windows include:* ARCHITECTURAL ANTIQUE CO., FLORIDA VICTORIAN ARCHITECTURAL ANTIQUES, *and* RAMASE.

Wood Stoves. *See* **Stoves**

Workshops and Courses. Workshops and courses in traditional building methods, architectural styles, and the interior design of period buildings are increasingly popular. Many of these educational programs are especially useful to the do-it-yourselfer, but they are also instructive for anyone who is about to become involved in restoration or renovation work. Listed here are just a few programs. There are many other seminars and lectures sponsored by preservation groups which are held from time to time throughout North America. The preservation organization in your area is likely to have information on similar programs.

CAMPBELL CENTER FOR HISTORIC PRESERVATION STUDIES
Campbell Center is a non-profit organization, offering courses in architectural preservation, care of collections, and refresher courses for conservators during the summer months, June through September. Courses vary in length from four days to four weeks. Although the Center's courses are intended primarily for professionals in the preservation and museum fields, some are of considerable interest to individuals concerned with the restoration and maintenance of their old houses or collections. Typical courses for interested laymen would include those on the preservation of architectural metals, the preservation of architectural stone, the conservation and restoration of historic plaster, the techniques of laying veneer and marquestry, the tradition of gilding, and the identification and analysis of historic paint. The Center is situated in the town of Mt. Carroll, Illinois, a registered historic district.

Literature available

CAMPBELL CENTER FOR HISTORIC PRESERVATION STUDIES
PO Box 66
Mt. Carroll, IL 61053
(815) 244-1173

EASTFIELD VILLAGE
Eastfield Village is both a living museum and a school for traditional trades and domestic arts. With over twenty buildings and a study collection of thousands of architectural elements, participants in

the one- to seven-day summer workshops are exposed to original documents dating from 1787 to 1840. They experience working with the tools and materials of the traditional trades taught. All instructors are well-respected in their individual fields. Workshops change from year to year, but typical subjects would include wall stenciling, fireplace and oven building, coopering, blacksmithing, stone cutting, flat wall and ornamental plastering, tinsmithing, slate roofing, shoemaking, historic house dating, historic millwork reproduction, restoration carpentry, and graining and marbelizing. While museum professionals have enjoyed these workshops, so have an equal number of interested private homeowners. Lodging is provided at the school, but students are on their own for meals.

Literature available, SASE

EASTFIELD VILLAGE
Box 143 R.D.
East Nassau, NY 12062
(518) 766-2422

HEARTWOOD OWNER-BUILDER SCHOOL
Heartwood's summer courses include a three-week house building course from the planning and design stages to framing and finishing, and a wide selection of one-week courses concentrating on the specific aspects of building design and construction. Topics for the shorter courses include contracting, cabinetmaking, finish carpentry, timber framing, renovation, and masonry. Heartwood's carpentry for women course, designed for those with little or no experience, is one of the most unique of all those offered. Taught by professional women contractors, it teaches self-sufficiency in home repair and remodeling. As is the case with all Heartwood courses, some classroom teaching is combined with practical application, working with both hands and power tools in the construction of a small building project. All tools and other materials for the Heartwood courses are available at the school, and local accommodation can be arranged easily.

Literature available

HEARTWOOD OWNER-BUILDER SCHOOL
Johnson Hill Rd.
Washington, MA 01235
(413) 623-6677

Workshops and courses are also offered by the ASSOCIATION FOR PRESERVATION TECHNOLOGY *and the* NATIONAL PRESERVATION INSTITUTE. THE NEW ENGLAND TOOL COMPANY LTD. *offers a number of forging workshops.*

Wreaths. *See* **Ornaments.**

Wrought Iron. *See* **Ironwork.**

Yardgoods. *See* **Fabrics.**

List of Suppliers

AA-Abbingdon Affiliates
2149 Utica Ave.
Brooklyn, NY 11234
(718) 258-8333

Abatron, Inc.
33 Center Dr.
Gilberts, IL 60136
(708) 426-2200
Fax (708) 426-5966

Abbey Garden Sundials
PO Box 102
Indian Hill Rd.
Pakenham, ONT K0A 2X0
(613) 256-3973

Acorn Manufacturing Co.
457 School St.
Mansfield, MA 02048
(800) 835-0121
(508) 339-4500 (MA)

The Adams Co.
100 E. 4th St.
Dubuque, IA 52001
(800) 553-3012

Aged Woods
147 W. Philadelphia St.
York, PA 17403
(800) 233-9307
(717) 843-8104 (PA)

Ahrens Chimney Technique
2000 Industrial Ave.
Sioux Falls, SD 57104
(800) 843-4417

Amazon Vinegar & Pickling Works
2218 E. 11th St.
Davenport, IA 52803
(319) 322-6800
(309) 786-3504
Fax (319) 322-4003

Amdega Conservatories
Boston Design Center
1 Design Center Plaza
Boston, MA 02210
(617) 951-2755

American Custom Millwork, Inc.
PO Box 3608
3904 Newton Rd.
Albany, GA 31706
(912) 888-3303 or 6848
Fax (912) 888-9245

American Wood Column Corp.
913 Grand St.
Brooklyn, NY 11211
(718) 782-3163

Amherst Woodworking & Supply, Inc.
Box 718, Hubbard Ave.
Northampton, MA 01061
(413) 584-3003
Fax (413) 585-0288

AMS Imports
23 Ash Lane
Amherst, MA 01002
(413) 253-2644

Anderson Corp.
Bayport, MN 55003
(612) 430-5018
(800) 426-4261

Anderson Building Restoration
923 Marion Ave.
Cincinnati, OH 45229
(513) 281-5258

Anderson-McQuaid Co.
170 Fawcett St.
Cambridge, MA 02138

(617) 876-3250

Antique Baths and Kitchens
2220 Carlton Way
Santa Barbara, CA 93109
(805) 962-8598

Antique Rose Emporium
Rte. 5, Box 143
Brenham, TX 77833
(409) 836-9051

Antiquity Reprints
PO Box 370
Rockville Center,
NY 11571
(516) 766-5585

Architectural Antique Co.
1240 Bank St.
Ottawa, ONT K1S 3Y3
Canada
(613) 738-9243
Fax (613) 738-9782

Architectural Antiques Exchange
709-15 N. Second St.
Philadelphia, PA 19123
(215) 922-3669

Architectural Antique Warehouse
PO Box 3065, Station D
Ottawa, ONT K1P 6H6
Canada

Architectural Components
26 N. Leverett Rd.
Montague, MA 01351
(413) 367-9441
Fax (413) 367-9461

Architectural Iron Co.
Box 126, Schocopee Rd.
Milford, PA 18337
(717) 296-7722
(212) 243-2664
Fax (717) 296-IRON

Architectural Lathe & Mill
316 S. Bernadette
New Orleans, LA 70119
(504) 482-0980

Architectural Reclamation
312 S. River St.
Franklin, OH 45005
(513) 746-8964

The Arden Forge Co.
301 Brintons Bridge Rd.
West Chester, PA 19382
(215) 399-1530

Artefact Architectural Antiques
130 S. Main St.
Doylestown, PA 18901
(215) 340-1213

Artefact Picture Framers
353 Upper St.
Islinton, London N1 8EA
England
(071) 226-8867

Artistic Woodworking Products
PO Box 4625
Englewood, CO 80155
(303) 721-6514

A. S. L. Associates
5182 Maple
Irvine, CA 92715
(714) 786-2407

Association for Preservation Technology
PO Box 8178
Fredericksburg, VA 22404
(703) 373-1621

The Astrup Co.
2937 W. 25th St.
Cleveland, OH 44113
(216) 696-2820

Authentic Designs
42 The Mill Rd.
West Rupert, VT 05776
(802) 394-7713
Fax (802) 394-2422

Backstrom Stained Glass & Antiques
PO Box 2311
71 Airline Rd.
Columbus, MS 39704
(601) 329-1254

Bailey's Architectural Millwork, Inc.
117-19 Slack Ave.
Trenton, NJ 08638
(609) 392-5137
Fax (609) 392-7151

Baldwin Hardware Corp.
841 Wyomissing Blvd.
Reading, PA 19612
(215) 777-7811

A. Ball Plumbing Supply
1703 W. Burnside St.
Portland, OR 97209
(503) 228-0026
Fax (503) 228-0030

The Balmer Architectural Art Studios
9 Codeco Ct.
Don Mills, ONT M3A 1B6
Canada
(416) 449-2155
Fax (416) 449-3018

Bangor Cork Co.
William and D Sts.
Pen Argyl, PA 18072
(215) 863-9041

The Bank Architectural Antiques
1824 Felicity St.
New Orleans, LA 70113
(504) 523-2702
(800) 2-SHUTTER

The Barn People, Inc.
PO Box 217
Windsor, VT 05089
(802) 674-5778

Bassett & Vollum Wallpapers
4350 N. Council Hill Rd.
Galena, IL 61036
(815) 777-2460

Stephen P. Bedard
PO Box 2, Durrell
Mountain Farm
Gilmanton Iron Works,
NH 03837
(603) 528-1896

Bedlam Beds
137 Rte. 4 Westbound
Paramus, NJ 07652
(201) 368-3500
Fax (201) 368-1850

Beech River Mill Co.
Old Rte. 16
Centre Ossipee, NH 03814
(603) 539-2636 (Fax and tel.)

Robert W. Belcher
2505 W. Hillview Dr.
Dalton, GA 30721
(404) 259-3482

S. A. Bendheim Co., Inc.
61 Willet St.
Passaic, NJ 07055
(800) 221-7379
(201) 471-1733 (NJ)
Fax (201) 471-3475

Bendix Mouldings, Inc.
37 Ramland Rd. S.
(800) 526-0240
(914) 365-1111
Fax (914) 365-1218

Bentley Brothers
918 Baxter Ave.
Louisville, KY 40204
(800) 824-4777
(800) 828-0271 (KY)
Fax (502) 581-0748

Bergen Bluestone Co., Inc.
PO Box 67, 404 Rte. 17

Paramus, NJ 07652
(201) 261-1903

Bernheimer's Conservation & Restoration
6439 Miller Dr.
Miami, FL 33155
(305) 770-6641

Besco Plumbing & Heating
729 Atlantic Ave.
Boston, MA 02111
(617) 423-4535

Blaine Window Hardware
1919 Blaine Dr., RD 4
Hagerstown, MD 21740
(301) 797-6500
Fax (301) 797-2510

Blake Industries
PO Box 155
Abington, MA 02351
(617) 337-3004
Fax (617) 335-3004

Blenko Glass Co., Inc.
PO Box 67
Milton, WV 25541
(304) 743-9081

Blue Ox Millworks
Foot of X St.
Eureka, CA 95501
(800) 248-4259
(707) 444-3437
Fax (707) 444-0918

Bona Decorative Hardware
3073 Madison Rd.
Cincinnati, OH 45209
(513) 321-7877

Bow House, Inc.
PO Box 900
Bolton, MA 01740
(508) 779-6464

Bradbury & Bradbury
PO Box 155
Benicia, CA 94510
(707) 746-1900
Fax (707) 745-9417

Philip Bradbury Glass
83 Blackstock Rd.
London N4 2JW
England
(071) 226-2919
Fax (071) 359-6303

Bradford Consultants
PO Box 4020
Alameda, CA 94501
(415) 523-1968

Sylvan Brandt
651 E. Main St.
Lititz, PA 17543
(717) 626-4520

Brandywine Garden Furniture
24 Phoenixville Pike
Malvern, PA 19355
(800) 722-5434

The Brass Knob
2311 18th St., NW
Washington, DC 20009
(202) 332-3370

Brass 'n Bounty
68 Front St.
Marblehead, MA 01945
(617) 631-3864

The Brickyard
PO Box A, 101 E. Wall
Harrisonville, MO 64701
(816) 884-3218

Broad-Axe Beam Co.
RD 2, Box 417
W. Brattleboro, VT 05301
(802) 257-0064

Richard A. Brunkus, Cabinetmaker
PO Box 451
Frenchtown, NJ 08825
(201) 996-7125

Brunschwig & Fils
75 Virginia Rd.

N. White Plains, NY 10603
(914) 684-5800
Bryant Stove Works
Box 2048
Thorndike, ME 04986
(207) 568-3665
Buckley-Rumford Fireplace Co.
PO Box 21131
Columbus, OH 43221
(614) 221-6918
Buckingham-Virginia Slate Co.
4110 Fitzhugh Ave.
Richmond, VA 23230
(804) 355-4351
J. R. Burrows & Co.
PO Box 1739
Jamaica Plain, Boston, MA 02130
(617) 524-1795
Fax (617) 524-5372
Cain Architectural Art Glass
Bremo Bluff, VA 23022
(804) 842-3984
California Products Corp.
169 Waverly St.
Cambridge, MA 02139
(617) 547-5300
Campbell Center
PO Box 66
203 E. Seminary
Mount Carroll, IL 61053
(815) 244-1173
Marion H. Campbell, Cabinetmaker
Barber & Plymouth Sts.
Bath, PA 18014
(215) 837-7775 (workshop)
(215) 865-3292 (home)
The Candle Cellar & Emporium
PO Box 135, South Station
Fall River, MA 02724
(401) 624-9529
Candlertown Chairworks
PO Box 1630
Candler, NC 28715
(704) 667-4844
Candy Tiles Ltd.
Heathfield, Newton Abbot
Devon, England
(0626) 834-668
The Caning Shop
926 Gilman St.
Berkeley, CA 94710
(415) 527-5010
John Canning & Co.
PO Box 822
Southington, CT 06489
(203) 621-2188
The Canopy Co.
Platts Rd., Amblecote
Stourbridge,
Worcestershire DY8 4YR
England
(0384) 370997
Fax (0384) 442128
Cape Cod Cupola Co.
78 State Rd.
N. Dartmouth, MA 02747
(508) 994-2119
Carlisle Restoration Lumber
HCR 32, Box 679
Stoddard, NH 03464-9712
(603) 446-3937
A Carolina Craftsman
975 S. Avocado St.
Anaheim, CA 92805
(714) 776-7877
Fax (714) 533-0894
Carson, Dunlop &

Associates
597 Parliament St.
Toronto, ONT M4X 1W3
Canada
(416) 964-9415
Carter Canopies
PO Box 808
Rte. 2, Box 2706
Troutman, NC 28166
(704) 528-4071
Fax (704) 528-6437
Castelnau Tiles of Barnes
175 Church Rd.
Barnes
London SW13 9HR
England
(081) 741-2452 or 748-9042
Fax (081) 741-5316
Cathedral Stone Co.
2505 Reed St., NW
Washington, DC 20018
(202) 832-1135

Cedar Valley Shingle Systems
943 San Felipe Rd.
Hollister, CA 95023
(800) 521-9523
(408) 636-8110 (CA)
Century House Antique Lamp Emporium and Repair
46785 Rte. 18 West
Wellington, OH 44090
(216) 647-4092
Chadsworth, Inc.
PO Box 53268
Atlanta, GA 30355
(404) 876-5410
Chelsea Decorative Metal
9603 Moonlight Dr.
Houston, TX 77096
(713) 721-9200
Cherry Creek Enterprises
3500 Blake St.
Denver, CO 80204
(800) 338-5725
Joseph Chillino
3 Emerald Ln.
Suffern, NY 10901
(914) 357-6772
Chilstone
Sprivers Est.
Hormonden, Kent
TN12 8DR
England
Chromatic Paint Corp.
PO Box 690
Stony Point, NY 10980
(800) 431-7001
(914) 947-3210
Fax (914) 947-3546
Cirecast
380 7th St.
San Francisco, CA 94103
(415) 863-8319
City Lights
2226 Massachusetts Ave.
Cambridge, MA 02140
(617) 547-1490
Clarence House Imports Ltd.
211 E. 58th St.
New York, NY 10022
(212) 752-2890
Classic Architectural Specialties
3223 Canton St.
Dallas, TX 75226
(214) 748-1668
Classic Illumination, Inc.
2743 Ninth St.
Berkeley, CA 94710
(415) 849-1842
Fax (415) 849-2328

G. R. Clidence
Box 386, James Trail
West Kingston, RI 02892
(401) 539-2558
Cohasset Colonials
Cohasset, MA 02025
(800) 288-2389
Cole & Son
18 Mortimer St.
London W1A 4BU
England
(071) 580-1066
Colefax & Fowler
See Clarence House Imports Ltd.
The Color People
1546 Williams St.
Denver, CO 80218
(303) 388-8686
Conant Custom Brass, Inc.
270 Pine St.
Burlington, VT 05401
(802) 668-4482
Conklin Metal Industries
PO Box 1858
Atlanta, GA 30301
(404) 688-4510
Conklin's Authentic Antique Barnwood and Hand Hewn Beams
RD 1, Box 70
Susquehanna, PA 18847
(717) 465-3832
Con-Test/William H. Parsons
2275 Silas Deane Hwy.
Rocky Hill, CT 06067
(203) 257-4970
Fax (203) 257-4967
Cook & Dunn Paint Corp.
Box 117
Newark, NJ 07101
(201) 589-5580
Coppa Woodworking, Inc.
1231 Paraiso Ave.
San Pedro, CA 90731
(213) 548-4142
Fax (213) 548-6740
The Coppersmith
PO Box 755, Rte. 20
Sturbridge, MA 01566
(508) 347-7038 or 9509
A. J. P. Coppersmith & Co.
20 Industrial Pkwy.
Woburn, MA 01801
(800) 545-1776
(617) 932-3700 (MA)
Counselor Profiles
40 Lawlins Park
Wyckoff, NJ 07481-1443
(800) 635-6285
Fax (201) 848-9867
The Country Bed Shop
RR 1, Box 65,
Richardson Rd.
Ashby, MA 01431
(508) 386-7550
Country Braid House
RFD 2, Box 29, Clark Rd.
Tilton, NH 03276
(603) 286-4511
The Country Iron Foundry
PO Box 600
Paoli, PA 19301
(215) 296-7122
Craftsman Lumber Co.
Box 222
Groton, MA 01450
(508) 448-6336
Crawford's Old House Store
550 Elizabeth St.
Waukesha, WI 53186
(800) 556-7878
Creative Openings

PO Box 4204
Bellingham, WA 98227
(800) 677-6420
(206) 671-6420 (WA)
Creative Woodworking Ltd.
26 Friendship St.
Westerly, RI 02891
(401) 596-4463
Fax (401) 596-3418
Cumberland General Store
Rte. 3, Box 81
Crossville, TN 38555
(615) 484-8481
Cumberland Woodcraft Co.
PO Drawer 609
Carlisle, PA 17013
(717) 243-0063
Gerald Curry, Cabinetmaker
Pound Hill Rd.
Union, ME 04862
(207) 785-4633
Cushwa Brick Inc.
PO Box 160
Williamsport, MD 21795-0160
(301) 223-7700
Custom & Historic Millwork
5310 Tennyson
Denver, CO 80212
(303) 480-1617
Fax (303) 480-5006
Custom Ironwork, Inc.
PO Box 180,
10619 Big Bone Rd.
Union, KY 41091
(606) 384-4122
Fax (606) 384-4848
The Dahlke Stair Co.
PO Box 418
Hadlyme, CT 06439
(203) 434-3589
Day Studio-Workshop, Inc.
1504 Bryant St.
San Francisco, CA 94103
(415) 626-9300
Decorative Textiles of Cheltenham
7, Suffolk Parade
Cheltenham GL50 2AB
England
(0242) 574-546
Fax (0242) 222-646
The Decorators Supply Corp.
3610-12 S. Morgan St.
Chicago, IL 60609
(312) 847-6300
Fax (312) 847-6357
Delaware Quarries, Inc.
River Rd.
Lumberville, PA 18933
(215) 297-5647
Denninger Cupolas & Weathervanes
RD 1, Box 447
Middletown, NY 10940
(914) 343-2229
Designer's Guild
6 Relay Rd.
London W12 7SJ
England
(081) 743-6322
Fax (081) 740-9582
Designs in Tile
Box 358, Dept. G
Mt. Shasta, CA 96067
(916) 926-2629
Devenco Products, Inc.
PO Box 700
Decatur, GA 30031
(800) 888-4597
Devoe & Raynolds Co.
PO Box 7600
4000 Dupont Circle

Louisville, KY 40207
(800) 654-2616
DeWeese Woodworking
PO Box 576
Philadelphia, MS 39350
(601) 656-4951
Diamond K. Co., Inc.
130 Buckland Rd.
South Windsor, CT 06074
(203) 644-8486
Dixon Brothers Woodworking
72 Northampton St.
Boston, MA 02118
(617) 445-9884
Fax (617) 445-4214
Dodge, Adams & Roy Ltd.
62 Mercy St.
Portsmouth, NH 03801
(603) 436-6427
Domestic Paraphernalia Co.
2a Pleasant St.
Lytham, Lancs. FY8 5JA
England
(02353) 736334
Domus Doorbells Ltd.
PO Box 190
Haywards Heath
Sussex RH17 5YG
England
(0444) 417571
Donnell's Clapboard
RR Box 1650, Country Rd.
Sedgwick, ME 04676
(207) 359-2036
Dovetail Woodworking
550 Elizabeth St.
Waukesha, WI 53186
(414) 544-5859
Eagle Eye Trading Co.
PO Box 17900
Milwaukee, WI 53217
(414) 374-1984
Early New England Rooms & Exteriors, Inc.
37 McGuire Rd.
S. Windsor, CT 06074
(203) 282-0236
Eastfield Village
RD, Box 143
E. Nassau, NY 12062
(518) 766-2422
Jon Eklund Restorations
80 Gates Ave.
Montclair, NJ 07042
(201) 746-7483
Elcanco, Ltd.
PO Box 682
Westford, MA 01886
(508) 392-0830
Elegant Entries
240 Washington St.
Auburn, MA 01501
(800) 343-3432
(508) 832-9898 (MA)
Especially Lace
202 5th St.
W. Des Moines, IA 50265
(515) 277-8778
EverGreene Painting Studios, Inc.
635 W. 23rd St.
New York, NY 10011
(212) 727-9500
Evergreen Slate Co.
PO Box 248
Granville, NY 12832
(518) 642-2530
Fax (518) 642-9313
Family Heir-Loom Weavers
RD 3, Box 59E
Red Lion, PA 17356
(717) 246-2431
Faneuil Furniture Hardware
163 Main St.
Salem, NH 03079

(603) 898-7733
Fax (603) 898-7839
Felber Studios, Inc.
110 Ardmore Ave.
Ardmore, PA 19003
(215) 642-4710
FerGene Studio
9986 Happy Acres W.
Bozeman, MT 59715
(406) 587-3651
Buddy Fife & Co.
9 Main St.
Northwood, NH 03261
(603) 942-8777
Fine Paints of France
PO Box 104
Blooming Grove,
NY 10914
(914) 496-8989
Finnaren & Haley
2320 Haverford Rd.
Ardmore, PA 19003
(215) 649-5000
Fireside Reproductions
4727 Winterset Dr.
Columbus, OH 43220
(614) 451-7695
David Flaharty, Sculptor
RD 2, 402 Magazine Rd.
Green Lane, PA 18054
(215) 234-8242
Fletcher's Paint Works
21 Elm St.
Milford, NH 03055
(603) 673-2300
Floorcloths, Inc.
920 Edgewater Rd.
Severna Park,
MD 21146
(301) 544-0858
Florida Victorian Architectural Antiques
112 W. Georgia Ave.
Deland, FL 32720
(904) 734-9300
Fax (904) 734-1150
Focal Point Inc.
PO Box 93327
Atlanta, GA 30377-0327
(800) 662-5550
(404) 351-0820
Fax (404) 352-9049
Forgeries
Old Butchery, High St.
Twyford, Hant SO21 1RF
England
(0962) 712196 (Fax and tel.)
Fourth Bay
Box 287
10500 Industrial Dr.
Garrettsville, OH 44231
(800) 321-9614
(216) 527-4343
Fax (216) 527-4346
The Fragrant Path
PO Box 328
Fort Calhoun, NE 68023
Anna French
343 Kings Rd.
London SW3 5ES
England
(01) 351-1126
Frog Tool Co., Ltd.
700 W. Jackson Blvd.
Chicago, IL 60606
(312) 648-1270
Fypon, Inc.
Box 365
22 W. Pennsylvania Ave.
Stewartstown, PA 17363
(717) 993-2593
Garrett Wade Co.
161 Ave. of the Americas
New York, NY 10013
(212) 807-1155

Gates Moore
River Rd., Silvermine
Norwalk, CT 06850
(203) 847-3231
Gazebo & Porchworks
728 9th Ave. SW
Puyallup, WA 98371
(206) 848-0502
Georgia Marble Co.
Blue Ridge Ave.
Nelson, GA 30151
(404) 735-2591
Giannetti Studios
3806 38th St.
Brentwood, MD 20722
(301) 927-0033
Fax (301) 779-5193
Glen-Gery Corp.
PO Box 7001,
1166 Spring St.
Wyomissing, PA 19618
(215) 374-4011
The Glidden Co.
925 Euclid Ave.
Cleveland, OH 44115
(216) 344-8000
Gloster Leisure Furniture
See Universal Gloster, Inc.;
Steptoe & Wife Antiques, Ltd.
Golden Age Glassworks
339 Bellvale Rd.
Warwick, NY 10990
(914) 986-1487

Good and Co., Floorclothmakers
Salzburg Sq., Rte. 101
Amherst, NH 03031
(603) 672-0490
Good Directions, Inc.
24 Ardmore Rd.
Stamford, CT 06902
(800) 346-7678
(203) 348-1836 (CT)
Fax (203) 357-0092
Virginia Goodman
Rte. 2, Box 770
Boone, NC 28607
(800) 735-5191
Gothom, Inc.
Box 421, 110 Main St.
Erin, ONT N0B 1T0
Canada
(519) 833-2574
Governor's Antiques
6240 Meadowbridge Rd.
Mechanicsville, VA 23111
(804) 746-1030
Grammar of Ornament
2626 Curtis St.
Denver, CO 80205
(303) 295-2431
Granville Manufacturing Co., Inc.
Rte. 100
Granville, VT 05747
(802) 767-4747
Greeff Fabrics
150 Midland Ave.
Port Chester, NY 10573
(800) 223-0357
(914) 939-6200
Fax (914) 939-8168
Green Enterprises
43 S. Rogers St.
Hamilton, VA 22068
(703) 338-3606
Jeffrey P. Greene, Furnituremaker
97 James Trail
W. Kingston, RI 02892
(401) 783-6614
Hamilton-Weston Wallpapers
18 St. Mary's Grove

Richmond,
Surrey TW9 1UY
England
(081) 940-4850
Fax (081) 332-0296
Hammerworks
6 Fremont St.
Worcester, MA 01603
(800) 777-3689
(508) 755-3434
Hampton Decor & Plastering
30 Fisk St.
Jersey City, NJ 07305
(201) 433-9002
Hartmann-Sanders Co.
4340 Bankers Circle
Atlanta, GA 30360
(404) 449-1561
Heads Up Sonoma Woodworks, Inc.
133 Copeland St.
Petaluma, CA 94952
(707) 762-5548
Heartland Appliances
5 Hoffman St.
Kitchener, ONT N2M 3M5
Canada
(519) 743-8111
Fax (519) 743-1665
Heartwood Owner-Builder School
Johnson Hill Rd.
Washington, MA 01235
(413) 623-6677
Hephaestus Pottery
2012 Penn St.
Lebanon, PA 17042
(717) 272-0806
Heritage Mantels
PO Box 671
Southport, CT 06490
(203) 335-0552
Heritage Rugs
Lahaska, PA 18931
(215) 343-5196
Hicksville Woodworks Co.
265 Jerusalem Ave.
Hicksville, NY 11801
(516) 938-0171
Allen Charles Hill, A.I.A.
25 Englewood Rd.
Winchester, MA 01890
(617) 729-0748
Historical Replications, Inc.
PO Box 13529
Jackson, MS 39236
(601) 981-8743
Historic Hardware Ltd.
PO Box 1327
North Hampton,
NH 03862
(603) 964-2280
Hoff's Custom Woodworking, Inc.
20 W. South St.
Greenfield, IN 46140
(317) 462-9522
Fax (317) 462-0776
Alvin Holm, A.I.A., Architects
2014 Sansom St.
Philadelphia, PA 19103
(215) 963-0747
Homestead Chimney
PO Box 5182
Clinton, NJ 08809
(201) 735-7708
Pat Hornafius
113 Meadowbrook Ln.
Elizabethtown, PA 17022
(717) 367-7706
The House Carpenters
PO Box 281
Leverett, MA 01054
(413) 367-2189

HouseMaster of America
421 W. Union Ave.
Bound Brook, NJ 08805
(800) 526-3939

Lyn Hovey Studio, Inc.
226 Concord Ave.
Cambridge, MA 02138
(617) 492-6566

Hurley Patentee Manor
RD 7, Box 98A
Kingston, NY 12401
(914) 331-5414

Hyde Manufacturing Co.
54 Eastford Rd.
Southbridge, MA 01550
(508) 764-4344

Inclinator Co. of America
PO Box 1557,
2200 Paxton St.
Harrisburg, PA 17105
(717) 234-8065

The Iron Shop
PO Box 547, 400 Reed Rd.
Broomall, PA 19008

Irreplaceable Artifacts
14 Second Ave.
New York, NY 10003
(212) 777-2900

Island City Shutters
1801 Mechanic St.
Galveston, TX 77550
(409) 765-5727

Marian Ives
Forget Rd.
Hawley, MA 01339
(413) 339-8534

Ned James, Wrought Metals
65 Canal St.
Turners Falls, MA 01376
(413) 863-8388

Kane-Gonic Brick Corp.
Winter St.
Gonic, NH 03867
(603) 332-2861

**Kayne & Son Custom
Forged Hardware**
76 Daniel Ridge Rd.
Candler, NC 28715
(704) 667-8868 or 665-1988

Kenmore Industries
PO Box 34
One Thompson Sq.
Boston, MA 02129
(617) 242-1711
Fax (617) 242-1982

Kentucky Millwork
4200 Reservoir Ave.
Louisville, KY 40213
(502) 451-3456
Fax (502) 451-6027

Kentucky Wood Floors
PO Box 33276
Louisville, KY 40232
(502) 451-6024
Fax (502) 451-6027

King's Chandelier Co.
Dept. OHC-VII
PO Box 667
Eden, NC 27288
(919) 623-6188
Fax (919) 623-1723

Jonathan Kline
5066 Mott Evans Rd.
Trumansburg, NY 14886
(607) 387-5718

Dimitrios Klitsas
705 Union St.
W. Springfield, MA 01089
(413) 732-2661

Mark A. Knudsen
1100 E. County Line Rd.
Des Moines, IA 50320
(515) 285-6112

Kohler Co.
Kohler, WI 53044
(414) 457-4441

Fax (414) 459-1656

Kraatz Russell Glass
RFD 1, Box 320C
Grist Mill Hill
Canaan, NH 03741
(603) 523-4289

Kyp-Go, Inc.
PO Box 247, 20 N. 17th St.
St. Charles, IL 60174
(312) 584-8181

J. & R. Lamb Studios, Inc.
PO Box 291
Philmont, NY 12565
(518) 672-7267

Lamp Glass
2230 Massachusetts Ave.
Cambridge, MA 02140
(617) 497-0770

Lampshades of Antique
PO Box 2
Medford, OR 97501
(503) 826-9737

D. Landreth Seed Co.
Ostend & Leadenhall Sts.
PO Box 6426
Baltimore, MD 21230
(301) 727-3922 or 3923

Langhorne Carpet Co.
PO Box 175
Penndel, PA 19047
(215) 757-5155

**Lawler Machine & Foundry
Co., Inc.**
PO Box 320069
Birmingham, AL 35232
(205) 595-0596

Lazy Hill Farm Designs
Lazy Hill Rd.
Colerain, NC 27924
(919) 356-2628

Lee Jofa
979 Third Ave.
New York, NY 10022
(212) 688-0444

**Lehman Hardware &
Appliances**
PO Box 41
Kidron, OH 44636-0041
(216) 857-5441 or 2931
Fax (216) 857-5785

**Lemee's Fireplace
Equipment**
815 Bedford St.
Bridgewater, MA 02324
(508) 697-2672

Brian F. Leo
7532 Columbus Ave. S.
Richfield, MN 55423
(612) 861-1473

Joe Ley Antiques, Inc.
615 E. Market St.
Louisville, KY 40202
(502) 583-4014

Liberty
210/220 Regent St.
London W1R 6AH
England
(081) 946-4700

Linen & Lace
4 Lafayette
Washington, MO 63090
(800) 332-5223

Linoleum City
5657 Santa Monica Blvd.
Hollywood, CA 90038
(213) 469-0063

Ludowici-Celadon, Inc.
4757 Tile Plant Rd.
New Lexington, OH 43764
(614) 342-1995
Fax (614) 342-5175

Kenneth Lynch and Sons
Box 488, 78 Danbury Rd.
Wilton, CT 06897
(203) 762-8363
Fax (203) 762-2999

Mad River Woodworks
PO Box 163
Arcata, CA 95521
(707) 826-0629

Mahantango Manor, Inc.
Hickory Corners Rd.
Dalmatia, PA 17017
(800) 642-3966
(717) 758-8000
Fax (717) 758-6000

Maizefield Mantels
PO Box 336
Port Townsend, WA 98368
(206) 385-6789

Frank J. Mangione
21 John St.
Saugerties, NY 12477
(914) 246-9863

Marmion Plantation Co.
RD 2, Box 458
Fredericksburg, VA 22405
(703) 775-3480

Marshalltown Trowel Co.
PO Box 738
Marshalltown, IA 50158
(515) 753-5999

The Martin-Senour Co.
PO Box 6709
Cleveland, OH 44101
(800) 542-8468

Marvin Windows
PO Box 100
Warroad, MN 56763
(800) 346-5128

Maurer & Shepherd Joyners
122 Naubuc Ave.
Glastonbury, CT 06033
(203) 633-2383

**M. J. May Building
Restoration**
505 Storle Ave.
Burlington, WI 53105
(414) 763-8822

**The Mechanick's
Workbench**
PO Box 668
Marion, MA 02738
(508) 748-1680

Metropolis
1210 46th Ave.
San Francisco, CA 94122
(415) 564-5776

**Michael's Fine Colonial
Products**
RD 1, Box 179A
Salt Point, NY 12578
(914) 677-3960

Monarch Painting
W. Redding, CT 06896
(203) 938-9016
(203) 322-7853

Montclair Restoration, Inc.
21 Cloverhill Pl.
Montclair, NJ 07042
(201) 783-4519

Benjamin Moore & Co.
51 Chestnut Ridge Rd.
Montvale, NJ 07645
(201) 573-9600

E. T. Moore, Jr. Co.
3100 N. Hopkins Rd.
Richmond, VA 23224
(804) 231-1823
Fax (804) 231-0759

Morgan-Bockius Studios
1412 York Rd.
Warminster, PA 18974
(215) 672-6547

Matthew Mosca
2513 Queen Anne Rd.
Baltimore, MD 21216
(301) 466-5325

Mountain Lumber Co.
Rte. 2, Box 43-1
Ruckersville, VA 22968
(804) 985-3646

Mrs. Monro
16 Motcomb St.
London SW1, England
(01) 235-0326

M. J. Mullane Co.
17 Mason St.
Hudson, MA 01749
(508) 568-0597

The Muralo Co., Inc.
148 E. 5th St.
Bayonne, NJ 07002
(201) 437-0770

Murphy Door Bed Co., Inc.
5300 New Horizons Blvd.
Amityville, NY 11701
(516) 957-5200

Nanik
7200 W. Stewart Ave.
Wausau, WI 54401
(715) 842-4653

**National Preservation
Institute**
National Building
Museum
Judiciary Sq., NW
Washington, DC 20001
(202) 393-0038

National Supaflu Systems
PO Box 89, Industrial Park
Walton, NY 13856
(607) 865-7636

Neenah Foundry
Box 729, 2121 Brooks Ave.
Neenah, WI 54956
(414) 725-7000

New England Firebacks
PO Box 268
161 Main St. S.
Woodbury, CT 06798
(203) 263-5737

New England Tool Co.
PO Box 30
Chester, NY 10918
(914) 782-5332 or 651-7550
Fax (914) 783-2554

New England Woodturners
PO Box 7242
75 Daggett St.
New Haven, CT 06519
(203) 776-1880

The New Jersey Barn Co.
PO Box 702
Princeton, NJ 08542
(609) 924-8480

Newell Workshop
19 Blaine Ave.
Hinsdale, IL 60521
(312) 323-7367

Newstamp Lighting Co.
227 Bay Rd.
North Easton, MA 02356
(508) 238-7071

New York Marble Works
1399 Park Ave.
New York, NY 10029
(212) 534-2242

W. F. Norman Corporation
PO Box 323, 214 N. Cedar
Nevada, MO 64772-0323
(800) 641-4038
(417) 667-5552 (MO)

North Woods Chair Shop
237 Old Tilton Rd.
Canterbury, NH 03224
(603) 783-4595

Nostalgia, Inc.
307 Stiles Ave.
Savannah, GA 31401
(800) 874-0015
(912) 232-2324
Fax (912) 234-5746

Nowell's, Inc.
PO Box 295
Sausalito, CA 94965
(415) 332-4933

Oak Crest Manufacturing

6732 E. Emory Rd.
Knoxville, TN 37938
(615) 922-1311

Oehrlein & Associates Architects
1702 Connecticut Ave. NW
Washington, DC 20009
(202) 387-8040
Fax (202) 265-0883

Old Carolina Brick Co.
Rte. 9, Box 77
Majolica Rd.
Salisbury, NC 28144
(704) 636-8850

Old House Journal Advertising Office
123 Main St.
Gloucester, MA 01930
(800) 356-9313

Old Lamplighter Shop
The Musical Museum
Deansboro, NY 13328
(315) 841-8774

The Old-Fashioned Milk Paint Co.
Box 222
Groton, MA 01450
(508) 448-6336

Old South Company, Inc.
PO Box 7096
Tarboro, NC 27886
(919) 823-8100

Old Stone Mill Factory Outlet
2A Grove St., Rte. 8
Adams, MA 01220
(413) 743-1042

The Old Wagon Factory
PO Box 1427, Dept. OC91
Clarksville, VA 23927
(804) 374-5787
Fax (804) 374-4646

Old World Moulding & Finishing Co., Inc.
115 Allen Blvd.
Farmingdale,NY 11735
(516) 293-1789

Omnia Industries, Inc.
Box 330, 5 Cliffside Dr.
Cedar Grove, NJ 07009
(201) 239-7272
Fax (201) 239-5960

The Original Cast Lighting
6120 Delmar Blvd.
St. Louis, MO 63112-1204
(314) 863-1895
Fax (314) 863-3278

Ornamental Mouldings Limited
PO Box 336
Waterloo, ONT N2J 4A4
Canada
(519) 884-4080
Fax (519) 884-9692

Osborne & Little
979 Third Ave.
New York, NY 10022
(212) 751-3333

Outdoor Designs & Service
197 George St.
Excelsior, MN 55331
(612) 474-8328
Fax (612) 474-60

Henry Page, House Restoration Consultants
PO Drawer T419
Gilmanton, NH 03237
(603) 524-0963

Pagliacco Turning and Milling
PO Box 225
Woodacre, CA 94973
(415) 488-4333

Pasvalco
100 Bogert St.
Closter, NJ 07624

(800) 222-2133

Patterson, Flynn, Martin & Manges, Inc.
979 Third Ave.
New York NY 10022
(212) 688-7700
Fax (212) 826-6740

Paxton Hardware Ltd.
PO Box 256
7818 Bradshaw Rd.
Upper Falls, MD 21156
(301) 592-8505
Fax (301) 592-2224

Peerless Rattan
222 Lake Ave.
Yonkers, NY 10701
(914) 968-4046

Pemaquid Floorcloths
PO Box 77
Round Pond, ME 04564
(207) 529-5633

Penn Big Bed Slate Co.
PO Box 184
Slatington, PA 18080-0184
(215) 767-4601
Fax (215) 767-9252

Pennsylvania Firebacks
308 Elm Ave.
North Wales, PA 19454
(215) 699-0805

Perkowitz
135 Green Bay Rd.
Wilmette, IL 60091
(708) 251-7700

H. Pfanstiel Hardware Co.
Rte. 52
Jeffersonville, NY 12748
(914) 482-4445

Philadelphia Architectural Salvage Ltd.
1214 N. 26th St.
Philadelphia, PA 19121
(215) 236-9339

Pipe Dreams
72 Gloucester Rd.
London SW7 4QT
England
(071) 225-3978
Fax (071) 589-8841

Pittsburgh Paints
One PPG Plaza
Pittsburgh, PA 15272
(412) 434-2400

Pompei & Co.
454 High St.
Medford, MA 02155
(617) 395-8867

Portland Stove Co.
PO Box 37, Fickett Rd.
N. Pownal, Me 04069
(207) 688-2254

Pratt & Lambert Paints
PO Box 22, Dept. GV
Buffalo, NY 14240
(716) 873-6000

The Preservation Partnership
345 Union St.
New Bedford, MA 02740
(508) 996-3383

Protech Systems
PO Box 1743
Albany, NY 12201
(518) 463-7284

Francis J. Purcell II
88 N. Main St.
New Hope, PA 18938
(215) 862-9100

E. W. Pyfer
218 N. Foley Ave.
Freeport, IL 61032-3943
(815) 232-8968

Queen City Architectural Salvage
PO Box 16541
Denver, CO 80216

(303) 296-0925

Ramase
Rte. 47
Woodbury, CT 06798
(203) 263-3332

Rambusch
40 W. 13th St.
New York, NY 10011
(212) 675-0400

Rastetter Woolen Mill
State Rte. 39 and 62
Millersburg, OH 44654
(216) 674-2103

Ravenglass Pty. Ltd.
PO Box 612
Goodland, KS 67735
(913) 899-2297

Red Fern Glass
HCR 68, Box 19A
Salem, AR 72576
(501) 895-2036

Tony Redgwick, Specialist Fabricator
35 Henhurst Hill
Burton upon Trent
Staffs. DE13 9TB
England
(0283) 65299
(0831) 415707
Fax (0283) 67761

The Reggio Register Co.
PO Box 511
Ayer, MA 01432
(508) 772-3493

Rejuvenation Lamp & Fixture Co.
901 N. Skidmore
Portland, OR 97217
(503) 249-0774
Fax (503) 281-7948

REM Industries
PO Box 504
Northborough, MA 01532-0504
(508) 393-8424

Remodelers & Renovators
Box 45478
Boise, ID 83711
(800) 456-2135

Renaissance Decorative Hardware Co.
PO Box 332
Leonia, NJ 07605
(201) 568-1403

Renaissance Marketing
PO Box 360
Lake Orion, MI 48035
(313) 693-1109

Renovator's Supply
Miller Falls, MA 01349
(413) 659-2211

Restorations Unlimited
24 W. Main St.
Elizabethville, PA 17023
(717) 362-3477
(Fax (717) 362-4571

Restoration Works, Inc.
PO Box 486
Buffalo, NY 14205
(800) 735-3535
(716) 856-8000
Fax (716) 856-8040

J. Ring Glass Studio, Inc.
2724 University Ave., SE
Minneapolis, MN 55414
(612) 379-0920

Rising & Nelson Slate Co.
W. Pawlett, VT 05775
(602) 645-0150

River City Restorations, Inc.
PO Box 1065, 623 Collier
Hannibal, MO 63401
(314) 248-0733

Roberts Lighting Craft
Rte. 5, Box 260-B
Santa Fe, NM 87501

(505) 455-3341

Robinson & Cornish
The Old Tannery
Hannaford Ln.
Swimbridge
Devon EX32 0PL
England
(0271) 830732

Robinson Iron Corp.
PO Box 1119, Robinson Rd.
Alexander City, AL 35010
(205) 329-8486

Rockingham Fender Seats
Grange Farm, Thorney
Peterborough PE6 0PJ
England
(0733) 270233

Barry Rose, Art in Action
1450 Logan St.
Denver, CO 80205
(303) 832-3250

Roses of Yesterday & Today
802 Brown's Valley Rd.
Watsonville, CA 95076-0398
(408) 724-3537

Roy Electric Antique Lighting Co.
1054 Coney Island Ave.
Brooklyn, NY 11230
(718) 434-7002
Fax (718) 421-4678

Rue de France
78 Thames St.
Newport, RI 02840
(401) 846-2084

E. Rumsey
721 East Shore Dr.
Ithaca, NY 14850
(607) 272-3020

Rutland Products
PO Box 340, Perkins Rd.
Rutland, VT 05720-0340
(802) 775-5519
Fax (802) 775-5262

Rye Tiles
The Old Brewery
Wishward, Rye
Sussex TN31 7DH
England
(0797) 223038
Fax (0797) 224834

Saco Manufacturing & Woodworking
39 Lincoln St.
Saco, ME 04072
(207) 284-6613

Samuel B. Sadtler & Co.
340 S. 4th St.
Philadelphia, PA 19106
(215) 923-3714

The Saltbox
3004 Columbia Ave.
Lancaster, PA 17603
(717) 392-5649

Salvage One
1524 S. Sangamon St.
Chicago, IL 60608
(312) 733-0098

Arthur Sanderson & Sons
979 Third Ave.
New York, NY 10022
(212) 319-7220

San Francisco Victoriana
2070 Newcomb Ave.
San Francisco, CA 94124
(415) 648-0313
Fax (415) 648-2812

Scalamandré
37-24 24th St.
Long Island City, NY 11101
(718) 361-8500

Conrad Schmitt Studios
2405 S. 162nd St.
New Berlin, WI 53151

(414) 786-3030
Fax (414) 786-9036
F. Schumacher & Co.
79 Madison Ave.
New York, NY 10016
(800) 423-5881
**Schwartz's Forge &
Metalworks, Inc.**
PO Box 205
Deansboro, NY 13328
(315) 841-4477
**A. F. Schwerd
Manufacturing Co.**
3215 McClure Ave.
Pittsburgh, PA 15212
(412) 766-6322
Select Seeds
180 Stickney Hill Rd.
Union, CT 06076
Seraph East
Rte. 20, Box 500
Sturbridge, MA 01566
(508) 347-2241
Seraph West
5606 State Rte. 37
Delaware, OH 43105
(614) 369-1817
Shady Lady
418 E, Second St.
Loveland, CO 80537
(303) 669-1080
Shakertown Siding
1200 Kerron St.
Winlock, WA 98596
(800) 426-8970
Shaker Workshops
PO Box 1028
Concord, MA 01742
(617) 646-8985
Sheppard Millwork, Inc.
21020 70th Ave. W.
Edmonds, WA 98020-6701
(206) 771-4645
(206) 283-7549
Fax (206) 672-1622
Shuttercraft
282 Stepstone Hill Rd.
Guilford, CT 06437
(203) 453-1973
**Silverton Victorian
Millworks**
PO Box 2987-OC7
Durango, CO 81302
(303) 259-5915
Fax (303) 259-5919
**Skyline Engineers of
Maryland, Inc.**
5905 Beall Dr.
Frederick, MD 21701-6839
(301) 831-8800
Smith & Hawken Ltd.
25 Corte Madera
Mill Valley, CA 94941
(415) 383-2000
**Society for the Preservation
of New-England
Antiquities**
185 Lyman St.
Waltham, MA 02154
(617) 891-1985
Somerset Door & Column
Box 328
Somerset, PA 15501
(814) 445-9608
Spanish Pueblo Doors
PO Box 2517
Santa Fe, NM 87504-2517
(505) 473-0464
**Spiess Antique Building
Materials**
230 E. Washington
Joliet, IL 60433
(815) 722-5639
Spring House Classics
PO Box 541
Schaefferstown, PA 17088

(717) 949-3902
Stair Specialist
2257 W. Columbia Ave.
Battle Creek, MI 49017
(616) 964-2351
(616) 964-3450
Standard Trimming Co.
306 E. 61st St.
New York, NY 10021
(212) 755-3034
Stark Carpet Corp.
979 Third Ave.
New York, NY 10022
(212) 752-9000
The Stencil Library
The Gatehouse
Naworth Castle
Brampton
Cumbria CA8 2HF
England
(091) 281-3899
Steptoe and Wife Antiques
322 Geary Ave.
Toronto, ONT M6H 2C7
Canada
(414) 530-4200
Fax (414) 530-4666
Sterling Publishing Co.
387 Park Ave. S.
New York, NY 10016-8810
(800) 367-9692
(212) 532-7160
Fax (212) 213-2495
**Stewart Iron Works
Company**
PO Box 2612
20 W. 18th St.
Covington, KY 41012
(606) 431-1985
**Stickney's Garden Houses
and Follies**
PO Box 32
One Thompson Sq.
Boston, MA 02129
(617) 242-1711
Fax (617) 242-1982
Strasser & Associates
35 Hillside Ave.
Monsey, NY 10952
(914) 425-0650
Fax (914) 425-1842
Structural Slate Co.
PO Box 187
222 E. Main St.
Pen Argyl, PA 18072-01
(800) 67-SLATE
(215) 863-4141
Fax (215) 863-7016
**Donald Stryker
Restorations**
154 Commercial Ave.
New Brunswick, NJ 08901
(201) 828-7022
Stuart Interiors
Barrington Ct.
Barrington, Ilminster
Somerset TA19 0NQ
England
(0460) 40349
Fax (0460) 42069
The Stulb Company
PO Box 597
E. Allen and Graham Sts.
Allentown, PA 18105
(800) 221-8444
Sturbridge Studio
114 East Hill
Brimfield, MA 01010
(413) 245-3289
Stuart Garden Architecture
Larchfield Estate, Dowlish
Ford, Ilminster,
Somerset TA19 0PF
England
Sunflower Glass Studio
RD 3, Box 93

Stockton, NJ 08559
(609) 397-1535
Sunningdale Oak
83, Chobham Rd.
Sunningdale
Berks SL5 0HQ
England
(0990) 26504
Fax (0990) 21822
Sunrise Salvage Co.
2204 San Pablo Ave.
Berkeley, CA 94702
(415) 845-4751
Sun Room Co., Inc.
PO Box 301
322 E. Main St.
Leola, PA 17540
(800) 426-2737
(717) 656-9391
Fax (717) 656-0843
**Sunshine Architectural
Woodworks**
2169 Sunshine Dr., Dept C
Fayetteville, AR 72703
(800) 628-8004
(501) 521-4329
Fax (501) 521-8863
Superior Clay Corp.
Box 352
Uhrichsville, OH 44683
(800) 848-6166
**Supradur Manufacturing
Corp.**
Box 908
Rye, NY 10580
(800) 223-1948
(914) 967-8230 (NY)
Swan Brass Beds
1955 E. 16th St.
Los Angeles, CA 90021
(213) 748-5315
M. Swift & Sons, Inc.
10 Love Ln.
Hartford, CT 06141
(203) 522-1181
**Tarkett Hardwood Division
of North America**
PO Box 300
Johnson City, TN
37605-0300
(615) 928-3022
Tennessee Fabricating Co.
1822 Latham St.
Memphis, TN 38106
(901) 948-3354
Fax (901) 948-3356
Textile Conservation Center
800 Massachusetts Ave.
N. Andover, MA 01845
(508) 686-0191
Thatching Advisory Service
Rose Tree Farm
29 Nine Mile Ride
Finchampstead, Berks
England R611 4QD
Richard E. Thibaut, Inc.
706 S. 21st St.
Irvington, NJ 07111
(201) 399-7888
The Tinner
PO Box 353
Spencer, NC 28159
(704) 637-5149
Tiresias, Inc.
PO Box 1864
Orangeburg, SC
29116-1864
(800) 553-8003
(803) 534-8478 or 3445
Fax (803) 533-0051
Traditional Line Ltd.
143 W. 21st St.
New York, NY 10011
(212) 627-3555
Tremont Nail Company
PO Box 111, 8 Elm St.

Wareham, MA 02571
(508) 295-0038
Tromploy Inc.
400 Lafayette St.
New York, NY 10003
(212) 420-1639 (Fax and
tel.)
Travis Tuck, Metal Sculptor
Box 1832
Martha's Vineyard, MA
02568
(617) 693-3914
Turncraft
PO Box 2429
White City, OR 97503
(503) 826-2911
The Twigs, Inc.
5700 3rd St.
San Francisco, CA 94124
(415) 822-1626
United House Wrecking
535 Hope St.
Stamford, CT 06906
(203) 348-5871
Universal Gloster, Inc.
1555-57 Carmen Dr.
Elk Grove Village, IL
60007
(708) 362-9400
Fax (708) 362-9430
**Vande Hey-Raleigh
Architectural Roof Tile**
1665 Bohm Dr.
Little Chute, WI 54140
(414) 766-1181
Vermont Soapstone Co.
PO Box 168
Stoughton Pond Rd.
Perkinsville, VT
05151-0168
(802) 263-5404
Fax (802) 263-9451
**Vermont Structural Slate
Co.**
PO Box 98
Fair Haven, VT 05743
(800) 343-1900
Victorian Lightcrafters Ltd.
PO Box 350
Slate Hill, NY 10973
(914) 355-1300
The Village Forge
Rte. 4, Box 124
Country Club Rd.
Smithfield, NC 27577
(919) 934-2581
Fax (919) 934-3298
Vintage, Inc.
336 N. 10th St.
Easton, PA 18042
(215) 258-0602
Vintage Lumber Co.
9507 Woodsboro Rd.
Frederick, MD 21701
(301) 898-7859
**Vintage Plumbing &
Sanitary Specialists**
9645 Sylvia Ave.
Northridge, CA 91324
(818) 772-6353
Vintage Wood Works
513 S. Adams
Fredericksburg, TX 78624
(512) 997-9513
Virginia Metalcrafters
1010 E. Main St.
Waynesboro, VA 22980
(800) 368-1002
(800) 572-1015 (VA)
Helene Von Rosenstiel, Inc.
382 11th St.
Brooklyn, NY 11215
(718) 788-7909
Walcot Reclamation Ltd.
108 Walcot St.
Bath BA1 5BG

Index